JESUS

D1395721

AND THE

WORD

And Other Essays

C. K. BARRETT

T&T CLARK
EDINBURGH

First published by: *Pickwick Publications, 4137 Timberlane Drive*
Allison Park, PA 15101-2932 USA

This edition published 1995 by *T. & T. Clark Ltd, 59 George Street,*
Edinburgh EH2 2LQ, Scotland, through special arrangement with
Pickwick Publications.

Printed on Acid Free Paper in the United States of America

ISBN 0 567 29306 8

British Library Cataloguing-in-Publication Data

A catalogue record for this book is available from the
British Library

CONTENTS

PREFACE

This volume owes its existence to a suggestion, or request, made by D. Y. Hadidian, of Pickwick Publications. I hope he was right to make it, and that I did not do wrong in selecting a few pieces that I thought some people might be glad to see, or to see again, and see in relation to one another. They are a fair mixture. Some cast a grateful and admiring but not uncritical glance at great New Testament scholars of the past—one of them an inadequate expression of thanks for inspiration that is still bright after nearly sixty years. Some could be regarded as additions to my *Essays on John* and *Essays on Paul*. And some look at the task of New Testament Theology. Between them they cover more than thirty years and there may here and there be differences between the pieces themselves, and between them and what I should say today. But I think they represent a fairly consistent point of view, which I still maintain.

C. K. Barrett
Durham
28 January, 1995

ORIGINS AND ACKNOWLEDGMENTS

1. This lecture was given in Cambridge, at the invitation of Westcott House, in 1958. It was published as a booklet by the Cambridge University Press in 1959.

2. This lecture was one of four delivered in Durham in December 1989 to mark the centenary of Lightfoot's death. It was published (with the three other lectures) in a special number of the *Durham University Journal* (1992), edited by J.D.G. Dunn.

3. This paper was given to the Durham University Lightfoot Society and repeated at Professor Hooker's Seminar in Cambridge at the centenary of Hort's death. It has not previously been published.

4. This paper on the two teachers who did more than any others to create in me a determination to study the New Testament was written at Dikran Y. Hadidian's suggestion for inclusion in this volume.

5. I was asked to lecture on Schweitzer as an interpreter of the New Testament in the Atlanta celebration of the centenary of his birth. The lecture was published in the *Expository Times* [87] (1978), 4-10.

6. A. M. Ramsey was Canon Professor in Durham, 1940-1950; subsequently Regius Professor at Cambridge, Bishop of Durham, Archbishop of York, and Archbishop of Canterbury. After his death in 1988 a Memorial Lecture was established by St. Mary's College, the Dean and Chapter of Durham Cathedral, and the Durham University Department of Theology. I was invited to lecture on this subject in 1991. The lecture was published by St. Mary's College.

7. This paper was commissioned as a contribution (Johanneisches Christentum) to a book, *Die Anfänge des Christentums,* edited by Jürgen Becker (Kohlhammer, Stuttgart; 1987). The German book was translated into English as *Christian Beginnings,* in which C.K. Barrett's "Johannine Christianity" appeared; edited by Jürgen Becker © 1993, Westminster John Knox Press.

8. This paper was given at the Colloquium Biblicum Lovaniense in 1992 and published in *John and the Synoptics,* 1992 BETL 101, edited by A. Denaux by permission of Peeters Publishers, Leuven.

9. Originally published in *The New Testament and Gnosis*, Essays in Honour of R. McL. Wilson, edited by A.H.B. Logan and A.J.M. Wedderburn (T. & T. Clark Ltd., Edinburgh; 1983), 125-137.

10. I gave this lecture (in German: "Paulus als Missionar und Theologe") at the opening of a Durham-Tübingen Symposium inTübingen in 1988. It was first published in *Zeitschrift für Theologie und Kirche* 86 (1989), 18-32, subsequently in the proceedings of the Symposium, *Paulus und das antike Judentum*, edited by M. Hengel and U. Heckel (Mohr, Tübingen; 1992), 1-15.

11. A paper given at the Colloquio Paolino Ecumenico in 1983, published in *Résurrection du Christ et des Chrétiens (1 Cor. 15)*, edited by Lorenzo De Lorenzi, Benedictina, Série Monographique, Section Biblico-Oecuménique, 8 (Rome; 1985), 99-122.

12. This paper appeared in *Eschatology and the New Testament*. Essays in Honor of George Raymond Beasley-Murray (edited by W. Hulitt Gloer: Peabody: Mass.; Hendrickson Publishers, 1988) 65-75. Used by permission.

13. Presidential paper at the meeting of *Studiorum Novi Testamenti Societas,* 1973, first published in *New Testament Studies* 20 (1974), 229-245.

14. Originally published in Rudolf Bultmann: *Werk und Wirkung*, edited by B. Jaspert (Wissenschaftliche Buchhandlung; Darmstadt; 1984) 81-91. This book celebrated the centenary of Bultmann's birth.

15. Published in *Wissenschaft und Kirche,* Festschrift für E. Lohse. Edited by K. Aland and S. Meurer. Luther-Verlag, Bielefeld, 1989.

16. Originally published in *Intergerini Parietis Septum (Eph. 2.14),* Essays presented to Markus Barth, edited by Dikran Y. Hadidian (Pickwick Press, Pittsburgh), 1-22; also in *Horizons in Biblical Theology* (1981), 1-22. The contents were given as a lecture at the Istituto Pontifico Biblico in Rome.

17. Originally published in *Die Mitte des Neuen Testaments*, Festschrift für Eduard Schweizer, edited by U. Luz and H. Weder (Vandenhoeck & Ruprecht, Göttingen: 1983) 5-21.

* * * * *

Publisher and author wish to thank the following who have given permission to republish the essays mentioned:

The Abbot of St. Paul's without the Walls, Rome, for No. 11.

Patrick H. Alexander (Hendrickson Publishers) for No. 12.

K. Aland and S. Meurer (Luther-Verlag) for No.15. Cambridge University Press, for Nos. 1, 13.

Durham University Journal (with Mr. P. Lewis, editor), for No. 2.

Dr. G. F. Green (T. & T. Clark Ltd.), for Nos. 5, 9.

D. Y. Hadidian (Pickwick Publications), for No. 16.

Miss J.M. Kenworthy (Principal of St Mary's College, Durham), for No. 6.

Mr. R.G. Jones, Editor of the *Epworth Review*, for some material used in No. 4.

W. Kohlhammer Verlag, Stuttgart, and Westminster John Knox Press. for No. 7.

P. Peeters (Peeters Publishers and Booksellers) for No. 8.

Dr A. Ruprecht (Vandenhoeck & Ruprecht, Göttingen), for No. 17.

Dr. G. Siebeck (J.C.B. Mohr (Paul Siebeck), Tübingen, with Professors M. Hengel and E. Jüngel, editors, for No. 10.

Wissenschaftliche Buchhandlung, Darmstadt, for No. 14.

ix

ABBREVIATIONS

In the notes the following abbreviations have been used:

E.R.	*Essays and Reviews* (London, 1860).
John	*The Gospel according to St John: The Authorized Version with Introduction and Notes*, by B. F. Westcott (London, 1881). Reprinted from 'The Speaker's Commentary.'
Ep. John	*The Epistles of St John: The Greek Text with Notes and Essays*, by B. F. Westcott (London, 1883).
Hebrews	*The Epistle to the Hebrews: The Greek Text with Notes and Essays*, by B. F. Westcott (London, 1889).
H.	*Life and Letters of Fenton John Anthony Hort*, by his son Arthur Fenton Hort (2 vols., London, 1896).
W.	*Life and Letters of Brooke Foss Westcott*, by his son Arthur Westcott (2 vols., London, 1903).

1

WESTCOTT AS COMMENTATOR

BROOKE FOSS WESTCOTT, Scholar and Fellow of Trinity, assistant master and house-master at Harrow, Regius Professor of Divinity, and Bishop of Durham, wrote commentaries on the Gospel according to St. John, on the Epistle to the Ephesians, on the Epistle to the Hebrews, and on the Epistles of St. John. Of his other writings, the *Essay on the Canon* is still in regular use, and many of the sermons and theological volumes deserve to be read more widely than they are; but undoubtedly it is primarily through his commentaries that Westcott continues to influence modern theological studies. Indeed, the recent republication of the commentary on the Fourth Gospel, three-quarters of a century after its first appearance, is a remarkable testimony at once to the vitality and enduring worth of Westcott's exposition, and to the inadequacy of more recent attempts to deal with the same subject.

To account for this vitality, attractiveness, and usefulness, which mark Westcott's commentaries, is our primary task. What are their characteristics? What qualifications enabled Westcott to write as he did? What were his methods, and the presuppositions with which he worked? What lessons may the commentary writer of the twentieth century learn from his predecessor of 100 years ago? It will perhaps not be amiss if I begin by quoting from the editorial of the *Durham University Journal*[1] of 10 May 1890. Westcott is apostrophized as "Before all things a Biblical student, bringing to the text of the Bible all the habits and resources of most accurate linguistic scholarship, along with a reverential affection to which no detail, however slight, was insignificant; unsurpassed in his command of all the statistics of text and matter, yet never mastered by them, never mechanical nor dry; resolute in insisting that exegesis must be, first and foremost, historical, yet never content with history as an end in itself; free from all verbal or mechanical ideas of inspiration, yet treating every syllable of Scripture with a reverent care which no maintainer of verbal inspiration could excel." This is, of course, the language of eulogy, addressed to the newly appointed bishop of the diocese and visitor of the University of Durham; but the anonymous writer (I have not found out who he was, but I am inclined to suspect Dr Alfred Plummer, himself a fertile writer of commentaries,

and at that time Master of University College, Durham) has accurately
picked out some of the essential features of Westcott's biblical work,
and much of what I shall say could be regarded as a development of his
paragraph.

Of all Westcott's qualifications for the interpretation of Scripture, the first and greatest was not his classical scholarship (though I
shall speak of that later) but his conviction that in handling the Bible he
was handling the Word of God, and his readiness, or rather his determination, to hear, faithfully and obediently, whatever should be spoken
through the written word. Great as were his literary accomplishments,
exegesis was never to him merely a literary exercise; it was an attempt
to hear the divine word in its fullness and richness, and to communicate
it to the fellow-student, on whomWestcott lays not only heavy academic demands, but also the heavier demand that he be equally willing to
hear and obey.

To illustrate this fundamental fact we may first of all go back
to the origins of Westcott's work as a commentator. This is of course a
story without which this lecture would in any case be incomplete. As
everyone knows Westcott's books were part of a complete commentary
on the New Testament, planned, but unfortunately not completed, by
Lightfoot, Westcott, and Hort. The final form of the scheme as planned
in 1860 was that Lightfoot should deal with the Pauline letters, Hort
with the synoptic gospels and with the epistles of James, Peter, and
Jude, and Westcott with the Johannine literature and Hebrews. (I include Hebrews in Westcott's list because he did eventually write upon
it, and for Macmillan's; in 1860 there was some doubt about it; it was
first assigned to Lightfoot, then to Westcott, "if it does not go to Benson."[2] But Benson—that is, of course, E. W. Benson, later Bishop of
Truro and Archbishop of Canterbury—was too much occupied with ecclesiastical affairs, and with his *Cyprian*.)

The market in commentaries was at this time open, and several publishers and editors were in the field. Dr Smith, whose *Dictionaries of Christian Biography* and of *Christian Antiquities* are still with us,
was, it appears, endeavouring to launch a new biblical commentary in a
series of dinners, which Westcott regretted his inability to attend (this
may be a reflection of Westcott's ascetic habit of life). Hort (who has
left on record that he enjoyed a good meal) was better informed, and
writes in a letter, "I have undertaken the Gospels, Wisdom, and Eccle-
siasticus. . . .Westcott takes Daniel and most of the Apocrypha; Temple
(of Rugby), Romans; Lightfoot, the Acts; Ellicott, some Epistles; Barry
is also to take part, and perhaps Scott; so one will be in good company.
Printing will not begin for nearly two years."[3] Alas, it did not begin at
all. I say "Alas," for even in a lecture on Westcott one may lament that
we have not "Lightfoot on Acts."

When Smith's plan fell through, at least as far as the New Testament was concerned—at this time Westcott still held to his agreement

to write on Daniel and the Apocrypha—Hort wrote to Lightfoot, "Might not we three venture to make a partition of the whole New Testament among ourselves?"[4] On the same day (29 April 1860) he wrote to Westcott to the same effect, and it is evident that there had been previous correspondence (which we do not possess) from these two, for Hort says to Lightfoot that his (Hort's) partition is into "three portions, which *contain* your and Westcott's suggested arrangements." It appears that the initiative had come from Macmillan the publisher, who was already in close touch with Westcott and Hort in regard to their revision of the text of the New Testament, not to mention many other projects. Already in 1859 Westcott had suggested to Macmillan that he should "persuade Mr Lightfoot to undertake St Paul's epistles," and proposed to reserve for himself "the writings of St John, including the Apokalypse (*sic*), and the Epistle to the Hebrews."[5] After Macmillan, Westcott and Lightfoot were the prime movers in the scheme. Westcott's letter to Macmillan was written in November; in December he was in correspondence with Lightfoot. There were minor points of disagreement between them. Lightfoot wished to print the Greek text; Westcott has no objection, though presumably he had not at first wished it; perhaps he did not wish to anticipate his and Hort's future publication. Lightfoot also wished to add a critical apparatus; here Westcott disagrees, unless the variants are confined to readings "which you regard as possibly true."[6] Lightfoot wished further to print, and apparently also to criticize, the English version; here Westcott saw great practical difficulties. But neither of the friends saw in these small differences any barrier to co-operation, and they considered possible collaborators. Hort is noted as having undertaken the synoptics for Smith. J. Ll. Davies was another possible helper. In an afterthought, Westcott mentions Benson as one who might take the Synoptists.

When he wrote to Lightfoot Westcott wrote also to Macmillan, and his letter includes the sentence, "Mr Hort above all men I should welcome as a fellow-labourer, because I know how heartily I could sympathise with all his principles where in detail I might differ from him, and so would Mr Lightfoot. . . . "[7] That Westcott should thus express confidence in his fellow-reviser of the New Testament text is only what might be expected; yet in fact it was precisely at this point that a misunderstanding arose between the friends, which reveals something of Westcott's approach to Scripture.

Between December 1859 and May 1860 Hort had visited Westcott at Harrow, and they had discussed the relations between the synoptic gospels. Their views on this subject were not those of Streeterian, or even of post-Streeterian orthodoxy, and need not concern us; but Westcott, though he did not show it at the time, had evidently been disturbed by what Hort had said—sufficiently disturbed to make him question whether Hort would after all be a suitable collaborator; whether, at any rate, he could be entrusted with the synoptic gospels. He had expressed his doubts to Lightfoot, who in turn communicated them to Hort. Hort, in some ways the most acute thinker of the three, was not satisfied with the suggested compromise that he should transfer from the Synoptists to another part of the New Testament, where historical questions would not arise. A principle was involved, and had to be treated as a principle.

What Westcott's complaint led Hort to fear was that collaboration with his friends would mean "an obligation to produce results of a predetermined colour."[8] All were agreed that their interpretation of the Bible must rest upon accurate and honest criticism; but Lightfoot and Westcott had made up their minds in advance (so it seemed to Hort) that the results of such criticism would not disturb "orthodox" assumptions. The question involved was (according to Hort) that of the absolute infallibility of the New Testament. Westcott had decided that the results of criticism could not prove errors in Scripture; if they seemed to do so, this was due simply to our imperfect knowledge and inadequate criticism. This conclusion Hort was unable to assume *a priori*. He wanted to find the Bible free from error, but he did not intend to assume the result in advance. "I shall rejoice on fuller investigation to find that imperfect knowledge is a sufficient explanation of *all* apparent errors, but I do not expect to be so fortunate. If I am ultimately driven to admit occasional errors, I shall be sorry; but it will not shake my conviction of the providential ordering of human elements in the Bible."[9] One suspects (and I shall return to the matter later) that Westcott was temperamentally unwilling to pay due attention to the "human elements" of which Hort was conscious.

The whole affair was wound up with the greatest cordiality and affection as a misunderstanding. Hort had all the time recognized a special Providence in the origin of the Bible. Westcott for his part found that he did not like the word *infallibility*, but preferred *absolute truth*. Lightfoot's position remains obscure, because his letters are not available. Up to a point, the matter may be regarded as a strife about words; yet not entirely so. There was in Westcott a streak of what, for lack of a better term, we may call the fundamentalist: a rigorist, ascetic, and somewhat intolerant vein, which had chosen its standard and resolved to fight under it, without asking too many questions.

It is right, and also for our purpose illuminating, to add that there was, precisely at this time, a special reason why Westcott should be touchy on precisely this issue. In February 1860 there had appeared a volume under the title *Essays and Reviews*; and it would not, I think, be outrageous to suggest that it was rather this event than Hort's very innocent views on the synoptic problem that had excited Westcott's doubts. There is no question that *Essays and Reviews* stirred Westcott deeply, especially the essay on "The Interpretation of Scripture" by Jowett. Jowett's commentary on several Pauline epistles had indeed been in print for some years, and had made clear enough his general position; but now he had formally declared his standpoint, and done so with the backing of a distinguished and influential group of collaborators—for though the authors of *Essays and Reviews* disclaimed any corporate responsibility they certainly shared a common outlook. And the whole volume was disturbing. F. Temple's essay on "The Education of the World," for example, led Westcott and Lightfoot to seek a private interview with Dean Stanley, in which the future of Temple's headmastership at Rugby was discussed. It is worth noting that Hort, though unlike his friends he was himself a Rugbeian, was not involved in this *démarche*.

Westcott differed from Jowett both in underlying principle, and in the practical method of exegesis. Early in his essay, Jowett lays down the considerations which are essential to the understanding of inspiration. (1) "The nature of inspiration can only be known from the examination of Scripture";[10] and if we consider the varied contents of Scripture it appears that the only tolerable principle is that of "progressive revelation,"[11] and this implies the imperfection of the earlier stages of revelation. "There is no more reason why imperfect narratives should be excluded from Scripture than imperfect grammar; no more ground for expecting that the New Testament would be logical or Aristotelian in form than that it would be written in Attic Greek."[12] (2) Another "consideration is one which has been neglected by writers on this subject. It is this—that any true doctrine of inspiration must conform to all well ascertained facts of history or of science."[13]

So much for principle. In practice, Jowett turned away from the minute verbal scholarship that Westcott practised so brilliantly and assiduously. "The minuteness of the study in our own day has also a tendency to introduce into the text associations which are not really found there. There is a danger of making words mean too much; refinements of signification are drawn out of them, perhaps contained in their etymology, which are lost in common use and parlance. There is the danger of interpreting every particle, as though it were a link in the argument, instead of being, as is often the case, an excrescence of style."[14] Anyone who is in the least familiar with Westcott's work can imagine the sparks that flew in the Harrow study when the last sentence was read. "Excrescence of style," indeed!

More was to follow, for Westcott found it hard to decide which he liked less: the errors of *Essays and Reviews,* or the episcopal counterblasts which pursued them. The scepticism and liberalism of the essays was bad enough, but the obscurantism and illiberalism of the bishops was worse. It is important for our understanding of Westcott as an interpreter of the Bible to imagine his anguish as he squirmed in a cleft stick. Whatever of sound theology and sound scholarship had escaped the Essayists, it seemed that the thick-headed defenders of orthodoxy would destroy. He tried in vain to get Hort and Lightfoot to join him in a volume of essays which should set forth the true *via media,* defending at once the authority of Scripture and the rights of criticism. "Let me introduce myself to you" (he writes to Lightfoot) "in the character of an agitator."[15] It was not a role that suited him well. Lightfoot and Hort were both busy, and probably felt that truth could be left to defend itself; the agitation had to remain within Westcott's bosom.

I hope that through these excursions into nineteenth century history we may have come to feel something of Westcott's approach to Scripture and the task of interpretation; but undoubtedly it is time we looked at the Commentaries themselves. The (shorter) commentary on St John, being a reprint from the Speaker's Commentary, is without any personal preface; but those on Hebrews and the Johannine Epistles have long and significant prefatory notes. On Hebrews Westcott declares, "No work in which I have ever been allowed to spend many years of continuous labour has had for me the same intense human interest as the study of the Epistle to the Hebrews. If this feeling, which must show itself in what I have written, moves others to work upon the book with frank and confident reverence, to listen to the voice which speaks to us 'today' from its pages, to bring to the doubts, the controversies, the apparent losses, which distress us, the spirit of absolute self-surrender to our King-priest, the living and glorified Christ, which it inspires, my end will be fully gained."[16] The "today" is of course drawn from Ps. xcv. 7, quoted in Heb. iii. 7, etc.; but it is far more than a literary allusion. To Westcott, Scripture did speak "today"; it was with that conviction that he worked.

His attitude to Scripture, however, was by no means the *sola Scriptura* of classical Protestantism. "The study of Scripture is, I believe, for us the way by which God will enable us to understand His present revelation through history and nature. When once we can feel the divine power of human words, which gather in themselves the results of cycles of intellectual discipline, we shall be prepared to pass from the study of one book to the study of 'the Divine Library'."[17] This may at first sound like Calvin's analogy of the pair of spectacles (*Institutes*, I, vi, 1), but in fact it differs. The Bible is the first step to a second and independent revelation, rather than the divine truth by which alone nature and history can be interpreted. The Bible is an interpreter of life. "From first to last God is seen in the Bible conversing with man. . . . In the main the Bible is the continuous unfolding in many parts and many ways of the spiritual progress of mankind."[18] On John i. 9, Westcott writes, "No man is wholly destitute of the illumination of 'the Light'. In nature, and life, and conscience it makes itself felt in various degrees to all."[19]

The fact is that Westcott lacks a *systematic* theory of inspiration and of the authority of Scripture; and this lack is not entirely compensated by his profound reverence for Scripture, and the exceptionally acute theological apprehension of the meaning of the text under discussion, to which Hoskyns draws attention in his own commentary on the

Fourth Gospel. This latter quality is indeed of immense importance. "When Westcott wrote his commentary the Fourth Gospel was still a great work of Christian Theology able to deliver up its secret only to those who were themselves sensitive to theological truth, prepared to assume that it is a 'good' book, and ready to listen to what it has to say without seeking to justify or defend it, or even to interpret and explain it, save on its own terms."[20] The theological apprehension of Scripture which Hoskyns demonstrates from one commentary could equally be shown in the others; but it may still be permitted us to regret that Westcott did not subject his beliefs about revelation to systematic criticism on the basis of his own wholly admirable exposition of the text of Scripture.

Westcott's own doctrine of Scripture may thus have been to some extent inadequate and inconsistent; but it was very clear to him that Jowett's doctrine would not do. He was equally dissatisfied with Jowett's methods of exegesis and interpretation. He, and Hort and Lightfoot with him, were prepared to accept Jowett's phrase and interpret the Bible "like any other book." As we shall see, he takes up the phrase, quotes it, and emphasizes it. But what does it mean to interpret Scripture like any other book? Whatever the formula may suggest to us there was no doubt about its meaning in the mind of the Senior Classic of 1848, who never forgot the grounding in linguistic discipline that Prince Lee had given him at King Edward's. It meant that the minutest attention must be paid to every detail, every syllable of the text. All the resources of scholarship must be employed and focused upon each sentence, each clause, each word. This was not Jowett's way. To him, the language of the New Testament was not the precise medium of the classical writers, and did not warrant the same treatment. There is, of course, a good deal in Jowett's contention, as no one today would dispute; though it might not be unjust to add that the cast of Jowett's mind seems to have been away from the minutiae of scholarship, whether he was dealing with Paul or with Plato. Readers of E. F. Benson[21] will remember with pleasure the picture of Swinburne, who had left Oxford without a degree, perusing the proofs of Jowett's *Plato* and from time to time calling out gleefully, "Another howler, Master!"

Westcott's mind moved in the opposite direction, and again and again he returns to the theme of the importance of minute verbal scholarship in the work of a commentator. Thus, "Some perhaps will think that in the interpretation of the text undue stress is laid upon details of expression; that it is unreasonable to insist upon points of order, upon variations of tenses and words, upon subtleties of composition, upon indications of meaning conveyed by minute variations of language in a book written for popular use in a dialect largely affected by foreign elements. The work of forty years has brought to me the surest conviction that such criticism is wholly at fault. Every day's study of the Apostolic writings confirms me in the belief that we do not com-

monly attend with sufficient care to their exact meaning. The Greek of
the New Testament is not indeed the Greek of the Classical writers, but
it is not less precise or less powerful."[22] We must not limit, Westcott
adds, the significance of an author's words to the significance actually
present in his mind when he wrote. Note the dig at Jowett in the following quotation: "It has been my main desire to call attention to the minutest points of language, construction, order, as serving to illustrate
the meaning of St John. I do not venture to pronounce that any variation is trivial or unimportant. The exact words are for us the decisive
expression of the Apostle's thought. I have therefore, if I may borrow
words which have been applied in a somewhat different sense, begun
by interpreting the Epistles as I should 'interpret any other book,' neglecting nothing which might contribute to a right apprehension of its
full meaning. I do not feel at liberty to set aside the letter of a document
till it has been found to be untenable."[23]

This principle of Westcott's could be illustrated from page after page of the many pages of his commentaries; but illustration of a detailed philological argument is difficult to give in the course of a lecture. Perhaps I may be permitted to say that when the New Testament
Seminar in Durham a few years ago studied Hebrews we found again
and again that Westcott had already given a lucid summary of all the
ways of construing a complicated sentence that occurred to us (and often several that had not occurred to us), and had given reasons for preferring one of them whose cogency it was very hard to dispute. Examples that come to mind are the expositions of Heb. iv.2, of the
beginning of x, and of the definition of faith in xi. 1. In passages such as
these, three things are likely to impress the reader most: the fine sense
Westcott has for the construction of a Greek sentence, and his ability to
convey this sense to his reader; the judicious use of patristic material,
which is not allowed to dominate the inquiry, but is brought in most
forcibly to cap an argument (for example, in the last passage mentioned
above: "This meaning [already established] is that which is uniformly
followed by the Greek Fathers in commenting on the passage [quota-
tions follow]");[24] and thirdly his use of the Latin (and sometimes Syriac) translations to illuminate the Greek text.

It is unnecessary to do more than mention Westcott's work, in
his commentaries, on textual criticism. It is of course true that the great
Introduction to the revised text of the Greek Testament was written by
Hort, and that Westcott several times remarks (in letters, for example)
that he has no interest in mere orthographical variants which do not affect the sense of the passage discussed; but it is also true that Westcott
was joint author of "Westcott and Hort"; that the principles of the *Introduction* were his no less than Hort's; and that he spent incalculable
hours in the drudgery of collation and analysis in which he professed to
have little interest. The textual work in the commentaries is what one
would expect it to be.

A special feature of the illuminating application of scholarship to the New Testament lies in the study of words. Here Westcott anticipates the word-study which in our own generation has received classical expression in Kittel's *Theologisches Wörterbuch.* I venture to give a list of some of the most notable word-studies that appear in the commentaries: τελείωσις; κληρονομία; Μελχισέδεκ; λειτουργεῖν, λατρεύειν; sacrifice (a group of words); συνείδησις; αἷμα; λυτροῦσθαι, λύτρωσις, etc.; διαθήκη; σῶμα Χριστοῦ; θυσιαστήριον; ἁμαρτία; ᾿Αντίχριστος; τέκνα (θεοῦ); titles of believers; ἀγάπη; psychological terms (σάρξ, ψυχή, πνεῦμα, καρδία); names of the Lord; ἱλασμός; μονογενής; θεός/ὁ θεός; the Christ; ζωή. Some of these are full New Testament studies; in others Westcott restricts himself to the book under consideration. All are based upon careful examination of the Old Testament, in both Greek and Hebrew, and most pursue the words under discussion into patristic usage. Sometimes Westcott strikingly anticipates recent conclusions. An outstanding example of this is his essay on ἱλασμός, where, after examining the biblical use of ἱλάσκεσθαι and ἐξιλάσκεσθαι, he concludes: "These constructions stand in remarkable contrast with the Classical and Hellenistic usage in which the accusative of the person propitiated is the normal construction from Homer downwards; a usage which prevails in patristic writers. They show that the scriptural conception of ἱλάσκεσθαι is not that of appeasing one who is angry, with a personal feeling, against the offender; but of altering the character of that which from without occasions a necessary alienation, and interposes an inevitable obstacle to fellowship. Such phrases as 'propitiating God', and God 'being reconciled' are foreign to the language of the New Testament."[25] This may or may not be an adequate account of the ἱλασμός group of words, but it has very often been repeated in the last seventy years, not always with acknowledgement to Westcott.

Both the range and the limitations of Westcott's scholarship may be illustrated by a simple list of the references he gives in his notes on Heb. x—a chapter I choose as sufficiently long and representative in subject-matter. Biblical references, which are innumerable and for all practical purposes exhaustive, may be excluded. It is clear that Westcott was only a little less familiar with the Greek Old Testament than he was with the New Testament, and that he used Trommius freely. "I have always seemed to learn most", he says, "from Trommius and Bruder. If to these concordances . . . the student adds Dr Moulton's edition of Winer's Grammar and Dr Thayer's edition of Grimm's Lexicon, he will find that he has at his command a fruitful field of investigation which yields to every effort fresh signs of the inexhaustible wealth of the Written Word."[26] Other references are listed in the following list.

Philo, 17	Primasius, 9
Chrysostom, 10	Theophylact, 6
Epictetus, 3	Isocrates, 1
Euthymius Zigabenus, 3	Justin Martyr, 1
Ambrose, 2	Leonidas Tarentensis, 1
Barnabas, 2	Liturgy of St James, 1
Cicero, 2	Lucian, 1
Sextus, 2	Macarius Alexandrinus, 1
Aeschylus, 1	Nicostratus, 1
Alcuin, 1	Pindar, 1
Ammonius, 1	Pliny Minor, I
Apostolic Constitutions, 1	Targum of Onkelos, 1
Aristophanes, 1	Testaments of the
Augustine, 1	Patriarchs 1
Didache, 1	Theodoret, 1
Dio Chrysostom, 1	Thomas Aquinas, 1
Hermas, 1	Vigilius Tapsensis, 1
Ignatius, 1	Xenophon, 1
Isaeus, 1	

The list is perhaps more interesting for what it does not than
for what it does contain. One is not surprised to note the presence of the
great classical writers, and other chapters would certainly add the
names of the most surprising absentees—Plato and Aristotle. There is
no question of Westcott's admiration for them. "Those hours which
were spent over Plato and Aristotle have wrought that in me which I
pray may never be done away."[27] Modern biblical scholars will be impressed by the wealth of patristic learning Westcott reveals. We have
today paid perhaps too much heed to Jowett's strictures on the Fathers
as guides to the interpretation of Scripture. They are indeed fallible
guides to biblical theology, but he must be a remarkable Greek scholar,
who, in construing a Greek sentence, can afford to ignore the instinc-
tive "feel" for words, style, and syntax, of those to whom Greek was
their native tongue. We have in these days so many other disciplines to
master that it is not, I think, likely that the latter half of the twentieth
century will witness the publication of commentaries so richly stored as
Westcott's with patristic material, and it follows that commentaries like
his will never become wholly out of date, if only because they provide
us with so fine a selection of materials which we are unlikely to quarry
for ourselves.

The classical writers and the Fathers speak for themselves. We
ought to note the presence of later Greek writers such as Epictetus, Dio
Chrysostom, and Lucian. In the period before the great discoveries of
papyri these represent the best attempt that could be made to illustrate
New Testament Greek by writing roughly contemporary with itself. It
goes without saying that the picture of Hellenistic Greek available to us

today is incomparably wider and more detailed than anything Westcott could have known; but I suspect that here too there may be a lesson for us to learn. There is an affinity, in objective and in tone, between Paul and Epictetus which can scarcely be found between Paul and the census papers of Egypt—illuminating as the latter are in their own context. The list of seventeen references to Philo is impressive, and I have heard Westcott spoken of as a great and independent authority on Philo. There is perhaps enough admiration in this lecture to allow me to prick this bubble. Westcott himself writes, in the introduction to Hebrews, "For illustrations from Philo I am largely indebted to the *Exercitationes* of J. B. Carpzov (1750), who has left few parallels unnoticed."[28] Carpzov's book covers only Hebrews (its full title is *Sacrae Exercitationes in S. Paulli Epistolam ad Hebraeos ex Philone Alexandrino*); and it is certainly true both that Westcott's references in his *Hebrews* are from Carpzov,[29] and that in his other works references to Philo are comparatively few.

The most striking absentees from the list we have drawn from Westcott's commentary on Heb.x are the writers of Judaism subsequent to the Old Testament. Apart from Philo we have one reference to the Testaments of the Twelve Patriarchs, and one to the Onkelos Targum. It may be interesting for comparison to glance at two more recent commentaries on the same chapter. In Moffatt (I.C.C., 1924) the following sources not used by Westcott are quoted: Plato (3), Aristotle (2), Comic Fragments (ed. Meineke) (1), Homer (1), Thucydides (1). These require no comment; their absence from Westcott may be regarded as accidental. A further group consists of Polybius (2), Apuleius (1), Florus (1), Galen (1), Plutarch (1), Seneca (1), and an inscription; the growing use of these later writers is significant of an attempt to place the New Testament more accurately in its linguistic, social, and religious environment. Clement of Rome (1), Cosmas Indicopleustes (1), Irenaeus (1), Maximus of Tyre (1), Odes of Solomon (1): the addition of these patristic writers is again scarcely significant. The Odes of Solomon were of course not known to Westcott. But there now follows a really important list: Aboth (2), Josephus (2), Sifre Numbers (2), Apocalypse of Baruch (1), Berakoth (1), Jubilees (1), Psalms of Solomon (1), Sanhedrin (1), Taanith (1), Yoma (1). We may add that Moffatt uses the Testaments of the Twelve Patriarchs much more freely than Westcott, and, if we seek further evidence, note that Windisch (*H.N.T.*[2], 1931) adds, on the Jewish side, Aristeas (3), Slavonic Enoch (2), Aristobulus (1), B. Berakoth (1), the Damascus Document (1), the Sibylline Oracles (1), and material bearing on Jewish Christianity from the Clementine Homilies and from Epiphanius.

To draw attention to these omissions is to pass no censure upon Westcott. A few of the works in question were not known to exist in Westcott's time, or were discovered towards the end of his life. None of them, perhaps, was as conveniently accessible, in trustworthy critical texts, as they are today. Between Westcott's death in 1901 and our own time there lies almost the whole of the work of R. H. Charles upon the Jewish Apocalypses, and of the great New Testament Rabbinists, both Jewish and Christian. During the last fifty years a vivid light, now intensifying almost daily as the Dead Sea Caves are investigated, has come to beat upon the Judaism out of which primitive Christianity emerged. It would be not unjust but merely fatuous to blame Westcott for not being aware of this light and employing it in his commentaries; but at the same time it would be stupid to overlook the greater illumination we now possess.

It is time to draw this lecture to a close, and the last observation may point the way to a suitable conclusion.

Westcott's greatness—as a man, a scholar, a theologian, a Christian, and certainly as a commentator—can be left to take care of itself. No praise from me could add to it, nor is it likely to be diminished by criticism. It would be hard to find a better example of ability, diligence, and devotion; of the capacity to take large views, and at the same time to scamp no detail and spare no pains. No man could expose more conclusively the fallacy that the labour of scholarship is inconsistent with vision and overall grasp. I may however be allowed to return briefly to a phrase of Hort's which I quoted earlier: the "human elements in the Bible."[30] In recalling these words it is not my intention to minimize the superhuman element in the Bible, or to return to those inadequate views of Scripture, and of the inspiration of Scripture, which grieved Westcott in *Essays and Reviews*; but rather (as Hort himself wished) to demonstrate the more clearly that "providential ordering" which overrules the human elements.

I have already indicated the profounder and more accurate knowledge of the human elements of the New Testament which is at our disposal today. Our Lord and the apostles belonged to a world which we are coming to know in increasing detail as more manuscripts are discovered, and more archaeological data disclosed. Beside the Gospels there stand on our shelves Josephus' Histories, the Psalms of Solomon, the Book of Enoch, the Mishnah, the Dead Sea Scrolls; and this contiguous literature forms a silent comment on the words: ὁ λό–γος σὰρξ ἐγένετο. The σὰρξ was that of a first-century Palestinian Jew. Westcott was never in danger of an Apollinarian Christology; but he was, it may be, in danger of an Apollinarian doctrine of Scripture. Sometimes it seems that he almost thinks of a vertical descent of—dare one say it?—a Westcott and Hort Greek Testament, with a divine significance in every mood, tense, and case.

Now the real objection to Apollinarian Christology is not that it is too supernatural and miraculous, but that it is not supernatural and miraculous enough. It fails to represent to us the supreme miracle, by which the divine nature was able to unite with itself, in complete harmony, a full, perfect, and real human nature. That is the true mystery and miracle of Christ. It is the same with Scripture. At times one feels that, with the opposite intent, Westcott has diminished the miracle of Scripture by neglecting its human element. There are in it, he suggests, no errors, no deficiencies, save only those which our own imperfections introduce. It may be that theology, exegesis, and history, are all of them better served when we see in Scripture a divine force, a divine authority, wrestling with human memory, human integrity, and human language, all of them subject to limitation, just as when we are speaking of Christology we must recognize that our Lord's own human nature was subject to human limitations. Scripture is not authenticated as the Word of God by the denial that the divine Word is spoken through a variety of human words.

The historical narrative of the Bible, and this includes the story of Jesus, comes to us through the medium of human tradition, with all the uncertainties of human tradition. The background against which the figure of Jesus stands is the fully human, religious, political, and social life of first-century Judaism, and the primitive Church reflects not a few of the interests and practices of societies contemporary with it. To recognize these facts with complete frankness is not easy even for the professional scholar, but it leads to a growing awareness of a supernatural control of the processes of tradition, of historical events, and of the interpretation of the events.

We may reach a similar conclusion by studying the language of the New Testament. This is related to Classical Greek, to the literary Koine of the Hellenistic and Imperial periods, to the vulgar Koine of the non-literary papyri, and to the Greek of the LXX; but it is not identical with any of these. The philologist who can trace in the New Testament the strands drawn from these sources, and control the underlying Hebrew and Aramaic too, has a unique opportunity of feeling the creative power which lies behind the New Testament and is constantly at work, moulding human speech, and sometimes doing violence to it, in order that it may become the divine Word.

Much then has happened in the fifty-seven years since Westcott died—enough to justify us, smaller men though we are, in writing new commentaries, which may do justice not only to the new historical and philological knowledge, but also through the use of these tools to a more radical and articulate doctrine of inspiration and authority. But we shall move backward, not forward, if we fail to build upon Westcott's foundation of rigorous scholarship, patient attention to every detail, personal piety, and reverent hearing of the voice of him that speaketh—today.

NOTES

1. Vol. IX, p. 41.
2. *H. I*, 422.

3. *H. I*, 396.
4. *H. I*, 4I7
5. *W. I*, 205.
6. *W. I*, 206.
7. *W. I*, 206 f.
8. *H. I*, 419.
9. *H. I*, 422.
10. *E.R.* p. 347.
11. *E.R.* p. 348.
12. *E.R.* p. 348.
13. *E.R.* p. 348.
14. *E.R.* p. 391.
15. *W.* 1, 214.
16. *Hebrews*, p. ix.
17. *Ep. John*, p. vi.
18. *Ep. John*, pp. vii, viii.
19. *John*, p. 7.
20. *The Fourth Gospel*, by E. C. Hoskyns, edited by F. N. Davey
(London, 1940), p. 34.
21. *As We Were* (Penguin Books, 1938), pp. 134 f.
22. *Hebrews*, p. vi.
23. *Ep. John*, p. v.
24. *Hebrews*, p. 352.
25. *Ep. John.* p. 87.
26. *Hebrews*, p. viii.
27. *W. I*, 175 f—in a letter of thanks for a wedding present!
28. *Hebrews*, p. viii.
29. On Heb. x, Carpzov has 117 references to Philo.
30. See p. 4 above.

2

J. B. LIGHTFOOT
AS BIBLICAL COMMENTATOR

I find my task in giving this lecture on Lightfoot in at least one respect an embarrassment. Eighteen years ago, here in Durham, I gave to the Lightfoot Society a paper on Lightfoot; I touched on other aspects of his work, but to a great extent the paper was devoted to his commentaries. It was published in the *Durham University Journal* in the following year, 1972.[1] I am not embarrassed because I am under the illusion that my hearers today have turned up their copies of the *DUJ* and perused my paper; that is in the highest degree unlikely. I am embarrassed simply by the prospect of inevitable repetition, which I should prefer to avoid. I shall avoid it as far as I can, and this paper will follow a different line from its predecessor. But to some extent I shall be obliged to repeat myself. It will be necessary to give a certain amount of fundamental information, and the basic facts about Lightfoot's life and work do not change, though we are now better aware of the Lightfoot manuscripts preserved in the Chapter Library at Durham;[2] these provide some biographical material and throw additional light on Lightfoot's work and thought.[3] My earlier lecture was on the whole—there were a few exceptions—laudatory. This is because it was in the main descriptive of Lightfoot's work, and what there is to describe is very good indeed. What Lightfoot set out to do he did with very great skill and very great thoroughness. In his own chosen line he has perhaps no equal in the English-speaking world. There is however room for a more critical examination. His own work suggests questions to which it does not, at least on the surface, provide answers. Did he do everything that may rightly be expected of a commentator? Were the methods that he used the right methods? Should his methods be replaced, or perhaps supplemented by others? Did he take his own methods as far as they would go? Did he draw from them all the conclusions to which they pointed?

We shall see as we proceed how these questions, or some of them, are raised, and what answers Lightfoot himself can supply. The result will not detract from our estimate of Lightfoot; he is great enough to abide our question. In any case, repetition or not, we must begin with some facts. Most of the biographical details may be found in my earlier lecture.[4] Lightfoot gained his equipment as a commentator in the first instance at King Edward's School, Birmingham, under James Prince Lee, later Bishop of Manchester, not only in a thorough training in Greek and Latin, and wide reading in classical literature and history, but in a firm Christian faith and a devotion to hard work. He learned the meaning of Prince Lee's own motto, *Virtus constat in agendo*. Thence to Cambridge, where he worked with Westcott, who had by three years preceded him from King Edward's to Trinity. Having taken first class honours in mathematics he took the Classical Tripos in 1851 and came out as Senior Classic. The legend that he wrote all his Tripos papers without a single mistake is perhaps credible as far as language papers are concerned. It cannot have been easy to find passages of classical Greek and Latin that were truly unseen to him, and composition presented few problems. Inevitably he was elected to a fellowship at Trinity, and proceeded to improve his linguistic knowledge yet further by the best of all methods—teaching the languages to others. Theology he was now learning in his spare time; that is, after others had gone to bed at night and before they got up in the morning. The same diligence that he had applied to reading the classics he applied to patristic literature, with results that appear not only in the editions of Clement, Ignatius, and Polycarp but in his contributions to the great Dictionaries, of Christian Antiquities and Christian Biography.[5]

In an even earlier lecture than that on Lightfoot to which I have already referred,[6] I described the way in which Lightfoot, Westcott, and Hort divided up the New Testament with a view to writing commentaries on the whole. Lightfoot was to take Paul, and, as everyone knows, he wrote commentaries on Galatians (1865), Philippians (1868), and, in one volume, Colossians and Philemon (1875). Each contains an introduction, dealing with the usual questions; the Greek text, edited by Lightfoot, in consultation but not in complete agreement with Westcott and Hort (who, as all know, were drawing up their text of the whole New Testament); notes on the text, which include brief explanatory paraphrases, which restate in English the meaning of the text; longer notes on special points of interest and difficulty; and dissertations on larger topics related to the contents of the several epistles. A summary such as this cannot do justice to the width and detail of Lightfoot's work; a brief outline is called for.

In *Galatians* there are extended notes on St Paul's sojourn in Arabia, St Paul's first visit to Jerusalem, The name and office of an Apostle, Various readings in ii.5, The later visit of St Paul to Jerusalem, Patristic accounts of the collision at Antioch, The interpretation of Deut. xxi.23, The words denoting "Faith," The faith of Abraham, St Paul's infirmity in the flesh, The various readings in iv.25, The meaning of Hagar in iv.25, Philo's allegory of Hagar and Sarah, The various readings in v.1, and The Patristic Commentaries on this Epistle. In addition, there are dissertations on Were the Galatians Celts or Teutons?, The Brethren of the Lord, and St Paul and the Three.

In *Philippians* there are extended notes on The synonymes "bishop" and "presbyter," The meaning of "praetorium" in i.13, The synonymes μορφή and σχῆμα, Different interpretations of οὐχ ἁρπαγμὸν ἡγήσατο, Lost epistles to the Philippians? "Clement my fellow-labourer," and Caesar's Household. There are dissertations on The Christian Ministry, and St Paul and Seneca, the latter with an additional note on the letters of Paul and Seneca.

In *Colossians* there are extended notes on Some various readings in the Epistle (Colossians), On the meaning of πλήρωμα, and On the Epistle from Laodicea. There are no dissertations, but the Introduction contains 72 pages on the Churches of the Lycus, and 41 pages on the Colossian Heresy, with an additional 66 pages On some points connected with the Essenes.

It has seemed worthwhile to read rapidly through these titles, which, taken together, give some impression of Lightfoot's wide-ranging learning. There is scarcely one that does not reveal such patristic learning as probably no living New Testament scholar could claim. Jewish material, in the original languages, is called on when it is needful, and the extended note on Hagar and Sarah required of the Cambridge University Press not only a Syriac but also an Arabic fount.

The three commentaries were published in Lightfoot's lifetime. He left lecture notes, and other notes, on other epistles which doubtless he would have used in published work had he lived, and had his interest not become absorbed in what must be regarded as his greatest work, that on the text of 1 Clement and the Epistles of Ignatius (with 2 Clement and Polycarp added in for full measure)—not to mention his conscientious, time-consuming work as bishop of Durham. The notes were edited after his death for his trustees and published under the title *Notes on Epistles of St Paul from Unpublished Commentaries* (1895). Here we have notes, similar to but less full than those in the finished commentaries, on 1 Thessalonians, 2 Thessalonians, 1 Corinthians 1-7, Romans 1-7, and Ephesians 1.1-14. We may note here that the Trustees did not publish all the available material. The Chapter Library at Durham contains a quantity of manuscript material which is interesting in that it shows both how probably the most popular teacher of theology at Cambridge in his time prepared and presented his material, and also how the finished commentaries first took shape.

It will no doubt be proper to attempt a brief characterisation of the commentaries that we have in finished form. The first characteristic the reader is likely to observe is their beautiful clarity. Except in the extended notes and dissertations, which are in the style of monographs rather than of commentary, there are no footnotes, and the reader takes in Lightfoot's exposition, and the grounds on which he bases it, without

distraction. It would be difficult to find a sentence that does not immediately tell the reader the author's meaning. Of course, some of the arguments are complex because the text on which Lightfoot is commenting is difficult, but even in such passages the meaning is not in doubt.
This appears pre-eminently in the explanatory paraphrases, of which I
quote, more or less at random, that on Col. 1.15-17.

> He is the perfect image, the visible representation, of
> the unseen God. He is the Firstborn, the absolute Heir
> of the Father, begotten before the ages; the Lord of
> the Universe by virtue of primogeniture, and by vir-
> tue also of creative agency. For in and through Him
> the whole world was created, things in heaven and
> things on earth, things visible to the outward eye and
> things cognisable by the inward perception. His su-
> premacy is absolute and universal. All powers in
> heaven and earth are subject to Him. This subjection
> extends even to the most exalted and most potent of
> angelic beings, whether they be called Thrones or
> Dominations or Princedoms or Powers, or whatever
> title of dignity men may confer upon them. Yes: He
> is first and He is last. Through Him, as the mediatori-
> al Word, the universe has been created; and unto
> Him, as the final goal, it is tending. In Him is no be-
> fore or after. He is pre-existent and self-existent be-
> fore all the worlds. And in Him, as the binding and
> sustaining power, universal nature coheres and con-
> sists.[7]

But this general note is followed by details, and here too, though the
details are followed out at length, there is comparable clarity. Thus the
note on εἰκών, which is far too long to quote in full, runs in outline
thus.

> This expression is used repeatedly by Philo, as a de-
> scription of the Logos [six quotations follow]... Still
> earlier than Philo,...the term was used of the divine
> σοφία personified in Wisd. vii.26...St Paul himself
> applies the term to our Lord in an earlier epistle, 2
> Cor. iv.4...Closely allied to εἰκών also is χα-
> ρακτήρ...

So much for usage. Now meaning:

> Beyond the very obvious notion of *likeness*, the word
> εἰκών involves two other ideas:
> (1) *Representation*. In this respect it is allied to χα-
> ρακτήρ, and differs from ὁμοίωμα. In ὁμοίωμα the
> resemblance may be accidental, as one egg is like an-

other; but εἰκών implies an archetype of which it is a copy. [Quotations of and references to Gregory Nazianzen, Philo, Trench, Basil, 1 Corinthians, 1 Clement, Clementine Homilies, follow.] The use which was made of the expression, and especially of this passage, in the Christological controversies of the fourth and fifth centuries may be seen from the patristic quotations in Petav. *Theol. Dogm.* de Trin. ii.11. 9sq., vi.5.6.

(2) *Manifestation.* This idea comes from the implied contrast to τοῦ ἀοράτου θεοῦ. St Chrysostom indeed maintains the direct opposite, arguing that, as the archetype is invisible, so the image must be invisible also. [Quotation.] So too Hilary [Quotation.] And this was the view of the Nicene and post-Nicene fathers generally. But the underlying idea of the εἰκών, and indeed of the λόγος generally, is the manifestation of the hidden [Quotations from Philo, Tertullian, Hippolytus, Origen, Basil, John, follow]...⁸

The example I have chosen to illustrate the clarity of Lightfoot's exposition and argumentation can and must serve other purposes also and illustrate other characteristics, notably his knowledge of the Fathers, and his independence. He always has at hand the right quotation to bring out the meaning of a passage and to support the interpretation that he offers; but he can also declare that on a point of considerable importance the Nicene and post-Nicene Fathers were mistaken. Naturally he is no less independent of—and hardly less well read in—the works of his contemporaries. There is a characteristic note early in the description of the Christian Ministry.⁹

> The origin of the Christian ministry is ably investigated in Rothe's *Anfänge der Christlichen Kirche* etc. (1837), and Ritschl's *Entstehung der Altkatholischen Kirche* (2nd ed. 1857).These are the most important of the recent works on the subject with which I am acquainted, and to both of them I wish to acknowledge my obligations, though in many respects I have arrived at results different from either.

Lightfoot's knowledge and use of patristic material can be illustrated by his account of patristic commentaries on Galatians.¹⁰ He knows Origen, Ephraem Syrus, Eusebius of Emesa, Chrysostom, Severianus, Theodore of Mopsuestia, Theodoret, Euthalius, Gennadius, Photius, Victorinus, Hilary, Jerome, Augustine, Pelagius, Cassiodorus, John of Damascus, the *Catena* published by Cramer, Oecumenius, Theophylact, Primasius, Sedulius, Claudius, Florus, Rabanus Maurus, Walafrid Strabo, and Haymo; Atto, Lanfranc, Bruno, and Herveus are added.

Equally striking and characteristic, but equally difficult to illustrate briefly and effectively, is Lightfoot's feeling for a Greek phrase or sentence, acquired over many years of familiarity with Greek literature of all kinds. For brevity, take these words, which provide a familiar problem in Gal. 1.19, εἰ μὴ 'Ιακώβου.

> Is James here styled an Apostle or not? Are we to translate, "I saw no other Apostle save James," or "I saw no other Apostle but only James"? It will be seen that the question is not whether εἰ μή retains its *exceptive* force or not, for this it seems always to do..., but whether the exception refers to the whole clause or to the verb alone... the latter is quite a possible construction....But on the other hand the sense of ἕτερον naturally links it with εἰ μή, from which it cannot be separated without harshness, and ἕτερον carries τῶν ἀποστόλων with it. It seems then that James is here called an Apostle....[11]

Lightfoot was perhaps even greater as a historian than as a grammarian. He has especially in Galatians a set of historical problems as difficult as any that the New Testament presents. His treatment of them is clear and in the main satisfying. His identification of the meeting described in Gal. 2 with the Council of Acts 15 is surely correct, and Lightfoot defends it with great force, though he labours under the difficulty that his principles made it impossible for him to answer adequately the two chief objections to it. He mentions them fairly.[12] How is it that Paul passes from his first Jerusalem visit to his third without a hint of the second (described in Acts 11.30; 12.25)? And how is it that Paul in Galatians makes no mention of the Decree decided on at the Council, according to Acts 15.29? These difficulties can be readily disposed of if one is prepared to say that the second and third visits in Acts are doublets, and that the Decree was promulgated in Paul's absence and without his consent. Lightfoot would not have felt free to adopt these explanations, which impugn the veracity of Acts. This sets a very serious limit to the value of his historical work, illustrated by his discussion of Acts 15 in which he settles the historical trustworthiness of the Acts narrative by confronting it with Galatians after, not before, reaching his decision.[13] Lightfoot was inhibited in his work as a historian by a false understanding of inspiration and authority; it is for this reason that his work on the apostolic fathers is even better, and is of more permanent value, than his work on the New Testament. Apart however from this defect he works out the historical relations of Galatians with reference to every scrap of evidence that the epistle affords with great skill.[14]

The story of the Council points forward to Lightfoot's long

dissertation on St Paul and the Three. It would not be proper to take this up in this lecture, for it will probably be dealt with in another of this week's lectures. In any case I dealt with it in some detail in my earlier Lightfoot lecture[15] and brought out its strengths and its weaknesses. Lightfoot recognizes as clearly as F.C. Baur ever did the conflict that lies at the heart of early Christian history and indeed treats it, or begins to treat it, even more radically than Baur in that he places the documents of strife and reconciliation at earlier dates than Baur. But he seems never quite to see how radical his understanding of early Christian development is, or, if he sees it, he shies away from it, stepping back from the brink of recognizing that the uneasy diversity, which he does clearly see, is part of the New Testament itself.

Let me add here, with a view to taking up the theme later, that Lightfoot did not neglect that other part of a commentator's duty, the theological evaluation of his text. Of this I shall give one example,[16] Lightfoot's treatment of the notorious problem in Gal. 3.16: οὐ λέγει καὶ τοῖς σπέρμασιν ὡς ἐπὶ πολλῶν, ἀλλ᾽ ὡς ἐφ᾽ ἑνὸς καὶ τῷ σπέρματί σου, ὅς ἐστιν Χριστός. First he deals with the language, with a neat quotation from Plato (*Laws* 9. 853c) to show that the plural σπέρμασι is not impossible, and the argument that the point Paul is making is that where a plural (e.g. τέκνα) might have been used the Old Testament in fact has a singular. "The singular collective noun, if it admits of plurality (as it is interpreted by S. Paul himself, Rom. iv.18; ix.7) at the same time involves the idea of unity." At this point Lightfoot takes the important step. "The question therefore is no longer one of grammatical accuracy, but of theological interpretation. Is this a legitimate sense to apply to the seed of Abraham?" Lightfoot goes on to show that the Christ "was the true seed of Abraham. In Him the race was summed up, as it were. In Him it fulfilled its purpose and became a blessing to the whole earth... He was not only the representative, but the embodiment of the race..."[17]

I have deliberately ended this sketch of Lightfoot's achievement as a commentator with a reference to theology because it is at this point that he has been attacked, and if this lecture is to be a critical discussion, as it must, it is here that we must begin. There cannot be many theologians still resident in Cambridge who remember Charles Smyth's provocative University Sermon.[18] It was in one of its less provocative parts that he referred, as Cambridge men often do—or did—to the three great figures of Cambridge theology. His hearers expected him to name them: Lightfoot, Westcott, and Hort. He said, Westcott, Hort, and Hoskyns. To take up the positive aspect of his substitution is a temptation I must firmly thrust aside. The negative aspect is relevant. Smyth of course was not denigrating Lightfoot the exponent of classical and sacred philology.[19] He had used the word theologian, and it was theologians of whom he was thinking. Lightfoot was a great man; was he a great theologian? Was he a theologian at all?

Disparagement of Lightfoot as a theologian goes back at least
to the year in which his *Galatians* was published and to his old friend
and colleague Hort. Some passages in Hort's letters[20] must be quoted.
He writes (2.35) to John Ellerton on 7 May 1865:

> . . . The main purpose of the volume [*Galatians*] is
> to determine precisely the nature of the Apostolic his-
> tory to which Galatians is the key, and that is its dis-
> tinctive merit. . . Doctrinal questions are almost en-
> tirely avoided, as Lightfoot means to keep them for
> Romans. However, that is certainly the weakest point
> of the book; and Jowett's notes and essays, with all
> their perversities, are still an indispensable supple-
> ment.

I have been unable to find where Lightfoot expresses the intention that Hort ascribes to him—of dealing almost exclusively with
the apostolic history and saving the Pauline theology for the Commentary on Romans (of which we have only the imperfect fragment in *Unpublished Commentaries*). This is not to say that Hort was mistaken;
Lightfoot may have said these things in conversation with his friend, or
written them in a letter now lost.

Nearly two years later (21 February 1867) Hort was writing
again to Ellerton, who had evidently asked Hort's opinion of several
books which he, Ellerton, had not read. Hort writes (2.79):

> Touching Lightfoot's *Galatians* ....[21] Certainly his
> doctrinal comments are far from satisfying me. They
> belong far too much to the mere Protestant version of
> St. Paul's thoughts, however Christianized and ra-
> tionalised. One misses the real attempt to fathom St.
> Paul's own mind, and to compare it with the facts of
> life which one finds in Jowett. On the other hand, he
> is surely always admirable on historical ground, and
> especially in interpreting passages which afford indi-
> rect historical evidence, as also in all matters of
> grammar and language and such like essential exter-
> nalities.

As myself a mere Protestant I find myself wondering what is
the mere Protestant version of Paul's thoughts; also how it may be, or
needs to be, Christianized and rationalized. It seems that, having resist-
ed the temptation to digress to Hoskyns, we shall be obliged to turn
aside for a few moments to Hort, though I shall do my best to keep the
digression within narrow limits, recognizing that a full account of
Hort's own theological position is matter for another occasion. It must
suffice to quote two letters, both written to Westcott. The first was written on 23 September 1864 (2.30f.):

>I believe Coleridge was quite right in saying that
>Christianity without a substantial Church is vanity
>and dissolution; and I remember shocking you and
>Lightfoot not so very long ago by expressing a belief
>that "Protestantism" is only parenthetical and tempo-
>rary. In short, the Irvingite creed (*minus* the belief in
>the superior claims of the Irvingite communion)
>seems to me unassailable in things ecclesiastical. Yet
>that is not after all the essential aspect of sacred
>things. If we may take St. Paul's life and work for
>our guidance (and St. Peter's "Of a truth, I perceive
>that God is no respecter of persons" goes even fur-
>ther), we may well be content to put up with compar-
>ative formlessness for I know not how many genera-
>tions rather than go back to "the elements of the
>world."

Westcott must have replied, for five days later (September 28)
Hort wrote again (2.31f.):

>We must not be tempted into discussing the Church
>and the Churches in the opening lines of a letter. I
>must take the chance of your misunderstanding me
>for the present, and merely state one comprehensive
>belief,—that perfect Catholicity has been nowhere
>since the Reformation (strictly, indeed, it was cruelly
>injured long before by the *Filioque* and the Athana-
>sian Creed), and that since then we have had the pre-
>eminence in constitutional Catholicity, and (not
>"Rome" but) the Churches that hold to Rome in his-
>torical Catholicity.

Looking at the matter from the outside, and without adequate
discussion, Hort, it seems, has all the appearance of a good middle-of-
the-road Anglican. The Reformation was a regrettable necessity, called
for by errors and excesses in the medieval church; it should have been
carried out with greater tact and moderation. Luther was a "great and
good man," but "he was sometimes violent and unwise."[22] It is interesting to reflect that of the three Hort was the only one who did not become a bishop; he seems to have been the likeliest candidate. One is almost disposed to see divine providence at work in the system of
appointment by royal prerogative. Westcott was saved by his mystical
piety and his profound sympathy with the unfortunate, Lightfoot by the
fact that he was a historian, a fact that made him too much of an anti-
sacerdotal presbyterian for Hort. Or was even this strong enough to
save him? The question will lead to a further development in the critical assessment of Lightfoot.

No more than any other commentator did Lightfoot come to

his work without presuppositions. What were they? I have said a little about theology, and I shall return to the theme. Two other kinds of presupposition call for consideration: philosophical and institutional. In one of my earlier papers[23] I compared Lightfoot and F.C. Baur. I pointed out, what is now generally recognized, that Baur did not impose a Hegelian view of history on the New Testament documents, but recognized, as is certainly true, that Baur was a Hegelian; this Hegelianism had in fact a far more powerful—and, I would add, harmful —effect on his theology than on his history. "Lightfoot, in contrast," I said (316), "was not a philosopher and showed no interest in a theory of history." He said himself,[24] "I brought to the task nothing more than ordinary sense." I went on however to say (317), "Lightfoot's presuppositions were theological or religious, but it may be that behind them we should recognize a way of apprehending reality....Does his 'ordinary sense' represent a kind of empiricism?" B.N. Kaye, in an important article,[25] with most of which I can heartily agree, takes issue with this. In a paragraph of conclusions he writes:

> The conflict between Baur and Lightfoot on early Christianity is really about the question of the origins of Christianity. It seems to me that in broad terms they agree about the importance of history and theology being related to each other. Their approach to historical method is very similar and they are both convinced that there is a vital connection between contemporary Christianity and its origins...They differ, however, as to the particular and precise definition of the character of that connection; Baur thinking in dynamic and developmental terms, Lightfoot in terms of a "given" in the incarnation and the struggle to maintain the truth of that "given" through the subsequent life of the Church with the aid of the institution of the Christian ministry. It seems to me therefore not at all the case that Lightfoot has no philosophy of history. Rather, he appears to me to represent not just an empiricist philosophy but a fairly traditional Anglican point of view, such as might be found in the writings of Richard Hooker, whom Lightfoot is wont on occasion to quote. It appears to me most certainly to be the case that Lightfoot is very importantly involved, in his New Testament writings, in English Church problems.

With most of this I agree—indeed with more of it than Dr Kaye appears to think I do, though I cannot but observe that a concern with English church problems is not the same as a philosophical standpoint. I return however to my suggestion that Lightfoot's "ordinary sense" might be thought of in philosophical terms as empiricism; and, if an outsider may be permitted to express an opinion on such a matter, few things seem to me more characteristic of a "fairly traditional Anglican point of view" than a devout empiricism.[26] I am inclined to think, though here in particular I would defer to the specialists, that this is by no means uncharacteristic of Hooker.[27]

It may be worthwhile to dwell briefly upon the last sentence in the paragraph that I have quoted from Dr Kaye. "Lightfoot is very importantly involved, in his New Testament writings, in English Church problems." It is arguable that increasing involvement in these problems led to changes in his critical attitude. Probably his most radical, most Baurian, work is to be seen in his earliest commentary, that on Galatians. I give one quotation only.[28] "The systematic hatred of St Paul is an important fact, which we are too apt to overlook but without which the whole history of the Apostolic ages will be misread and misunderstood." Lightfoot does not, I think, return to this vehement expression of the turbulent and disunited apostolic age. His language in *Philippians*, though firm, is more moderate.

> If these sectarians resolutely opposed St Paul they were hardly less zealous in preaching Christ. The incentive of rivalry goaded them on to fresh exertions. Their gospel was dwarfed and mutilated; it ignored the principle of liberty which was a main feature of the true Gospel: but though their motives were thus unworthy and their doctrine distorted, still "Christ was preached"; and for this cause, smothering all personal feeling, the Apostle constrained himself to rejoice. (p.18)

Most important however is the fact that Lightfoot found it necessary, after he had become bishop of Durham, not to retract his long dissertation on the Christian Ministry[29] but to point out that it had been misunderstood. In this dissertation it is plainly stated that "the functions of the Apostle and the bishop differed widely" (196). Originally, the terms bishop and presbyter were synonymous (argued in a special note, *Philippians* 95-99); hence it is deduced (196) that "the episcopate was formed not out of the apostolic order by localisation but out of the presbyteral by elevation; and the title, which originally was common to all, came at length to be appropriated to the chief among them." This is worked out in detail in the following pages. The last part of the dissertation (244-269) is devoted to an attack on sacerdotalism, defined (245) as the view that designates "the Christian minister as one who offers sacrifices and makes atonement for the sins of others." This, though it subsequently developed rapidly, is not to be found in the New Testament.

Lightfoot on the origins of the episcopate is radical enough; but he can go farther. I allow myself to quote again passages I used in the past.[30]

> This then is the Christian ideal; a holy season extend-
> ing the whole year round—a temple confined only by
> the limits of the habitable world—a priesthood coex-
> tensive with the human race. (*Philippians* 183f.)
> It may be a general rule, it may be under ordinary cir-
> cumstances a practically universal law, that the high-
> est acts of congregational worship shall be performed
> through the principal officers of the congregation.
> But an emergency may arise when the spirit and not
> the letter must decide. The Christian ideal will then
> interpose and interpret our duty. The higher ordi-
> nance of the universal priesthood will overrule all
> special limitations. The layman will assume functions
> which are otherwise restricted to the ordained minis-
> ter. (*Philippians* 268).

A pity, one might think, ever to live by the letter rather than by the
Spirit, by the lower rather than the higher ordinance. That Lightfoot
never said; but he had said more than enough for some of his readers.

> It would seem that partial and qualifying statements
> ...have assumed undue proportions in the minds of
> some readers, who have emphasized them to the ne-
> glect of the general drift of the Essay.[31]

The general drift was that "from the Apostles time there have
been these orders of Ministers in Christ's Church, Bishops, Priests, and
Deacons." But Lightfoot had made it clear that in the Apostles' time,
bishops were the same as priests (or presbyters), and that priests were
to be understood in an entirely unsacerdotal sense. These were not the
points that he now, in 1881, wished to bring out.

No one could accuse Lightfoot, whose integrity was beyond
question, of springing to the defence of an order simply because he had
entered it. But it is probably true that he did, in the last decade of his
life, feel greater responsibility for the traditions and order of the Church
of England.

Apart from such considerations, before perhaps they began to
weigh heavily with him, how did Lightfoot understand the business of a
commentator, and how did he set about carrying it out? To answer
these questions I shall draw upon two sources.

The first is the introductory lecture to his course, given several
times in Cambridge, on the Acts of the Apostles.[32] Systems of interpretation (he says) depend on views of inspiration—a statement that can be
made a priori and is confirmed by the history of Biblical criticism.
There are two extreme views, which stress either the human element in
Scripture or the divine, each to the exclusion of the other. The latter
stress is irrational, the former rationalistic. Neither is satisfactory. It is
essential to give due weight to each element; this method only is in ac-

cordance with the highest reason and the fullest faith. In modern times
the irrational method came first. It reduces Scripture to featureless uniformity. and falls immediately to the assaults of criticism; in falling it
has carried with it the faith of some. The rationalist method arises by
reaction. The divine element is virtually if not actually denied, and inspiration is lowered because it is claimed not only for Scripture but also
for writers such as Homer, Aeschylus, Pythagoras, and Plato.

The combination of divine and human elements is of fundamental importance; it makes it possible to recognise those differences
in natural gifts and circumstances which enable us to understand how
Paul saw the Gospel as the abrogation, James as the fulfilment of the
Law. It is when the human element is lost sight of that criticism and
grammar are disregarded in a loose system of interpretation. Such indo-
lence has not disappeared in England; and Lightfoot illustrates it. "I see
no ground whatever for supposing that the language of the inspired
writers is careless or ungrammatical." It is not "pure," but it is "exact."
'Aristotle himself is not more exact in his use of terms than St Paul."
With precise study of language must go the attempt to reproduce the
historical circumstances under which the Gospel was first preached.

The irrational method of interpretation is to be avoided but at
least it is better than the rationalistic which boasts that it approaches
Scripture free from prepossessions. But is this possible? Is it desirable?
There are two kinds of prepossession; There are those that result from
outward circumstances, such as education and social position. These
must be resigned. There are also those that come from the inward dic-
tates of the heart, from God speaking within us. These we must cling
to.

> The human indeed must be tried "in foro rationis".
> The text must be discussed, the interpretation fixed,
> historical questions decided before this tribunal. But
> there is a higher court of appeal—the conscience.
> Spiritual things are spiritually discerned; spirituality
> is necessary in the interpreter.

One specific piece of advice follows: young students should
avoid German criticism, or at least approach it in a "spiritual frame of
mind." This is not a wholesale condemnation. There is much to learn
from German scholars: they have done so much work, there must be
something of value in their results. "Then and then only shall we as a
nation have a right to inflict this indiscriminating censure when we
have spent as much time and pains over the sacred writings as they
have and produced results as considerable."

Finally Lightfoot stresses the importance of prayer. If you
study a historian such as Thucydides or Tacitus you must transport
yourself into his time so as to think and feel as he did. In regard to the
Bible, this means the Spirit. Lightfoot does not say, though he probably

meant, You must also learn to live in the biblical history.
A profound belief in the divine element in Scripture; a readiness to study its vocabulary, grammar, and history with the whole of a
Senior Classic's resources; a devout spirit of prayer and readiness to
hear the word of God: we cannot doubt that Lightfoot brought these to
his lectures and to his commentaries.
My second source is Lightfoot's critical essay[33] on "Recent
Editions of St Paul's Epistles," in which he reviews the commentaries
of Ellicott, Stanley, and Jowett. Ellicott is soon dismissed; he offers
grammatical criticism only. Evidently Lightfoot, for all his stress on
grammar, regarded this as no more than preliminary to a commentary.
The treatment of Stanley can only be described as savage. Stanley "has
taken upon himself a task for which he was unfitted either by his intellectual constitution or by his previous training. . . he seems to be entirely wanting in that habit of strict accuracy, which is the first second and
third requisite for a successful critic" (90). Examples, dealing with text,
exegesis, lexicography, grammar, and history follow. "The treatment of
tenses. . . in these volumes is so hopelessly confused and contradictory, that any attempt to analyse it would be vain" (96f.). "If our belief in
Mr Stanley's efficiency as a commentator has not received its death-
blow already, it will scarcely survive his self-contradictions" (98).
So much for Mr Stanley.
Jowett was a different matter and had to be taken seriously,
though his "greatness appears in the Essays rather than in the commentary" (102). Here are discussed the questions which (I suspect) the mere
Protestant in Lightfoot did not bring into commentaries, though he was
capable of understanding and appreciating them when he met them.
"How has this or that metaphysical question presented itself to different
minds, or to the same mind at different times? Under what contradictory aspects may a particular religious sentiment or moral truth be
viewed? What phenomena does an individual mind exhibit at different
stages in its growth? What contrasts do we find in the ancient and modern world of thought?" (117f.). These are not improper questions. It is
Jowett's exegetical methods that evoke criticism. He "applies entirely
different principles of interpretation to the language of St Paul, from
those by which he would investigate Sophocles or Xenophon. He removes him beyond the pale of ordinary grammatical considerations.
We cannot argue therefore from these volumes what treatment he
would adopt with a classical writer" (102). He exaggerates the changes
in the Greek language since the days of Pericles (106) and—worse—
makes the unwarranted assumption that degeneracy in a language implies indefiniteness. "It was impossible that Prof. Jowett's views of the
language of St Paul should not to a great extent vitiate the character of
his commentary" (109). Lightfoot gives examples, but is also able to
say that Jowett's "practice is better than his theory" (103).
The charge of inexact scholarship (which, if we put it into re-

verse, tells us much about Lightfoot's understanding of the commentator's task) may be taken a little further. It will bring us back to Hort, who joined in the criticism of Jowett. There was much in Jowett's work that he liked; much also that he disliked. One quotation will suffice. In November 1855 Hort wrote to Gerald Blunt

> About Jowett, I don't think you could go beyond me in enjoying and praising him. His wonderful sympathy, depth of insight into men, and thorough love of truth and fact are above praise; but, alas! his theological *conclusions* seem to me blank atheism, though he is anything but an atheist. Even the learning and scholarship of the book you must not accept on trust. It is nearly always second-hand, and often quite wrong.[34]

It is not surprising that criticism such as Lightfoot had published and Hort had written privately were brought into the controversy at Oxford over the endowment and remuneration of the Greek professorship which Jowett held. It was probably Jowett's contribution to *Essays and Reviews* that precipitated the trouble but the adequacy of his Greek scholarship was brought into it. It is surprising that Hort leapt to Jowett's defence in a letter to *The Record*.[35] It is too long to quote, but Hort makes the points that Lightfoot (in the *Journal of Classical and Sacred Philology*) had referred to a disagreement in opinion, not to lack of knowledge, and that Jowett had in any case not been asked to lecture on the New Testament. "Marcus"[36] replies that Lightfoot had referred to confusion of the perfect and aorist tenses, and that if Oxford had not asked Jowett to lecture on the New Testament there may have been good reason for the omission. I find it impossible to acquit Hort of a measure of disingenuousness. This however is not a point that I may allow myself at present to pursue. Strictly relevant to a consideration of Lightfoot's biblical commentaries is the disagreement between him and Jowett about biblical Greek. We have already seen something of Lightfoot's criticism of Jowett. Let Jowett now speak for himself. He is right when he complains,[37] "There is a danger of making words mean too much; refinements of signification are drawn out of them, perhaps contained in their etymology, which are lost in common use and parlance." That might have been written by James Barr! When he asks for a lexicon not of the entire Greek Testament but of significant theological words (he mentions πίστις, χάρις, δικαιοσύνη, ἁγιασμός, νόμος, πνεῦμα, παράκλητος, ἀπόστολος, ἐπίσκοπος, πρεσβύτερος, ὁ καὶ ἡ διάκονος, ἀγάπαι, ἡ κυριακὴ ἡμέρα) he is anticipating Kittel. But to him the language of the New Testament was simply degenerate.

> The degeneracy of the Greek language is traceable in the failure of syntactical power; in the insertion of

prepositions to denote relations of thought, which classical Greek would have expressed by the case only; in the omission of them when classical Greek would have required them; in the incipient use of ἵνά; (sic) with the subjunctive for the infinitive; in the confusion of ideas of cause and effect; in the absence of the article in the case of an increasing number of words which are passing into proper names; in the loss of the finer shades of difference in the negative particles; in the occasional confusion of the aorist and perfect; in excessive fondness for particles of reasoning or inference; in various forms of apposition, especially that of the word to the sentence; in the use, sometimes emphatic, sometimes only pleonastic, of the personal and demonstrative pronouns. These are some of the signs that the language is breaking-up and losing its structure.[38]

Lightfoot knew better. The language was developing, and the New Testament is part of the development. It is possible to be too nice in handling the language of the New Testament[39] but it is also possible to be not nice enough, and it can usually be assumed that the New Testament writers, not least Paul, said what they meant to say, even though by classical standards they did not say it in the most elegant, in the most "correct" way. Lightfoot's insight in anticipating the papyrus discoveries of "everyday" Greek has often been celebrated,[40] but the words must not be made to mean too much. He writes explicitly:[41]

We do not believe that St Paul can be said in any strict sense to have written in the Greek of every day life. He wrote perhaps in the religious Greek of the day. A language formed partly by the influence of the LXX. version, and partly by other traditional influences, but in many respects very different in colour from the language spoken every day at Athens or Antioch, or even Alexandria.

This seems to me well observed.

Comparison with Jowett, which illuminates some of Lightfoot's basic principles, may also serve to bring us to the last section of this sketch of Lightfoot as commentator. After dealing, in *Essays and Reviews*, with the language of Scripture, that is, with interpretation in the narrow sense, Jowett turns (404) to application. This is partly a matter of recognizing ourselves, especially in the parables, which speak immediately to "well-satisfied Pharisees; repentant Publicans" (414); partly selection.

It is impossible to gather from a few fragmentary and apparently not always consistent expressions, how

> the Communion was celebrated, or the Church or-
> dered, what was the relative position of Presbyters
> and Deacons, or the nature of the gift of tongues, as a
> rule for the Church in after ages;—such inquiries
> have no certain answer, and at the best, are only the
> subject of honest curiosity. But the words,—
> "Charity never faileth," and "Though I speak with the
> tongues of men and of angels, and have not charity, I
> am nothing,"—these have a voice which reaches to
> the end of time.[42]

Over against this, Lightfoot has only one method of interpretation and application: the historical-critical method. The primary and in-
escapable task of exegesis is to determine the precise meaning of the
words in question in the context in which they were first spoken or
written. This task Lightfoot achieved with unsurpassed success. 'Lightfoot's strength lay in the historical interpretation of the documents
which he handled.'[43] The New Testament commentaries set out to state,
with the utmost accuracy and clarity, what Paul wished to say to the
Galatians, to the Philippians, to the Colossians, and to Philemon. There
is a tacit assumption that this is also what Paul would have wished to
say to Christian Englishmen in the nineteenth century. This assumption
comes, I believe, pretty near to what Hort meant by "mere Protestantism," though whether Hort had found the best terms for denoting it is
questionable. It is also questionable whether the assumption is justified;
it is our last question in regard to Lightfoot as commentator. Does he
complete his task? Does there not remain untouched a hermeneutical
process which Lightfoot owed to his readers, but did not give them?

It goes without saying that nothing will be found in Lightfoot's works of modern linguistic or semantic theory. It also goes without saying that we shall not be fair to Lightfoot if we do not study along
with his commentaries his many sermons—many published and many
more that are still available to us in manuscript. These are interesting
and instructive in their form; and in what they say and do not say. I take
one, preached in St Paul's, on Septuagesima Sunday, 1877, on 2 Cor.
3.6, The letter killeth, but the spirit giveth life. It begins with matter
that could have been used in a lecture or commentary. The contrast of
spirit and letter was coined by Paul; it occurs in three places in his letters; each passage is given straight-forward historical exegesis. Then
comes the turning-point.

> This is the primary sense, in which the Apostle
> speaks of the letter killing and the spirit giving life.
> But, like many another maxim of St Paul, the saying
> is far too full to be exhausted by its primary meaning.
> It has applications as wide as human life is wide, as
> human thought is wide. On one such application—

perhaps the most important of all—I shall venture to
dwell for a few moments.[44]

Lightfoot then goes on to deal with the way in which practical
moral conclusions are to be drawn from difficult sayings such as "Give
to him that asketh thee."
In other words, a general truth was given to the Corinthians in
a particular context. This context, reached by the skill of the historian
and helped out by parallels, enables us to determine the precise meaning of the general truth. The general truth may then be applied to other
contexts which were not in Paul's mind when he wrote to Corinth.
Thus historical exegesis has not only the negative function[45] of saying
to the modern theologian or moralist, No, you may not base your proposition on that text, but the positive function of providing solid ground
for inferences relevant to ages long after the original truth was stated.
Lightfoot assumes—and if the assumption is valid he may be vindicated not only as a philologist and historian but also as a theologian—that
the language and the historical circumstances of Scripture have a quality of universality that gives them a perennial applicability. Lightfoot's
extraordinary familiarity with the Fathers is enough to show that he was
by no means unmindful of the post-biblical tradition and its value. It
helped him in exegesis and provided examples of the way in which
Scriptural truth had been applied to post-biblical situations earlier than
his own. He speaks also with admiration of Luther as well as of post-
enlightenment biblical scholars in Germany and elsewhere. There remains for him however an absolute qualitative distinction between the
words of Scripture and all other words, and it is this, together of course
with his splendid scholarly equipment, that places him securely in the
line of great biblical expositors, from Origen and Chrysostom to Calvin
and Bengel.

NOTES

1. *DUJ* 64 (n.s. 33), 193-204.
2. I gladly take this opportunity to express my gratitude to Roger
Norris, of the University and Chapter Libraries, who has helped me in every
possible way.
3. See especially the identification by G. R. Treloar and B. N. Kaye
of Lightfoot's Norrisian Prize Essay, *DUJ* 79 (n.s. 48, 1987), 165-200.
4 See also the late J. A. T. Robinson's 1981 Durham Cathedral Lecture, *Joseph Barber Lightfoot*.
5. Notably the great essay on Eusebius of Caesarea, *DCB* 2. 308-348.
6. *Westcott as Commentator*, The Bishop Westcott Memorial Lecture
1958; CUP, 1959.
7. *St Paul's Epistles to the Colossians and to Philemon*, London,
Macmillan, 1875, 210.

8. *Colossians* 210-212.
9. *Saint Paul's Epistle to the Philippians,* London, Macmillan, 1868, 187.
10. *Saint Paul's Epistle to the Galatians,* London, Macmillan, 1865, 227-236.
11. *Galatians* 84f.
12. *Galatians* 127.
13. I have drawn attention to this in *NTS* 28 (1982), 314.
14. As an example of historical knowledge that goes far beyond the New Testament see e.g. the discussion of the meaning of πραιτώριον (*Philippians* 99-104).
15. *DUJ* 64 (33; 1972), 199-203.
16. It is given less fully in *DUJ* 64, 197.
17. *Galatians* 142f.
18. Printed, with suitable omissions, in *The Cambridge Review* 68, no. 1661, 1 February 1947, 269-271.
19. I borrow the apt title of the journal Lightfoot helped to found and, through its short life, to edit.
20. *Life and Letters of Fenton John Anthony Hort,* by his son, A. F. Hort, two volumes, London, Macmillan, 1896.
21. The running dots are in the *Life and Letters*, presumably indicating an omission made by the editor. Of what? Of something too uncomplimentary to repeat?
22. 2.306; a letter of 17 November 1883.
23. "Quomodo historia conscribenda sit," *NTS* 28 (1982), 303-320.
24. *Essays on the Work entitled Supernatural Religion,* London, Macmillan, 1889, 180.
25. "Lightfoot and Baur on Early Christianity," *NovT* 26 (1984), 193-224; the quotation is on 223.
26. Cf. the reference in *NTS* 28.317 to J.W. Rogerson's phrase, "a Lockean sort of supernaturalism."
27. Lightfoot quotes Hooker perhaps less frequently than this suggests; in re-reading for this lecture I have noticed only one example, though there are doubtless more.
28. From p. 311, in the dissertation, St Paul and the Three. There is more to this effect in *DUJ* 64, 199-203.
29. *Philippians* 181-269.
30. *DUJ* 64, 203f.
31. *Philippians*, 6th edition, p.x. The dissertation was reprinted separately (London, Macmillan, 1910). In the reprint the quotation is on 138f.
32. Durham Chapter Library MS. Since my lecture was written and delivered Lightfoot's lecture has been published, with Introductions, by B.N. Kaye and G.R. Treloar in *DUJ* (July 1990), 161-175.
33. In *The Journal of Classical and Sacred Philology* 3 (1857; reprint 1970), 81-121.
34. *Life and Letters* 1.315.
35. Supplement, Wednesday evening, 27 April 1864, 4.
36. I do not know who hides behind this pseudonym.
37. *Essays and Reviews*, London, Parker, 1860, 391.
38. *Essays and Reviews* 398.
39. Perhaps Westcott was.

40. E.g. by J. A. Robinson, in *Lightfoot of Durham*, ed. G.R. Eden and F.C. Macdonald, CUP, 1932, 126.
41. *JCSPh* 4 (1859), 107f.
42. *Essays and Reviews*, 415.
43. F. F. Bruce, in *New Testament Interpretation*, ed. I.H. Marshall, Exeter, Paternoster, 1977, 45.
44. *Sermons preached in St Paul's Cathedral*, London, Macmillan, 1891, 206-217, quotation on 214.
45. *Biblical Interpretation*, R. Morgan, with J. Barton, OUP, 1988, 181.

3

F. J. A. HORT

Hort was born in Dublin on 23 April 1828, of an originally English family. His greatgrandfather, Josiah Hort, was a friend of the hymn-writer Isaac Watts, and attended the same Dissenting Academy; he was, according to Watts, "the first genius in the academy." Later Josiah conformed to the Church of England and went to Clare College, Cambridge; ordained in the Church of England he became chaplain to Earl Wharton, Lord Lieutenant of Ireland. Established in Ireland he eventually became Archbishop of Tuam. The family prospered in Ireland, but when FJA was nine his father, who was fortunate enough to need no gainful occupation, moved from Leopardstown to Cheltenham, where at ten Hort went to his first school. It must not be thought that his education had previously been neglected. He was now ready to read Homer and Xenophon, with Horace or Virgil and Cicero.

The Horts were, by modern standards, a fairly large and undoubtedly a happy and united family. Fenton Hort (the father) is said to have required obedience, but to have been gentle and tender. He loved to read aloud to the children after 6 o'clock dinner, especially Scott. Mrs Hort was a remarkable character, of high intelligence. She was an old-fashioned evangelical, with a firm faith and a deep knowledge of Scripture. There was a close link between her and her eldest son (FJA) which survived the theological differences that developed as he moved in a different direction—a matter to which we must return. It grieved him very much to disagree with her, but each of them knew that truth, as either saw it, must come first. No doubt he learned from her favourite saying, "I hate mediocrity." And he absorbed too a sense of truth, uprightness, and duty.

---

*This paper was given first at Durham, later (in celebration of the centenary of Hort's death) at Cambridge. I have removed introductory paragraphs, intended to accommodate the paper to Durham and Cambridge respectively, and a very small number of other local allusions.

References to the indispensable *Life and Letters of Fenton John Anthony Hort,* by his son Arthur Fenton Hort, two volumes, London 1896, are given in the form (1.123).

In 1841, at the age of thirteen, Hort moved on to Rugby—
Arnold's Rugby, though Arnold was to die in 1842. There are letters-
which show (to the late 20th century reader) a quite astonishing maturity, and not only in the writer, who was, of course, to become an outstanding scholar. I cannot forbear to quote the postscript of his first
Rugby letter to his *young* brother Arthur. (1.20)

> I should write more, if I had time, but I shall soon
> write again. Over the door of the chapel is written
> εὐφράνθην ἐπὶ τοῖς εἰρηκόσιν μοι Εἰς οἶκον
> Κυρίου πορευσόμεθα. I leave it to you to translate
> it.

Hort left the translation to his ten-eleven year old brother; I
will not insult my readers by translating it for them.

A narrow education, you may say. But he was also at work on
mathematics (at Cambridge he would have to take honours in the Mathematical Tripos before being allowed to take honours in Classics), he
was learning German (he writes in the same first letter of having four
pages of Schiller to learn by heart), and reading widely in history and in
English literature. In his spare time he was not only acquiring a practically professional knowledge of botany but constructing an electrical
machine. In addition he was not a brilliant but an enthusiastic and fear-
less player of football—of Rugby football, of course, whose earliest
rules he helped to codify. In 1845 he wrote in a letter to his father, (l.
31)

> Our football rules are to be out this week, and if the
> book is as small as I hear, I will send you a copy by
> post. I believe we are the only school who make it a
> scientific game with an intricate code of laws.

Another letter, dated on Easter Day 1846 and again of astonishing maturity, tells his father and mother of his intention to be ordained.

In October 1846 Hort went up to Trinity, Cambridge. In the
long chapter of the *Life and Letters* dealing with his undergraduate career I notice no reference to Lightfoot, one to Westcott—an apology for
absence from tuition, caused by illness.

It was not as successful a career as others, and no doubt Hort
himself, had hoped. At the time of his examination in Mathematics he
was ill, and was adjudged no more than Junior Optime (a kindly Cambridge expression for a third). He had hoped to follow Lightfoot as Senior Classic, but was bracketed third—a result good enough for most
purposes, but Tait, for example, who had succeeded Arnold at Rugby,
was disappointed. Hort blamed himself for his laziness; there is a sense
in which this could be said to be true, not in that he idled his time away
but in the width of his interests. He had not forgotten Rugby football,

though it is not clear that he played very much.

> Our Club rules are as bad as can be, having a basis of
> the vile Eton system for making skill useless with
> merely one or two Rugby modifications. On the other
> hand, our Rugby rules are very complicated and hard
> to learn (though excellent), and require much expla-
> nation. (1.127f.).

More than this: he was reading very widely, including a great
deal of fiction and general literature that fell well outside the limits of
the Tripos. He was also very interested in politics. There is an enormous letter (thirteen pages of print) in which (at the age of not quite 22)
he gives a history of his political opinions. Passing through the influence of Arnold and of Maurice he was coming out as something of a
Tory. The discussion of politics involves at point after point theological
principle, and it is clear that, though he was not at this stage officially
studying theology, theology was his deepest interest. Here too there are
changes to record. When he went up to Cambridge he retained much of
the evangelicalism he had inherited from his mother, though Rugby had
to some extent loosened its hold. Arnold's influence was now largely
replaced by that of F. D. Maurice, to whom Hort wrote a long letter
(1.116-123), asking for guidance primarily on the question of eternal
punishment but incidentally on a great many things beside. He received
a long and kind reply, which confirmed him for the present—and a
good deal of the future—as something like a disciple of Maurice, and
friend of his associates, not least of Kingsley. Notwithstanding the To-
ryism referred to above, Hort had a great deal of sympathy with the
Christian Socialists.

He also had a stronger taste for examinations than most. At
Cambridge two new Triposes had been inaugurated to accompany those
in Mathematics and Classics: Moral Sciences and Natural Sciences.
Hort decided to go in for both, though in the same year he was also taking the examination for a fellowship at Trinity. He had first classes in
the two Triposes but just failed to win a fellowship, narrowly beaten by
men who were senior to himself, and with such a good performance
that his success in the following year was confidently predicted. Indeed
it duly came off, so that he was established in Cambridge for life, provided that he did not marry. In fact he stayed till 1857, when he was 29.

They were well filled years, filled not entirely with work,
though there was plenty of that. There was one long tour on the main-
land of Europe and a number of shorter excursions, mainly for the purpose of visiting glaciers and climbing mountains. In the middle of the
19th century English mountaineers were pioneers, and it is pleasing to
picture Lightfoot and Hort spending the night in a Swiss mountain cha-
let, lying on one bag of straw and covered by another, while the Swiss
guides made the most of loose straw on the floor. Hort seems to have

dreaded nothing in this experience but the possibility of being bitten by insects. Fortunately the straw was clean. At another place a local inhabitant encouraged the travellers; they would not be cold during the night; they were on the upper floor and *les vaches sont en dessous, et vous en aurez la chaleur.* Hort notes that there were not only vaches but cochons.

Work included university committees. Perhaps in those days Professors knew how to make the young men in their twenties do the work. There was the *Journal of Classical and Sacred Philology.* He shared the editing with Lightfoot and one or two others and wrote in both fields: an essay on the date of Justin Martyr, and one on the meaning of the Latin word *limes.* He wrote (you will note the width of his interests) an essay on Coleridge. He was concerned in the Cambridge translation of Plato, which in the end came to nothing. Having taken the new Triposes he was soon examining in them. He was teaching, though, as he explained to his mother, this did not mean lecturing. It was a matter of reading texts with undergraduates, correcting their mistranslations, explaining the grammar, annotating the more obscure words.

He had not forgotten the intention that he had already formed in his last year at school of being ordained, and in preparation took the so-called Voluntary Theological Examination. Ordination to the priesthood was, as a ceremony that should have been memorable, eminently forgettable. He wrote to his mother (1.322),

> You will perhaps have been expecting to hear something about my ordination at Ely last Sunday week, but really there was nothing about it on which I could write with any pleasure. Nothing could well be more frigid and perfunctory without being absolutely offensive.

The two great events that touched Hort closely may be mentioned now though I shall have to return to one of them later. One was the project for producing a critical edition of the Greek New Testament. Hort had not been well, and went to Umberslade Hall, near Birmingham, to take a hydropathic cure. Westcott was at the time staying with his parents at Moseley; Hort paid him a visit; they took walks together.

> One result of our talk I may as well tell you [Ellerton]. He and I are going to edit a Greek text of the N.T. some two or three years hence, if possible. Lachmann and Tischendorf will supply rich materials, but not nearly enough; and we hope to do a good deal with the Oriental versions. Our object is to supply clergymen generally, schools, etc., with a portable Grk. Test., which shall not be disfigured with

> Byzantine corruptions. But we *may* find the work too
> irksome. (1. 250).

Hort's mind had already begun to turn in this direction. Earlier
(1.211) he writes (also to Ellerton):

> I had no idea till the last few weeks of the importance
> of texts, having read so little Greek Testament, and
> dragged on with the villainous *Textus Receptus*.
> Westcott recommended me to get Bagster's *Critical*,
> which has Scholz's text, and is most convenient in
> small quarto, with parallel Greek and English, and a
> wide margin on purpose for notes. [This is shocking;
> but I am sure Hort was thinking of the wide mar-
> gins!] This pleased me much; so many little altera-
> tions on good MS. authority made things clear not in
> a vulgar, notional way, but by giving a deeper and
> fuller meaning. But after all Scholz is very capricious
> and sparing in introducing good readings; and Tis-
> chendorf I find a great acquisition, above all, because
> he gives the various readings at the bottom of his
> page, and his Prolegomena are invaluable. Think of
> that vile *Textus Receptus* leaning entirely on late
> MSS.; it is a blessing that there are such early ones.

In view of the later collaboration between Hort, Westcott, and
Lightfoot it is interesting that Daniel Macmillan suggested a compre-
hensive "New Testament Scheme." Hort and Westcott were to edit the
text, Westcott would supply a commentary (presumably on the whole
NT), and Lightfoot would contribute a NT Grammar and Lexicon. This
was dropped, but "Westcott and Hort" went ahead. They little knew
how much they had taken on. On 4 November 1853 Hort wrote to Gerald Blunt (1.264)

> We came to a distinct and positive understanding
> about our Gk. Test. and the details thereof. We still
> do not wish it to be talked about, but are going to
> work at once, and hope we may perhaps have it out in
> little more than a year.

It took twenty eight.

A second event that touched Hort deeply, though it did not
concern him directly, was F. D. Maurice's dismissal from his chair (or
chairs) at King's College, London. The cause was that on which the undergraduate Hort had written to Maurice; Maurice had now publicly
called in question the fact, or at least the meaning, of eternal punishment. This is not a paper on Maurice and I must not discuss the matter,
though later I shall refer again to Hort's indebtedness to Maurice. It
was at this time that Hort came to know Kingsley and to value him as a

friend. He writes with special admiration of Kingsley's *Westward Ho!*
Just how Tory were the Christian Socialists? That too is not a question
for discussion now.

In 1857 Hort married Fanny Dyson Holland, and accepted the
college living of St Ippolyts-cum-Great Wymondley, near Hitchin. He
was incumbent here till 1872, but I shall say little about this part of his
life. He was not really cut out to be incumbent of a country parish. He
was absolutely sincere in his profession; he worked hard at the sermons
that he preached to his rural congregation; but he was shy and diffident,
and there was little community of interest between himself and his pa-
rishioners. They respected him, and some at least were capable of per-
ceiving and appreciating his genuine good will and desire to be of service to them. But he continued to live in a rarefied academic
atmosphere, which, it seems, most of them found inpenetrable. All the
time, though with frustrating (often self-induced) interruptions, the
work on textual criticism was going on, and in 1864 he wrote (but did
not publish) a first draft of the famous *Introduction*, to which we shall
come in due course. This fell during an interruption of his parish ministry; from 1863 to 1865 he took leave from St Ippolyts, partly because
he himself, in the interests of his health, needed rest, partly to care for
his mother. Both purposes call for some qualification. "Rest" really
meant rest from the parish; he took the Greek NT and its textual problems away with him; and he left his mother (and his wife—but not textual criticism) for some months every summer while he wandered in the
Alps, proving incidentally that his physical health was not in too bad
shape. In addition to the text there were other literary pursuits, which
never reached publication: a NT Greek Grammar (an edited translation
of Winer), contributions to a biographical history of England; and of
course the commentary, which was to be shared with Lightfoot and
Westcott. Work was not only assigned; it was timetabled to come out in
three issues. Alas for such careful planning. Hort did not in his lifetime
succeed in publishing a single line. On the problem that arose over the
assignment to him of the Synoptic Gospels I have spoken in my lecture
on Westcott.

Already in 1867 Hort had his eye on Cambridge, and applied
for the Knightsbridge Chair of Moral Philosophy. Maurice was elected—apparently to Hort's surprise, and, as he said, to his great pleasure.
Increasing contacts with Cambridge, including several examinerships—
in Moral and Natural Sciences rather than theology—followed, and inclusion among the Revisers, charged with producing the Revised Version, must have helped to bring Hort to the middle of the stage both academically and ecclesiastically. At the end of 1871 or the beginning of
1872 he received a letter from Emmanuel College informing him of a
statute that permitted the College to elect to a fellowship "Aliquem vir-
um ob literas vel scientiam insignem, etiamsi uxorem duxerit, qui nec
beneficium in Ecclesia extra Universitatem habeat nec Magister sit nec

socius alii Collegii." The College wished to promote the study of theology and to appoint Hort to lecture on theological subjects. He accepted.

Before we follow him back to Cambridge there are a few matters belonging to the St Ippolyts period that we may note with a view to taking them up again in the assessment that we must in the end attempt to make.

How seriously are we to take this letter to Lightfoot (April 1864; 2.7)?

> I shall be glad to hear whether you think Syriac can be profitably learned without a good preliminary study of Hebrew. I have almost made up my mind to make either Hebrew or Syriac my holiday task this year, and incline to think Syriac the more useful. But of Hebrew I know only the letters, a smattering of the grammar, and a very few words. With great labour and loss of time I can make out any single word or verse that I want to study, but only piecemeal.

He had been at work on NT textual criticism for ten years and knew no Syriac. And Hebrew! Do we detect feet of clay? Of course his interests were moving strongly in a philosophical direction, but he had undertaken to write commentaries on the Synoptic Gospels and Acts. And what of this (to Westcott, August 1866; 2.69)?

> I fear I could not construe Aeschylus now. You [Westcott, a master at Harrow] certainly have some compensation for drudgery in being compelled to read so much of the great Greeks. Sometimes I have a yearning to read nothing else, and often seriously think of assigning them a fixed number of hours per week.

There are hints at Hort's theological position, on which we must collect, as we proceed, as much evidence as we can get. In November 1865 he writes to "A Friend" (2.63):

> In Theology itself I am obliged to hold a peculiar position, belonging to no party, yet having important agreements and sympathies with all, and possessing valued friends in all. What I am chiefly is no doubt what Rugby and Arnold made me. In other words I have perhaps more in common with the Liberal party than with others, through a certain amount of agreement in belief, and because in these days of suspicion and doubt I look upon freedom and a wide toleration as indispensable for the well-being of the Church. At the same time I feel most strongly that there can be no higher aim than to help to maintain a genuine

> Christian faith, and a reverence for the Bible at once
> hearty and intelligent.

He refused to sign a petition (even at Lightfoot's request)
against the abolition of religious tests at Cambridge.

> Now I have come to the conviction that the Colleges
> as well as the University must be thrown open . . . If
> we are wise now, I think we may keep our position as
> the *standard* "denomination," though not as the *ex-
> clusive* one; and if so, the most important parts of the
> religious machinery may be preserved, and I believe
> neither Church nor religion will suffer in the long
> run. (2.94f.).

I write this on the day (7 February 1990) on which the Russian commu-
nist party said, mutatis mutandis, exactly the same thing.

Also significant are Hort's relation with Maurice and his attitude to *Essays and Reviews*.

Towards the end of his time at St Ippolyts he was invited by
the Bishop of Ely (Harold Browne) to be his Examining Chaplain. Hort
feared that his views were too far off-centre for such an appointment
and gave the bishop every opportunity to withdraw his invitation. What
of his relation with Maurice?

> Mr Maurice has been a dear friend of mine for twen-
> ty-three years, and I have been deeply influenced by
> his books. To myself it seems that I owe to them
> chiefly a firm and full hold of the Christian faith; but
> they have led me to doubt whether the Christian faith
> is adequately or purely represented in all respects in
> the accepted doctrines of any living school. (2.155).

This does not tell us in any detail *what* he had learnt from Maurice,
only *that* he had learnt.

Hort was invited by Rowland Williams to contribute to *Essays
and Reviews*. He declined as follows (1.399f.).

> The chief impediment is a wide difference of princi-
> ples and opinions from the body of your coadjutors. I
> can go all lengths with them in maintaining absolute
> freedom of criticism, science, and speculation, in ap-
> pealing to experience as a test of mere *a priori* dog-
> ma; and in upholding the supremacy of spirit over let-
> ter in all possible applications. . . But I fear that in
> our own positive theology we should diverge widely.
> I have a deeply-rooted agreement with High Church-
> men as to the Church, Ministry, Sacraments, and,
> above all, Creeds, though by no means acquiescing in

their unhistorical and unphilosophical treatment of theology, or their fears and antipathies generally. The positive doctrines even of the Evangelicals seem to me perverted rather than untrue. There are, I fear, still more serious differences between us on the subject of authority, and especially the authority of the Bible; and this alone would make my position among you sufficiently false in respect of the great questions which you will be chiefly anxious to discuss.

When *Essays and Reviews* appeared, and raised the storm that Hort had expected, Westcott, Hort, and Lightfoot reacted in different ways. Westcott, though disliking the episcopal counterblasts, wished to express public disapproval. For Hort, the balance lay on the other side, and he proposed the following pronouncement (1.439):

We, the undersigned clergymen of the Church of England, desire to protest publicly against the violent and indiscriminate agitation now being directed against a book called *Essays and Reviews*, and against the authors of it. Believing that the suppression of free criticism must ultimately be injurious to the cause of truth and religion, we especially regret the adoption of a harsh and intolerant policy, which tends to deter men of thought and learning from entering the ministry of the Church, and to impel generous minds into antagonism to the Christian faith.

Thus Westcott, and thus Hort. Lightfoot was for doing nothing; and nothing was done.

There are two more passages which are revealing. One is a long letter (1.460-469) to a "Lady who meditated joining the Church of Rome." It is an interesting defence of objectivity against subjectivity; whether Hort finds these in the right places is of course open to discussion. The other deals with the American Civil War (1.458-460). It contains remarks about the United States against which Americans can be trusted to defend themselves effectively, but what it says about the black population of America I cannot bring myself to quote; it is appalling beyond words, though no doubt one must allow for a change in outlook over the last 125 years.

We resume the narrative, and find a bitter disappointment. One thing that drew Hort back to Cambridge was the prospect of regular intercourse with Maurice. This was not to be. Hort reached Cambridge in March 1872; on April 1 Maurice died. It was a severe blow, but it was mitigated by the fact Hort found a house only a few yards from Westcott's. He was soon busily engaged in university affairs (with so many unfinished literary projects why did he not avoid them?) and of course fulfilled the terms of his fellowship by lecturing on theological subjects. In his six years at Emmanuel he lectured on Origen, *Contra Celsum*; Ephesians; Irenaeus, *Haereses* III; 1 Corinthians; James; Clement, *Stromateis* VII; Apocalypse 1-3. There were publications. He contributed, with most of the best theologians of the day, to the *Dictionary of Christian Biography*. He undertook to deal with the Gnostics, but characteristically got no further than the letter B. Even so his entries were numerous, though mostly brief; the most important were Abrasax; Adam, books of; Adamantius; Antitactae; Apelles; Archon; Archontici; Arsinous; Ascodrugitae; Aseneth, history of; Barbelo; Bardaisan (10 pp.); Basilides (12 pp.). More important were the *Two Dissertations* (printed in one volume) which he submitted for the degrees of B.D. and D.D. To this book I shall return in order to say something of its contents. For the present it will suffice to observe that, in my opinion, it provides the perfect model of what dissertations ought to be, and though Hort's dissertations were submitted for the two higher degrees those who are aiming at Ph.D.s could with advantage take note of them. It is worth noting too that though Hort wrote the second dissertation (on the origin of the Constantinopolitan creed) purely as an academic exercise he hoped that it might prove "really favourable to the Bonn policy in the long-run" (2.212)—an allusion, I presume, to the attempt to unite the Orthodox and the Old Catholics (with Lutherans and Anglicans thrown in). But that is another story, though one which has a Durham connection and might some day provide entertainment for this Society.

Hort had not, he tells us, thought of his Emmanuel fellowship as a step on the way to a chair. This did not however prevent him from applying in 1875 for the Hulsean Professorship; J. J. S. Perowne was elected, but did not last long. In 1878 he became Dean of Peterborough, and Hort was elected to the again vacant chair.

From the ensuing narrative it might seem proper to infer that professors have less to do than lecturers. The inference might be misleading. For the first three years of his professorship Hort was hard pressed with the last stages of the production of the RV, and even more with the publication of his and Westcott's Greek Testament, for it was felt that this must be published before RV came out. It goes without saying that Hort and Westcott, backed up by Lightfoot, had been very influential members of the translating Committee. When the work on the NT was done Hort and a few others continued with the translation of the Apocrypha. He continued to lecture on the same topics as those with which he had fulfilled his fellowship, adding Cyril of Jerusalem, Tatian, the Clementine Recognitions, Tertullian, *Adv. Marcionem* IV, V, Romans, and Judaistic Christianity. He busied himself with the decoration of Emmanuel Chapel in view of the College's tercentenary. I draw attention to two letters which are important for any attempt to understand Hort's thinking and his theological and ecclesiastical position. The former indeed is not a letter but a declaration by a small group "On

Disestablishment and Disendowment of the Church of England"; it was however essentially Hort's work. The Declaration seeks not so much to show advantages that accrue from establishment as to consider "the evils which establishment and endowment are alleged to involve. These fall mainly under two heads, injustice to Nonconformists and injury to the higher interests of the Church itself."

"Nonconformists have unhappily much to forgive." But to disestablish and disendow the Church of England would make it more rather than less unkind to Nonconformists. (That is my way of putting it.) And what the Church needs is precisely the national and lay element that it is in the power of Parliament to provide.

The case is well put (at very much greater length than this inadequate summary), but I question whether any one would defend it, at least in Hort's terms, today. There is a thirteen-page letter, followed by another page of reply to a supplementary question, to a Mr H. Brinton, an Oxford undergraduate, who was in difficulty over subscription to the XXXIX Articles. This letter is worth careful consideration. (2.324-337)

It begins with a history of the Articles, moving backward from the present time, for the most important feature of the history was the Parliamentary Act of 1865, based on the report of the Royal Commission of 1864. This introduced a measure of relaxation of the old requirement that every candidate for ordination should give unfeigned consent and assent to all and everything contained in the Book of Common Prayer and accept each and every of the Articles.

Having thus cleared the ground Hort goes on to deal severally with the articles that were likely to cause difficulty. These were

IX. Of Original or Birth-sin. After a very sensible discussion of the problem, not least in the light of the NT use of *flesh*, Hort refuses to ask how a good God could create human beings capable either of "original sin" or of actual sin. This is the inscrutable mystery of evil. But the Gospel reveals to us a God who brings good out evil.

X. Of Free-will. Hort approves. "We can will and do what is well pleasing to God, but only in virtue of a divine power inspiring us."

XIII. Of works before Justification, evidently troubled Mr Brinton. Hort observes that "nothing is said about 'conscious' faith in Jesus Christ, and I do not see why we may not read the Article in the light of such passages as Matt xxv.34-40, Rom ii.14-16."

XVII. Of Predestination and Election. Hort's main point is that these must not be understood in an individualist sense, and that election is to a *function*.

XVIII. Of obtaining eternal Salvation only by the name of Christ. The Article is not, Hort thought, happily expressed. Hort's own distinction, however, between higher and lower forms of salvation, the former available only to Christians (John xvii.3), the latter to Jews and heathen before Christ, and to non-Christians now (John i.3,4) is also less than satisfactory.

XXII. Of Purgatory. It is only the Roman doctrine of Purgatory that is condemned. "But the idea of purgation, of cleansing as by fire, seems to me inseparable from what the Bible teaches us of the Divine chastisements." Mr Brinton was evidently still unhappy about article XIII, for Hort returns to it in a very interesting answer. (2 337f.)

> There is but one mode of access, faith; and but one perfect and, as it were, normal faith, that which rests on the revelation in the person of Jesus Christ. But faith itself, not being an intellectual assent to propositions, but an attitude of heart and mind, is present in a more or less rudimentary state in every upward effort and aspiration of men. Doubtless the faith of non-Christians (and much of the faith of Christians, for that matter) is not in the strict sense "faith in Jesus Christ"; and therefore I wish the article were otherwise worded. But such faith, when ripened, grows into the faith of Jesus Christ . . . .

Much of this is good and helpful, though I do not like "every upward effort and aspiration."

In 1887 Hort moved up to the Lady Margaret chair, but there is little more to tell by way of a story. He had spent his strength, and the long holidays in the air of Swiss mountains and glaciers were no longer sufficient to restore him. Two things especially drained him of his last stores of energy. In December 1889 Lightfoot died. That in itself, the breaking of a long friendship, was a severe blow, but it was compounded by the fact that Lightfoot was succeeded at Durham by Westcott. Several of Hort's old Cambridge friends died at this time; Westcott's elevation removed in another way perhaps the oldest and closest of all, the partner of nearly thirty years of collaboration. More: Westcott wanted Hort to preach at his consecration. Preaching had always been a burden to Hort, but no sermon cost him as much as this. He hesitated for weeks before he could bring himself to accept the invitation. The service was to be held on May 1. He sat up over his sermon nearly the whole night of April 29, as indeed he had for several nights previously. On the 30th he travelled up by the last train from Cambridge to London, working all the way while candles were held for him. He sat up nearly all the rest of the night. No wonder the strain brought on illness. Then came the request to write on Lightfoot for *DNB*. The strain was physical as well as spiritual, but the duty one that he could not refuse. The task was finished on November 10, 1892. On November 30 he died.

I have now spent longer than I intended on a sketch of Hort's life; in a way uneventful, yet full of unexciting incidents which nevertheless cast so much light on Hort's character and intellectual equipment that an analytical summing up may, as it must, be reasonably brief.

It is clear at once that Hort shared to the full in the fundamental virtue of his colleagues Lightfoot and Westcott. He knew and was always governed by the primary texts. There is a famous story of one who asked him to recommend the best books for the study of the synoptic problem. He replied, "I should advise you to take your Greek Testament, and get your own view of the facts first of all." It was not that he neglected the current literature. It used to be said, of the most obscure subjects, "Dr Hort will tell you all the literature." And he actually possessed the books. If the young men in Cambridge wanted to consult some rare book they did not say, "It will probably be in the University Library," they said, "Dr Hort is sure to have it." Even if he got rusty with Aeschylus (and I doubt it), he lived in the ancient Greek and Latin texts and knew them with complete familiarity.

Take the posthumous fragment of a commentary on 1 Peter 1.1-2.17. This contains a special note on the provinces Pontus, Galatia, Cappadocia, Asia, and Bithynia mentioned in 1.1. In this excursus I have noted quotation of and references to the following ancient authorities: Aelian, Agathemerus, Appian, Chrysostom, Cicero, C.I.G., C.I.L., Diodorus Siculus, Diogenes Laertius, Dion Cassius, Dionysius, Ephraemius, Epiphanius, Eusebius, Eustathius, G. Acropolita, Herodotus, Hierocles, Irenaeus, Jerome, Josephus, Juvenal, Livy, Lucian, Marcianus, Memnon, Orosius, Philaster, Philo, Philostratus, Plato, Pliny Major, Pliny Minor, Plutarch, Polyaenus, Polybius, Pseudo-Scymnus, Pseudo-Tertullian, Ptolemy, Strabo, Suetonius, Suidas, Tacitus, Tertullian, Valerius Maximus (46 names). The following modern writers are named: Le Bas, Blümner, Borghesi, Bunbury, Clinton, Dressel, Eckhel, Wald, Fallmerayer, Finlay, Friedländer, Grotius, Hamilton, Huizen, Keil, Krebs, Kuhn, Lightfoot, Lipsius, Marquardt, Michaelis, Migne, Mommsen, Müller, Oehler, Orelli, Renan, Schmitz, Schoene, Schürer, Streuber, Waddington, Weiss, Wesseling, Wilmanns, Zumpt (36 names). This is certainly a special piece, but the style is characteristic of the commentary as a whole.

The commentaries have, I suspect, been somewhat neglected because of their incompleteness. If one wishes to make a study of James, 1 Peter, or Revelation it is natural to choose a commentary that covers the whole book. The commentaries are however of great value and (this is my impression on looking at them afresh) remarkably little dated. They are fuller than Lightfoot's—or, you may prefer to say, they lack Lightfoot's sharp, incisive style, his readiness to leave fools to their folly. They are less full than Westcott's—or, you may prefer to say, Hort avoids Westcott's tendency to squeeze out of the text a little more than it contains. Sometimes Hort's silence is significant. In contrast with some more recent authors he is able, for example, to discuss 1 Peter 1.22-25 without a reference to baptism. This is correct; it is clear that the regenerating agency thought of here is the preached word. This is not to say that Peter had no interest in baptism; he certainly had such an interest (3.21), but it is rash to find the interest where Peter does not express it. The *Two Dissertations*, as I have said, reveal Hort at his academic best. Does John 1.18 refer to the μονογενὴς υἱός, or to μονο–γενὴς θεός? It is of course easy to set out the evidence; Hort does it with care and fullness. It is not hard to discuss questions of transcriptional and intrinsic probability, though the argument that since θεός occurs in v. 1 we may expect it also in v.18 is slight. One may question also Hort's deduction from the fact that μονογενὴς θεός is a patristic phrase that occurs frequently in passages where there is nothing to suggest that John 1.18 is in mind. This in fact points to the standing problem in textual arguments, a problem which Hort perhaps did not solve as completely as he supposed. What should we infer from this widespread patristic use of μονογενὴς θεός? We may infer the likelihood that it is what John wrote and intended, or that the popular expression was introduced into a statement that did not originally contain it. This is an example, an outstandingly important example, of the difficulty that always accompanies arguments about intrinsic and transcriptional probability; we shall meet it again. If a form of words can be held to be suitable to the context, does this mean that the author used it, or that copyists inserted it? The difficulty is compounded if the same proposition is true of both readings. I used not to be convinced by Hort's argument, but the occurrence of his reading in the two recently discovered papyri, P[66] and P[75], probably means that he was right.

It is his note on μονογενὴς θεός in the Nicene Creed that leads to the second dissertation, in which Hort argues that the " 'Constantinopolitan' Creed is not a revised form of the Nicene Creed at all, but of the Creed of Jerusalem" (76). The briefest statement of the argument would occupy the whole of a further paper, and I shall content myself with the observation that Hort's thesis has been widely accepted, though for my own part I have been impressed by Badcock's counter-argument.

We come to the *Introduction and Appendix*, the second volume appended to the *New Testament in the Original Greek* (A title as unfortunate as the famous *textum nunc ab omnibus receptum* of Elzevier's 1633 edition). This book is a classic, and everyone who professes a serious interest in the NT and its text reads it. It is of course over 100 years old and is therefore out of date—out of date in the same sense as Newton's *Principia*, though not to the same extent.

After a brief account of the way in which errors arise in MS transmission and of the way in which he and Westcott had collaborated, Hort begins with an exposition in general terms of the methods of textual criticism (19-72). These are subdivided into Internal evidence of readings (Intrinsic probability and Transcriptional probability), Internal evidence of documents, and Genealogical evidence. Next, these Principles of criticism are applied to the NT (73-287, the backbone of the book). Finally (288-324) there is an account of the Nature and details of this edition.

The central section begins with an account of the material available—Greek MSS, versions, quotations, lectionaries. It is made clear that Westcott and Hort did not regard themselves as collectors of MSS, adding to the available materials, as, for example, Tischendorf had recently done with the discovery of Codex Sinaiticus in St Catherine's Monastery. They were prepared to take over collations made by others if they had reason to think them trustworthy. Next comes genealogical study, with the fundamental discovery that "an overwhelming proportion of the variants common to the great mass of cursive and late uncial Greek MSS are identical with the readings followed by Chrysostom (ob. 407) in the composition of his Homilies" (91), leading to the conclusion that "all the important ramifications of transmission preceded the fifth century" (93). The Syrian (Antiochian) text is therefore late. This leaves three groups of MSS, containing three characteristic texts, labelled by Hort Western, Neutral, and Alexandrian. Of these, he and Westcott chose, mainly on internal grounds, the Neutral, represented by the two ancient codices Vaticanus and Sinaiticus, best of all by the former.

It is with considerable diffidence that I develop this ridiculously brief summary mainly in a negative direction.The magnitude of the achievement made by Westcott and Hort in the third quarter of the 19th century cannot be exaggerated; it is enhanced rather than diminished by the fact that the last 100 years have thrown up important questions. These are among the questions I would put to Hort.

First, I question whether he recognized as fully as he should have done the awkward fit of his two probabilities. He recognized it in theory. "The insufficiency of Transcriptional Probability as an independent guide is most signally shown by its liability to stand in apparent antagonism to Intrinsic Probability" (26). The word *apparent* indicates Hort's intention to minimize the difficulty; often the difficulty is not apparent but substantial.

Second, his insistence that "knowledge of documents should precede final judgement upon readings" (31) has been widely and rightly criticised. It leads him to take three steps: (1) Deal with variations individually, forming a provisional judgment on the basis of general considerations; (2) Evaluate the MSS on the basis of these provisional judgments; (3) Follow, where possible, those MSS which are judged best. Against this it has been said (with some exaggeration but on the whole rightly), that there are no good and bad MSS, only good and bad readings.

A third point is a compound one. On 9 August 1892, not long before his death, Hort sent a postcard from Switzerland to Rendel Harris. It began (2.449)

> Man is an inquisitive animal. Would you mind put-
> ting on a card some few salient particulars about your
> new Old Syriac MS?

This is a reference to the Sinaitic Syriac, unknown at the time when "Westcott and Hort" was produced. It is good to see Hort's continuinig inquisitiveness—and one hopes that he had by now acquired enough Syriac to appreciate the MS! But I mention the matter as representative of the fact that the last 100 years have witnessed a conisiderable number of MS discoveries, which have complicated the fairly straightforward picture drawn by Hort. In particular, we must say (a) the Western text is not a geographically Western but a universal phenomenon; (b) there is a good case for adding a fourth text-type, the Caesarean; and (c) the great variations had arisen much earlier than Hort supposed; we must say not "Before 400" but "Before 200."

I turn now to the posthumous works, of which I have already mentioned the commentaries. There are two that show us something of Hort as a historian of NT life and thought: *Judaistic Christianity* (1894) and *The Christian Ecclesia* (1897). Out of these, with limited time available (and my mind still running on Lightfoot) I shall take up only one point. In the 1880s Hort could think of the Tübingen School almost as belonging to the past.

> The subject [Judaistic Christianity] would indeed be
> not only more extensive but very much more impor-
> tant, if Judaistic Chrstianity had really in the first and
> second centuries included all the Christianity which
> twenty or thirty years ago was so described by the
> great critical school on the Continent. If what is
> known as the Tübingen theory were true, the Chris-
> tianity of the Twelve remained always Judaistic, and
> so also all that Christianity of the Apostolic Age
> which was governed by their influence. It was further
> a part of this theory that the Roman Church of the
> second century was Judaistic in doctrine and custom,
> and that to this source is to be traced that organisation
> of the several churches, and ultimately of the Church
> at large, which grew up in the latter part of the sec-
> ond and in the third centuries. (*Judaistic Christianity*
> 6f.).

The only comment I can make is that Hort fails to state—does he fail to see?—the serious questions asked by Baur and his colleagues; still more does he fail to answer them. I say this with primary reference to his account (which is briefly repeated in *The Christian Ecclesia*) of the Jerusalem Council (Acts 15; Gal 2) and of the subsequent encounter between Peter and Paul. He does ask why Paul in Galatians makes no reference to the Decrees, and answers that "there was no real reason why he should confuse his very rapid sketch by a reference to a measure the importance of which had probably long already passed away" (75). But Paul is not merely silent; he says, μόνον τῶν πτωχῶν ἵνα μνημονεύωμεν (Gal. 2.10)—μόνον. And he goes on to give some detail of his altercation with Peter, the importance of which according to Hort passed even more quickly away. Moreover, in parts of Christendom the Decrees continued to be observed for hundreds of years. There was no "antagonism in principle between the two Apostles," says Hort (77); yet on the next page he himself writes, "What it amounted to was that multitudes of baptized Gentile Christians, hitherto treated on terms of perfect equality, were now to be practically exhibited as unfit company for the circumcised Apostles of the Lord who died for them" (78). Hort, I suspect, did not approach the modified Baurianism that Kümmel rightly finds in Lightfoot. His presentation of the early church is very smooth.

No final assessment of Hort, of his beliefs and achievement, can be made without reference to another posthumous work, *The Way the Truth The Life*. This contains the Hulsean Lectures given by Hort in 1871. Like all his public utterances this course of four lectures cost him much. The first and second were in the end revised for publication and in them we may read essentially what Hort wished to say. The third was partially revised and the printed form is based on two drafts; the fourth was never revised and as delivered was not regarded by Hort as satisfactory. It was composed under enormous pressure. It is not a book that can be summarized in a paragraph. A single sentence may serve better: the theme is the unity of truth, and Hort reflects, I think in philosophical rather than theological terms, on what he had learned from the Natural and Moral Sciences and seen to be focused in the incarnation. Take as a sample the concluding pages (76-94) of the second lecture (on The Truth). Like the Eleven in the first century the church today is called "to know as truth what it has hitherto chiefly held as sacred tradition..." (86). And the individual will use "the past of parental teaching, or the past of an authoritarian creed..." as bonds which "exist that men may be free" (90).

This is strong and heady stuff; different from Westcott and different from *Essays and Reviews*. But the book is a torso; no more than half of it was Hort content. It was dashed off in a hurry, against the 28 years he gave to the text. There is a significant letter which he wrote to William Sanday on 28 August 1889.

> It is only by accident, so to speak, that I have had to occupy myself with texts, literary and historical criticism, or even exegesis of Scripture. What from earliest manhood I have most cared for, and what I have at all times most longed to have the faculty and the

opportunity to speak about, is what one may call fundamental doctrine, alike in its speculative and on its historical side, and especially the relations of the Gospel to the Jewish and Gentile "Preparations," and its permanent relations to all human knowledge and action. Some aspects of the subject were treated in a course of Hulsean lectures which I delivered nearly eighteen years ago while still a parish Priest, and a large part of which went soon afterwards into type. Unluckily the last lecture was written in a state of dull exhaustion, and so fell disproportionately below its intention, as indeed did also, less egregiously, its predecessor. But the time has never yet come when there has been a quiet space of at once tolerable vigour and tolerable undistractedness for completing even these unpretending little discourses, unmolested by imperious claims of more pressing pieces of work; and so the sheets and slips lie imprisoned in a box... (2.406).

It is hard to avoid the impression of a rather sad and somewhat disappointed man. Twenty eight years on textual criticism; sixteen years at St Ippolyts; eleven years on the Revised Version; and the lectures that meant most to him driven through in a few sleepless nights. Banished, as he must have felt, from Cambridge, failing to get the professorship in philosophy that seemed made for him, in the wilderness until there came, to this outstanding scholar, the offer of a college lectureship, followed by yet another rejection of an application for a chair. The one thing that suggests that this impression may be mistaken is part of Westcott's Prefatory Note to *The Way The Truth The Life*. Hort visited Westcott at Auckland Castle in Summer 1890. They spoke of their late friend, Lightfoot.

We talked of what the great scholar had done at Cambridge and the great bishop at Durham; of the new work which had been most strangely committed to me at the close of life: of the work which remained to be done at Cambridge towards the fulfilment of old designs which we had cherished for enterprises at home and in the Mission Field. And where much seemed to be shadowed with anxious uncertainty, one thing I recognized with unqualified joy. Hort felt that at length he was truly known by those among whom he had laboured without one thought of self for nearly twenty years, and looked forward to the future with confident hope, conscious that he should be strengthened for every duty by the eager and reverent affection of younger men. The hope was amply justified by two years of happy and varied activity continued without intermission through failing health. (xii).

There is no doubt that the young men at Cambridge respected, no, venerated him; and there is much satisfaction in that. But how little there was to show, in comparison with what might have been! And how fully Hort was aware of it!

4

HOSKYNS AND DAVEY

It was Dikran Y. Hadidian's suggestion that I might add to the essays collected in this volume (which itself was his suggestion) a new piece, matching, though on a smaller scale, those on Lightfoot, Westcott, and Hort; a piece that should deal with two Cambridge men of a later generation. I am diffident about the response that the suggestion has elicited, but I am glad that it was made. I can hardly hope to write a great deal more, and it might be not inappropriate to conclude my career as a professional theologian with an account of the two men who set me on my way.

Hoskyns and Davey: the names belong together. Indeed, I thought of hyphenating them in the title: Hoskyns-and-Davey. Through two generations many New Testament teachers have begun their instruction by saying, You had better read Hoskyns and Davey;[1] better than anything else it will give you an idea of what New Testament study is, and why it is important and exciting and creative. There are interesting questions behind this advice. Who wrote *The Riddle*[1]? What was the relation between the two men whose names appear on the title page and how did it work on the literary level? We may for the present leave these questions. Hoskyns-and-Davey would have expressed a truth but it would not have expressed the whole truth and would have concealed or distorted more than it expressed. For these were not simply two distinct persons; though united in theology and churchmanship they were different in manner and style.

This is not a biography; I have nothing except personal reminiscence to add to the biographical material contained in *Crucifixion-Resurrection*.[2] I shall refer again to this doubly posthumous book, but Gordon Wakefield's editorial work leaves little for gleaners in the field. To it however should be added the book by Richard E. Parsons, *Sir Edwyn Hoskyns as Biblical Theologian*,[3] which originated in a degree dissertation supervised by C.F. Evans, who knew and understood "Hoskyns-and-Davey" as well as anyone. His brilliant lecture, published in the *Epworth Review*,[4] is the prime source (after Hoskyns's own writing) for Hoskyns's thought, though it may be supplemented by Wakefield and Parsons.

Let me introduce them with one memory that is clearly not the stuff of book or lecture. It was in 1936 that I relinquished the study of mathematics, not without regret, for I had enjoyed it, and turned to the theology which I knew (no son of my father could fail to know) that I should need if I was to be a Methodist minister. At that time Pembroke had no theology don, and I was sent along the road to Corpus Christi to see Noel Davey, of whom I had never heard. He seemed, I thought, a little remote; after telling me what to read during the long vacation he said, "Sir Edwyn does not need to see you at present." Who Sir Edwyn was I had no idea; I suppose Davey was still fairly new to supervising and that Hoskyns was keeping an eye on his young colleague. At the beginning of next term I carried my first essay along Trumpington Street from Pembroke to Corpus. It was on the Synoptic Problem, and I remember thinking that it was not a bad essay. When I had finished reading it Noel said, "Is that all?" He had not wanted an account, even a fairly full and reasonably accurate account, of the various theories that have been evolved in the attempt to solve the Synoptic Problem. He had wanted me to dig into Huck, to examine the text, to describe the phenomena that give rise to the problem. I do not tell this story as an interesting little reminiscence of my own but because it is characteristic and fundamental not only for Davey but for Hoskyns too. The texts: What does the text actually say? What does it mean? What is its place in the Christian tradition? I have heard Hoskyns's lectures on the Theology and Ethics of the New Testament (my own too, incidentally, but that is derivative) criticised as not really theology, just exegesis. But that, to Hoskyns and Davey, was what theology was. What did the evangelists, what did Paul wish to say? What was God saying through them? This could only be theology. It was what the writers meant, what they intended, that mattered. The "response" of "readers" was useful only in so far as it helped us to understand the text itself. The text: and then a certain amount of coordination to bring the various parts into relation with one another and so to form a whole, comprehensible as a whole.

In my second paper on Lightfoot (p. 21) I referred to a university sermon, notorious enough in its day, preached by Charles Smyth,[5] who spoke of the three great names in Cambridge theology. His hearers expected him to continue, as Cambridge theologians are wont to do, by naming Lightfoot, Westcott, and Hort. Smyth named Westcott, Hort, and Hoskyns. Whether this was fair to Lightfoot I have considered elsewhere. Undoubtedly he was greater as a historian and philologist than as a theologian in the usually accepted sense of the term. It was a just recognition of Hoskyns, though his greatness as a theologian is to be seen primarily, and unsatisfactorily, in the unfinished commentary on John,[6] and of course in his lectures. These were reshaped year by year, and it is probable that the substance of them changed as Hoskyns's own thought developed. It was characteristic of him that he should in one

year begin his lectures with a study of 2 Peter, one of the least studied
books of the New Testament. His purpose was to show that even if you
started on the periphery of the New Testament questions were raised
which, as you sought the answers, drove you inward till you arrived at
the theology of Paul or the story of Jesus.

It is not easy to describe Hoskyns's developing theological position. Mr Parsons can hardly avoid using such terms as Liberal Catholic, Liberal Protestant, Modernist, in his account of the background and
of Hoskyns's relation to it. Labels are useful, but they have the effect of
making the environment look more static than it was and of represent-
ing Hoskyns as either espousing or reacting against a party-line, whereas in fact the environment was fluid and marked not only by theological
attitudes but by personal antagonisms, not always theological, and Hoskyns was thinking things out for himself. Liberal catholic he may have
been to begin with, but already before his teaching career began he had
attended Harnack's lectures in Berlin and entertained high respect for
the most notable of liberal protestants, and he became a friend of Albert
Schweitzer's, whom he must have thought a heretic in Christology. As
a teacher he was still thinking his way through, and thinking for himself, but in the process he came under two powerful influences. The
first was Karl Barth, whose commentary on Romans he translated. This
was a great literary achievement; Barth's German is not easy, and Hoskyns's English reproduced the energy and force of the original together
with its occasional obscurity—obscurity due to the complexity and
depth of the thought. But it was more than that: to wrestle as Hoskyns
must have done with five or six hundred pages of Barth at his most explosive and creative must have been a profound experience. Davey
made me read the translation; I doubt whether, as a first-year theologian, I understood much of it, but the impression it made has lasted
now for nearly sixty years. It is not easy to define the influence of Barth
on Hoskyns. Barthian rhetoric and early Barthian existentialism (Hoskyns picked up some of the former, next to nothing of the latter) are not
important. It would be nearer the truth (if we may try to put the truth in
a sentence) if we say that Hoskyns moved from an interest in the religious experience of the apostolic church to a theology of the Word of
God. I remember, perhaps not quite accurately, an analogy that he used.
You look down your critical microscope at the New Testament text
with a view to descrbing the religious life of the first-century Christians, and you find that God is looking back at you through the microscope and declaring you to be a sinner. What mattered was to find out
what Paul and the evangelists were saying; or rather, what God was
saying through their human word. It would be ridiculous to claim that
Hoskyns ever became a Calvinist or a Lutheran (the early Barth, though
his colleagues at Barmen sometimes looked askance at him, was more
Lutheran than the Barth of the *Dogmatics*). Hoskyns remained an Anglican Catholic, but he had learned that what distinguished the New

Testament was not religious experience or liturgy but a theology of the word of God. And there was no denying that the word of the cross was a word of grace that looked for no sort of merit to account for its readiness to justify the ungodly and asked for nothing but faith. It is probably true that Hoskyns would have said that the word of grace was sacramentally expressed. Baptism was a crystallization of the gracious acceptance of the sinner; the eucharist was a common meal at which the Friend of sinners invited his friends to his table, never making grace clearer than in so doing. Yet strong as his sacramental background must have been I have at the end of my undergraduate notes of Hoskyn's lectures the words, "I have not dealt with baptism and the eucharist; ask your supervisors." We all know what it is to run out of time at the end of a course, but I have often wondered why this of all themes had to suffer.

The second influence on Hoskyns was that of Gerhard Kittel, founder and, till his death, editor of *Theologisches Wörterbuch zum Neuen Testament*.[7] Behind this, one of the most notable contributions to biblical theology in the 20th century, was the conviction that through the biblical message they conveyed, the words of the New Testament were themselves charged with a theological content, so that the study of words became an important avenue into the meaning of the Gospel. This we can now recognize (more clearly perhaps than either Kittel or Hoskyns) is a dangerous proposition. Words do not have a built-in theological content; they derive their specific meanings from the contexts in which they are used. To a great extent the criticism brought to bear on the "Wörterbuch" method, notably by James Barr,[8] is justified. It was a method easy to use in exaggerated ways. But it was, and is, a method that can be used with moderation and with profit. Hoskyns did not learn it from Kittel; his course of sermons on The Language of the Church[9] was preached in Corpus chapel in the year 1932-1933. But there is no doubt that Kittel encouraged him in the use of it. This essay is not an attempt to defend Hoskyns and Davey from all attacks on all fronts. It is however fair to say that they were less exposed to criticism than some of those who followed them, that the philosophical aspects of the study of semantics, of which Barr is a master, did not come over their horizon—they were even less philosophers than they were systematic theologians—and that when they found theological significance in a word they were in fact often drawing that significance from the context and attributing it to the word. When this is said, however, it should perhaps be added that they chose to adopt a philological method with something less than adequate philological equipment. I doubt whether either was well equipped in Hebrew—an unfortunate lacuna in the resources of exegetes who (rightly) laid great weight on the Old Testament for the understanding of the New. Another important gap might be found in failure to give attention to the interaction—philological, social, philosophical—of the New Testament with its non-biblical environment. Moulton and Geden, Hatch and Redpath, are primary and indispensable guides to the interpretation of the New Testament, but they are not quite sufficient guides.

It will be worth while to turn aside for a moment to put together the two names, Barth and Kittel. Barth had not only been present at the Synod of Barmen in 1934, he had to a great extent been responsible for drafting the Barmen declaration. He was driven by Hitler out of his German professorship and obliged to take refuge in his native Switzerland. Kittel was if not a member of the Nazi party at least a sympathizer. It is, I think, fair to infer that Hoskyns's contact with each was in the realm of theology, not politics, and this is all that need be said about the invitation (probably given by him, though the visit took place after his death) to Kittel to lecture in Cambridge. Kittel wore his swastika badge, which did not go down well in Cambridge, but he lectured quite straightforwardly on the Wörterbuch and its method—I was present and can answer for this. I cannot answer in the same way for the earlier visit of Karl Fezer of Tübingen, one of the "German Christians." He was invited privately by Hoskyns and spoke in Hoskyns's rooms in Corpus to a small gathering of pupils of Hoskyns and of Davey. He spoke in German, which I could not then understand; Hoskyns translated, but when Fezer said anything that particularly interested him he forgot to translate and instead replied in German, upon which an unintelligible dialogue ensued. At the end of the paper (which was on Justification) Hoskyns said, "There are no doubt many questions you would like to ask Professor Fezer. You must remember that he is here as theologian and exegete and ask questions only in that field." It was Joe Sanders (who died, alas, so young) who had the wit to ask for an exegesis of Rom 13.1-7. The point of these contacts is not that Hoskyns was a Nazi sympathizer (though there were few in England in 1937 who were aware of the full extent of Nazi wickedness). He was a universal sympathizer. This was in part (it would not have sounded old-world in the thirties) the attitude of the English gentleman who insists on fair play even for his enemies; in part the result of ministry in working-class parishes and as an army chaplain; but much more than this it was the result of what Hoskyns had learned from a New Testament that asserted of Jews and Greeks that they were all under sin. The man with a pocketful of money might be the poor man whom we must love and cherish, the great athlete the sick man whom we must care for (*Cambridge Sermons*, pp. 132-136). With universal sympathy went universal interest; few theologians are regular readers of *The Farmer and Stockbreeder*, as Hoskyns was. And out of it arose an eloquence created by the Gospel as it came into contact with the various departments of human life.

Anyone who wishes to make a serious study of Hoskyns's theology must turn to the early essays in *Essays Catholic and Critical* (1926) and *Mysterium Christi* (1930), and to the posthumous and unfinished commentary on John and to the few lines of the posthumous *Crucifixion-Resurrection*. I shall not attempt such study here. I have reread my notes of his lectures. In their form what impresses me now is the freedom with which he moves through Scripture even while keeping close to the point he is discussing. When he is speaking of the Synoptic Gospels Paul is always putting in an appearance; when he is discussing Paul John is quoted; and always the Old Testament is at hand. But it is memory rather than the written page that rekindles the fire and revives the enthusiasm.

I turn to Davey, the junior partner, himself a pupil of Hoskyns, too often thought of as no more than a *fidus Achates* to his principal. Hoskyns I listened to three times a week for two terms and spoke to hardly more than half-a-dozen times before his unexpected death in 1937. Davey lived till 1973 and became not only a supervisor but a dear friend. He came up to Cambridge, a little older than most undergraduates, in 1925; after reading the Modern and Mediaeval Languages Tripos at Corpus Christi he read the Theological Tripos as Hoskyns's pupil. Soon afterwards he was collaborating with him. It is certainly true that it was Hoskyns who made a theologian of Davey; it is also true that without Davey Hoskyns would hardly be known. It was Davey who got him on to paper. I shall come shortly to *The Riddle*; what is beyond question is that without Davey it would never have been written. It was Davey who rescued, edited, and supplemented the torso of a commentary; it was Davey who wrote nearly all we have of *Crucifixion-Resurrection*, a theologian, and a profound one, in his own right. His career as a university teacher was short. Some time after Hoskyns's death he held for a little while a university lectureship, but his tenure was soon terminated on the charge that his lectures were obscure. The basis of the charge seems to have been a university sermon[10] which he had had to deliver in the afternoon after hearing in the morning that his mother had died. I am not aware that any senior person attended his lectures; I attended one or two and so far from finding them obscure thought them perhaps unnecessarily easy—but at that time I was, or thought I was, a rather clever young man; at any rate, I was three or four years older than the undergraduates for whom the lectures were intended. It was, I think, old animosity, which Hoskyns with his baronetcy and his Corpus fellowship could shrug off, that brought his successor down.

After Cambridge he became Rector of Coddenham, but not for long; he was summoned to be Editorial Secretary, later Director, of S.P.C.K. His work in publishing is described by Gordon Wakefield in *Crucifixion-Resurrection*. We saw each other from time to time, in London and in Durham. At the time of the Anglican-Methodist Conversations and the attendant disputes we contemplated producing jointly a book on Episcopacy in the form of letters addressed to each other. I am rather sad that we were both too busy to put the plan into effect.

The Riddle of the New Testament was published in 1931, when Davey was twenty six. On its title page it bears both names, Hoskyns and Davey. Now that some misleading stories, arising probably out of Davey's exaggerated modesty, have been discounted it is clear how the book was written. That it should be produced was Hoskyns's idea, and he thought of the topics of the chapters. It is worth while to add here, what is not often observed, that most of these were probably the subjects of essays that he had set for Davey, and other pupils too, no doubt. At least, they were the topics of essays that Davey required of me—the Synoptic Problem, the Language of the New Testament, Textual Criticism, Form Criticism, and so forth. Davey brought his chapters—revised and expanded essays?—to Hoskyns; they discussed them; and Davey probably did some rewriting. The dual ascription of authorship was correct in that without Hoskyns there would have been no book and without Davey there would have been no book. Hoskyns thought of it; Davey wrote it; Hoskyns improved and approved. It was translated into many languages and has been very widely used. It is now over sixty years old and out of date; it does not deal with the latest kinds of criticism, about which the beginner has in these days to be informed. But the question from which it starts—Did Christianity begin from Jesus or start in some other way?—is still the fundamental question, and no one would regret the time he spent in reading it.

Davey's own theological work is to be found in a few small pieces,[11] in the Introductory Essay prefixed to Hoskyns's commentary, and in the greater part of *Crucifixion-Resurrection*. The Introductory Essay on the Fourth Gospel and the Problem of the Meaning of History, stands on the same level of percipience and profundity as the most mature and finished parts of Hoskyns's work in the commentary. It has been criticised because Davey asks the question which no writer on the Fourth Gospel can avoid, "Did Lazarus rise from the dead?"(p. xxiv) and replies, "The answer cannot be either a simple 'Yes' or a simple 'No'." Why can he not give a plain answer? A man either does or does not believe that Lazarus came out of his tomb alive. But this is a grave over-simplification. "To say, on the basis of the existing documentary evidence that Lazarus, having died, was, or was not, restored to life, is a judgment that cannot be made by a Biblical theologian, and not even by a natural scientist, since the New Testament does not furnish any record of the event comparable to the minute analysis demanded by scientific observation" (p. xxv). Moreover, John was working on earlier tradition, such as the Synoptic tradition, not "writing upon a clean slate" (p. xxvi). And John does go out of his way to emphasize that Lazarus was physically dead. These observations, Davey adds, do not tell us in what sense the story can be regarded as historical. We must go further. "Can it be that, faced with the alternative of handling the material as a chronological historian or as a theologian, the fourth Evangelist chose, deliberately and under the pressure of his function as an evangelist, the latter course?" (p.xxvii). From this point Davey enters into a profound analysis of the Evangelist's interpretation of history. To follow him here would expand this essay to an impossible length; to abbreviate or summarize would be beyond my ability. This is a good point at which to begin a summing up. What Hoskyns and Davey had in common was the ability always to show me (and of course many others) how much more there was in a text, in a question, than I had seen. They did this in different settings, Hoskyns in lectures, as he moved swiftly from one passage in the gospels to another, sometimes from the gospels to Paul, sometimes from Paul to John, Davey in supervisions, as he interrupted the reading of my immature essays to bring out more fully the meaning of passages I was dealing with, sometimes the implications, unnoticed by me, of what I had myself written. In Hoskyns the lecturer there was the manifest conviction that the study, interpretation, and proclamation of the New Testament was both the most exciting and the most responsible task open to men. Here was what I had always, no doubt hazily, observed in my father's preaching, given now an academic status. The ecumenical significance of the harmony between catholic and protestant I did not observe till later. Hoskyns died at the end of my first year of theology. Friendship with Davey lasted and developed. I never submitted a manuscript to him, enjoyed a talk with him, without some re-creation of the days when I used to take my essays from Pembroke to Corpus and found that the subject I was dealing with, and even what I had said about it, had far greater depths and were far more exciting than I suspected.

I used to regret that they had not written, published, more. Perhaps they wrote enough; and even that mattered less than what they were.

NOTES

1. Meaning, *The Riddle of the New Testament* (Faber and Faber, London, 1931 and subsequent editions).
2. Edited by G. S. Wakefield (SPCK, London, 1981).
3. Hurst & Co., London, 1985. I am indebted to the editor for permission to draw on my review of Mr Parsons's book in *Epworth Review* 13.3 (1986), 80-83.
4. *Epworth Review* 10.1 (1983), 70-76; 10.2 (1983), 79-86.
5. *Cambridge Review* Vol. lxviii, No. 1661, 1 February 1947.
6. Faber & Faber, London, 1940 and later editions.
7. English translation, *Theological Dictionary of the New Testament*.
8. *The Semantics of Biblical Language* (OUP, Oxford, 1961).
9. In the posthumous *Cambridge Sermons*, with a memoir by Charles Smyth (SPCK, London, 1938), 89-150. For Hoskyns's sermons see also *We are the Pharisees* (SPCK, London, 1960).
10. In *Crucifixion-Resurrection*, 16-26.
11. His long review—*JTS* 4 (1953), 234-246—of C. H. Dodd's *The Interpretation of the Fourth Gospel* should not be missed.

5

ALBERT SCHWEITZER AND
THE NEW TESTAMENT

A Lecture given in Atlanta on 10th April 1975
as part of the Albert Schweitzer Centenary Celebration

To take part in the Albert Schweitzer Centenary celebrations, and especially here in Atlanta, is at once a great public honour and a notable private satisfaction, for which I cannot thank too warmly those who have invited me to speak on this theme and in this setting. Of the public honour there is no need for me to say much. There can be few in the world to-day who do not recognize in Albert Schweitzer one of the outstanding representatives of our common humanity. His magnificent and wide-ranging mental ability and manual dexterity, and his profound and creative concern for mankind as a whole, are far too well known to call for elaboration from me, and any attempt on my part to praise them would look more like an insult than a eulogy. He takes his place now among the great of all the ages; the world is richer, intellectually and morally, because he lived in it; and the rest of us may congratulate ourselves on any kind of contact we may have with such greatness. I spoke also of private satisfaction. I read all Schweitzer's books on the New Testament while I was an undergraduate, nearly forty years ago, and I have been occupied with them ever since. One of my own greatest teachers, E. C. Hoskyns, was a friend of Schweitzer's, and understood him well; another, C. H. Dodd, was, I suppose, one of the outstanding opponents of Schweitzer, at least in the understanding of the eschatology of the New Testament, and (among many other things) helped to keep the primary issues Schweitzer raised before my mind. To some extent at least these issues have been, or have suggested, the questions that have been in the forefront of my own thought in the interpretation of the New Testament text and the understanding of early Christian history. And it may be not altogether irrelevant to add that, when I can take a little time off the study of the New Testament, there is nothing I like better to do than listen to the music of J. S. Bach (or even, if no one else is listening, to play it myself), and to read up the music I am studying in Schweitzer's great book on Bach.

This lecture, however, is to be about neither me nor even

Bach, but Schweitzer, and Schweitzer's work as a New Testament scholar, so that at least for the moment we must forget Lambarene, and Goethe, and the music, and attend to business. Some other opportunity will, I am sure, occur in the course of these celebrations to give an account of Schweitzer's life, including his birth and boyhood in Alsace, and there must be many here who know the story better than I. He studied in Strasbourg, but again it is unnecessary for us to spend time on a sketch of the university there and the teachers under whom he worked. Schweitzer dedicated his first New Testament book to one of the greatest of his teachers, H. J. Holtzmann, "with sincere respect and devotion," but this did not prevent him from attacking in the course of the book most of the things that Holtzmann stood for. Indeed it is perhaps not unfair to say that both Schweitzer's work on Jesus and his work on Paul are introduced with the proposition, "Up to the present everyone has got this topic wrong; I will now tell you what is right." In most men, especially in most young men, this would give the impression of a quite intolerable egotism and cocksureness, and seventy years ago it can hardly have increased Schweitzer's popularity. But closer reading shows the genuine respect that Schweitzer had for his predecessors, and his readiness to learn, as well as his determination to read the texts for himself and make up his own mind about their meaning. What we must do is hear what he said, examine his grounds for saying it, and then consider not so much where it came from as what it has led to.

If this lecture is not biographical neither is it bibliographical; fortunately there is only quite a small number of publications to cover, and they come in easily intelligible and indeed logical sequence. I shall confine myself to the four main books, three and a half of which are easily available in excellent English translations. In 1901, when he was twenty-six, Schweitzer published a small book in two parts. Its overall title was: *Das Abendmahl im Zusammenhang mit dem Leben Jesu und der Geschichte des Urchristentums*. The first part of the book dealt with the Lord's Supper, the second with the life of Jesus, viewed in particular (as the subtitle makes clear) in the light of the *Messianitäts- und Leidensgeheimnis*. The second part has been translated as *The Mystery of the Kingdom of God*. It was a young man's book; it took little note of earlier work on the same subject, even when (as with J. Weiss and Kabisch) this was favorable to his own view, and the response it won may perhaps be described as a resounding tinkle. For the most part it was ignored; for the rest, it ran into heavy criticism. Schweitzer, it was alleged, had made up his mind in advance on a bizarre interpretation of Jesus and his message, and had determined to dig it out of the gospels at any price. He was, men said, a systematic theologian rather than a New Testament scholar; and they implied, or stated, that they did not think much of his systematics. For he took the disturbing view that the mind of Jesus had been dominated by eschatological conviction and the belief that the world would shortly end—a view not immediately reconcilable with orthodox Christology or (what mattered more, probably, to most of his readers) with the evolutionary liberalism of the nineteenth century. The orthodox conservatives probably lumped Schweitzer together with the liberals (and may not in the end have been far wrong); those who had been engaged in reconstructing 'liberal lives' of Jesus—the term means both that they used an uninhibited literary and historical criticism of the Bible and that the Jesus they found there harmonized with their liberal humanitarian principles—saw their work negated in the extraordinary picture that young Schweitzer had drawn. At this stage there were few who loved, or even admired, him.

We all know now that a few minor discouragements of that kind were unlikely to deter Schweitzer; if anything, they served to make him more determined, and the little book was followed by a much bigger one, *Von Reimarus zu Wrede: eine Geschichte der Leben-Jesu-Forschung*, published in 1906. It was not long before this was published in English translation with the brilliantly chosen and memorable title, *The Quest of the Historical Jesus* (1910). Schweitzer was not content to restate his own views: two other factors made the new book what it was. First: the patrons of "the liberal Jesus" had objected to his work. Well, he would show them that their work had now come to a full stop, indeed that they, with all their fine intentions and great learning (which Schweitzer recognized unreservedly), had been marching resolutely up a cul-de-sac, and had now come to the end of the road. Secondly: there had been published simultaneously with his own earliest work another small book by another young New Testament scholar, William Wrede. This was his *Das Messiasgeheimnis in den Evangelien*. Equally with his own (in Schweitzer's view) Wrede's book put an end to the old liberal Quest, but the two were alternatives. No more than man can serve God and mammon could New Testament scholarship accept both Wrede and Schweitzer; and Schweitzer did his best to make the alternative clear. It is, I believe, the most striking example of Schweitzer's clarity of perception that he saw the significance of these two books of 1901, which have in fact dominated and directed the New Testament world (which has not been without its giants) for three-quarters of a century; and there is today hardly a more important question than that which asks whether they are truly alternatives, or we may in some way combine the wisdom and eliminate the faults of both.

Schweitzer had now reached a point at which it was—academically—impossible to stop. In all other respects it is a wonder that he carried on, but logically he had to do so. Suppose at least for a moment that Schweitzer was right about Jesus, that in or about A.D. 30 Jesus went up to Jerusalem to engineer his death in order that the kingdom of God might immediately come, and died in despair because God showed no sign of doing what he hoped; that Jesus trusted in, and gave his life for, a hope that the inexorable march of history proved false. What next? The disappearance, you would suppose, of Jesus into the limbo of deluded and deluding prophets. But it was not so. Less than a hundred years later we see in Ignatius of Antioch the clear-cut structures of early catholicism—a three-fold ministry, an orthodox faith, a fixed and exclusive liturgical life. Earlier still we find the great Hellenistic Christian mystic John; and, a mere decade or two after Jesus, Paul. Jesus was not forgotten. The organized society and mystical piety of the Christian church not merely looked back to him but also looked up to him as the pre-existent Son of God who now again lived in heaven. How did this result follow from that cause? The key-figure is obviously Paul, and to Paul Schweitzer turned, in two books which perform separately what was brought under one cover in *The Quest*. First came *Paul and his Interpreters* (German, 1911; English, 1912), and, much later, the companion volume *The Mysticism of Paul the Apostle* (German, 1930; English, 1931). Especially in the latter Schweitzer explained how historic Christianity came into being after and in dependence on the historical Jesus. These are his main New Testament publications and will provide more than enough material for us to work on. They will also provide, what is indeed evident enough, the framework within which this lecture must be constructed, though time forbids me to follow Schweitzer in his critical survey of his predecessors; this is unfortunate, for his account of others often leads him to contributions of his own, made sometimes with a characteristic and attractive wit. But we must confine ourselves to his own work, apart from his notice of Wrede, which I shall come to at a later point.

Perhaps a writer—historian or theologian or both—is fortunate when he can start with the conviction that his predecessors and contemporaries are fundamentally in error. It makes for clarity of analysis. When the conviction springs simply from a desire to be, or to be thought to be, original, the results are distasteful; when it is genuine they are apt to be electric. Schweitzer begins *The Mystery* by distinguishing the four assumptions on which the current understanding of the message and work of Jesus, and especially his own understanding of his death, was based. To recall these, and his comments on them, will serve as a useful introduction to his thought. They were (pp. 63f.):

> 1. The life of Jesus falls into two contrasted epochs. The first was fortunate, the second brought disillusion and ill success.
> 2. The form of the Synoptical Passion-idea in Mark 10:45 (his giving himself a ransom for many) and in the institution of the Lord's Supper (Mark 14:24: his blood given for many) is somehow or another influenced by the Pauline theory of the atonement.
> 3. The conception of the Kingdom of God as a self-fulfilling ethical society in which service is the highest law dominated the idea of the Passion.
> 4. If Jesus' Passion was the inaugural act of the

> new morality of the Kingdom of God, the success of
> it depended upon the Disciples being led to under-
> stand it in this sense and to act in accordance with it.
> The Passion-idea was a reflection.

This was shrewdly observed, and a just analysis of much that
was being written at the end of the nineteenth century. Schweitzer takes
up each assumption in turn, and concludes as follows (pp. 81f.):

> 1. The assumption of a fortunate Galilean peri-
> od which was followed by a time of defeat is histori-
> cally untenable.
> 2. Pauline influence cannot have conditioned
> the form of the early Synoptic sayings about the Pas-
> sion.
> 3. Not the ethical but the hyper-ethical, the es-
> chatological, notion of the Kingdom dominates the
> Passion as Jesus conceived it.
> 4. The utterances of the Passion-idea did not
> occur in the form of an ethical reflection but it was a
> question of an incomprehensible secret which the
> Disciples had not the least need to understand and in
> fact did not.

Of these, the third is the point that demands a certain amount
of exposition before we move on. Most scholars at the beginning of this
century understood the biblical phrase "kingdom of God" in the way in
which, I suspect, many who are not biblical scholars still understand it
today. Men think of it as an ideal state of brotherhood, charity, and
good will, and we are urged to establish, or to build it. There is no need
to defend such an ideal; and it is fortunate that we can add that few men
have done more than Albert Schweitzer to plant brotherhood, charity,
and good will in our world. For he, more than anyone else, has made it
unmistakably clear that this is not what the kingdom of God means in
the gospels. The background of the phrase is the apocalyptic of first-
century Judaism. Men felt that they could no longer look, as the Old
Testament prophets had done, for a manifestation of God's will in ordinary historical circumstances; things were now too bad for that. For
some reason of his own, inscrutable to men, God had permitted the
reins of power to be taken out of his hands, and they were now held by
the devil, whose sovereignty over mankind was attended by evil of every kind—sin, oppression, physical suffering, and death. The only hope
was that God, the rightful ruler of mankind, would assert his own royal
power—his kingdom—defeating and driving out the devil and putting
an end to his works. This was not man's task, but God's; all men could
do was hope for it, believe in it, pray for it; and there is preserved in the
Qaddish an ancient prayer, similar to the "Thy kingdom come" which
Jesus taught his disciples: "May he establish his kingdom during your

life and during your days, and during the life of all the house of Israel, even speedily and at a near time." It was this divine act by which God would assert his sovereignty and set up his kingdom that Jesus proclaimed .

This, the hyper-ethical, eschatological notion of the kingdom of God, is not only the point that may have needed some elucidation; it is also the fundamental point in Schweitzer's new interpretation of the work and the passion of Jesus. The whole force of Jesus' person was directed towards the coming of the kingdom. He taught his disciples to pray for it, and he also taught them how to live in a manner suited to it—not suited to life within it but to hasten it. His ethics were interim ethics, intended for the short period before the coming of the kingdom. He accepted what was something of a commonplace in the apocalyptic teaching of his time, the notion of a "messianic tribulation." Things must get worse before they got better; or, in mythological language, Satan would embark upon his last and fiercest struggle before his final destruction, and in this struggle the people of God, his elect, must expect to be hurt. If the coming of the kingdom was to be hastened the people of God must pay the price, and Jesus sent out his twelve disciples in pairs to bring down upon themselves the final woes. "Behold, I send you forth as sheep in the midst of wolves".... Beware of men; for they shall hand you over to councils and in their synagogues they shall scourge you.... Brother shall deliver up brother to death.... Fear not those who kill the body but are not able to kill the soul.... Think not that I came to put peace on the earth; I came not to put peace (on earth) but a sword" (Mt 10:16-34). He did not expect to see them back in this age: "You will not have completed the cities of Israel before the coming of the Son of man" (Mt 10:23). But they came back; and there was no sign of the affliction, still less of the kingdom of God. What then? The new discovery that Jesus made was that he himself must bear the suffering that the rest might go free; and with this determination he went up to Jerusalem to bring about his own death. "But now God does not bring the Affliction to pass. And yet the atonement must be made. Then it occurred to Jesus that he as the coming Son of Man must accomplish the atonement in his own person. He who one day shall reign over the believers as Messiah now humbles himself under them and serves them by giving his life a ransom for many, in order that the Kingdom may dawn upon them. That is his mission in the estate which precedes his celestial glory. 'For this he is come' (Mk 10:45). He must suffer for the sins of those who are ordained for his Kingdom. In order to carry this out, he journeys up to Jerusalem, that there he may be put to death by the secular authority.... That is the secret of the Passion. Jesus did actually die for the sins of men, even though it was in another sense than that which Anselm's theory assumes" (*The Mystery*, pp. 235f.).

So Jesus died; and with him died the framework of thought

and belief within which he had lived. He had lived and died for the apocalyptic hope of the supernatural establishment of the kingdom of God, and not even under the pressure of his own religious devotion and sacrifice did the kingdom come. It is no longer possible to accept the eschatological world-view. The quest of the historical Jesus has reached its self-destroying goal. Men, impatient with the dogmatic structures of the church which seemed to them remote and unacceptable, pushed past them to the Jesus of history, and many had found in him what they looked for—an ideal nineteenth-century liberal, who confirmed their own values and encouraged them in their ethical endeavor. But this was the product of bad history."The Jesus of Nazareth who came forward publicly as the Messiah, who preached the ethic of the Kingdom of God, who founded the Kingdom of Heaven upon earth, and died to give His work its final consecration, never had any existence. He is a figure designed by rationalism, endowed with life by liberalism, and clothed by modern theology in an historical garb"(*The Quest*, p. 396). The real Jesus of history is even stranger than mediaeval theology, for his eschatological worldview is more remote from ours, and could not survive his death.

Yet Christianity came into being; Jesus himself lived on, and not only as the heroic figure whom Schweitzer described in the Postscript of *The Mystery of the Kingdom of God*, the aim of which was "to depict the figure of Jesus in its overwhelming heroic greatness and to impress it upon the modern age and upon the modern theology" (*The Mystery*, p. 274). It lay as an obligation upon Schweitzer the historian, and he saw it clearly, to explain how the work and person of Jesus led to Christianity, and this meant the study of Paul. I have already observed that this led to two books, one a review of the history of Pauline study, which we have no time to consider, and the other Schweitzer's own exposition of Paul's mysticism and its place in the development of Christian thought. Schweitzer was writing at the time of vigorous attempts to place Paul's theology against the appropriate religious background. Thus it was argued that Paul's theology was Greek; it must have been Greek because in the second century Christianity was part of the Greek world and presented a hellenized appearance; and who could have hellenized it but Paul? John, Ignatius, and others no doubt contributed to the process, but alone they could not have initiated it. Paul, the Hellenistic Jew, had hellenized the Jewish religion of Jesus. The influence of the mystery cults, streaming in from the orient, absorbed into and at the same time modified by the world of Hellenism, was stressed by Reitzenstein; Bousset took a similar line but placed the influence further back—not only upon Paul but on the church at Antioch; Deissmann saw the impact of Hellenism on Paul as mediated by Hellenistic Judaism. All this, Schweitzer maintained, was beside the point. Paul's presentation of the Christian faith owed nothing to Hellenism; it was based, like the teaching of Jesus, simply upon Jewish eschatology.

All the features of that mysticism, which Schweitzer saw as the core of Paulinism, could be derived from this source. "Our review of the characteristics of the Pauline mysticism has shown that it is closely connected with the eschatological world-view; that it finds no place for the conceptions of rebirth or deification; that it is dominated by the eschatological idea of predestination; that it has a kind of realism which is foreign to the Hellenistic mysticism; that its conception of the Sacraments is quite different from the Hellenistic; and that the symbolism which plays so essential a part in the sacramental side of Hellenistic mysticism here plays no part at all" (*The Mysticism*, p. 26).

This is said on the basis of a preliminary survey. Schweitzer goes on—and we can follow him only to the extent of noting where he goes—to deal in detail with Paul's eschatological mysticism and to show how the great themes of Pauline theology, which have always been recognized as such, grow out of this as their root: the mystical doctrine of the dying and rising again with Christ; suffering as a mode of manifestation of the dying with Christ; possession of the Spirit as a mode of manifestation of the being-risen-with-Christ; mysticism and the law; mysticism and righteousness by faith; mysticism and the sacraments; mysticism and ethics. Jesus had died, and his dying was the messianic affliction that must precede the glory of the age to come; Jesus had been raised from the dead and was thus the first-fruits of them that slept, the beginning of the resurrection that must usher in the age to come. Those who were "in Christ" and had thus shared his death and resurrection were thereby brought into the age to come; this was the salvation they experienced in and through Christ, their righteousness and sanctification. Always the central and indispensable factor is the mystical being-in-Christ. Thus Schweitzer can write of what has been, and still is, often taken as Paul's fundamental theme, "The doctrine of righteousness by faith is therefore a subsidiary crater, which has formed within the rim of the main crater—the mystical doctrine of redemption through the being-in-Christ" (*The Mysticism*, p. 225).

Paul did not himself hellenize Christianity but by transforming eschatology into mysticism he put it into a form in which it could be hellenized. The next steps were taken by John and Ignatius. Here we have not an eschatological but a Hellenistic conception of redemption through union with Christ. To move directly from pure eschatology to pure Hellenistic mysticism would have been impossible, even for John; Paul provided the indispensable middle term. To Schweitzer it is quite clear why John "writes, and why he makes Jesus speak and act as he does: it is to show the historic Jesus preaching the mystical doctrine of redemption through being-in-the-'Logos-Christ'." (*The Mysticism*, p. 349). A further quotation will be worth bearing in mind: "Paul's mystical doctrine of the union with Christ does not need to come to terms with the tradition of the doings and sayings of Jesus, because it simply takes an independent place alongside of the latter, as being derived from a direct revelation of the Spirit. The Hellenized mystical doctrine of union with Christ, on the other hand, claiming as it does to be the proper understanding of the teaching of Jesus, is forced to choose between history as required by its own logic, and history as embodied in the tradition. . . . The Pauline Mysticism does violence to the facts of the natural world; the Johannine to those of history" (*The Mysticism*, pp. 366f.).

For all that, Paul and John had provided a vehicle through which the living spirit of Jesus continued to impinge upon the world's conscience—as none knew more vividly than Schweitzer himself, who had, not only as a historian, perhaps not mainly as a historian, apprehended a good deal of the heroism of Jesus. The time is come now for an appraisal, not of his work, or of his character, but of the question whether he was as admirable as a historian and theologian as he was as a practical Christian and exponent of the spirit of Jesus. Before this can be done, however, one preliminary question, to which I have already alluded, must be considered.

Schweitzer's great review of the quest of the historical Jesus we must pass by, but we cannot disregard his special attention to the work of Wrede, because this will help us both to grasp and assess Schweitzer's own views, and to move on to the question which he would surely not wish us to neglect: What next? What are the tasks and opportunities for our post-Schweitzer generation? Like Schweitzer, Wrede was concerned with a mystery or secret in the gospels—*das Messiasgeheimnis*. Read the gospels, especially Mark, and you will find, possibly to your surprise, that Jesus, so far from urging men at large to accept him as the Messiah, seems rather to conceal his status. When Peter, in the region of Caesarea Philippi, acknowledges, "You are the Messiah," Jesus instantly commands him to be silent and keep his views to himself. It is the same with the demons when they recognize him. When miracles are performed, Jesus forbids the beneficiaries to tell anyone what has happened. Sometimes the prohibitions are carried to hardly credible lengths, as when Jesus commands the parents of a girl, publicly believed dead, to conceal the fact that she is now alive. Not only is this so, a supernatural hardening falls upon men, even at times upon the disciples, preventing them from understanding what Jesus is about. Why is this so prominent and pervasive a feature of Mark? Wrede's answer, too simply and crudely put, is: Jesus did not believe himself to be the Messiah, and did not proclaim himself as Messiah, during his ministry, which consequently was free of messianic categories and ideas. Later, when his disciples came to believe that he had risen from the dead, they concluded that he must have been the Messiah. But how, they asked themselves, could it be that the Messiah, now vindicated by resurrection, had not been recognized as such during his earthly life? Their answer was, He had chosen not to be recognized; he had kept his secret, and God himself had co-operated by closing and hardening men's minds. Such (in rough outline) was Wrede's theory of the messianic secret. But the really significant thing about Wrede was not this particular theory but the conviction, worked out with a wealth of detail and historical insight, that the gospels were theological rather than historical works, and that the tradition on which they were based was dominated by theological motivation. The evangelists, on whom those who had gone in quest of the historical Jesus had inevitably depended, were themselves not in the least interested in the historical Jesus, but only in their own non-historical, theological Jesus.

Schweitzer claimed that Wrede's "thoroughgoing scepticism" had equally with his own "thoroughgoing eschatology" put an end to the quest of the historical Jesus. In at least one sense it could be said that Wrede had done this even more effectively than Schweitzer. It was Wrede rather than Schweitzer who had argued that the historical Jesus was completely unattainable since the bridges that might appear to connect us with him never reached the other side of the river but simply pointed into space—into theological thin air. Wrede indeed was not consistent, for he believed he had found a non-messianic historical Jesus, but in the process he had denied the validity of all the evidence. Schweitzer had ended the quest by successfully discovering the historical Jesus and showing that he was unintelligible and unacceptable, a historical Jesus of whom we could make nothing and whom we should be better without. Wrede had reached the conclusion that the evangelists were not historians but theologians; Schweitzer believed that Jesus himself was a theologian, and one of a particularly obscure and unintelligible kind, belonging to and comprehensible in his own age but totally out of tune with ours. And that, you might suppose, was that.

But it was not. It is not for me in this lecture to tell the—doubtless already well known—story of Schweitzer's career, of his long self-denying activity as a medical missionary in West Africa. Jesus might appear to be an incomprehensible and mistaken first-century apocalyptic Jew, but no one could deny that he meant something to Schweitzer, or that the something that he meant was not simply a hypothetical reconstruction of the study. "The truth is, it is not Jesus as historically known, but Jesus as spiritually arisen within men, who is significant for our time and can help it. Not the historical Jesus, but the spirit which goes forth from Him and in the spirits of men strives for new influence and rule, is that which overcomes the world" (*The Quest*, p. 399). "That which is eternal in the words of Jesus is due to the very fact that they are based on an eschatological world-view, and contain the expression of a mind for which the contemporary world with its historical and social circumstances no longer had any existence. They are appropriate, therefore, to any world, for in every world they raise the man who dares to meet their challenge, and does not turn and twist them into meaninglessness, above his world and his time, making him inwardly free, so that he is fitted to be, in his own world and in his own

time, a simple channel of the power of Jesus" (*The Quest*, p. 400).
Schweitzer as a New Testament scholar is a paradox. He
shows that the quest of the historical Jesus is a failure; yet claims that
he has in fact pursued it to a successful conclusion, in that he has found
out what the historical Jesus truly was—an apocalyptic prophet who
lived on the edge of the age to come and died to bring it into the
present, but, in the event, like Samson, pulled the whole house down
about his ears, destroying for ever the framework of thought and belief
to which he had committed himself. That world is gone and cannot be
reconstructed, and in the different world in which we live it is no longer
possible to accept or even to understand Jesus as a historical character.
He is and must always remain a stranger. Yet Schweitzer, whose concern has been the historical Jesus, turns about to say that the historical
Jesus is after all irrelevant; it is his heroic spirit, alive in the hearts of
men, that matters. And this spirit does live on, and men may know it
and be inspired by it. Schweitzer on the one hand describes the ethical
teaching of Jesus as interim ethics, designed for the short period between the present and the coming of the kingdom of God in power, and
on the other puts that ethic into practical effect with a sacrificial greatness that the world will not readily forget .

This paradox presents us with the question whether we can be
content to leave the study of the New Testament where Schweitzer left
it. Without abating a jot of my admiration for Schweitzer not only as a
man but as a scholar, I believe that we cannot. It is a relatively minor
matter that new techniques have been brought into use since Schweitzer's books were written. Since his work on the gospels both form criticism and redaction criticism have been developed, and owe perhaps
more to Wrede than to him. The gospels are analysed not only in terms
of their written sources but also in terms of the units of tradition of
which they are composed, and the way in which the evangelists used
and arranged these units is seen to throw light on their theological and
other presuppositions. Paul has been studied not only with reference to
his background (whether Jewish or Hellenic) but also with reference to
earlier Christian belief, and in his epistles we seek to distinguish between traditional material that Paul takes over and the editorial process
by which he incorporates it in his own thought and writing. The new
techniques, valuable as they are, do not alter the essential task. A
phrase that has been much used in the last fifteen or twenty years is the
"New Quest of the Historical Jesus." This quest, of course, is the old
quest, though the old quest, renewed after an interval, is now being pursued not only with new techniques but also from a new angle. The
quest Schweitzer described arose from a desire to bypass dogmatic theology and arrive at a simple untheological "Jesus of History." The new
quest asks why the theology of the early Church came to be fastened
upon Jesus of Nazareth. This lecture is not an occasion for me to develop my own views, but it seems to me that our starting-point must be the

recognition that we do not have to choose, as Schweitzer thought, between himself and Wrede. Both are right. The work of the evangelists and their predecessors was governed by theological motives; Jesus himself was directed by theological conviction. It is easy to state this in such a way as to invite misunderstanding. I do not mean to suggest that Jesus and the evangelists had swallowed a book of systematic theology and regurgitated it, or that they constructed events on the basis of a theological timetable; rather that both he and they were aware of profound theological significance in the actions he performed and they recorded. Their theological interests were related and often parallel, but they were not identical; here is the difficulty and the fascination of gospel study. It sometimes happens that layer after layer of theological interpretation can be observed, painted, as it were, over some incident; but we seldom or never get down to an incident devoid of theological concern. And I must make it clear that when I speak about theology I do not refer to the kind of speculation that enquires how many angels can dance on the point of a needle but to the ultimate questions about the meaning of human life in relation to the divine. Of all this theology Jesus himself is the theological source.

Of this theological process the outstanding example is Paul, who makes little use of the gospel tradition yet stands beside it as a second fixed point in the story of early Christianity. Schweitzer was absolutely right to fasten on him with his second great question mark. Paul is the decisive stage on the path between following Jesus and belonging to the Church. In many things Schweitzer is right—in, for example, the fundamental one: the basis of Paul's thought, as of that of Jesus, was eschatological. But Paul was a theologian rather than a mystic. He was, as H.J. Schoeps has said, a thinker of the postmessianic situation. Jesus had borne the messianic affliction; the risen Jesus was the first-fruits of the dead. But when Paul asserts that we too, in Christ, have passed these milestones in the story of salvation he is making an objective theological not a subjective mystical proposition. I do not mean that Paul was unconcerned about the Christian's consciousness of salvation; this would not be true; but what the Christian knows subjectively is objectively true. It will follow from this that justification is rehabilitated as the cardinal Pauline doctrine, and it proves to be one that he shares with Jesus, for the doctrine of the justification of the ungodly, which Paul taught, is the doctrine Jesus lived when he consorted with publicans and sinners and ate at their tables.

I have ventured in the last few minutes to express or imply a few critical judgments: uncritical adulation would be no way to honour a man like Albert Schweitzer. But I cannot draw this lecture to a close without emphasizing once more the debt we owe him. He worked, often in unbelievably difficult conditions, with an industry and devotion that must be a challenge to us all. He was irrevocably committed to the historical method, and proved how rewarding, practically and theologically, this method can be, when handled with freedom and courage. He posed questions which no New Testament scholar today, seventy-four years after the appearance of his first book, can afford to avoid. Not all his answers have been, or will be, or deserve to be, universally accepted; but he has made the point that Jesus is not an artificial mystery but a real mystery, of unplumbed depths and creative energy, and that when historical science has made its indispensable contribution and done its best to disclose him there remains still another dimension. What this is, the most famous paragraph Schweitzer ever wrote may do something to reveal. "He comes to us as One unknown, without a name, as of old, by the lake-side, He came to those men who knew Him not. He speaks to us the same word: 'Follow thou me!' and sets us to the tasks which He has to fulfil for our time. He commands. And to those who obey Him, whether they be wise or simple, He will reveal Himself in the toils, the conflicts, the sufferings which they shall pass through in His fellowship, and, as an ineffable mystery, they shall learn in their own experience Who He is" (*The Quest*, p. 401).

6

THEOLOGY IN DURHAM IN THE RAMSEY PERIOD

The subject of this lecture is not one that I chose myself. Take that, if you will, as an excuse; I have serious doubts about my competence to deal with it. I am grateful for the choice, however, and not only because it has saved me the not inconsiderable trouble of thinking out for myself what might be a suitable way of handling a weighty responsibility. The subject is one that calls for one or two prefatory remarks. By the Ramsey period is meant, I suppose, 1940 to 1950; my only qualification for dealing with it is a measure of longevity. Of those who were teaching theology in Durham at that time there are few survivors, and of them one is 5000 miles away in the heart of Canada. There are, I think, two others, one of whom I have consulted, but I have had to depend to a great extent on my own memory and knowledge, and these are as deficient as my understanding of the theological issues I shall be obliged to discuss.

Another prefatory remark had better be made frankly and at once. I should do no sort of justice to this distinguished occasion if I did not bring to my subject such critical judgment as I possess, and criticism of opinions is bound on occasion to spill over into criticism of those who hold and propagate the opinions. I need not say that I do not mean criticism of their motivation and integrity. I shall speak of others, but inevitably, in a lecture under this title and in this series, I shall speak of Michael Ramsey himself. This, I am sure, was intended by the Committee that proposed the subject. I am not aware that any claim has ever been made for the infallibility of the Archbishop of Canterbury, and I am not going to initiate such a claim in this lecture. For that reason, and because in any case I want to say it, let me say publicly as I have said often enough in private, that as long as I live I shall count myself fortunate to have begun my university teaching career in a Department led by Michael Ramsey. No young lecturer ever had a better senior colleague, a colleague too who maintained a close and affectionate friendship for nearly forty years after colleagueship in the official sense had ended. After such a beginning it would be easy to proceed with what I should regard as a misinterpretation of my title, and speak not of theology but of theologians active in Durham between 1940 and 1950. I shall avoid this danger to the best of my ability. Names of course will frequently appear; it would be difficult and tedious, and indeed unreal, to dispense with them. We need some of them at the beginning to set the scene. In any case, I know my limitations: I can approach theological issues only along historical and biographical lines, and we shall have to consider the different contributions made by different theologians. Ramsey and Greenslade must have been an unusual pair of Canons of Durham; neither of them had been brought up as a member of the Church of England. As converts they had trodden different paths. I recall a meeting of the Lightfoot Society, not (I fear) the speaker or his subject but that in the discussion that followed each of the Canon Professors made a characteristic remark. "It was (among other reasons) because the Church of England was a national church that I felt that I must join it," said Greenslade. Ramsey countered at once with, "And because it was a national church I almost decided not to join it." As every one knows, Ramsey was the son of a Cambridge mathematician, who was a Congregationalist. It was (if one may sum up a long pilgrimage in not too long a sentence) the influence of an Anglican mother and an Anglican school that first communicated to him a love of Anglican spirituality and Anglican liturgy that led him to confirmation and eventually to ordination in the Church of England. In a word (which even after last year's lecture by the Archbishop of York will continue to defy brief definition), it was catholicity, understood in terms of the Anglican tradition, that won him to the national church. Greenslade's family was Methodist; he too went to an Anglican school. At Oxford he fell in with the most evangelical wing of the Church of England, and it was by this route that he too arrived at Anglican ordination. To these two must be added a third figure of great distinction. W.A. Whitehouse was a Congregationalist who remained a Congregationalist. Like Ramsey, he was a Cambridge man—a first class mathematician; like Greenslade, he learned theology at Oxford. He came to Durham to occupy the readership vacated through the retirement of E.G. Pace (a well loved figure in the Durham of those days); not, like Pace, to teach the Old Testament, but Systematic and Philosophical Theology.

I have now hinted at a mixture that could hardly be less than interesting; in fact it was, to a greater extent than might at first appear, potentially explosive. Ramsey might perhaps (though he would find it hard to forgive me for attaching to him a party label) be called an Anglo-Catholic, but he was undoubtedly an Anglo-Catholic of an unusual color, for he had been a hearer of Hoskyns. It is true that later[1] he would speak of his relation with Hoskyns in no more than measured terms, but he had undoubtedly learned from him, and continued to be a friend of Noel Davey's. I must not allow myself to digress to speak at length about Hoskyns, but it is relevant to recall the diverse strands in his development which indirectly contributed to Ramsey's. By his own account Hoskyns learned little at Cambridge—not even to think for himself, an art which he acquired in Germany as he sat under Harnack, the prince of liberal protestants. He developed a close relation with Albert Schweitzer, though he must have regarded him as in many respects a heretic. It was understandable enough that he should become (again I must apologize for the use of a label) a liberal catholic; and this is what he must have been at the time when Ramsey heard his lectures. It was Barth who turned Hoskyns from religion to theology. If it is true that Barth "broke like a bomb shell over the sleeping tents of Anglicanism"[2] (looking at the matter from without one is impressed by the profundity of slumbers that not even Barth could disturb) it was Hoskyns's translation of Barth's *Commentary on the Epistle to the Romans* that provided the fuse. No one who has read that commentary can remain quite what he was before he read it; to translate it, weighing every word and transposing the words from their German to an English context, must have shaken Hoskyns to the core. For him, New Testament theology was no longer a matter of the religious experience of the primitive church; it was the theology of the word of God. Ramsey can never have experienced this as those of us who heard Hoskyns a few years later did, but he was aware of it and lived, as it were, along side it. It is not surprising that when Barth and Ramsey met at the World Council of Churches at Amsterdam in 1947 there was rapport between them: "My very good neighbour Canon Ramsay [sic] from Durham, an authentic Anglo-Catholic, with strange views concerning tradition, succession, ontology, and so on, but also with a very convincing twinkle in his eye . . . a man with whom I more often agreed than disagreed . . . *the* outstanding figure in the picture of my first ecumenical experience!"[3] I do not know whether it ever occurred to Barth that the connection between Ramsey and Hoskyns might have something to do with this. But there were stronger influences on Ramsey than Barth ever was.

This leads me back to Whitehouse, for Whitehouse had an intimate acquaintance with the German Confessing Church, of which Barth (though a Swiss and a Calvinist) was a leading and inspiring member. Whitehouse had already translated H. Vogel's *Iron Ration of a Christian*,[4] and before Barth's *Kirchliche Dogmatik* was translated he was already communicating its substance to English-speaking theologians in a series of review articles published in the *Scottish Journal of Theology* (which Whitehouse had himself helped to establish on the basis of *The Presbyter*—"a journal of confessional and catholic [note the word] churchmanship"). These review articles, or at least some of them, were first communicated to a theological book reviewing circle, founded by Alan Richardson (then a Canon of Durham) and meeting in his house. Here then was Ramsey's senior colleague on the side of Dogmatics: a representative of that orthodox dissent (I borrow of course Bernard Manning's title[5]—Cambridge, and indeed all, free churchmen owed him an incalculable debt) which was as certain of its own catholicity (in all that it considered the proper meaning of the word) as any "catholic," and, instructed by P.T. Forsyth, did not need Barth to tell it the meaning of the theology of the word of God, though it gladly welcomed him as a most powerful ally.

I must return briefly to Greenslade, whom the critical study of history had led far beyond some of his earlier convictions—or rather, perhaps, beyond some of the ways in which those convictions, which fundamentally he retained, had been expressed. His main published product in the Durham years was the book containing his Cadbury Lectures on *Schism in the Early Church*.[6] I remember that I reviewed this book in the *Durham University Journal* (this was before I established for myself the principle that I do not review books by colleagues) and began my review by recalling (and it seems worth while to recall it again now) that the study of the Donatist schism had been one of the factors that led Newman out of the Church of England into the Church of Rome: *securus judicat orbis terrarum*. Study of the schisms, including the Donatist, was to lead Greenslade in a different direction with regard to the relation between the churches. This is by no means all there is to say about Greenslade; I mention it specifically because it relates him to the area of theological discussion that Ramsey and Whitehouse have already suggested.

This may be the point at which to mention one other name. It was in 1945 that R. R. Williams, later to be Bishop of Leicester, succeeded Canon Wallis as Principal of St John's College. In 1950 he published a small book on *Authority in the Apostolic Age*.[7] This was written from a base in the "Liberal Evangelical school of thought," but showed "a balance of emphasis not always associated with liberalism or with evangelicalism" (124). The discussion of "the contemporary problem of authority" (124-142) seems to me worthy of more attention than it has received. Williams recognizes the new situation brought about by Ramsey's *Gospel and the Catholic Church* on the one hand and D.T. Jenkins's *The Nature of Catholicity*[8] on the other. Again one can regret a too early departure from Durham.

This brief setting of the scene requires in addition one note on matters exterior to Durham. It was a time of rising interest in relations between the churches—to say "in ecumenism" would be anachronistic both in the sense that the word was not at that time in common use, and in the sense that, for the most part, the οἰκουμένη was only distantly envisaged. Even Scotland was a special case to be treated, if at all, on its own. In 1946 Archbishop Fisher had preached at Cambridge a sermon in which he suggested that, short of complete unification, the Church of England and the English Free Churches (he was of course thinking of the Evangelical Free Churches, not of the Roman Catholic Church, equally in this country unestablished) might come close enough to enjoy intercommunion if the Free Churches were prepared to take episcopacy—that is, I need not say, the historic episcopate, in the apostolic succession—into their non-episcopal systems. Were they at least prepared to discuss the possibility?

It is no part of my task or my intention to describe and comment on the wide-ranging discussions and proposals that arose out of this suggestion, except so far as they entered into the theological work of Durham theologians. The debates were too often conducted on the basis of expediency and ecclesiastical politics; it was too seldom recognized that the decisive issues were theological. And my point, some might think the only point of substance in this lecture, is that there was in Durham the possibility of a positive and creative approach to these theological issues. I doubt whether this was perceived at the time; and this may have contributed to the fact that the story I have to tell is one of failure—one is tempted to overstate and speak of tragic failure—to reach a goal that could have affected the story of the church in England through the latter half of the twentieth century and beyond. The work—the fundamental theological work—is still to be done; and it remains to be seen whether it is capable of being done, whether it is possible to hold together in one ecclesiastical framework the view that one particular form of church order is, and the view that it is not, essential to the being of the church. If however it is to be done it must be done by one (or more) catholic theologians who are prepared to take the New Testament seriously, by one (or more) reformed theologians who are aware of their responsibility to the church and know that systematic theology, though it learns from and uses the language of the philosophers, is based on Scripture, and one (or more) church historians who recognize that the vital component in church history is not sociology but theology (even when the theology is heretical theology).

To say this is not to discount the importance of ecclesiastical politics. We live in this world and cannot do without politics. *The City of God, Civitas Dei*, is ἡ πόλις τοῦ θεοῦ, and the πόλις will have its politics. Moreover, both Ramsey and Whitehouse, though theologians, were aware not only of the necessity but also of the technique of administration. Durham knew Whitehouse as a most effective Principal of St Cuthbert's Society, and Canterbury was later to know him as the founding Master of Eliot College. Ramsey was a "Liberal Prime Minister" *manqué*; perhaps an Asquithian sort of Prime Minister, yet one capable, when roused, of getting things done. One of the few points on which I would venture to disagree with Owen Chadwick's biography[9] lies here. According to Chadwick, once Ramsey was established as Canon Professor in Durham it was generally thought that he had embarked decisively on an academic career. I know that I did not think so. I thought he would never leave Durham except for a bishopric, and when on occasion I expressed this view in conversation I do not remember that anyone disagreed. When he left Durham for the Regius Chair at Cambridge I was astounded and concluded that I must have been mistaken.

In fact I was only two years out. Both, then, in their own way and when they wished it, practical men; but primarily theologians. Greenslade was a church historian, and church historians see plenty of the administrative as well as the seamy side of life. And Williams was head of a house as well as a theologian.

It is necessary now to embark on the central task of this lecture and inquire what sort of theologians these men were, or rather, since I have disavowed any specifically biographical intention, what kinds of theology they represented, and what happened not so much to them as to their theologies.

Ramsey had already written before be came to Durham what I still think his best and most important book, even though I know that, according to Chadwick (p. 63), in thinking so I am disagreeing with Ramsey himself. I say this, too, aware of the fact that there are other books, notably some of the later ones, that I have not read and for which possibly a case could be made. But for originality and creativeness I doubt whether any of them can match *The Gospel and the Catholic Church*,[10] though I suspect that some of them may work out with greater maturity thoughts that were not fully developed in the earlier book. It was written before Ramsey came to Durham, but it was, in a sense, on this book that he came to Durham, and there can be no doubt that it continued to mark his thinking.

It is a crass oversimplification to say that Catholics believe and find their source of authority in the church; Protestants believe and find their source of authority in the Bible. Oversimplification; yet it has been said, and, wrapped up in impressive verbiage, by many who should have known better. Of course there is truth of a sort in it. When one turns for guidance to the living magisterium of the church the other turns immediately to Scripture. From point to point Thomas Aquinas based his *Summa* on the words of Scripture, but it was the teaching of the church that he was establishing. There has never been a higher churchman than Calvin, but the church he valued so highly was ruled at every point by Scripture. Both were great Christian theologians, but there remains a difference between them.

Ramsey was as concerned as any catholic with tradition, but not with tradition set over against Scripture. I do not think he was trying to make a move by which he could steal the enemy's guns and turn them against their owners. He had learned—whether from his early family background, or from Hoskyns, or from his own head and heart—that Scripture was a theological object and was to be interpreted theologically, as both the Fathers and the Reformers had interpreted it. One of its leading theological themes was the people of God, the catholic church. The Gospel, the evangelical scriptural message of good news, implied the church, just as the church lived by the Gospel. The two, Gospel and church, were neither opposites nor alternatives; they belonged together. You could not have the church without the Gospel;

you could not have the Gospel without the church.

I cannot forbear to point out here how close Ramsey is to Hoskyns. I think there must have been a measure of dependence; if not there was a striking development on parallel lines. In the Preface to the volume of *Cambridge Sermons*[11] J.O. Cobham wrote of Hoskyns's lectures, "If Evangelicals within the Church of England were less appreciative [than members of Wesley House], that is perhaps because Hoskyns was never tired of insisting that the Gospel implied the Church." Cobham went on to assert (*ibidem*), perhaps with some exaggeration but not without insight, that for many years in Cambridge Hoskyns had been fighting the cause of Evangelicalism almost single-handed. I clearly remember the indignation with which this was received—and repudiated—by J. M. Creed. Ramsey works on this theme in greater detail, but it is worth noting how close parts of Ramsey's book, published in 1936, are to *The Riddle of the New Testament*,[12] published in 1931. In *The Gospel and the Catholic Church* there is, if I may trust the joint witness of the Index and my own observation, no reference to Hoskyns or to Davey, even though there is a discussion of the biblical use of the word truth which is akin to that in *The Riddle*. One must suppose that this chapter of *The Gospel and the Catholic Church* was written before Ramsey had read *The Riddle*; the parallel development is very striking. Or had Ramsey read and forgotten?

We must see how Ramsey sets out his argument. His intention appears clearly in the opening pages.

> The debates between the two traditions [Catholic and Protestant] are often wearisome and fruitless. A fresh line of approach seems needed. Those who cherish the Catholic Church and its historic order need to expound its meaning not in legalistic and institutionalist language, but in evangelical language as the expression of the Gospel of God. In these pages Church order, with its Episcopate, Creeds and Liturgy, will be studied in terms of the Gospel. It will be asked, for instance, what truth about the Gospel of God does the Episcopate, by its place in the one Body, declare? And what truth about the Gospel is obscured if the Episcopate is lacking or is perverted? If the historic structure of the Church sets forth the Gospel, it has indeed a meaning which the Evangelical Christian will understand, and it may be possible to show that reunion without that structure will impair that very Gospel which the Evangelical Christian cherishes (8).

This from the introductory first chapter. The next three are (in my opinion) the best in the book; which may mean that they are most strongly in the vein of Hoskyns; or perhaps simply that they are the chapters with which I can agree most whole-heartedly. They show that the New Testament as a whole points as a witness to Christ crucified, and that since he died for all and in his dying all died, the crucifixion and resurrection mean the coming into being of a body, a *Corpus Christi*, a σῶμα, into which men and women are integrated by faith. This is the basis of the assertion that the Gospel of the Cross and the doctrine of the church belong together. You cannot, if you mean to play fair with the New Testament and not pick and choose your texts according to your fancy, have the one without the other. The influence of Hoskyns is apparent. The point may be overstressed here and there. In the 1956 edition of the book Ramsey in an additional note (42) refers the reader to J.A.T. Robinson's *The Body*;[13] and there is some kinship between what Ramsey himself says and Robinson's confusion (as it has always seemed to me) of the physical body of Christ, the resurrection body, and the body which is the church. However closely these may be related they are not identical, and the New Testament never says they are. I do not make this point simply as criticism; the confusion is related to what follows.

For from this point the book loses strength; and I do not think that I feel this simply because I agree with it less. The reason is probably that Ramsey tried to cover too much ground in one small (234 pages, including two appendixes and two indexes) book. It is a common error of judgment in the young: there are so many things to say and there may never be another chance—one may die at thirty five. But perhaps in a sense it was necessary—necessary to go on to establish not only the being but the form of the church, its worship, liturgy, and doctrine, and then to trace the right and the wrong understanding of all this in the Fathers, in the Middle Ages, in Tridentine and post-Tridentine Roman Catholicism, in the continental Reformers, and in the Church of England; and finally to draw conclusions with regard to Reunion. For this book was in some sense an *Apologia pro vita sua* (not so far a long life, but he must justify his having left his father's church), a tract for the times, and a confession of faith. Perhaps it was necessary to attempt all this, but there are places where the argument. and the requisite knowledge of the texts, though never to be despised or easily dismissed, runs a little thin.

There has always been a problem in relating second and third century bishops to first century apostles, and in relating the role, in maintaining essential Christian truth, of a succession of trusted Christian teachers to the establishing of a canon of Scripture. The vital contrast between a succession of persons and a succession of the Word is not handled. The paradox of a sacramentally based and ordered society in the light of a New Testament that does not even know the word *sacrament* is not seen. Most of the rest of the book is beyond my competence to judge in detail; there is no doubt that Ramsey makes a great effort to be fair to the Reformers, and that he learned from them. All the churches could profit from his emphasis on the 62nd of the 95 Theses:

"The true treasure of the church is the Holy Gospel of the glory and the grace of God," but he does not draw out its radical implications, and there are places where one feels that justice is not being done—this is not intentional, but arises out of less than perfect knowledge of the facts.

Durham should have provided an ideal setting for the hammering out of such matters. I do not say that a conclusion could have been reached. There are some theological issues where, so far as I can see, there is no possibility of agreement without a change of opinion on one side or the other. It cannot for example be both maintained and denied that a certain form of ministry is necessary for the being of the church; the maintainers and deniers may learn to live together in godly love but they cannot live in complete unity—and for myself I am inclined to add that in the end it may not matter very much. A conclusion would have been too much to hope for; a profitable conversation should surely have been possible.

As far as I know, it did not take place. For this there were several reasons. One is that all the potential participants had other things to do—in addition, that is, to a fairly heavy teaching load, in which our small numbers made excessive specialization impossible; Whitehouse, for example, found himself teaching the Greek New Testament. At the same time he was keeping up with Barth and making him available to English theologians, not only in linguistic but in cultural and epistemological terms. As one who has found the *Dogmatics* in English pretty heavy going I can imagine what working on it before the appearance of a translation was like. Moreover, Whitehouse's mathematical past gave him a special set of interests in the field of philosophical theology. Far too good a Barthian to deal in Natural Theology of a conventional kind, he was aware—as of course Barth was—of the need for a theology of nature. The first Christian proposition about God is that he is the Creator of heaven and earth, and it is proper to inquire what he was up to in the business of creation. I cannot but recall the occasion when Whitehouse was asked in a radio programme why God created the world, and provoked furious correspondence by answering, "For fun." He meant of course for the joy of creating, and in particular for the joy of creating such absurd and lovable creatures as we see going about on four legs or two, and meant it as serious theology.

This interest appears already in *Christian Faith and the Scientific Attitude* [14] and somewhat later in the Riddell Memorial Lectures of 1960,[15] but it will be convenient here to pursue it, and to observe the abundant scope there was for discussion, in a work of somewhat later date, the paper on "Authority, Divine and Human,"[16] though serious treatment of this would call for philosophical ability that I do not possess. Take for example this passage (230f.). Whitehouse quotes from Augustine (*Of True Religion* vii. 13-14) and continues:

Christian religion, according to what is said in that

passage, provides an answer to a serious question: the
question about the source from which our existence
(and that of everything else) is *ordered and authorized* . . . At present I would merely draw attention to
the ways in which St.Augustine's answer to it involves acknowledgement of authority: first in the ro-
bust assertion of an "Author," from whom all is derived and to whom all is subject by necessary,
indefeasible and just laws; second, in the claim that
this state of affairs may be certainly known in virtue
of authoritative information. The statement contains
quite remarkable correctives of the human tendency
to make do with superstitious credulity and to think
of obedience in terms of institutional legalism—
which is why I approve so highly of it.

At this point, of course, Whitehouse is speaking of authority
as it is exercised in the world at large, though what he says about institutional legalism may be recognized as having ecclesiastical corollaries.
It is at a later point (234) that he invites "attention to that particular
place in the universe of human experience where, so Christians maintain, divine authority reaches through with unambiguous and final clarity and establishes men and women in the obedience of Christian faith."
He continues (and it will immediately appear that it is at this point that
the conversation between himself and Ramsey should take place), "The
reality to which Christian faith is a response is, in the first instance, the
authority of a Gospel (formulated news) and the *authority* of the person, Jesus Christ, whom the news is principally and finally about." If
this seems to point in the direction of Christological rather than ecclesiastical discussion it may function as a valuable reminder (which Ramsey would certainly have echoed) that the doctrine of the church is rooted in Christology.

For it is at once striking that in the elaboration of this theme
Whitehouse is as concerned as Ramsey with the existence not only of
persons but of a people, indeed of a people ideally, or potentially, coex-
tensive with the human race. "He [Jesus] evidently believed that in the
actuality of his life-work taken as a whole, a link was being established
between historical mankind in its entirety and the divine Judge-Saviour
of whose reality Israel had become vividly aware" (236). But (and this
is the point at which conversation could—should—have broken out)
unlike Ramsey he makes no attempt to demonstrate a particular ordering of the people as alone constituting an adequate instrument of the authority inherent in the Gospel. This is partly because, in the paper
which I am quoting, Whitehouse was writing as a theologian in the
most precise sense of the term, elucidating the meaning of the propositions "Jesus is Lord" and "God was in Christ." Moreover, he is soon
back with authority widely understood, that is, with authority not specifically religious but (as it might appear) secular. Here too however

(and *a fortiori* this will be more certainly true within the church) he is unwilling to speak of intermediate authorities. There is a place where authority is to be found, the place "where man and all his enterprises have been subjected to the divine action of the holy and saving God, and may now be seen in faith to be thus subjected" (260).

It is impossible not to regret that these two great theologians seem not to have discussed these matters. Even before his departure to Cambridge, Ramsey was from time to time drawn away from Durham. It was no doubt as the author of *The Gospel and the Catholic Church* that he was elected chairman of the Anglo-Catholic group appointed by Archbishop Fisher to "examine the causes of the deadlock which occurs in discussion between Catholics and Protestants and to consider whether any synthesis between Catholicism and Protestantism is possible." The report of this group was published in 1947 under the title *Catholicity: A Study in the Conflict of Christian Traditions in the West*.[17] It has been interesting to reread this report in parallel with *The Gospel and the Catholic Church*. They have a great deal in common; no one can doubt that most of the drafting came from Ramsey's hand. But there is a difference in—mood, atmosphere, flavor? It is hard to find the right word, but there are signs of a shift (and it is fair to say in view of the agenda prescribed by Fisher an inevitable shift) in the direction of institutionalism. For the young Ramsey, episcopacy was something inherent in the Gospel; grasp the Gospel in its fullness and the essence of episcopacy was there. It would be an unfair caricature to say that the Report takes the line that something very much like the Anglican episcopate is the right way, the only right way, to run the church; but it does begin to move in that institutionalized direction, and the contrast between the book and the report reminds me of the epigram of a Roman Catholic friend who said to me, "I can see the argument that episcopacy is of the *esse* of the church, but I can't see that it is of the *bene esse*."

It is perhaps more important that Ramsey's own interests were shifting, were perhaps somewhat uncertain. The first three fifths of *The Gospel and the Catholic Church* is a New Testament study. While at Durham Ramsey published two more books on the New Testament, *The Resurrection of Christ*[18] and *The Glory of God and the Transfiguration of Christ*.[19] Of the former the bias is on the side of theology, but it deals also with the difficult questions of the literary and historical relations between the various pieces of evidence concerning the resurrection that the New Testament contains. It is characteristic of Ramsey's thought that the corporate aspect of resurrection is stressed. "The thought of my resurrection is inseparable from the thought of the resurrection of all the members of Christ" (114). It is the resurrection that gives the Bible and its message coherence. "The Bible has the resurrection as its key. Its God is the God who raised up Jesus Christ from the dead, and in so doing vindicated His word in the Old Testament and in the Cross of Christ" (122). Lake and Gardner-Smith are there, but so, significantly, is Westcott, and, as in *The Gospel and the Catholic Church*, there is some awareness of Barth, though it does not go beyond Hoskyns's *Romans*. The book on *Glory and Transfiguration* looks to me like Ramsey's farewell to New Testament study—that is, to New Testament study as an end in itself; it would be quite misleading to suggest that he ever ceased to look to the New Testament as the ultimate source of all theological thinking. Indeed, if I may be allowed a personal reference, I shall never forget the fact that when, in retirement, Ramsey returned to his beloved Durham, he returned to the New Testament Seminar which in the 1940s I had persuaded him to found and over which I now, in the 1970s, presided, and sat among us with his Greek Testament before him, never obtruding himself but offering from time to time his mature reflection on the text we were studying.

But I believe that he was losing interest in the technicalities of New Testament study, and though his exposition of the New Testament passages containing the word δόξα pays some attention to the linguistic background it is clear that his heart was not in this, and when he turns to Transfiguration the historical treatment is passed over quickly and he moves to the Transfiguration in Christian festivals, in Patristic interpretation, in the Eastern church, in the English church, and in some English collects. I note from Chadwick's biography (70) that during Ramsey's short spell at Cambridge he gave two courses of lectures, one on the New Testament and one on the Christian idea of redemption. I suspect that the shade of Hoskyns may have drawn him back a little into the New Testament field. Chadwick's bibliography (409-411) contains no further New Testament books, unless *Jesus and the Living Past* [20] is to be included.[21]

There is one other publication of the Durham period that should be mentioned, both for its own sake and for its historical and biographical significance. In 1948 Ramsey gave the Maurice Memorial Lectures at King's College, London, and in 1951 they were published, with some additional material, as *F.D. Maurice and the Conflicts of Modern Theology*.[22] Maurice's influence was already apparent in *The Gospel and the Catholic Church*; indeed this book of Ramsey's could be regarded as a twentieth century version of the book, *The Kingdom of Christ*, that Maurice had written a century before.[23] Both were young men's books; in 1837 Maurice was 32; in 1936 Ramsey was 32. In *The Kingdom of Christ* Maurice (brought up a Unitarian) addresses primarily a Quaker, but cannot prevent himself from going on to speak to Lutherans, Calvinists, Unitarians, Methodists, and Philosophers and Politicians of various kinds, treating all with sympathy, willing to learn from all, but showing how much better the episcopal system of the Church of England was than the systems that they had evolved. In *The Gospel and the Catholic Church* Ramsey is surely addressing the English Dissenter he might have become and that his father was, but includes (in his much smaller book) Luther, Calvin, and Barth, and reaches the same conclusion: how much better the catholic Church of England is than any of the alternatives. In both books there is a profound respect for and use of Scripture, set in the light of tradition—especially, in Ramsey's book, the tradition of the Eastern Church. I do not mean to suggest that Ramsey deliberately set out to imitate Maurice's book, but there is already so much of Maurice in *The Gospel and the Catholic Church* that Chadwick's paragraph (63)—"He decided to make Maurice understood by the undergraduates of Durham University"—surely gives an inadequate account of the matter. The lectures and the book on Maurice represent the payment of a debt that had been building up over many years. I have time to illustrate the importance of this book, which I hope I have sufficiently indicated, with no more than one quotation. Let it be this. "The 'Cambridge School' has come to mean Lightfoot, Hort, Westcott and those who succeeded them in their own tasks; but perhaps the final verdict of history will recognize a 'Cambridge School' which begins with Hare and Maurice and reaches beyond the specific labours of the great Trio into an era when theology will recover the wider range which Maurice believed it to possess" (105). It is, I believe, as an explorer and colonist of that wider range that Ramsey himself is most deserving of our admiration. One may add, however, that the more explicit concern with Maurice made less probable that theological interaction that might have electrified the Durham years and the Durham scene.

I shall conclude this lecture with a return to one who has— very regrettably—dropped out of the last few pages. Ramsey—the Ramsey of *The Gospel and the Catholic Church* and still more of *Catholicity*—was eventually deeply committed to the scheme for uniting the Methodist Church with the Church of England under the umbrella of the historic episcopate. When the scheme failed, rejected even by his Durham colleague Williams (Bishop of Leicester), he was more hurt than most people knew (Chadwick, 345f.) and wondered whether he ought to resign his see. Not that; but he could write, "What has vanished is the idea that being an Anglican is something to be commended to others as a specially excellent way" (346). A long way from Durham, 1940-1950.

But there was another way. His Durham colleague Greenslade, wrestling with the Donatists, with Cyprian of Carthage, Stephen of Rome, and Augustine of Hippo, stated it. I see no way of tracing here the beautifully clear exposition of the complicated doctrinal and historical developments that Greenslade gives. But his conclusion is plain. Corporate reunion is not the first step; nearer the last. It will be easier to take if first there has been intercommunion. And this there ought to be.

> If we find a denomination so far sound in faith that it
> preaches the Gospel on the basis of the Bible and af-
> firms the Apostles' Creed (and a fortiori the Nicene),
> if we find that it uses the sacraments of Baptism and

Holy Communion and that it solemnly sets apart men
to be ordained by Christ, through the prayers of the
Church there represented, as its ministers, and if we
find that this denomination, so far as we can judge,
has produced the fruits of the Spirit and shown its
power to survive, then we ought to assume that Christ
has given it a ministry endowed with His own authority and we ought to acknowledge it to be within the
Una Sancta. Between any denominations which acknowledge each other, on such a basis, to be sister-
churches, there ought, I believe, to be intercommunion and the possibility of an ordered (but not
indiscriminate) interchange of ministers, even though
there will be not unimportant differences between
them. I am not content to say, there could be intercommunion between them. No, there should be, it is
wrong if there is not; there is enough unity of spirit to
demand it, and to be injured if it is refused (218f.).

It is Greenslade's way that seems to be in process of realiza-
tion. It does mean postponing the really difficult problems, but post-
ponement will certainly make them no harder to solve; and perhaps a
solution does not matter as much as we sometimes think.

A good deal of theology was going on in Durham in the
1940s; and I have said nothing of work being done on the edge of biblical, dogmatic, and systematic theology, such as the magnificent work
of H.F.D. Sparks in editing the Vulgate, and T.W. Thacker's establishing of the School of Oriental Studies, once Durham's glory but now so
sadly dismembered. It is interesting to speculate what might have happened had those early figures whose work I have sketched decided to
remain here and to stimulate one another. But it has been my task in
this lecture to describe, to comment just a little, but not to speculate.

NOTES

1. I am thinking of his Foreword in *Crucifixion-Resurrection*, E. C.
Hoskyns and F. N. Davey, ed. by G. S. Wakefield (London, SPCK; 1981), xi,
"Hoskyns had a remarkable influence, and I was one of those who as a young
student came under his spell. Though I never became an uncritical devotee, I
learned from him, more vividly than from anyone else, that the study of the
New Testament is an exciting adventure . . . ."
2. C. H. Smyth, in *Cambridge Sermons*, E. C. Hoskyns (London,
SPCK; 1938), ix.
3. Owen Chadwick, *Michael Ramsey, A Life* (Oxford, Clarendon
Press; 1990), 67.
4. London, SCM; 1941.

5. *Essays in Orthodox Dissent*, B. L. Manning (London, Independent Press; 1939).

6. London, SCM; 1953

7. London, SCM; 1950.

8. London, Faber & Faber; 1942. This book contains a very percipient and sympathetic criticism of Ramsey's position. "The significance of the rise and growing power of this point of view [that of Ramsey] we are only just beginning to grasp, but one thing is clear about it. Its criterion of the nature of catholicity is theological and not merely historical. This makes discussion with modern Reformed churchmen possible at once" (p. 13). Cf. however fn. 2 on 80f.

9. See n. 3.

10. London, Longmans, Green & Co.; 1936; 2nd edn, 1956; new impression, London, SPCK; 1990.

11. London, SPCK; 1938; xviii.

12. By E. Hoskyns and N. Davey; London, Faber & Faber; 1931; many subsequent impressions and translations.

13. Studies in Biblical Theology, No. 5; London, SCM; 1952.

14. Edinburgh, Oliver & Boyd; 1952.

15. *Order, Goodness, Glory.* London, OUP; 1960.

16. First published in *The Authority of Grace*, by W. A. Whitehouse, ed. by Ann Loades (Edinburgh, T. & T. Clark; 1981); 225-243. A revision of the Boutwood Lecture delivered at Corpus Christi College, Cambridge, in 1967.

17. Westminster, Dacre Press.

18. London, Geoffrey Bles: The Century Press; 1945.

19. London, Longmans, Green & Co.; 1949.

20. Oxford, OUP; 1980.

21. For completeness we must add the *SNTS* paper, "What was the Ascension?", published in *SNTS Bulletin* 2 (1951), 43-50.

22. *F. D. Maurice and the Conflicts of Modern Theology* (Cambridge, CUP; 1951).

23. The first edition was published in 1837; an enlarged edition appeared in 1842.

7

JOHANNINE CHRISTIANITY

A. The Basic Problem

Nowhere is it easy to describe the relation of early New Testament Christianity with the society that surrounded it. The reason for this difficulty is evident. Not one New Testament author had as his goal the comparing or contrasting of the new group of which he was a member with other groups and with the population at large or of working out their mutual interaction.[1] This fact is generally true for all early writers of history, though in various degrees. Social history is a modern invention, and little of it can be observed in antiquity: very little in Thucydides, for example; more in Herodotus, basically because Herodotus was in a way a less serious historian than Thucydides. Herodotus stops and reminisces once in a while, thus from time to time relaying to us pieces of information that, though not necessarily required for his reporting, are in fact of great interest to us. In Plutarch's *Moralia* we find more social history than in his biographies; the latter deal with history that, when it is not strictly biographical, is largely military and political. The *Moralia*, on the other hand, or at least parts of them, convey a large amount of information about people's life-style and the structure of their society.

It is possible to make a similar observation in the comparison of Paul's letters with Acts, all of which at least appear to refer to the same period and to a great extent to the same people. In its own way, Acts is history, yet it provides little information (it would be wrong to say that it provides no information) on the personal and social life of the average Christian and his or her Jewish or pagan contemporaries. Although the letters are certainly theological, they provide the reader who is willing and able to read between the lines a great deal of information about social matters.[2] Yet even so, one does not find much. Social history (and to an even higher degree sociology as a science), which is undoubtedly of interest to the twentieth century, was of no interest to the first century, and perhaps least of all was it of interest to the Christians of the first century. It is surprising that we even have

Acts as a "history of the church." Up to the end of the first century, it was not expected that the following generations would continue to pass on history to their readers. The author was much more concerned to proclaim the gospel in his own way and to impress upon his readers the gospel's goals and consequences than to describe the past, especially in its individual and social details.

If we turn to the writings of John, the characteristics of the New Testament that have just been described become even clearer for two reasons. The first arises out of John's theological purpose. It is not necessary to show here in detail that this is a subject that has been discussed at great length by many authors.[3] For example, it has been considered proved that the Fourth Gospel is a Palestinian Jewish work originating in Palestine on the basis of Palestinian traditions of the life of Jesus and written for Palestinian readers who would fully understand the Gospel's allusions to the Torah and to the circumstances of Palestinian life. It has also however been taken as proved that the Gospel's background is Hellenistic, that it was written for the Hellenistic world, a process in which the original terms and language used by the historical Jesus were translated into a new, Greek, more or less philosophical form. A view related to this is that the Gospel rests on a Gnostic basis and thus presents the reader with the historicizing and Christianizing of a Gnostic myth. Then again it has been argued that the Gospel of John was indeed a Jewish work but was intended for readers in the Diaspora rather than for Palestinian Judaism. Palestinian Judaism had rejected Jesus; speeches and signs were now interwoven in a new way in the hope that the Jews outside Palestine would not repeat the terrible mistake of their brothers living in the land of Israel. In this view the Gospel is a work of Judaism in the Diaspora and has to be understood in connection with debates in the diaspora synagogue.

This vast diversity of opinions contributes greatly to what may be considered a better understanding of John's theological intention. "When we turn from this study of the Synoptic Gospels to John, we may occasionally find that John has adapted traditional material to yet another historical setting; but much oftener we find that John has liberated his material from particular settings to give it universal applicability."[4] John employs a multitude of theological concepts and expressions. It is also true that he writes with such simplicity that common people throughout the Christian centuries have accepted the Gospel and understood it by no means badly, though they knew nothing about Palestinian or diaspora Judaism, or about Hellenistic religious and philosophical concepts or about gnosis. If John did not intend to give his work universal appeal, he was the victim (or the beneficiary) of a uniquely happy coincidence. So far as these observations are true, one will have to conclude that only an extremely limited amount of information concerning John's environment can be expected. It was precisely not his intention to make his Gospel conform to a particular form of society.

The more completely people are placed and considered *coram Deo*, the less they will differ from each other. A person described thus appears primarily as non-God; as created, not as creator; as mortal, not as immortal; as changeable, not as unchangeable; as sinful, not holy. And this person appears, unless at second glance, not as Jew or non-Jew, male or female, old or young, civilized or barbarian.

The second reason why John—and he more than the other authors of the New Testament—is of little help to the social historian is that his theology prompts him to speak in a special way of the "cosmos," which is portrayed as almost completely evil. The cosmos was created by the Word; yet when the Word appeared in it, the cosmos would not acknowledge it (John 1:10). The world lies wholly in the evil one (1 John 5:19). One could add many other passages, especially that the world will hate believers as it hated Jesus (John 15:18; 1 John 3:13). This means that John and his congregation believed that for their part they were different and separate from the world. Only those who never truly belonged to "us" go out into the world, speak of the world, and are heard by the world (1 John 4:5). It can therefore hardly be expected that John would give information about the world, about life in the world, and about the way the world presents itself. The world is a creature that has turned its back on the Creator. It may be of marginal interest to examine the reasons for this decline, but it is not really important to describe them: the world passes away together with its desires (1 John 2:17). It is therefore of no lasting interest. It corresponds to this that the Christian community can have only negative relations with the world and cannot accept the world's life-style or worldly social patterns. Of course, it is possible that the community nonetheless does accept them unconsciously.

Accordingly, the Johannine literature (from which, for the purpose of the present discussion, Revelation is excluded) is hardly a promising field for an examination of "Christianity and society." It would be misleading to begin such an examination without explicitly acknowledging this fact. The prospect, however, is not quite as unfavorable as it may at first appear. Few great theological works have been written in complete isolation from the things of this world. Augustine's *City of God* is unintelligible without some knowledge of the break-up of the Roman Empire. For Calvin's *Institutio* one must be aware of the attempt to transform Geneva into a city of God. Barth's theology presupposes not only familiarity with the history of liberal Protestantism in the nineteenth century but also awareness of the Great War of 1914-1918 and the Third Reich. There is no reason to assume that John alone lived in an ivory tower and remained untouched by his environment. It is his greatness that he viewed contemporary events under theological rather than sociological aspects; it is our misfortune (as far as the present study is concerned) that theology may be drawn directly from the text but social history only by means of hints and inferences. Even the world has a theological meaning, and a positive one at that. However er much it may revolt against God, the world is still the object of his love (John 3:16). Jesus does not pray for the world (17:9), and it cannot receive or understand the Holy Spirit (14:17); that, however, does not mean that it is without hope, but the hope consists only in its ceasing to be what it is.

Up to this point I have used the name John as if the entire Johannine corpus had been written by only one author. This is in fact most improbable. This essay is not the place to discuss the question of authorship; I shall presuppose that we are dealing with at least four authors, who wrote, respectively, John 1-20, John 21, 1 John, and 2 and 3 John.[5] In addition, there may have been those who interpolated and edited the texts. It is impossible at this point to probe into this question in detail, though it will be mentioned occasionally. The question of authorship is, however, important; references already made in this discussion to the Johannine understanding of the cosmos may suggest that a distinction exists between the Gospel and the letters. A distinction, however, exists not only in this respect but also in regard to the interest shown in the Christian society and the behavior of Christians in the world.

Naturally, such distinctions would be unavoidable even if there were no question of differing authorship. *Prima facie*, the Gospel tells the story of the words and deeds of Jesus of Nazareth. So far as the story is historically correct, these date from the time before the existence of any Christian congregation. So far as it is based on old tradition, their background is that of Palestinian Judaism. It is a matter of debate how far these presuppositions are correct. Even if, however, the Gospel were completely fictional, it would still be true that the evangelist uses the form of a story played out in Galilee, Judaea, and Jerusalem. Certainly, the Gospel writer wrote for his contemporaries, but the writer of the letters wrote to his contemporaries, and what he wrote had to relate to the conditions under which they lived if it was to be of any value to them. From this it follows that we shall do well to begin by gathering data from the letters, and first from the two shorter ones.

B. T'.e Situation in the Johannine Letters

The second and third letters of John offer a picture of a precisely delimited and strictly disciplined Christian community. They are of special importance since they observe this community from two points of view; better, perhaps, they describe this community as divided into two parts, each of which could be described as the mirror image of the other. Each letter claims to have been written by someone who describes himself as "the elder" (2 John 1; 3 John 1) . The second letter is addressed to a church (that is the most likely meaning of "the elect lady"; 2 John 1), the third to a person named Gaius (3 John 1). In addition, the third letter refers with great disapproval to another person, Diotrephes, who is accused of defaming the elder, of wanting to be in first place in his group, and of attempting to exclude those whom the group wants to include (3 John 9-10). Gaius, on the other hand, has helped these brothers on their way. These are said to have ventured out "for the sake of the name" without accepting anything from those who stood outside the congregation ("They went out 'for the name' [i.e., for Christ], without accepting anything from the Gentiles"; 3 John 6-7). The brothers are evidently traveling Christians, that is, not Christians traveling on their own business but Christians doing the business of the church, of Christ. They are missionaries and depend on the support of Christian congregations, which they find and try to turn into their base of operations. They are not simply wandering prophets (like those mentioned in *Didache* 11-13), for such travelers could not have made claims on the "Gentiles." They are rather evangelists, itinerant preachers, who as such have dealings with non-Christians yet are not willing to be supported by them, lest they should undermine their own purpose by making it appear as if they worked for personal gain. There are other Christian travelers.

The elder hopes to meet Gaius soon (3 John 14). Who it is that will visit the other is not mentioned explicitly; perhaps the intention was to meet halfway. Why did Diotrephes oppose the elder, and why did he refuse to accommodate the Christian travelers? The third letter of John gives no answer to that question. Since no reasonable explanation for the refusal exists, one gains the impression, which the elder certainly sought to create, that Diotrephes was motivated by baseness and jealousy. He wished to be in first place and therefore did not want to accept the authority of the elder (whether as an equal or possibly as an ecclesiastical official who was responsible for an area that included Diotrephes's district); he did not want to grant support to the itinerant preachers because they were from the elder's church and not his own.

For further information we turn to the Second Letter of John, where a similar situation appears. Here no one is mentioned by name. The reason for this may be that the leading man of the church with which the letter deals is Diotrephes himself, and that the only way to address the church is to circumvent him (3 John 9: "I have written something to the church; but Diotrephes, who likes to put himself first, does not acknowledge our authority"). Perhaps. But it is more probable that another church is meant here, since the "elect lady" and her children are commended for their good behavior and are warned not to accommodate traveling missionaries—perhaps from the heretical church headed by Diotrephes? This time a reason is given for the refusal of recognition: it is doctrinal. "Do not receive into the house or welcome anyone who comes to you and does not bring this teaching" (2 John 10). Whoever does so makes himself a partner in his evil deeds (his false doctrine is an evil work; 2 John 11). Of course, it might be that

Diotrephes, if given a chance to explain, would have given a reason for rejecting the preachers similar to that recommended by the elder. It is possible that the unfriendly remarks he made about the elder were based on the same identification of heresy and moral baseness.

In the second letter of John the elder suggests two tests for wholesome orthodox Christianity by which one could identify the antichrists and deceivers. Deceivers do not confess Jesus Christ as coming in the flesh (2 John 7). Second, it is required of Christians that they love one another. Love is defined as walking in agreement with the commands of God, and walking in agreement with God's commands appears to lead back to the confession of faith mentioned earlier (2 John 5-7). In this confession of faith there has been a long debate on the meaning of the present participle "coming"[6]; either an aorist or a future tense would have been much more readily intelligible. The words of the elder as they stand sound like a slogan or catchword in which the time scheme is of no importance, as one might say (without using a verb), "Jesus Christ in the flesh," meaning that this is how he came (in the incarnation) and how he will come (at his return). Catchwords in theology are always dangerous. They prevent thought, and behind the second and third letters of John there are few indications of active theological thinking. One finds here, however, at least an endeavor to maintain a theological position and a strict order. This is important for any attempt to discover what the respective Christian congregations were like.

In a remarkable essay E. Käsemann[7] contends that Diotrephes was an early bishop who believed that he was acting wholly in the interests of the Catholic church, while the elder presided over a group of enthusiasts who still lived the Christian life-style that can be discovered in early passages in the New Testament. The one maintained a formal discipline based on what one could almost call canon law. The other considered a certain kind of spiritual experience to be an unconditional requirement for membership in the church. This distinction does not seem to match the observations we have made up to this point. Both congregations, or at least their leaders, the elder and Diotrephes, appear to act in similar ways. We know (for he tells us) that the elder practised excommunication on the basis of doctrine and behavior. Diotrephes does not have a chance to speak for himself, so that if one of the two acted on the basis of enthusiastic criteria, it must have been he. It is more likely, however, that he too expected doctrinal and ethical conformity.

Both congregations are surrounded by "Gentiles," a word we can understand in the sense of "outsiders." Its origin, however, is important. The word does not signify non-Jews in the ethnic sense; it has etymological overtones (cf. Matt.18:17) that suggest the relation between the Jewish and the non-Jewish world. From this we might conclude that both congregations stood in some danger not only of living in an isolated fashion but also of becoming inwardly directed. It is not that the synagogue always or necessarily directed its vision inward, but that congregations in this situation are always inclined to develop in this direction. We are certainly not dealing here with an extreme tendency, for it seems that the congregations had sent out missionaries whose purpose must have been to convert "Gentiles" and to bring them into the communities as new members. But conversion in itself presupposes the existence of a clearly recognizable borderline, which the converted have to pass in order to leave the old life and enter into the new. And "loving one another" (2 John 5) is a rule of behavior that can be easily understood in a delimiting sense if one looks inwardly. Thus the phrase "loving one's neighbor" (before Christianity and within Christianity) has often led to hating one's enemies. That the two congregations formed a closed front toward the world around them is most convincingly confirmed by the fact that they also formed a closed front against each other. It is bad enough not to confess "that Jesus Christ has come in the flesh" in the interest of some heretical view, but the total rejection of Jesus Christ is worse.

It seems impossible to say much about the inner structure of these two closed groups. Both seem to have been monarchical. Diotrephes wants "to put himself first" and seems to have been a person capable of acting with authority, since those of whom he disapproves he excludes from the church (3 John 9-10). The elder writes in a way that indicates that he has equal or even greater authority. This is the general style of his letters, and it becomes especially clear in his threat to put Diotrephes in his place (3 John 10). That could mean that the elder exercised jurisdiction over a fairly large region that included the area over which Diotrephes presided. Or they may have been rivals in neighboring cities. The elder, like Diotrephes, could exclude those whom he did not wish to welcome "into the house." House could mean a house owned by a single member of the congregation or a place used by the church itself, or perhaps, to judge from Paul's letters (Rom. 16:5; 1 Cor. 16:19; Philemon 2; cf. Col. 4:15), the house of a church member where the congregation met. It is not important whether Diotrephes and the elder were termed bishops. There are many indications[8] that suggest that the two terms elder (or presbyter) and bishop had the same meaning and that the monarchical episcopate grew out of the college of presbyters.[9] The term presbyter is perhaps not used in a fully technical sense. On the one hand, there are passages in the New Testament (1 Tim. 5:1, 17, 19; Titus 2:2; 1 Peter 5:1-5) that make it fairly clear that presbyters, or elders, were originally older members of the congregation. This term remained in use (advanced by the Jewish example) even when it became clear that not all older men possessed in notable measure the appropriate gifts. On the other hand, one finds indications among the authors of the second century[10] that "presbyter" was a term that did not identify men who held a particular office but men of high standing in the earlier days of the church. It seems as if the churches in question moved towards a monarchical form of congregation leadership, whatever the term may have been that was used to denote it. When we turn to the first letter it becomes clear that we are still in the same general environment. This emerges from the basic doctrinal affirmation of Jesus Christ's incarnation (1 John 4:2) and the basic Christian commandment to walk in love and to keep the commandments (2:3,7,10 and passim). It is almost as clear that we have moved back in time. Both doctrine and commandments appear in a less strict and schematized fashion. Ecclesiastical reprimands have not yet assumed such a clear and drastic form. The writer is evidently someone who has, or assumes that he has, authority among those whom he addresses. He addresses fathers, young men, and little children (2:12-14) always in the same commanding way and can speak to an entire congregation as his little children (2:1,18), reminding, admonishing, directing, with no trace of any lack of self-confidence. He does not write, however, as elder or with the application of any other title. We may suppose that his authority was of a personal rather than an institutional kind. He can expect attention and obedience simply on the ground that he is known to be who he is.

        In some matters the longest—and probably earliest—letter gives us fuller information, which nevertheless is in full agreement with the general picture that we were able to form from the second and third letters. Three things in particular call for mention here. First, it is clear that the author was confronted with the problem of sin in the church. Exegetes have always found difficulty in his observations on this theme, but this is not the place for a detailed discussion. It seems that there were members of the church who asserted that they were free from sin. The author evidently questions the validity of their assertion. "If we say that we have no sin, we deceive ourselves, and the truth is not in us" (1 John 1:8). "If we say that we have not sinned, we make him a liar, and his word is not in us" (1:10). Sinlessness means righteousness and perfect love (4:7-12). Were these people, who asserted of themselves that they were without sin, Käsemann's enthusiasts, people filled with religious ecstasy and incapable of applying serious criticism to their own behavior and of distinguishing between excitement and moral perfection?

        The author's critical discussion is complicated and obscures the fact that he is compelled to admit that these enthusiasts are in a sense right. "He was revealed to take away sins.... The Son of God was revealed for this purpose, to destroy the works of the devil" (1 John 3:5, 8). "If anyone does sin, we have an advocate with the Father . . . and he is the atoning sacrifice for our sins" (2:1-2; cf. 4:10). These are theological assertions. One could argue that they do not go beyond the Pauline doctrine of justification. "In Christ" the believer is without sin since he or she receives the righteousness of Christ. It is, however, difficult not to accept that there are also passages that go beyond this. "Those who have been born of God do not sin, because God's seed abides in them; they cannot sin because they have been born of God" (3:9; cf. 5:18). John seems to expect not only a forensic but also a moral freedom from sin.   Fortunately it is not our task in this study to tackle the theologically difficult problem of amalgamating these remarks into a theological unity. Our task is to grasp that upon the author was laid a heavy practical responsibility in that he was obliged to deal with those who wrongly claimed to be without sin (wrongly, for they did not love their brothers, 3:10), without at the same time invalidating the fundamental Christian conviction that Christ died to put an end to sin, and that there was a Christian obligation to love. Were those who caused the difficulty enthusiasts? Along with the assertion, "We are without sin," we should note also the assertion, "I have come to know God" (2:4). For this one can hardly find another term than gnosis, although gnosis of a primitive, undeveloped kind. Gnosis is not the same as enthusiasm, though it may be connected with it.

Second, we can better understand enthusiasm if we note that the author of 1 John had to deal with the phenomenon of inspiration and accordingly was forced to insist on the church's duty to test the spirits so as to determine whether they came from God (4:1). But here also we again encounter an intellectual, dogmatic element, since the test the prophets have to undergo is a doctrinal one. "By this you know the Spirit of God: every Spirit that confesses that Jesus Christ has come in the flesh is from God, and every spirit that does not confess Jesus is not from God" (4:2-3). No other test is proposed. No attempt is made to measure the degree of inspiration or ecstasy. And here one finds again a connection with gnosis, for the false prophets or antichrists are presumably Docetists. When it is said that they do not confess Jesus, what is meant is that they do not confess that he has come in the flesh. Had they surrendered all interest in Jesus, they would not have claimed to be Christians, as they evidently did. Again, John responds to the Gnostic claim with the counterclaim that he and his friends are the true Gnostics because they keep God's commandments. "Now by this we can be sure that we know him, if we obey his commandments. Whoever says, 'I have come to know him,' but does not obey his commandments, is a liar" (2:3-4). "I write to you, not because you do not know the truth, but because you know it" (2:21). The truth or insight that the Christians possess is due to an anointing (*chrisma*) that they have received. "I write these things to you concerning those who would deceive you. As for you, the anointing that you received from him abides in you, and so you do not need anyone to teach you. But as his anointing teaches you about all things, and is true and is not a lie, and just as it [or: he (Christ)] has taught you, abide in him" (2:26-27) .

Thus we see rival groups, both claiming and striving to be without sin, but in different ways. Both claim to be enlightened, but each by its own gnosis. Both concentrate, but in different ways and in terms of their own understanding, on the person of Jesus. This leads to the third point that we have to consider. John relates his opponents to the cosmos. In the first reference to antichrists the word cosmos is not used: "They went out from us, but they did not belong to us; for if they had belonged to us, they would have remained with us. But by going out they made it plain that none of them belongs to us" (1 John 2:19). There is no doubt, however, that we are dealing here with the same group that is referred to in 4:1, 5-6: "Many false prophets have gone out into the world. . . . They are from the world; therefore what they say is from the world, and the world listens to them. We are from God. Whoever knows God listens to us, and whoever is not from God does not listen to us."

It is true that John theologizes the meaning of the cosmos and that to him worldliness is not a matter of wine, women, and song but of that which had the appearance of a highly spiritual gnosis. It is possible, however, and in the present context even necessary, to take his word in both a historical and a theological sense and thereby to see a congregation from which members set out to acquaint themselves with the world and especially with the philosophical and religious language of the world, which they then use with some success. The world listens to them. Theologically speaking, they may have been antichrists, but it is not necessary to question their motives, unless this is justified by such pictures as John offers in 1 John 3:17: "How does God's love abide in anyone who has the world's goods and sees a brother or sister in need and yet refuses to help?" In fact it may not only be generous but completely correct to suppose that their intention was to offer to the world what they held to be the Christian message, and that it was their method to learn and use the language of the world. This, however, was the language of gnosis, and the result was that they adopted a Docetic Christology. From what they learned from the world, they may also have drawn the conclusion that since all matter was essentially evil, the ethical or unethical actions of their physical lives were of no significance, so that no moral value was inherent in loving one's neighbor or Christian brother. About such people the author of 1 John can only sadly shake his head and say: They never really belonged to us. This is a more favorable attitude than that of the elder or of Diotrephes, but one can hardly call it positive.

In addition to its Gnostic language and theology, the author of 1 John seems to know of the world outside the church only that it is connected with "desire" and "pride" (2:16-17). He is much too good a theologian to assume that "the desire of the flesh" is the only kind of desire there is. He points to the basic characteristics of life in the world: selfishness and boastful clamor. Both belong to the cosmos, not to God. But does not the cosmos itself belong to God? I cannot find that the author seriously examines this question. That must mean that in the end he had no theology of society, or perhaps we should say that in this letter he did not intend to develop one. He leaves us a picture of this world no more than he leaves us with a theology of it.

C. The Gospel of John and the Past Social World of Jesus

We now turn to the Gospel and must recall that in our treatment of "Christianity and society" at least two societies are involved: that of Palestine in or about A.D. 30 (for whatever our estimate of the historical value of the Gospel may be, its story is set in this framework) and that of the region and time in which the Gospel was written.

Gospel passages about the social and religious conditions in Palestine before the fall of Jerusalem (and about the kind of Judaism that existed after the catastrophe) have often been gathered. To enumerate and describe them in detail is not necessary. Jesus is depicted as one who existed within the religious framework of Jewish life, even though he does not always observe its regulations. His contemporaries complain that he does not keep the Sabbath (John 5:9-16; 9:14-16). He replies not only in theological pronouncements (5:17), which need not be discussed here, but also by referring to the well known argument in which the Sabbath law and the law of circumcision were weighed against each other (7:22-23). He keeps the Jewish feasts, though it may be doubtful whether he will go to the Passover feast in Jerusalem (11: 56). He chooses not to go to the feast of Booths at the usual time (7:14). He does, however, celebrate the relatively unimportant feast of Temple Dedication (10:22). He interprets the Old Testament by rabbinic methods; for this we can cite especially the ' al-tiqre' interpretation of Ps.78:24 in John 6. It is not surprising that the sermon of this chapter is placed in the synagogue in Capernaum (6:59), an appropriate place for a sermon in this form. Jesus can make use of a recognized legal basis of proof: the testimony of two persons is valid (8:17).

Some of the statements made in the Gospel are of dubious correctness. The statement in 11:49 (cf.18:13) that Caiaphas was high priest "that year" has been used on both sides. Here it is sufficient to say that should John have had the impression that the office of high priest was one that changed hands every year, he was mistaken. It is, of course, possible that he meant only that Caiaphas was high priest in the year of the crucifixion. More questionable is the statement in 18:28 that the Jewish officials were unwilling to enter the Praetorium, so as not to be defiled and thereby prevented from participating in the Passover feast. Whether that was so is disputable. Questionable in another sense is the remark in 4:9: "Jews do not share things in common with the Samaritans." There is manuscript evidence for the omission of this phrase,[11] so that we may be dealing here with a late redactional interpolation (but this is unlikely). It is also disputed whether the meaning is only that "Jews have nothing to do with Samaritans" (which would re-

quire only superficial knowledge of Palestinian conditions), or that
"Jews do not use dishes with Samaritans" (which would require familiarity with the opinion that Samaritan women had to be considered as
menstruating from birth [*Niddah* 4.1] and therefore always unclean).
There is much more material of this kind to be found in commentaries.
All of this forms a picture, nebulous and blurred in some details, of Jesus as a Palestinian Jew who lived within, yet in tension with,
the structure of Palestinian Jewish society. In the end the tension becomes strong enough to result in Jesus' complete rejection ("It is better
for you that one man should die for the people than that the whole nation should be destroyed" [11:50]), in his being handed over to the Roman judiciary ("Your own nation and the chief priests have handed you
over to me. What have you done?" [18:35]), and in his crucifixion.
    This leads to a second element in Palestinian society: the Ro-
man prefect Pontius Pilate and his assistants in the provincial govern-
ment. We may note that Galilee under its ruler Herod Antipas, who
plays an important part in the Synoptic Gospels, remains in the Fourth
Gospel relatively insignificant and does not at this point call for special
consideration. In fact Pilate too appears only at the end of the story in
the only place where, according to John, Jesus has any dealings with
secular, political society. It is important here to make a distinction. The
exactness of the historical material reported by John is extremely questionable. In John's narrative of Jesus' arrest (18:1-11) a cohort of soldiers is accompanied by a band of retainers from the high priest and the
Pharisees, the entire group being apparently under the command of a
military tribune (18:12). Yet the Roman part of this surprisingly mixed
group is ready to permit Jesus to be taken immediately to Annas, not to
the Roman governor. Throughout the entire story Pilate appears favora-
bly inclined toward Jesus and much less inclined toward shedding
blood than other indications would suggest. He permits the Jews to address him with incredible impudence. "What accusation do you bring
against this man?" "If this man were not a criminal, we would not have
handed him over to you" (18:29, 30). After deciding that Jesus is innocent, Pilate nevertheless has him flogged (19:1) and permits his soldiers
to ridicule him (19:2, 3). He seems to expect that the Jews will carry
out the crucifixion (19:16). The Johannine passion story thus contains
little material that can be considered to be of great historical value.
    To be distinguished, however, from this lack of historical in-
formation are two dialogues between Jesus and Pilate (18:33-38; 19:9-
11) and also some of the conversations between Pilate and the Jews (especially 18:31-32, 38b-40; 19:6-8, 12-13). These passages are not of
importance because of their historical value, which is in fact nil—who
was in a position to report what private conversations (if indeed there
were any) took place between the prefect and his prisoner? They are,
however, of great importance for the Johannine understanding of authority and the theological significance of the state. Moreover, this

combination of historical worthlessness and weighty theological content means that this material must be regarded as shedding light on John's relationship with the second society or environment with which his book is concerned, that is, the environment that surrounded John as author. We shall return to this later.

The Johannine relationship to history is curious. The fact that a historical Jesus existed, of whom one could know at least certain things, was a central and indispensable element in his thought. To tell the story of this Jesus, the incarnate Word of God, to tell it with exact and verifiable details, was a task that for John had no theological or other significance. Had Jesus been other than he was, John could not have written as he did. His main concern, however, was to describe Jesus as he is, or rather, perhaps, to tell the consequences resulting now from what he was then. All that we should at present conclude from this is that we should not be surprised if the Gospel has little to tell us about the relationship between Jesus and the religious and political groups of his day. What we may hope to find in the Gospel is an implicit representation of the Johannine reaction (a theological rather than a sociological reaction) to John's own environment. It is this reaction that we shall examine now.

D. The Environment of the Fourth Evangelist

It would lead far beyond the limits of this study if more than brief reference were made to one of the essential elements in the background of the Fourth Gospel: I refer to gnosis. In an investigation of "Christianity and society" it must be left almost completely out of account. This is not because gnosis is unimportant but because in the first century it did not represent a society. In fact, it was hardly a sharply defined religious or philosophical form of thought, though it became that later, and in the second century it became a society, a kind of church. In John's time it resembled rather an atmosphere that one inhaled than a clearly distinguishable entity or even a formulated myth. For this reason it need not be considered here, important as it is for an assessment of Johannine theology.

Judaism, on the other hand, offers an almost exact opposite. Within Judaism theology is very various. The author (or authors) of Enoch did not think in the same way as Philo. Yet Judaism is above all the embodiment of an institution, of a firmly established and strictly organized society with no essential confession apart from the monotheism of the Shema, with a disciplined life regulated by the precepts of the Torah, at least of the written Torah, for many expanded and explained by the additional precepts of the oral Torah. John shows that he is aware of precisely this kind of institutional Judaism. He is an heir of the Old Testament and makes it his own, since Moses wrote of Christ (John 5:46), Isaiah saw his glory (12:41), and Abraham rejoiced to see his day (8:56).

As many generations of commentators have pointed out, John tends to refer to "the Jews" in general. This is unlike the Synoptic Gospels, which prefer to speak of certain groups or classes among the Jews: Pharisees, Sadducees, Herodians, teachers of the law, priests. Various reasons have been suggested to explain why the Johannine treatment differs. Most of them have at least some validity. Especially important is the fact that John wrote (in all probability) at a time when earlier distinctions had disappeared with the disaster of A.D. 70. Most important of all, however, is the fact that the expression "the Jews" points to Judaism as an institution—one that had rejected Jesus and now stood over against the church in apparently irreconcilable detachment. John writes (9:22; 12:42; 16:2) with knowledge of the Benediction[12] that had the effect of excluding Jewish Christians from the synagogue. At the first mention of this action it is attributed to "the Jews": "For the Jews had already agreed that anyone who confessed Jesus to be the Messiah would be put out of the synagogue" (9:22).

The phrase *the Jews* is characteristic of the Gospel as a whole. "The Jews" had sent to John the Baptist (1:19); the feasts are feasts of "the Jews" (e.g., 2:13); "the Jews" were intent on killing Jesus (e.g., 5: 18); "the Jews" who believed are in an insecure and dangerous situation (8:31: " . . . if you continue in my word"); and so on. John is fully aware that the entire story of Jesus took place within Judaism, up to the point when he was buried "according to the burial custom of the Jews" (19:40) . Yet, finally, by the end of the first century, the Jews had separated themselves from the Christians. For John, salvation comes from the Jews (4:22). But this is in the first instance a historical statement. Salvation was to come out of Judaism and had been predicted by the prophets, but from that point onward Christianity no longer needed Judaism. When modern authors search for signs of anti-Semitism, or rather of anti-Judaism, in the New Testament, they begin quite naturally with John. There is no indication in the Gospel that the evangelist and his companions were aware of a continuing special mission to Israel. John has no parallel to the terrible sentence in Matthew, "His blood be on us and on our children" (Matt. 27:25), but "We have no king but the emperor" (John 19:15) is in many respects an even clearer proclamation that those who speak thus reject their position as the people of the one king, God. For the Johannine church the synagogue represents a threat and a warning. The synagogue is not a sister nor even a mission field.

The last paragraph referred to Johannine statements concerning the Jews in general—"the Jews"; some remarks about the Pharisees could be taken in the same way. Are there exceptions? Are there Jewish groups who were exempt from the process by which John distanced himself from his compatriots? Before the military catastrophe of the year 70 Judaism was a manifold religious phenomenon. The universal applicability of the Torah to the whole of Judaism inevitably produced a certain measure of uniformity, as I have already indicated. But the Torah had to be interpreted. The interpretations differed, and they differed more in the earlier time than in the later. We know today that the term "normative Judaism" is an expression that must be used, if at all, with great caution, and that sectarian groups existed with their own interpretations and customs, a situation in which each viewed itself not as sectarian but as the central group, as the only soldier within the troop who kept step. Early Christianity must have appeared as such a sectarian group within Judaism at large. Did Christianity then have in those early days, and did it continue to have later, a special kind of relation with any other sectarian group?

Since the discovery of the Dead Sea Scrolls a relationship of this kind between Johannine Christianity and the Qumran sect has often been maintained. On the whole, however, this relationship has over the years come to seem increasingly improbable. A few superficial similarities are misleading. The sect shows antipathy to the temple; John declares that the Father will be worshiped "neither on this mountain nor in Jerusalem" (4:21). The two attitudes, however, differ substantially. Essentially the sect had nothing against the temple; it would have used the temple had it been allowed to do so in its own way, which differed from what the sect considered the temple's desecration by the officiating priests. The Johannine rejection of the temple resulted from the conviction that the temple had been fulfilled and thus abolished by Jesus, since he had taken its place and now served himself as the link between God and humanity. Much has been made of the modified dualism that, as has been repeatedly claimed, can be found in both John and the Qumran literature. In its essential features, however, this modified dualism can be found also in the Old Testament.

The differences between *Qumran* and the Gospel are fundamental. The Qumran community had its own understanding and interpretation of the Torah, but it insisted with extreme rigidity that the Torah, thus understood and interpreted, should be strictly kept. That was the foundation of the community's piety. For John the law had at best a subordinate status ("The law indeed was given through Moses; grace and truth came through Jesus Christ"; John 1:17). Moses is important because "he wrote about me" (5:46). Jesus does not keep the Sabbath law in a literal sense (5:16; 9:16). Qumran is not sufficient to explain the Gnostic traits of the Gospel.

We know far too little of the variety, the subdivisions, and the crosscurrents in the Judaism of the first century to be able to affirm that no contacts ever existed between the traditions that eventually found their way respectively into the Fourth Gospel and into the Qumran sect and its writings. We can probably accept that the first Christian group displayed in many respects parallels and similarities with the groups that settled by the Dead Sea. Further than that we cannot go, unless it is in more detailed similarities between the organization of the Johannine communities (which are described more clearly in the letters than in the Gospel) and the organization of the sect. The parallel between the group of twelve disciples in the Gospel and the twelve merciful judges of Qumran (lQS 8.1)[13] is neither remarkable in itself nor specifically Johannine. At best it could indicate an early contact of Christians with Qumran, but no particularly Johannine interest lies there. The fact that the letters show an increasingly monarchical structure (as pointed out above) is no special parallel with the Teacher of Righteousness or any other Qumran figure.

There is another group of Jewish origin that deserves brief mention. It has often been taken as proved that one of the motives that contributed to the fact that the Gospel was written down was the necessity felt by the Christians to counter the claims made in their master's name by the *disciples of John the Baptist*, who continued to exist as a group after the deaths of both John and Jesus. This was done (it is held) by integrating these claims into the demands made for Jesus. Some who believe that behind the extant Prologue to the Gospel (John 1:1-18) there lies an *Urprolog* are of the opinion that it originated in Baptist circles.[14] Here, however, there is a danger of building one hypothesis upon another.[15] Still, it is correctly observed that the Gospel contains a number of passages that, though ranking John the Baptist highly, assert emphatically that he is inferior to Jesus. Thus he himself declares that he is not the Christ or Elijah or the prophet (1:20-23). The disciples leave him in order to follow Jesus (1:37). He welcomes the greater success that Jesus has and compares himself to the friend of the bridegroom—an important but secondary figure: "He must increase, but I must decrease" (3:26-30; cf. 4:1). The Baptist is an important witness to Jesus but not the most important (5:33-36). The difficulty we encounter here lies in the lack of concrete evidence for the existence of a Baptist sect.[16] For such evidence it is natural to point to the narratives in Acts that deal with Apollos (Acts 18:24-28), who knew "only the baptism of John," and with the disciples (19:1-7) who had been baptized "into John's baptism." It is not possible at this point to appraise the historical value of these two reports. Nor would it be wise to make too much of them or of whatever may be hidden behind the infancy narratives in Luke 1-2. It is certainly correct to argue that the fourth evangelist would not have written in such a pointedly negative way about the Baptist had he not known some who made equally pointed positive assertions about him. It is probable therefore that such people existed and certain that if they existed, John the evangelist could not have agreed with them, and it is likely that he would express his lack of agreement. We cannot, however, on the basis of this lack of agreement draw any conclusions about the social structure of the two groups, the one following John the Baptist and the other gathered about John the evangelist. Here as elsewhere John's interests lie more in the theological than the sociological realm.

The Fourth Gospel shows without doubt an interest in Samaria and the Samaritans. Not only are the important words about the water of life spoken in Samaria (John 4:4,5) and directed in the course of conversation to a Samaritan woman. The passage also concludes with the statement that Jesus was accepted by many Samaritans as "the Savior of the world" (4:39-42). There is perhaps more to be learned from this chapter. After the woman's departure the disciples return to Jesus and invite him to eat some of the provisions they have brought. He replies, "I have food to eat that you do not know about." When the disciples take this literally (a typically Johannine development, which shows that we have here Johannine rather than traditional material), he explains that his food is to do the will of him who sent him and to accomplish his work. This in turn leads to a series of sayings about the work of sowing and reaping and finally to the statement: "I sent you to reap that for which you did not labor. Others have labored, and you have entered into their labor" (4:38). Taken in the light of Acts 8, this passage has been understood to mean that Samaria was converted to Christianity by the Hellenists and had subsequently been taken over as a mission field by the church's nucleus, the Twelve.[17] This in turn has led to the conclusion that there was a connection between the Gospel and the Hellenists. The connection, however, is too hypothetical and problematic to mean much to us. It is exegetically uncertain. In 4:38 the mention of "others" may be a concealed reference to Jesus himself.[18] It was he who began the work of evangelizing in Samaria; now it is up to his disciples to bring in the harvest. The word Samaritan appears once more in the Gospel (8:48), where it is used as a Jewish accusation against Jesus: "Are we not right in saying that you are a Samaritan and have a demon?"

Where do these references to the Samaritans lead? There can be no doubt that John, or the Johannine tradition, was aware that the Samaritans formed a group that was related to the Jews but repudiated by them. The Samaritans worship the same God but in a different place (4.20). The Samaritans expect the coming of a Messiah, a prophetic and teaching Messiah ("He will proclaim all things to us"—4:25; "...a man who told me everything I have ever done! He cannot be the Messiah, can he?"—4:29), and Jesus can say with reference to the Samaritan expectation, "I am he" (4:26). This seems to indicate a greater willingness on John's part than on that of some Jews to accept the Samaritans as part of God's people. One can hardly claim, however, that it proves more than that. There is a prophetic component (based on Deut. 18) in at least the Qumran form of Judaism (1QS 9.11; 4QTestim 5-8) and in early non-Johannine messianism (Acts 3:22). One may reasonably suppose that the Johannine Christians had at a certain stage come into sufficiently close contact with Samaritans to have an interest in and sympathy for them. There is nothing in John 4 that could not have taken place (from the standpoint of the narrative) in Galilee, for example. It may very well be significant also that in John the Samaritans are the first to hail Jesus as the Savior of the world, even though significance may lie in the fact that other representatives of the world outside Judaism are hardly mentioned in the Gospel and that there is some appropriateness in having this truth proclaimed by the despised and undervalued. Contacts between the Johannine community and the Samaritans could have led to the rejection of Jesus as a Samaritan (8:48). The insinuation that Jesus was born out of wedlock (8:41, in the same context) is an accusation that was made at a later time, possibly as late as when the Fourth Gospel was written, and that may be true of the Samaritan accusation too. But John makes no comment on it. Only the criticism that Jesus has a demon (8:49) receives a reply. The most that can be said is that a number of doors open up to speculations regarding the social environment of Johannine Christianity; valid proofs hardly exist.

The Samaritans have led us a step outside Judaism. It remains to consider John in relation to *Roman society*. We have already seen that Rome plays only a relatively small part in the story told in the Gospel. Fear of Rome is represented as contributing to the Jewish decision to get rid of Jesus (John 11:48). Pilate proves to be a partner in the conspiracy, though a reluctant one, so that eventually, in spite of his assertions of Jesus' innocence (18:38; 19:4, 6, 12), Pilate hands him over to be crucified (19:16). John himself, however—whether he wrote in Ephesus, Antioch, or Alexandria—wrote under the law of the empire. He must have known, though there is no evidence for it in the letters, that he had his own local Pilate, an authority to which he and the church to which he belonged were inevitably bound, whether in a positive or a negative sense. This means that the conversations reported in chapters 18 and 19 must be considered, regardless of their historical origin, as expressing his opinions about the relationship between his church and the state and in particular about his understanding of the state's authority.

The main thought in John 18:29-32 (we ignore here many particular problems and additional statements) is that the Jews have decided on Jesus' death for their own reasons. They demand nothing less than his death; that is why they hand the case over to Rome. Pilate has Jesus called before him and asks immediately, "Are you the King of the Jews?" (18:33). From the fact that the death sentence was demanded we are perhaps expected to infer that it had already been stated that Jesus had declared himself king, but it is much more likely that John is simply borrowing from the source he used, shortening it by omitting this feature. Jesus' evasive reply (18:34 and especially 18:37) is strongly reminiscent of the Synoptic narrative (e.g., Mark 15:2).

What follows is a discussion about the nature of kingship. Jesus insists that he possesses a kingdom but proves that his kingship is not of this world by pointing out that his followers are not fighting in order to prevent his falling into the hands of the Jews. It is a natural characteristic of a this-worldly kingdom that its followers fight for it, but for Jesus' kingdom his followers do not fight. This argument overlooks the fact that the true reason why the disciples are not fighting is not that they understand Jesus' kingship but that they have run away out of cowardice. Or is it hinted that had they been encouraged by Jesus, they would have been brave enough to fight? At any rate, Jesus confirms that his kingship is not rooted in this world (it is not "from here"; John 18:36). By his words Jesus in fact admits that he is a king. "So you are a king?" (18:37). The "you" may be emphatic: you, wretched man, a king! The reply, "You say that I am a king," is not a renunciation of kingship but probably means that kingship was not the word that Jesus would have chosen. Politicians like Pilate may use it, but Jesus prefers to speak of the "truth." The meaning of his life is to be a witness to the truth. Pilate can only reply by another question: "What is truth?" (18:37-38). This seems to mean that a conversation between Jesus (and those whom he represents, who also represent him, namely, the Christian community) and Pilate (and the society he represents) can only lapse into silence, since the two parties speak different languages. The language Pilate chooses is that of political dominion. Christians will use his language only if they are allowed to turn its meaning upside down. To Pilate, kingship is only a matter of this world and of power understood in terms of this world. For Jesus, however, kingship is precisely not of this world and carries in itself a repudiation of this-worldly power. Jesus is concerned with the truth, but that is a word that Pilate does not understand.

The next conversation begins when the Jews inform Pilate that Jesus claims to be the Son of God. The assertion that Jesus is of supernatural origin puts fear into Pilate. He asks, "Where are you from?" (19:9), a question that shows that we are dealing here with a typical Johannine development of traditional material, for it originates in Pilate's discovery, reported in the Synoptics (Luke 23:6ff.), that Jesus is from Galilee and can therefore be remitted to Herod. But the matter is no longer a question of Jesus' country of origin, and there is no reply. Jesus' silence prompts Pilate to a further question, intended to make the prisoner talk. Is he not aware that Pilate has the power to set him free or to crucify him (John 19:10)? This claim to power is true in so far as Pilate's decision, whatever it may be, will be carried out. The rights that Pilate has as Roman governor, however, are not something that he possesses in himself. He has power only because it has been given him from God ("from above"; cf.3:3). It follows that Pilate cannot be considered an entirely free agent. In regard to Jesus' death he has less guilt on his shoulders than "the one who handed me over to you" (commentators disagree on the question, here irrelevant, whether the phrase refers to Judas, Caiaphas, or the Jewish people as a whole). From this

point onward (19:12) Pilate tries to release Jesus, partly because he is
now convinced of the supernatural (if not divine) origin of his prisoner.
But he is overruled by the political threat: "If you release this man, you
are no friend of the emperor. Everyone who claims to be a king sets
himself against the emperor."

The primary Johannine interest in these conversations is theological and especially christological. John asserts that Jesus will die as
an innocent man, for he does not claim for himself kingship, and thus
power, as the world knows it. Rather, he sees it as his task in the world
to bear witness to the truth. He also dies as a divine being who rules a
kingdom that is not of this world, and he thus has a power that Pilate
does not share. At the same time it is admitted that earthly rulers like
Pilate have a measure of power that has been granted them by God.
This is depicted in the form of a record of Jesus' historical confrontation with Pilate. Since, however, this report is clearly a Johannine addition to the passion narrative, it must be understood as containing also
John's commentary on his own situation, in which he and the congregation to which he belonged found themselves confronted with the Roman state. John 16:2 indeed points primarily to resistance from the Jewish side. That becomes clear in the reference to expulsion from the
synagogue and also in the death threat, for those who "kill you" and believe that "by doing so they are offering worship to God" can only be
Jews. It is doubtful, however, whether at the time at which John wrote,
Jews often had the opportunity to execute Christians. Probably John's
train of thought is intended only to indicate the general dislike that
Christians experienced (15:18). With this in mind, John uses the confrontation between Jesus and Pilate, on the one hand, for its own sake
(in order to bear witness to the truth about Jesus, that is, about Christology) and, on the other, as a prime example of the relationship between
church and state.

It is of the highest importance, and absolutely characteristic,
that John views this confrontation much more from the standoint of theology than from that of sociology. Social and political relations have a
theological basis in so far as the power exercised by the state and applied in part in persecutions is given to it by God. This takes the matter
one step beyond Rom. 13:1-7, where the state suppresses baseness and
vice, rewards virtue, and is thus quite naturally regarded as God's servant, empowered and approved by God. For John the state is the perse-
cuting power[19] with undisputed authority to acquit or to crucify. Yet
this power, too, which includes the power to do evil and to oppose the
work of God, is based on an authority of command that comes from
God. It is a different version of the doctrine of the two swords, in which
the one can be turned against the other. Presumably, John does not
mean that it is God's will that the state should attack the church, but
that the power given to the state by God is given without any conditions
attached to the gift. The power may be abused as well as used for good.

This attitude was adopted by the early church. "We respect in the emperors the ordinance of God, who has set them over the nations. We know that there is that in them which God has willed; and to what God has willed we desire all safety, and we account an oath by it a great oath" (Tertullian *Apology* 32). It is important to recognize that in the beginning this attitude was based mainly on theological grounds rather than on grounds of expediency. We have already pointed to John 15:18 at an earlier point: "If the world hates you, be aware that it hated me before it hated you." With that we may compare 1 John 3:13: "Do not be astonished, brothers and sisters, that the world hates you." As we have seen above, the world, the cosmos, is a fundamental theological theme in the Johannine literature, especially in the Gospel and in the first letter (cf. also 2 John 7). The theological theme has two historical, social forms of expression. One appears in the Gospel in the frequently used term the Jews. This term is not used in the Prologue, but the idea is present. "He was in the world, and the world came into being through him, yet the world did not know him; he came to what was his own, and his own people did not receive him" (John 1:10-11). The world is God's creation, which has used the freedom given to it to rebel against its creator. To the world has been given the power to release or to crucify, and it chooses to crucify. According to the Johannine view, the Jews are the best example of this abuse of power; the words of 19:11 must be understood in this way. The Jews deserve more reproach than the Romans, for while Pilate can only ask, "What is truth?" (18:38), the Jews are supposed to know the truth. Israel's teacher should understand what is said to him (3:10). Salvation comes from the life and traditions of the Jews (4:22). The most painful rebellion against God is that of the pious. In addition, however, there is also the rebellion of the worldly power, which also abuses what has been entrusted to it. Although John exonerates the governor rather than the Jews in his passion story—mainly for theological reasons but in part also perhaps out of prudence—he cannot avoid the conclusion that Pilate handed Jesus over to be crucified (19:16). Jesus was *crucifixus sub Pontio Pilato*. In this clause the cosmos is written into the confession of faith. This observation is true only for the Gospel. Strangely enough, the cosmos seems to assume another meaning in the first letter. The state disappears, and *cosmos* becomes a word belonging to the realm of thought rather than to that of political action and power. People leave the church and go out into the world (1 John 2:19; 4:5). They go out in order to speak the world's language in such a way that the world may listen to them, as it was not listening to John and his associates. The world has now become not the source of persecution but the fount of unbelief and heresy. This theme has been discussed earlier and now leads to the last question to be raised in this study.

E. Tensions in the Johannine Community

We have examined the Christian congregation or congregations as they are set forth in the Johnine literature in relation to various groups in their environment: Jews and Romans, Samaritans, Qumran sectarians, and disciples of John the Baptist. We must now examine the Christian group in relation to itself, that is, in relation to claims and tensions that were caused not by external but by internal pressure. To a certain degree this topic also has already been dealt with. The letters clearly show that there were those who went out into "the world" and learned to speak as the world speaks and no doubt to live as the world lives, at least to the degree that they separated themselves from the circle of Christian love. So it appeared at least to the authors of the letters. Those who went out, however, would describe what they did in a different way.

The Gospel also shows traces of controversy and schism. At this point we should note the passages that Bultmann and others have attributed to an ecclesiastical redactor, who believed that the Gospel in its original version was unsatisfactory in regard to eschatological doctrines and sacramental practice and accordingly inserted passages such as John 3:5 (with its clear reference to baptism) and 6:51-58 (with its allusion to eating and drinking at the Eucharist), as well as references to the "last day" 6:39, 40, 44, 54). The possibility must not be excluded that these passages belonged to the many-sided dialectical theology of the evangelist.[20] If, however, they are correctly considered to be insertions, they testify to sacramental and non-sacramental elements in the congregation and to rival convictions regarding whether eschatology was or was not to be completely transposed into the present. In any case, it must be emphasized that the Gospel as it stands testifies to a theology and a practice that were able to accommodate both a futuristic and an already realized eschatology, as well as an adoption of baptism and eucharist as critical as that which can be seen in Paul's writings.

Less problematic is another group of passages, which tell explicitly of dissensions among the disciples. Such passages are found in John 6:60-71 ("When many of his disciples heard it, they said, 'This teaching is difficult; who can accept it?' But Jesus, being aware that his disciples were complaining about it, said to them, 'Does this offend you?...But among you there are some who do not believe.' For Jesus knew from the first who were the ones that did not believe, and who was the one that would betray him.... Because of this many of his disciples turned back and no longer went about with him. So Jesus asked the twelve, 'Do you also wish to go away?' "). In addition one may point to the following passages: 7:5 ("Not even his brothers believed in him"); 8:30-59 ("As he was saying these things, many believed in him. Then Jesus said to the Jews who had believed in him, 'If you continue in my

word, you are truly my disciples.... You are trying to kill me.... You
are from your father the devil' "); 10:1-16 ("Anyone who does not enter by the gate into the sheepfold but climbs in another way is a thief
and a bandit.... All who came before me are thieves and bandits");
12:42ff. ("Nevertheless many, even of the authorities, believed in him.
But because of the Pharisees they did not confess it, for fear that they
would be put out of the synagogue; for they loved human glory more
than the glory that comes from God"); 13:11 ("Not all of you are
clean"); 13:30 ("After receiving the piece of bread, he immediately
went out"); 15:1-10 ("He removes every branch in me that bears no
fruit.... Whoever does not abide in me is thrown away like a branch
and withers; such branches are gathered, thrown into the fire, and
burned");16:32 ("The hour is coming, indeed it has come, when you
will be scattered, each one to his home, and you will leave me"); 18:17
("[Peter] said, "I am not' "); 18:25-27 ("He denied it and said, 'I am
not.' . . . Again Peter denied it").

If we are unwilling to accept the view that John included all
this material in his Gospel only in order to preserve the memory of
some interesting past events, which is highly unlikely, we have to conclude that the material reflected divisions in the post-Easter congregation, divisions John believed to have been prefigured in events that took
place during the course of Jesus' life or are presented as if they had tak-
en place there. The texts listed above do not simply deal with the unbelieving. If they did, they would belong to a different category, one that
has already been examined. In the passages cited here we encounter,
rather, those who did believe, but out of fear did not confess their faith,
and those who did believe but abandoned their faith either for doctrinal
reasons (they find Jesus' teaching "difficult") or succumbed to moral
temptation (as, for example, in the case of Judas, to the love of money);
also we have those who deny their faith when under pressure, like Peter, even though one cannot say that they have actually given up their
faith; finally, there are those who in truth were never really branches of
the vine. It is not difficult to speculate on the circumstances in a Christian congregation in the first century in which things of this kind could
occur, if only because they occur in every generation of Christian history. Because of the lack of clues, however, it is impossible to lay one's
finger on particular events in the history of the Johannine congregation
that could be brought into relation with the foreshadowings so cleverly
described in the Gospel. Rather, we see in the Gospel only in general
terms the reflection of a congregation in which such events took place.
There was persecution. (No one in the England of the twentieth century
could have written such a sentence as John 16:2, for in England people
are not killed because they are Christians.) Some broke down under
persecution. For some, temptation proved too strong. Doctrinal disagreements existed, possibly in connection with the sacraments, more
probably in regard to Christology. Not all who separated from the Jo-

hannine church believed that they thereby ceased to be Christians. At
least some probably believed most profoundly that they were maintaining the faith in its purity over against Johannine corruptions.
This leads us almost back to the point from which we started.
In the letters also one observes this turning away from the Johannine
church, and in them it appears to be treated with increasing harshness.
It is not, however, that the evangelist discusses such matters only superficially; rather, he discusses them theologically.[21] The authors of the letters, on the other hand—especially the author of the second and third
letters—view such matters from an institutional point of view. It may
be possible to make conjectures about this historical variation; it may
simply have happened with the lapse of time: theological insight disappeared as the church became increasingly institutionalized. It may be,
however, that there is a clue in John 21, if it is correct to consider this
chapter an addition to the Gospel in its original form. It is often thought
and probably rightly, that John 21:23 reflects the death of the disciple
whom Jesus loved, and that one motive for writing the chapter was not
only to point out that Jesus had not predicted that this disciple would
live to see Jesus' return but also to point out the different though com-
plementary roles that he and Peter would play in the life of the church:
Peter would be the shepherd; the beloved disciples the witness. It is unlikely that the chapter would have been added to the Gospel if the beloved disciple had not been connected in some way with the writing of
it as its link to the earliest beginnings (or unless it was believed, or alleged, that he had been so connected with it). His death accordingly denoted the end of an era: an era in which the current of theological
thought flowed strongly and the church could cope with a high degree
of elasticity in form and discipline. In the new era strict discipline replaced creative theological thought. To weather the storm the church
battened down the hatches and left no doubt that the end of freedom
had arrived. "Do not receive into the house or welcome anyone who
comes to you and does not bring this teaching; for to welcome is to participate in the evil deeds of such a person" (2 John 10-11).

BIBLIOGRAPHY

In addition to the commentaries on the Johannine writings and
works on the social history of the New Testament generally (e.g., those
by H. C. Kee, A. J. Malherbe, W. A. Meeks, and G. Theissen), the following may be mentioned.

Boismard, Marie Emile, and Arnoud Lamouille. L'Évangile de Jean, Synopse
    des quatre Évangiles. Vol. 3. 1977.
Brown, R.E. The Community of the Beloved Disciple. 1979.

Cullmann, Oscar. *The Johannine Circle*. 1976.

Culpepper, Richard Allan. *The Johannine School*. 1975.

Lieu, Judith. *The Second and Third Epistles of John: History and Background*. 1986.

Malherbe, A. J. "The Inhospitality of Diotrephes." In *God's Christ and his People*, FS for N. A. Dahl, edited by J. Jervell and W. Meeks, 222-32. 1977.

Martyn, J. Louis. *History and Theology in the Fourth Gospel*. 1968, rev. ed. 1979.

_____ *The Gospel of John in Christian History*. 1978.

Meeks, Wayne A. "The Man from Heaven in Johannine Sectarianism." *JBL* 91 (1972): 44-72. .

Painter, John. "The Farewell Discourses and the History of Johannine Christianity." *NTS* 27 (1980/81): 525-43.

___*The Quest for the Messiah. The History, Literature and Theology of the Johannine Community*. 1991.

Purvis, James D. "The Fourth Gospel and the Samaritans." *NovT* 17 (1975): 161-98.

Robinson, John A. T. "The Destination and Purpose of the Johannine Epistles." *NTS* 7 (1960/61): 56-65.

Smith, D. Moody. *Johannine Christianity*, esp. 1-36, 1984.

Thyen, Hartwig. "Entwicklungen innerhalb der johanneischen Theologie und Kirche im Spiegel von Joh. 21 und der Lieblingsjüngertexte des Evangeliums." in *L'Évangile de Jean*, edited by M. de Jonge, 259-99, 1977.

NOTES

1. To say this does not mean to deny the value of an attempt to write the social history of early Christianity. But it is important to recognize the difficulty of such an undertaking and to point out that the success of the undertaking is bound to be limited.

2. Cf. the bibliographical listing by Robin Scroggs, "The sociological Interpretation of the New Testament: The Present State of Research," *NTS* 26 (1979/80): 164-79.

3. Cf., e.g., C. K. Barrett, *The Gospel According to St John* (1978), 96-99, 139-44; *The Gospel of John and Judaism* (1975), 1-19.

4. C. K. Barrett, *Essays on John* (1982), 131.

5. Barrett, *St John*, 59-62, 133ff.

6. Cf. the recent discussion by R.E. Brown, *The Epistles of John* (1983), 669ff.; also J. Lieu, *The Second and Third Epistles of John* (1986).

7. E. Käsemann, "Ketzer und Zeuge," in *Exegetische Versuche und Besinnungen* 1 (1960), 168-87.

8. Acts 20:17, 27; Titus 1:5, 7.

9. The classical account of this view is found in J.B. Lightfoot, "The Christian Ministry," a dissertation appended to his commentary on Philippians (1st ed., 1868), 181-269.

10. See the material collected by Günther Bornkamm in *TWNT* 6:676-80.

11. Omitted by the manuscripts D a b e j.

12. See Barrett, *St John*, 362; *Judaism*, 47ff.

13. It is uncertain whether the group consisted of twelve all told, of whom three had to be priests, or of twelve Israelites together with three priests. CD 10:4-6 requires a group of ten judges.

14. Cf. especially R. Bultmann, *The Gospel of John* (1971), 13-18.

15. Cf. C. K. Barrett, *St John*, 149-51; *New Testament Essays* (1972), 27-48.

16. Cf. John H. Hughes, "Disciples of John the Baptist" (Durham University thesis, 1969).

17. O. Cullmann, *The Johannine Circle* (1976).

18. E.g., Barrett, *St John*, 243.

19. It would be appropriate, though it would go beyond the appointed limits of this study, to consider in this context the role of the state in the Johannine Apocalypse. Even when the state has given itself over to evil, its power is from God.

20. See Barrett, *New Testament Essays*, 49-69; also *Essays on John*, 128-30.

21. In John 8 we can perhaps observe the evangelist at work as he re-theologizes accusations that are merely insulting. The Jews insist that their freedom and ancestry stem from Abraham (v. 33) and on that basis accuse Jesus of being illegitimate (v. 41). John, in turn, insists that freedom and ancestry have to be interpreted in a theological sense. There is no true freedom unless it is freedom from sin; ancestry manifests itself in behavior.

8

THE PLACE OF JOHN AND THE
SYNOPTICS WITHIN THE EARLY
HISTORY OF CHRISTIAN THOUGHT

It was perhaps with false hopes that I submitted the title of this paper to the Chairman of the Colloquium. The old ways of approach to the question before us have been trodden smooth, and there does not seem to be much to pick up from them; I hoped that a fresh approach might produce interesting results. I am not at all sure that it has done; but I shall do my best to use it.

Since the publication in 1938 of Gardner-Smith's little book[1] the opinion that had previously been pretty widely held[2], that John had made use of at least Mark among the Synoptic Gospels, possibly Luke, and maybe even Matthew,[3] has been frequently discussed and the debate has ebbed and flowed one way and another. So many matters of detail have been discussed, so many parallels or alleged parallels compared, that it is hard to know where to turn if the debate is to be continued—not to say, brought to a conclusion. It is in fact interesting to turn back to Gardner-Smith, who converted to his view C. H. Dodd[4] and many others, and to note how much ground that has since been fought over inch by inch was already outlined by him. His primary observation is that though there are agreements between Mark and John the disagreements are more common and complete; they must be weighed against each other. "The attention of critics has generally been concentrated on the points of agreement, and insufficient regard has been paid to the very important divergences which are everywhere apparent" (p.88).This argument has a superficial logic, but it is perhaps not as strong as Gardner-Smith, and many others since his time, have supposed. Agreement does not prove knowledge; the critic must never altogether discount the possibility of coincidence, and in any case, however many differences and nuances of interest and intention there may be, both Mark and John profess to recount the same historical event, to present the life and teaching of Jesus of Nazareth: small wonder therefore if they choose to narrate the same incidents, that there should be occasional or even frequent agreement. The same story will sometimes be found in *The Times* and in *The Daily Mirror*—and incidentally when this occurs the agreement will often be found to run back to the use of some agency source. Again, disagreement does not prove lack of knowledge; all it proves is disagreement, and it often presupposes knowledge.[5] Who should know this better than theologians and historians? Sometimes the disagreement is absolute. "You think it happened like that, or that this is what he meant—or at least that is what you want us to think. I think it happened differently, and that he meant something else." Sometimes, and this is particularly significant, the difference is qualified. "Yes, you are right, but I can express it better, tell the story more effectively." Or again, to put the matter in a form appropriate to a discussion of Mark and John, the difference may be expressed thus. "You think that out of the whole tradition events A, B, and C are the most important and on no account to be omitted. I think that they are less important than X, Y, and Z, and it is these that I intend to include." The importance of this is that it is bound to rest upon the different intentions of different authors, which will be expressed in the selection of material as well as in the way each uses the material that they have in common. I am of course not saying that the discussion of agreements and disagreements is irrelevant to our debate; it is hard to know what else to argue about. I do suggest that the logical basis of the argument needs some consideration. Agreement at least suggests the possibility of knowledge, though (unless on a very large scale) it does not prove it; disagreement does not disprove it. I observe also that "agreement" is, in a literary context, a concept very difficult to quantify. For example, Gardner-Smith sets side by side Mark 1:7 and John 1:26, observing that "the phraseology of the Fourth Evangelist is not very close to that of Mark" (p. 3). In the Marcan sentence, as quoted, there are 17 words. Of these, 7 appear identically in John; a finite verb (ἔρχεται) is paralleled by a participle (ἐρχόμενος); an infinitive (λῦσαι) by ἵνα and the subjunctive (λύσω)[6]; a plural noun, with article (τῶν ὑποδημάτων) by the singular (τοῦ ὑποδήματος), with no change in meaning. It is thus not unreasonable to say that 11 of Mark's 17 words have verbal parallels; that Mark's κύψας is a superfluity, quite unnecessary to the sense (how do you deal with someone's shoes without bending down?); and that John's ἄξιος is a more suitable word than Mark's ἱκανός. Of Mark's 17 words there are now left an article (ὁ), and the phrase ὁ ἰσχυρότερός μου, and of the latter at least the comparative sense appears in John's πρῶτός μου (1,15.30).[7] There is in the Fourth Gospel a great deal more about John the Baptist, and I am not proposing to discuss the matter in detail. What I am saying is that we shall not get very far on the basis of subjective estimates of what constitutes agreement and what does not. No one in his right mind could affirm that John the Evangelist gets all he says about John the Baptist, not only in ch. 1 but in chs. 3, 4, and 5, from Mark; some he got from another source and some he developed for himself. But that is not the same thing as the proposition that John the Evangelist had never seen what Mark does say about John the Baptist.

There is another respect in which the logical foundation of the arguments used, whichever way they are held to point, may be examined. Gardner-Smith complains as follows: "Points of similarity are picked out and discussed in isolation; it is concluded that John must have known Mark, or Mark and Luke; then, when the matter has been thus decided, an attempt is made to account for the much more numerous discrepancies between [the] several Gospels" (p. 91). It would be better, Gardner-Smith argues, to start from the greater area of disagreement, reaching presumably the conclusion that the gospels were independent, and then set out to explain the few agreements, or apparent agreements, that occur. The question that is raised here is that of the logical relation between agreement and disagreement, or difference, and the different senses in which each may be explained; for agreements and discrepancies are not like votes, given respectively for and against a certain proposition, which may be counted, with victory going to the majority. There is a difference between agreement and difference which, it seems to me, Gardner-Smith and some others have overlooked. Difference can always be explained by means of what may be called internal considerations, considerations, that is, that are internal to the mind of the writer. If I give a different account of a sequence of events from that given by my colleague, this will be either because I deliberately modified his account, or modified the same source of information that he used, changing what lay before me so as to make it square with presuppositions of my own; or because I used a different source of information. If it was for the latter reason it may be that I simply did not possess the source my colleague used, or his own account; or it may be that for reasons of my own I rejected my colleague's (or his source's) account in favour of another, which might of course be my own personal knowledge. The latter possibility—that I knew my colleague's account but rejected it in favor of another—is bound to remain open unless some additional information excludes it. In a modern book, a bibliography may be provided which can show what accounts were, and what accounts were not, available to the author. Ancient books were not provided with bibliographies in the modern sense; but it is very clear, for example, that Josephus[8] knew the story of the Jewish War as it was told by Justus of Tiberias, though he had good reasons for preferring his own version. We come back to the conclusion that difference, including omission, does not in itself prove lack of knowledge; one cannot therefore start where Gardner-Smith would have us start. Agreement, however, can hardly be explained otherwise than by external considerations, considerations that arise not from the mind of the writer but from objective circumstances in his environment. The only alternative is coincidence. This, of course, is not to be excluded, though the probability that both John and Mark independently invented

stories of the feeding of 5000 men in the desert on five loaves and a
few fish is not high.[9] Agreement is not the same sort of thing as disagreement, or difference, or discrepancy. Where agreement between two
authors exists there must be either fortuitous coincidence or, if not the
use of the one by the other, the use of identical or at least similar sources.
    This suggests a further area in which careful use of language is
called for. It is by no means unfamiliar, but is so important that it must
be recalled. What do we mean by knowledge and ignorance, use and
disuse? There is a world of difference, nowadays usually but perhaps
not always observed, between a painful copying out of a text, in which
occasionally a word or construction is modified, and a recollection that
someone, somewhere, has written on the subject on which I am now
writing, and has done so in a way that has provoked me to thought, and
therein to a measure of disagreement; he may even have said things
which I find myself happy to borrow, whether consciously or subconsciously. Whatever else may be said about the Fourth Evangelist he did
not work like Wellhausen's Pentateuchal editor, leaving behind him
clearly identifiable blocks of J, E, D, and P. Rather he has left the print
of his own mind and hand throughout.
    I have in the past dealt with a number of Johannine passages,
more or less parallel to passages in Mark, in such detail as is possible in
a fairly detailed commentary[10], and I do not propose to discuss them
afresh now. The whole ground has been laboriously and acutely examined by others, of whom one thinks (not least in Leuven) especially of
Professor Neirynck. One continues to learn, especially in matters of detail, from one's colleagues, but I confess to being unchanged in my
opinion. There seem to me to be, in the detailed examination of the parallels, good ground for holding that John knew, respected, modified, rethought either Mark or some source—conceivably but improbably
oral—very much like Mark. I do not profess to be able to distinguish
between Mark and some other source, of which all we can say is that it
was like Mark; and on the general principle of Occam's razor I am inclined to think that the odds are on Mark. If it comes down to word-by-
word analysis this is where the probability seems to me to lie. But I
have been concerned in these opening paragraphs to look at the logic
involved in the kind of debate that has now been going on for over 50
years, and the conclusion of the examination is that no one will ever be
able to be certain whether John had read Mark or not (though, as I say,
I think I know where the probability lies). If this is so, it may be possible to do something more profitable than examine once more the material that is already in some danger of falling to pieces in our fingers. At
least, I hoped so.
    We are concerned with two books that come to us from the
first century of church history. They are part of a small but remarkable
body of literature[11] from which we gain practically all the knowledge

we have of the first three or four generations of Christians. It may be possible to learn something about John and Mark by viewing them as constituents of this literary corpus—a corpus which must be viewed from theological and historical standpoints, and not only as literature. We may begin with a few fairly general observations.

1. So far as the slight evidence at our disposal goes, the earliest Christian generations were not interested in chronological or topical order in such accounts as they possessed of the ministry of Jesus. This may be observed as a phenomenon of the gospels themselves. It is an old form-critical observation, not falsified by the processes of redaction criticism or any other more recent kind of criticism, that Mark is not a biography in the sense of a book that traces the physical, mental, and spiritual development of its hero. For the most part, Jesus stays in one area; most of the incidents could be reshuffled and would continue to make as good sense as they do now. Gardner-Smith's remark that "the outline of any written Gospel was determined not only by the natural sequences of history, but also by the form of the Preaching of the Apostles and their immediate followers" (p.89) hardly goes further (as the context shows) than the recognition that the baptism of Jesus must have preceded his public ministry, his public ministry his death, and his death his resurrection; true, but scarcely worth saying. And crucifixion and resurrection are a theological rather than a narrative or psychological climax. Does it matter that a leper is cleansed in the synagogue (1:40-45) before the epileptic boy is cured (9:14-27)? Would it matter if the stories were reversed?

There is external evidence to support the internal. Papias in a well known passage[12] complains that Mark's gospel, though written ἀκριβῶς, was nevertheless οὐ τάξει. The meaning of τάξις in this judgement has often been discussed; does it refer to narrative order, or to systematic presentation of the teaching and preaching of Jesus? There are two pointers to the answer to this question. The first is in the passage itself. Papias goes on to say that Mark did not write as one who was making a σύνταξις of the Lord's sayings.[13] It was systematic rather than chronological order in which Papias was interested. Secondly: he declares that Matthew did what Mark did not do. He συνετάξατο[14] τὰ λόγια, that is, he made a σύνταξις of them. Now Matthew's chronological order is nearly identical with Mark's. If he wrote so as to make a σύνταξις which Mark did not make, the order (τάξις) was systematic rather than historical; and incidentally it related to sayings rather than to events. We shall see as we continue that such interest as early Christian writers show in the material of the gospels relates more to teaching than to incident. And it is clear that Papias was not interested in chronological order; there is no reason to think him unique in this respect. Matthew, indeed, followed Mark's order; this was not because it seemed to him correct and important but because it was conveniently available and he had no interest in historical research which might have led him to change it. It was a labour-saving device; using Mark's order he did not need to think for himself. Luke, who was more interested in history, changes Mark more. John, who was very interested in theology, made the narrative order serve his theological interests.

2. The early church showed little interest in the order of events in the life of Jesus; it showed hardly more respect for the words in which his sayings and deeds were recorded. This familiar observation can be verified by a few minutes' study of a Synopsis and need not be demonstrated here. Matthew and Luke both used Mark as a major source of their work and undoubtedly each possessed a written copy of the gospel[15]; neither hesitated to modify and abbreviate where it suited him to do so. Sometimes a different view of an incident is given; often the Greek is improved; occasionally the changes are theological. Consider for example what Matthew (13:13-15) makes of the profound but difficult saying of Mark 4:11f.; it is enough here to recall that the difficult ἵνα disappears, lost in an easy but somewhat platitudinous ὅτι. Each of the evangelists gives the words of Jesus at the Last Supper not in accordance with a historical source but in agreement with the liturgical form used at the Supper in his own church.[16] John, whatever sources he used, was not out to simplify the theology that he found, but to enrich it, not to reproduce familiar liturgy, but to get behind liturgy.[17] It may be said that if John, who certainly had at his disposal other source material of great importance, did use Mark, he would probably use it with great freedom in regard both to its wording and to its order. The fact that verbal and chronological differences between John and Mark exist is no proof that John had not read, and did not make some use of, Mark.

3. An observation that needs careful statement, and perhaps (in view of the existence of the Synoptic Gospels) some qualification, is that, in the early years of the church there was considerably greater interest in the teaching of Jesus than in the events of his ministry. It may be that different groups of Christians entertained different interests. The tendency to neglect events can be seen (along with the gospels) in the New Testament itself. Paul refers only seldom to the teaching of Jesus, but to only one incident in his life—the supper taken in the night in which he was betrayed; and here it is clear that the interest focuses on the words of Jesus over the loaf and the cup, rather than on the fact that the group met for a meal, and that Paul's motivation in mentioning the incident was pastoral rather than historical. There is in 2 Peter 1:16-18 a reference to the Transfiguration,[18] and in Hebrews 5:7 a somewhat more obscure reference to the agony in Gethsemane. Acts (not surprisingly in view of the fact that its author wrote also a gospel) shows more interest in the events and sayings of the gospel narrative,[19] but with one exception these are given in very general terms: Jesus was set forth by God with mighty works, portents, and signs (2:22); he went about doing good and healing all who were overpowered by the devil (10:38).

The same verse refers in almost explicit terms to the baptism of Jesus by John.[20] Of course, in Acts as in the epistles the death and resurrection of Jesus are mentioned, but in general they are treated as theological factors rather than described as happenings. This is true even of Acts, though there the theology is on a relatively superficial level. Thus Herod and Pontius Pilate are mentioned (4:27) not for their own sake but because they fulfil Ps 2:2.

The Apostolic Fathers move within a similar field of interest. There are for example two places[21] where Clement bids his readers remember the words of the Lord Jesus (1 Clement 13:1; 46:7) and proceeds to quote what he has in mind. He does not bid them remember the actions of the Lord Jesus; he may be said at most to presuppose the call and commissioning of the apostles.[22] 2 Clement similarly quotes sayings of Jesus, some similar to sayings contained in the canonical gospels, some different; but there are no incidents. The same is true of Barnabas and of Polycarp. Hermas quotes nothing much; the Didache alludes only to teaching. The odd man out—relatively speaking—is Ignatius, who does refer to incidents that are familiar to us, but even he does so in scanty fashion. At Eph 17:1 he says that μύρον ἔλαβεν ἐπὶ τῆς κεφαλῆς αὐτοῦ ὁ κύριος, and we know to what he is referring,[23] but he can hardly be said to tell the story (though it is fair to say that he assumes that his readers could), and his interest in the anointing is that it happened ἵνα πνέῃ τῇ ἐκκλησίᾳ ἀφθαρσίαν. Eph 19:1,2 refers to the birth of Jesus from a virgin, and claims that at his birth a star shone in heaven, brighter than the rest; its light was unspeakable and the novelty of it caused astonishment. The sun and moon and other stars formed a ring round the new star. This however can hardly be called narration, myth rather; it is not in itself teaching, but Ignatius's interest is in the cosmic interpretation of the myth.

The apocryphal gospels manifest an uninhibited interest in miraculous narrative, but some of the earliest show a marked concentration on teaching. This is very notably true of the Gospel of Thomas, and the same interest is present in the groups of sayings which occur mostly in fragmentary form in the Oxyrhynchus Papyri.[24] Again however qualification is called for in view of the fact that the so-called Unknown Gospel[25] contains along with some teaching a paragraph which begins with an attempt to stone Jesus and continues with the cleansing of a leper.[26] We possess however so little of this gospel that any attempt to estimate the relative proportions of narrative and teaching would be foolish. The same is true of the fragments preserved from the Gospel according to the Hebrews and the Gospel of the Ebionites. It is however perhaps a useful pointer that the word Agrapha[27] has come to suggest unwritten sayings rather than unwritten stories.

The point of these observations is that if John shared the tendency to concentrate on teaching to the neglect of incident (and he did) it is not surprising that he used so little of Mark. His omissions require no special explanation, for most of Mark is narrative. It is true that John contains some notable non-Synoptic stories—the wedding feast (2:1-11), the lame man at the pool (5:1-9),[28] the man blind from birth (9:1-41), Lazarus (11:1-46)—but John needs these for his special teaching material.

4. Another tendency that must not be exaggerated but carefully evaluated was to disparage written records in favor of oral tradition; this was combined with the tendency to use written material with some freedom. The distinction between oral material, carefully written up, and written material, freely edited, is by no means easy to see or to describe with confidence.

The explicit evidence for the tendency to value oral above written sources is provided by the well-known saying of Papias, who declared[29] that he made a practice of inquiring into the oral teaching of the men of old (πρεσβύτεροι), οὐ γὰρ τὰ ἐκ τῶν βιβλίων το– σοῦτόν με ὠφελεῖν ὑπελάμβανον, ὅσον τὰ παρὰ ζώσης φωνῆς καὶ μενούσης. We may recall as parallel Irenaeus's account[30] of his acquaintance with Polycarp. Polycarp had recounted his intercourse with John and with others who had seen the Lord, remembering their words "and what he had heard from them concerning the Lord, and concerning his miracles and his teaching." What Polycarp had passed on, Irenaeus in his turn clearly remembered—or so he claimed. That is, Polycarp in his day had valued the oral tradition (he is never quoted as stating that John had written a gospel); and Irenaeus, in the last third of the second century, valued it still. Alongside this must be put the claim of the gnostics to possess a secret apostolic tradition, different from, or at least supplementing, the public tradition handed down in the church, and regarded by them as of special value. Of this gnostic tradition Irenaeus was well aware, and there can be no doubt that it encouraged his support of the written gospels in which the true apostolic tradition was, he believed, crystallized.

It may be that the passages in 1 Clement referred to above (p. 125) provide an illustration. Whence did Clement draw his references to the teaching of Jesus? To take one example: 1 Clement 13:2 runs

> Ἐλεᾶτε ἵνα ἐλεηθῆτε
> ἄφετε ἵνα ἀφεθῇ ὑμῖν
> ὡς ποιεῖτε, οὕτω ποιηθήσεται ὑμῖν
> ὡς δίδοτε, οὕτως δοθήσεται ὑμῖν
> ὡς κρίνετε, οὕτως κριθήσεσθε
> ὡς χρηστεύεσθε, οὕτως χρηστευθήσεται ὑμῖν
> ᾧ μέτρῳ μετρεῖτε, ἐν αὐτῷ μετρηθήσεται ὑμῖν.

There is not a sentiment in this quotation that cannot be found, more or less explicitly, in the canonical gospels, but the parallels have to be sought in three chapters of Matthew and one of Luke. Clement does not quote the traditionally Roman gospel, Mark; the material that he wants is not to be found there. If he was not making his own excerpts from Matthew or Luke, and it is at least doubtful whether they were known at Rome at this time, he was presumably drawing on oral tradition—not necessarily however preferring it. There may have been no alternative. It may not have been firmly fixed; probably then as now every Christian knew that the Lord had said something about being treated as you had treated others; showing mercy, therefore, in order that mercy might be shown to you; and so on. Probably, within a general pattern of uniformity, people phrased the sayings as they remembered them and as the occasion required.

To return to Papias. I quoted the Greek version of his words as it stands in Eusebius. There is a Latin version given by Jerome,[31] which has an interesting addition. It runs: "Non enim mihi tantum libri ad legendum prosunt, quantum viva vox, usque hodie in suis auctoribus personans." The addition gives a somewhat different sense to the statement. Presumably it is intended to interpret μενούσης, but *in suis auctoribus* suggests that we are dealing not with a continuous tradition handed down from one to another in ecclesiastical circles but with what the *auctores* are themselves still saying—*usque hodie*. This however seems too much, even if it is how Jerome understood Papias. Even if Papias was writing as early as A.D. 120-130 we may be sure that Peter and John were no longer alive; Aristion and the Elder John (to whom Papias refers) may have been.

How does this bear upon the question we are discussing? At first sight it seems to weaken the case for John's use of Mark and strengthen the belief that he used quasi-Marcan oral tradition. In fact it may not do much for either side of the argument. If John preferred oral tradition to books, he preferred oral tradition to Mark. But it may not have been quite so straightforward. He certainly did prefer non-Marcan material to Marcan material, and used far more of it. This may have been (though I doubt it) because Mark was written and the other material was oral. If he used Mark at all he undoubtedly handled it very freely. Papias tells us that Mark was the reservoir of Petrine tradition; if this was already common opinion, and if there was no corresponding oral source of supply, John would no doubt be glad to use the written material that was available. We must remember too that Papias and Clement were not writing gospels. It is one thing to use memory and oral tradition for the purpose of an occasional quotation; writing a continuous narrative is a different exercise, and most would find it helpful to have a written document that could be consulted, copied, and considered.

5. It is natural to consider next the tendency to favor writings or traditions that could be traced back to an apostle. The connection between Mark and Peter began at least as early as Papias[32] and it gave

Mark a kind of apostolicity; but it was a second-hand apostolicity and it would not be surprising that in consequence Marcan material should be swamped by what was believed to have originated in the testimony of John. To take this further would involve a comparison of the figures of Peter and the Beloved Disciple, and this cannot be undertaken now. In such a comparison John 21 would be important.

6. It is not possible to trace in detail a development of doctrine in the apostolic and post-apostolic ages. The evidence is not sufficient, and such evidence as there is suggests a confusing mixture of progress and retrogression. There are however some features in regard to which it is possible to observe trends, and it may be said that, especially in regard to eschatology and Christology, there was a general trend that could be described as a movement away from Mark and towards John. This was due in great measure to the lapse of time, which made it increasingly difficult and eventually impossible to believe that the End would come within the first Christian generation, and to the growing pressure of gnosticism, which furnished both a general atmosphere and categories suitable for the development of "realized eschatology" and of Christology. These are not matters which it is necessary here to illustrate in detail. The Fourth Gospel (still more 1 John) is not without futurist eschatology; certainly in the form in which we read it today, the form, that is, that was given it by its final editor (if there were more editors than one), it refers to the last day (6:39, 40, 44, 54). But it never hints (contrast Mark 9:1; 13:30) that the last day is coming in the near future, and the last chapter (certainly part of the book as published) explains that some ways of understanding Jesus' predictions regarding the future were mistaken. Again, John's Christology has linguistic roots in the Old Testament and in the earlier Christian tradition[33]; but the picture of Jesus as the heavenly Envoy who reveals the Father, communicating knowledge of the divine name, owes not a little to the gnostic environment with which the church had to come to terms. A theologian writing a gospel towards the end of the century would, if he used Mark at all, have to use it in something like the way John appears to have done.

7. At this stage I shall make one further general observation, which may lead us further. There is in the New Testament what may be called an element of deuterosis. We have long been familiar with the term deuteropauline. Exactly where the line is to be drawn between Pauline and deuteropauline is not settled: on which side does Colossians stand? But there were writers who admired Paul and had learned from him (even if they had misunderstood some of their lessons); who wished to make his voice heard in the generation after his death, and to do so attached his name to their writings. In their work his voice can be heard, but it is modulated in a new way. The old sharpness of the discussion of law, sin, grace, righteousness is gone. One would be inclined to call the Fourth Gospel deuteropauline, except that it does not use

Paul's name and is so rich in fresh and independent thought. It is almost certainly true that there is deuterojohannine literature. In comparison with the gospel the epistles are of lower power; less profound, more traditional. They were written, I believe, by one or more writers who venerated John and did their best to apply his universal Gospel (and gospel!) in particular situations. It may be that we should speak of a deuteropetrine literature without being able to point to anything that can properly be called protopetrine. The existence of 1 and 2 Peter, with confirmation not to be wholly discounted from Acts, and not to be discounted at all from 1 Corinthians, Galatians, and perhaps 2 Corinthians, bears witness to the fact that Peter was a name to be reckoned with in the early church, though he may never have written a word—nothing in the story suggests that he was a literary man. His name however was such as to add weight and authority to a document that bore it, and there is no reason to doubt that the authors of 1 and 2 Peter were seeking to perpetuate his beliefs (as they understood them) and authority as conscientiously as the authors of 1 and 2 Timothy were attempting the same task for Paul. Was Mark early thought of in these terms?

These remarks have in the present context one purpose: to make the point that there was in the age in which John was written a strong sense of the value of the tradition that came down from an earlier age. A desire to perpetuate, and at the same time to modify and apply, the Marcan traditions would be entirely in place.

It is not easy to make more precise observations within early Christian literature that bear specifically on the question of the relation between Mark and John. It is to be feared that much of what can be said on the basis of the early Christian literary corpus is either too obvious or too far-fetched to be worth saying. Some attempt however may be made to collect evidence which has at least the merit of not being dependent on particular comparisons of specific passages (though it may be said once more that this kind of comparison, inconclusive as it must always be, provides the fundamental data of our discussion).

It is of prime importance that Mark is a document that spread rapidly and widely. It was known to the authors of the First and Third Gospels. It is a fair guess (not to be discussed here) that Mark was written not far from A.D. 70 and that Matthew and Luke were written in the 80s or perhaps the 90s. Matthew was written probably in Syria; perhaps in Antioch; almost certainly at the eastern end of the Mediterranean. Luke has been located in Caesarea, Achaea, Decapolis, Asia Minor, Rome.[34] If the traditional place of origin of Mark is correct the book must have passed with great rapidity from West to East; even if Mark itself is placed further east its rapidity of diffusion is remarkable. And though Papias's opinions about the authorship and Petrine background of Mark may be worth little—they may be based on inferences from the gospel, on 1 Peter 5:13, or on some more direct tradition—there is no doubt that he knew the gospel as a book, well enough known and wide-

ly enough used for it to be worth his while to offer information about it
and an assessment of it. After this good beginning, Mark seems, so far
as we know, to have dropped out of use; this was probably because the
two "bigger and better" gospels, Matthew and Luke, supplanted it, and
would apply only to areas in which they were current (and therefore
probably not to the area in which John originated). The disappearance
of Mark (of which there is scarcely a trace in the Apostolic Fathers[35])
was in any case only temporary. Papias is joined by the early Gospel
Prologues described by De Bruyne and Harnack as Anti-Marcionite,
but dismissed, not quite convincingly, by J. Regul[36] as neither early nor
anti-marcionite. The Marcan Prologue shares with Hippolytus[37] the curious designation of Mark as *colobodactylus*, which is best explained as
originating (though the Prologue will not have it so) in attacks on
Mark's integrity as an apostolic man. Justin, who refers several times[38]
to the ἀπομνημονεύματα of the apostles, speaks specifically (*Trypho*
106) of the ἀπομνημονεύματα of Peter. These, he says, name the two
sons of Zebedee as Boanerges, explained as Sons of Thunder. This
must almost certainly be based on Mark; no other canonical gospel, or
other gospel known to us, contains the name. These facts make it very
probable that Mark was in circulation in most places in Asia Minor except those in which another gospel was already established. Is there not
a balance of probability that John, himself intending to write a gospel,
would familiarize himself with the work of a predecessor?

Consider another line of thought. I have spoken (above, pp.
128f.) of what may be called a Johannine school. If I may once more
set out conclusions without providing proof, it seems that the Fourth
Gospel was the centre of the group's literary production; the Apocalypse (possibly in a form earlier than that which we have) came first,
the epistles later than the gospel.[39] These four works were not written
by the evangelist but they were written in the same environment, and
the question of the evangelist's use or disuse of Mark may therefore be
expanded into a consideration of the use or disuse of Mark in the whole
Johannine corpus. At this point I draw attention to an interesting section of E. Schüssler Fiorenza's book on Revelation.[40] On pp. 101-108
she discusses "The School Traditions and the School Tradition of Revelation." It is fair to say that the evidence for knowledge of Mark as a
book is no more conclusive than it is in the gospel, but that there is contact between Revelation and the apocalyptic element in Mark is certain.
Some 13 or 14 verses of Mark 13[41] have parallels, more or less close,
in Revelation, and it seems reasonable to conclude that something like
the so-called Little Apocalypse was known to John the Apocalyptist;
not necessarily of course in its Marcan form, for this apocalypse probably circulated independently. The sayings about confessing and denying Jesus (Rev 2:13; 3:8; cf. 3:5) have parallels of a sort in Mark 8:35,
38, but these sayings also circulated independently and were part of
general Christian paraenesis.[42] It is however a fact that a form of the

saying, and the paraenesis, are found in Mark. The sayings about confessing (ὁμολογεῖν) Christ appear in Johannine style in the first epistle also (2:22; 4:3, 15), and there are a few other parallels.[43] If the relative dating (Revelation, Gospel, Epistles) of the Johannine works is correct there is thus a thread of Marcan material running through all five works and centered on the gospel, and though this could be due to quasi-Marcan oral tradition it tends to support the permanence of the written (*pace* Papias) word. That there is a much greater number of parallels in the gospel is due to the evangelist's greater percipience, and of course to the fact that John is a gospel and Mark is a gospel.[44]

Three further sources of information may be briefly mentioned as contributing, with some uncertainty, to our knowledge of the early history of Mark and thus to our consideration of the likelihood or otherwise of its being known, and in his own way used, by the author of the Fourth Gospel.

Marcion is well known *Lucam. . . elegisse, quem caederet.*[45] Why Luke? Why not Matthew, Mark, or John? Reasons why Marcion should have rejected Matthew are not hard to find, but one would have thought that Mark and John would have needed no more, and possibly less, cutting and emendation than the canonical Luke. The question was discussed by Harnack,[46] who concluded that the reason for Marcion's preference for Luke was not internal to the gospel but external; one might say fortuitous. "Das erste Evangelium, welches in den Pontus gekommen ist, war wahrscheinlich das Lukas-Evangelium; mit ihm war Marcion am frühesten vertraut gewesen sein, wenn es nicht gar Jahre hindurch in seiner pontischen Heimat sein einziges Evangelium gewesen ist." This however was not the kind of reason for preferring Luke that Marcion could publish; accordingly (presumably in his *Antitheses*) Marcion "connititur ad destruendum statum eorum evangeliorum, quae propria et sub apostolorum nomine[47] eduntur, vel etiam apostolicorum,[48] ut scilicet fidem, quam illis adimit, suo conferat."[49] Thus Mark was already, before Marcion wrote, circulating and known as a written work. Known as a written work and used by Matthew and Luke, A.D. 80-90; known as a written work and contrasted with oral tradition by Papias, 120-130; known as a written work by Marcion, 140; is it not probable that Mark was readily available to John, and taken seriously by him?

The second source of information may be dealt with briefly. More clearly than Marcion, but somewhat later, Tatian knew Mark as a written work, to be used in a gospel harmony along with Matthew, Luke, and John.[50] I think it probable that the harmony was originally drawn up in Syriac and used in the Syriac-speaking church, but, like Marcion, Tatian had originally acquired his knowledge of the gospels much further west.

Third and last is the Gospel of Thomas. Of the 114 sections

into which this gospel is commonly divided, 37[51] have been held to show some possible contact with Mark. Some of these possible contacts seem in fact to be most improbable, and in nearly every case the question is complicated by the existence of Synoptic parallels in Matthew or Luke or both. The question of the relation between Thomas and the Synoptic gospels is a very difficult one—by no means unlike that with which we are at present concerned. I shall draw attention to two observations that seem to me important. The first was made by C.M. Tuckett.[52] In Thomas 20 (the parable of the mustard seed) and Thomas 9 (the parable of the sower) Thomas seems to show acquaintance with redactional elements in the Marcan versions; this strongly suggests that he is dependent not only on general tradition but specifically on Mark. The date of the Gospel of Thomas is a matter of debate, but it may well go back to the first half of the second century, and thus provide further evidence for the early distribution of Mark. The second observation goes back to B. Gärtner's *The Theology of the Gospel of Thomas* (1961). Many of the sayings in Thomas recall those "compound texts" (Gärtner's term) which are to be found in various early authors, and not least in gnostic works. The early fathers "considered themselves far less tightly bound to the precise formulation, than to the content of the text. When we consider the Gnostics, we notice that there may also have been, at the back of their quotations, some attempt at a harmonization of the text of the New Testament. This may well be an expression of the same striving which gave rise to Marcion's single gospel and the Diatessaron of Tatian" (p. 42). "We must naturally not ignore the possibility that certain logia may be expressions of a gospel tradition outside that of the New Testament. But with the background of these 'compound texts' in the early Church, we must be very cautious in passing judgment, particularly in those cases in which we have no proof available from manuscript traditions" (p. 43).

Here is a process which distinctly recalls the way in which Mark appears in John; with it we may end this not very productive examination of the background of the phenomenon, and return to a search for traces of Marcan redaction and perhaps of "compound texts" in the Fourth Gospel.

NOTES

1. *Saint John and the Synoptic Gospels*, Cambridge, 1938.
2. For example, J. H. Bernard, *The Gospel according to St John* (ICC), Edinburgh, 1928, pp. xciv-cxxi.
3. So H. F.D. Sparks in *JTS* 3 (1952) 58-61.
4. *The Interpretation of the Fourth Gospel*, Cambridge, 1953, p. 449; *Historical Tradition in the Fourth Gospel*, Cambridge, 1963, p. 8.
5. John seems to correct Mark with regard to the relative dates of the

work of Jesus and of John the Baptist (Jn 3:24) and with regard to the dates of the Last Supper and the Crucifixion (Jn 13:1; 18:28; 19:14).

6. As is well known the development has continued into Modern Greek, in which the infinitive is no longer used (A. Thumb, *Handbook of the Modern Greek Vernacular. Grammar, Texts, Glossary*, Edinburgh, 1912, p. 116).

7. See J. H. Moulton, *A Grammar of New Testament Greek*, Vol. I *Prolegomena*, Edinburgh, [3]1908, pp 79, 245.

8. See Life 40; and E. Schürer, *The History of the Jewish People in the Age of Jesus Christ*, rev. and ed. by G. Vermes and F. Millar, Vol I, Edinburgh, 1973, pp. 34-37.

9. For Gardner-Smith's rather lame explanation of the agreement between Mark and John in connecting the feeding miracle with the crossing of the lake see his book, p. 33.

10. Especially of course outstanding passages, such as those dealing with the Baptist, the feeding miracle and the adjacent water miracle, Peter's confession, the anointing, the entry, and the relevant events in the Passion Narrative.

11. For the present purpose attention must not be confined to books contained in the New Testament.

12. Quoted in Eusebius, *H.E.*, 3.39.15.

13. It makes little difference whether λόγων or λογίων be read; see McGiffert *ad loc*.

14. The variant συνεγράψατο makes rather more difference, but not much. For συγγράφειν see L.S. s.v. III; the middle is much used for drawing up legal contracts and thus implies orderly arrangement.

15. There are of course other views of the Synoptic problem; I state the commonest, which I believe to be correct.

16. Luke seems to combine Mark with his own liturgical form.

17. For the flesh and blood sayings in John see my commentary, pp. 297-300; also my *Essays on John*, London, 1982, pp. 42-49, 84-92.

18. 1 Peter 5:1 does not refer to the Transfiguration (*pace* Selwyn).

19. For the sayings see my contribution *Sayings of Jesus in the Acts of The Apostles*, in *A cause de l'Évangile. Mélanges offerts à J. Dupont*, Paris, 1985, pp. 681-708.

20. Ἔχρισεν αὐτὸν ὁ θεὸς πεύματι ἁγίῳ καὶ δυνάμει.

21. For some detail see below, p. 126.

22. See 1 Clement 42.

23. In saying that the head of Jesus was anointed Ignatius agrees with Matthew and Mark rather than with Luke and John.

24. POxy 1, 654, 655 contain sayings parallel to the Gospel of Thomas; see also POxy 840 and 1224. Some other papyri also contain sayings.

25. PEgerton 2; *Fragments of an Unknown Gospel*, London, 1935 eds. H. I. Bell and T. C. Skeat.

26. Lines 5-10. The paragraph seems to combine John and Mark, thus suggesting that the two gospels were current in the same environment.

27. See the classical work by A. Resch, in *TU* 54, 1889; [2]*TU* 15: 3-4, 1906.

28. But there are hints of Mark (2:1-12) in this Johannine story.

29. Eusebius, *H.E.* 3.39.4.

30. In his letter to Florinus, quoted in Eusebius, *H.E.* 5.22.49.

31. *De Viris Illustribus* 18.

32. Or rather, as early as 1 Pet 5:13.

33. He seems, for example, to give a theological interpretation of Mark's "Messianic Secret."

34. W. G. Kümmel, *Einleitung in das Neue Testament*, Heidelberg, 1978, p. 120.

35. *The New Testatment in the Apostolic Fathers*, Oxford, 1905, finds a doubtful trace in Hermas and some very doubtful traces in Ignatius.

36. Accepted by W. G. Kümmel, *Einleitung* (n. 34), p. 206, but some anti-Marcionite interest seems clear.

37. *Refutatio*, 7. 30.1.

38. *Trypho*, 100, 101, 102, 104, 106.

39. R. E. Brown (*The Community of the Beloved Disciple*, London, 1979) agrees that the epistles follow the gospel but finds that "the relationship of Revelation to the main Johannine corpus remains puzzling" (p. 6). For Judith Lieu's more complicated view of the relation between gospel and epistles see her *The Second and Third Epistles of John*, Edinburgh, 1986. M. Hengel (*The Johannine Question*, London, 1989) thinks that at least the final redaction of the gospel is to be put later than the letters (p. 52). See also *Essays on John* (n. 17), pp. 116-131.

40. *The Book of Revelation, Justice and Judgment*, Philadelphia, 1985.

41. Verses 5, 6, 10, 14, 19, 22, 24, 25, 26, 33, 34, 35, 37.

42. See my "I am not ashamed of the Gospel" in *Foi et Salut selon S. Paul* (AnBib, 42), Rome, 1970, pp. 19-41.

43. 1 Jn 2:18 and 4:1 (Mk 13:5, 6:22); 3:22 and 5:14 (Mk 11:23f.); 4:21 (Mk 12:29-31); 5:6 (Mk 1:10); 5:16 (Mk 3:28).

44. The following incidents in John have parallels in Mark; in that gospel they occur in the order given in brackets; The Baptist and baptism (1); Naming of Cephas (3); Cleansing of Temple (11); Jesus' πατρίς (5); Lame man - paralytic (a weak parallel) (2); Feeding of multitude (6); Crossing Lake (7); Peter's confession (8); Blind man (a weak parallel) (9); Anointing (12); Entry (10); Agony (15); Isaiah 6 (4); Last Supper (13); Betrayal and denial foretold (14); Arrest (16); Jesus with Jews (17); Peter denies (18); Jesus with Pilate (19); Barabbas (20); Mockery (22); Pilate's decision (21); Titulus (24); Division of clothes (23); Drink (25); Death (26); Woman (women) at the tomb (28).

45. Tertullian, *Adv. Marcionem*, 4.2. f.

46. A. von Harnack, *Marcion: Das Evangelium vom Fremden Gott*, Leipzig, 1921, p. 39 (²p, 42); cf. J. Knox, *Marcion and the New Testament*, Chicago, 1942, p. 155.

47. Matthew and John.

48. Mark.

49. Tertullian, *Adv. Marcionem* 4.3.

50. And perhaps the Gospel according to the Hebrews? Diapente? So Victor of Capua; see B. M. Metzger, *The Early Versions of the New Testament*, Oxford, 1977, p. 28.

51. 4, 5, 6, 8, 9, 11, 12, 13, 14, 20, 21, 24, 25, 31, 33, 35, 38, 41, 44, 47, 48, 55, 63, 65, 66, 67, 75, 79, 82, 88, 96, 99, 100, 101, 104, 106.

52. *NovT* 30 (1988) 148-157. In JTS 35 (1984), 140, the same author argues that the Gospel of Truth seems to have used only Matthew.

9

GNOSIS AND THE APOCALYPSE OF JOHN

An invitation to contribute to this *Festschrift*, and thus to have the pleasure and privilege of a share in the honoring of an old and good friend, was not to be refused. A request however to write on Gnosticism in relation to the Johannine literature was another matter, for several reasons. In the first place, who knows so much about Gnosticism and the Fourth Gospel as Robin Wilson? To write on such a subject in a volume dedicated to him could only make the writer look a fool. In the second place, fool or not, I have already written on the subject, and would have little that is really fresh to say; moreover, my own immediate interests have moved on from John to Acts. It occurred to me that I might go on to consider the Johannine Epistles instead of the Gospel. There would be not a little to be said for this, but the epistles do not offer an untouched field, and where for example Dodd[1] and Bultmann[2] have reaped it is unlikely that much will be left for the gleaner. It might however have been interesting to see how, and if, ideas and relationships that have been detected in the first epistle are reflected in the practical circumstances disclosed by the second and third. It seems that, at this period, theological issues connected with Gnosticism (Jesus Christ coming in the flesh; 2 John 7) evoked strong ecclesiastical measures (2 John 9-11; 3 John 9f.). I decided however to take the bull by the horns and deal with a subject which, so far as I know, has been less frequently discussed: Gnosis and the Book of Revelation. At first sight the relation between the two may seem to be nil, but the matter may prove worthy of consideration.

A moment's reflection is, in fact, sufficient to show that the topic is a reasonable one. It is a cheering thought that in *Gnosis and the New Testament* (Oxford, 1968) Dr Wilson's references to Revelation seem to be limited to a consideration of the question whether various Gnostic documents quote or allude to the book—an important question to which we shall return but one that is not sufficient to determine the relation between the thought of Revelation (and of Apocalyptic in general) and Gnosticism.

A second preliminary observation is that there seems to have existed a Johannine school, community, or circle,[3] of which John the

Divine, the author of Revelation, was a member, and that if some members of the circle were deeply implicated in the beginnings of the Gnostic movement it is unlikely that John the Divine should have had no contact with it at all.

Again, there is a relation of some kind (on which study of Revelation may throw light) between Apocalyptic and Gnosticism. In an early study of Gnosticism[4] F.C. Burkitt took the view that the developing Christian Gnosticism of the second century was intended in part to replace the no longer credible eschatological mythology of Apocalyptic. "... 'Chiliasm' had begun to fade into the background of the Christian consciousness. In the East the Apocalypse of John was already dropping out of favour, and documents such as the Apocalypse of Peter began to take its place, documents in which attention was concentrated on the state of good and bad souls immediately after death, rather than on a general resurrection at an anticipated return of Christ to earth with attendant rewards and punishments" (op. cit., 90f.). This view is open to criticism as perhaps an over-simplification of the facts. It has given place in some more recent studies to a more positive understanding of the relation between Apocalyptic and Gnosticism. This was powerfully put by R.M. Grant,[5] though he too begins from the view that disappointed Apocalypticism was one source of Gnosticism. What were Jewish believers to do when predictions not merely that Jews would become the rulers of the world but that their city and temple would remain inviolate were proved false? "Faith was shaken in God, his covenant, his law, and his promises. Out of such shaking, we should claim, came the impetus toward Gnostic ways of thinking, doubtless not for the first time with the fall of Jerusalem but reinforced by this catastrophe" (op. cit., 34). "When his predictions were not realized, the apocalypticist of the first century had several options. (1) He could postpone the time of fulfillment and rewrite his apocalypse; such revisions were actually made. (2) He could abandon his religion entirely. (3) He could look for escape rather than victory, and could then reinterpret his sacred writings in order to show that the revelation had been misunderstood. It would appear that most Gnostic teachers did reinterpret not only the Old Testament but also some of the apocalyptic writings or their ingredients" (op. cit., 35).

Later, Dr Grant brings out specific connections between Apocalyptic and Gnosticism."Origen suggests that a Gnostic doctrine known to Celsus came from the book of Enoch [Orig., *Cels.* v, 52, 54]; in *Pistis Sophia* we read that the *Books of Ieu* were written by Enoch in paradise [*Pist. Soph.* 99, 134]; and the later Manichees and Bogomils used both 1 Enoch and 2 Enoch [See also Söderberg, *La religion des Cathares*, 130, n. 1, 131]. The Ascension of Isaiah, part of which may have originated at Qumran [D. Flusser, "The Apocryphal Book of Ascensio Isaiae and the Dead Sea Sect," *Israel Exploration Journal* 3 (1953), 30-47], was used by the Archontics [Epiphanius, *Haer.* 40,

2:2]. More significant is the way in which the apocalypse form flourished in various Gnostic sects. Many of the books found at Nag-Hammadi are apocalypses—one of Adam to Seth, one of Dositheus, one of Sêém or the Great Seth. The Gnostic Justin wrote a book called Baruch, presumably because he knew something of the tradition in which revelations were ascribed to the Old Testament personage (though for Justin Baruch has become an angel). [Note that Irenaeus, *Haer*. II, 24:2 (Harvey 336) regards Baruch as the name of God] (op. cit., 41f.).[6] This clear and positive relation between Apocalyptic and Gnosticism has been recently supported by Christopher Rowland.[7] "Knowing one's origins and destiny is just as much a concern of apocalyptic as [of] gnosticism, though in the former this knowledge has not yet become in itself a means of salvation" (op. cit., 21). It may be that Revelation has something to contribute here (see below, pp. 145f.)[8]

Finally among preliminary observations we should note that Revelation is the first Christian book to refer by name to a Gnostic sect or group. At 2:6,15 it refers to the Nicolaitans, who were evidently active at Ephesus and at Pergamum. It seems probable that the teaching of Balaam (2:14) and Jezebel the false prophetess (2:20) were connected with the same erroneous doctrine and that this included *ta bathea tou satana* (2:24); see further below. It is of course clear that the author of Revelation looked on this sect and its teaching with severe disfavor. This is not to say that he was necessarily uninfluenced by it. His colleague, the author of the Fourth Gospel, was both Gnostic and anti-Gnostic,[9] and there is no reason why John the Divine should not have shared this double attitude. In any case the Gnostic movement existed in his environment, and action and reaction must have been inevitable.

It is at this point that we may begin to make a more particular study of Revelation and its relation to Gnosticism. Who were the Nicolaitans?[10] The short, and correct, answer is: we do not know. Patristic statements rest upon the references in Revelation, helped out by the conjecture[11] that the sect of Nicolaitans was founded by the Nicolas of Acts 6. Thus Irenaeus, *Haer*. I, 26:3: The Nicolaitans are the followers of that Nicolas who was one of the seven first ordained to the diaconate by the apostles. They lead lives of unrestrained indulgence. The character of these men is very plainly pointed out in the Apocalypse of John, as teaching that it is a matter of indifference to practise adultery, and to eat things sacrificed to idols. Wherefore the Word has also spoken of them thus: "But this thou hast that thou hatest the deeds of the Nicolaitans, which I also hate." *Haer*. III, 11:1 adds nothing of substance to this, nor do other patristic writers, except that Clement of Alexandria does his best to save the reputation of Nicolas (*Strom*. III, 4:25; Eusebius, *Hist. Eccl*. III, 29:1-4). Since the fathers seem to have had no information about the Nicolaitans that we do not ourselves have we turn to the passages in Revelation. The first, 2:6, tells us only that their works were, in the writer's opinion, odious. The second, 2:15, compares the teaching of the Nicolaitans with that of Balaam, who taught Balak to put a stumblingblock before the children of Israel; this consisted (taking the infinitive *phagein* to be epexegetical of *skandalon*) in leading them to eat food sacrificed to idols and to commit fornication. This suggests a further parallel in 2:20 in the woman Jezebel, who calls herself a prophetess and teaches my servants to commit fornication and to eat food sacrificed to idols. The combination of food sacrificed to idols and fornication recalls the so-called Apostolic Decree (Acts 15:20, 29; 21:25) and the Old Testament allusion in 1 Corinthians 10:6-10. The letter to Thyatira speaks also of those who claim to have knowledge of *ta bathea tou satana*, which was evidently a current phrase (*hōs legousin*, 2:24). This is important because it points in a Gnostic direction[12] and suggests that the action of the Nicolaitans, which John condemns, arose not out of mere licentiousness but out of false doctrine; indeed, out of a kind of Satanology. The phrase is commonly interpreted in one of two ways.[13] It is sometimes claimed that the author deliberately perverted what the persons in question said. They professed to know the deep things of God (cf. 1 Corinthians 2:10); John the Divine countered: Deep things of Satan I call them. This is not impossible; compare for example the Old Testament substitution of *bōšet* for *ba'al*,[14] and, perhaps a better comparison, Colossians 2:8, where the writer appears to mean something like "philosophy—empty deceit I call it." Nevertheless this interpretation does not seem to do justice to *hōs legousin*. The usual alternative is to suppose that the Jezebelites (no doubt Nicolaitans) of the idolatrous worship and practice that went on around them. Given that heathen sacrifice and temple prostitution were the work of demons it was proper that Christians—who of course could not be harmed by the demons because they were protected by gnosis or sacraments or both—should know by experience what the demons were doing. They might safely eat idolatrous food and practise fornication, discover the deep things of Satan and so beat him at his own game. This could have been represented as a logical step beyond Paulinism, though it involved a step that Paul refused to take. He went along with his Corinthians in accepting the argument that since both food and the organs that digest it are alike on the way to destruction Christians were bound by no food laws (1 Corinthians 6:12f.; 8:1, 4; 10:23, 25, 27), but he declined to draw a parallel conclusion regarding fornication, since sexual union is not (though it may appear so) the work of one organ but the action of the *sōma*, the whole human person, who is to be united to Christ. It could have been argued against Paul, how can we know the power of Christ to keep the body that has been united to him if it is never exposed to fornication? Or, how can sexual relations any more than eating affect the non-material spirit, which is all that matters?

These interpretations of *ta bathea tou satana*, especially the second, must be allowed to be possible, but I doubt whether either is satisfactory. Knowing the deep things of Satan is a boast, a claim of which certain people are proud; it seems to imply that Satan is one with whom it is well to be acquainted. In some of the later Gnostic systems the name Satan appears among the aeons and emanations.[15] There is however a good deal more to say than this.

The Nicolaitans are compared with Balaam (Revelation 2:14f.; the *houtōs* at the beginning of 2:15 connects Balaam's practice with the teaching of the Nicolaitans, thereby suggesting that teaching as the basis of immoral practice is what is common to the two). This calls to mind two other New Testament passages, which are undoubtedly related to each other: Jude 11 (They went in the way of Cain and for the sake of reward abandoned themselves to Balaam's error) and 2 Peter 2: 15 (They left the straight path and went astray, following the way of Balaam the son of Bosor, who loved the reward of unrighteousness). The persons in question here appear to practise moral licence (possibly appealing to Paul's example, 2 Peter 3:15f.). Their free attitude to angels and other authorities (Jude 8; 2 Peter 2:10, 11) may be connected with the claim to know the deep things of Satan. Their questioning of the Parousia (2 Peter 3:4) has been connected[16] with a statement attributed to Hippolytus, in which it is alleged that Nicolas was the first to assert that the resurrection had already happened; he understood by "resurrection" that "we believe in Christ and receive the washing," but denied a resurrection of the flesh.

The name Satan occurs five times in the Seven Letters (2:9, 13(*bis*), 24; 3:9); subsequently in Revelation three times (12:9; 20:2, 7). In the first two of these Satan is explicitly identified with *ho drakōn, ho ophis ho archaios*. This means that we may reasonably expect to find a connection between those who profess to know the depths of Satan and the sect known as the Ophites (or Naassenes, the alternative name being derived from *naḥaš*, serpent; cf. also the Cainites, noting Jude 11).[17] The snake is not only a widespread religious symbol; it recalls the myth of Genesis 3, where the snake is the being who encourages man to take (what is thought to be) lifegiving knowledge by eating the fruit of the forbidden tree. The snake thus becomes man's champion against the jealous God of the Old Testament who wishes to deny man knowledge; the patron saint, as it were, of Gnostics.[18]

There is no space in this paper, nor would it be relevant, to pursue the little that is known of the later history of Ophites, Nicolaitans, Cainites and Carpocratians. It is enough to observe that there seems good reason to believe that early Gnostic groups existed in Asia Minor when Revelation was written. Their doctrine was antinomian; John the Divine was aware of it, and fought against it.

This leads to the questions that this paper must answer if its existence in this *Festschrift* is to be justified. Is Revelation simply a work opposed to the Gnostic movement? Does it have any positive relevance to the study of that movement?

There are several ways in which this question may be approached. We may ask, for example, what the Christian Gnostic heretics of the second century and later made of Revelation as a book. The answer to this question appears to be, Not very much. Dr Wilson, in *Gnosis and the New Testament* (above, p. 135), draws attention to the following passages.[19]

The Apocalypse of Adam 78:18-26:

> The third kingdom says of him that he came from a virgin womb. He was cast out of his city, he and his mother; he was brought to a desert place. He was nourished there. He came and received glory and power. And thus he came to the water.

On this passage Dr Wilson (op. cit., 67f., 138) notes Böhlig's suggestion that there may be a reference to Revelation 12:5, or to its mythological background. His conclusion is cautious: "In short, while we may perhaps suspect an allusion to Revelation 12:5 in the Apocalypse of Adam, we cannot be certain; we have to make allowance for the possibility of other influences" (op. cit., 68). No doubt it is wise to be cautious. When however the context is considered the repeated references to the child's mother as a virgin suggest, though they do not prove, that the author was a Christian,[20] and 78:9-14 (And a bird came, took the child who was born and brought him onto a high mountain. And he was nourished by the bird of heaven. An angel came forth there) adds to the possible parallels with Revelation 12 (v. 5, *hērpasthē*; 14, *hai duo pteruges tou aetou tou megalou*; 7, *ho Michaēl*)

The Apocryphon of John 2:16-20:

> Now [I have come to teach] you what is [and what was] and what will come to [pass], that [you may know the] things which are not revealed [and the things which are revealed, and to teach] you the [... about the] perfect [Man].

Cf. Revelation 1:19.

4:21, 22:

> This is the spring of the water of life which gives to [all] the aeons and in every form.

Cf. Revelation 22:1.

As far as these parallels are concerned (those alleged with other parts of the New Testament are not under consideration here) it is impossible not to share much of Dr Wilson's scepticism. "Even such allusions [to the New Testament] as have been detected must be considered doubtful" (op. cit., 105).

The Sophia of Jesus Christ 111: 16-20:

> And [the] gods of the gods by their wisdom
> revealed gods. By their wisdom they revealed
> lords. And the lords of the lords revealed lords
> by their thinking.

Dr Wilson (op. cit.,115), writing before the complete publication of the texts, refers to the titles "God of gods" and "King of kings", and notes that these "may reflect knowledge of Revelation 17:14; 19:16." One must now be even more cautious in drawing any conclusion about a literary relation here.

This is not a complete list of references to Revelation, and of course Dr Wilson does not suggest that it is. Nor will any such claim be made in the present brief discussion. A few passages, however, are interesting enough to add, especially a group from the Gospel of Truth. Of these the first is the most important.

The Gospel of Truth 19:34-20:14:

> There was revealed in their heart the living book of
> the living the one written in the thought and the mind
> [of the] Father, and which from before the foundation
> of the all was within the incomprehensible (parts) of
> him—that (book) which no one was able to take
> since it is reserved for the one who will take it and
> will be slain. No one could have appeared among
> those who believed in salvation unless that book had
> intervened. For this reason the merciful one, the faith-
> ful one, Jesus, was patient in accepting sufferings un-
> til he took that book, since he knows that his death is
> life for many.

This passage recalls especially Revelation 5, in which the author laments that no one is found worthy to open the sealed book. He is cheered by the elder who tells him that the Lion of the tribe of Judah, the Root of David, has conquered so as to open the book and its seven seals. He looks, and sees not a lion but a lamb standing as though slain. The Lamb's victory leads to the ascriptions of praise that fill the rest of the chapter. Other chapters in Revelation refer to the book, described as the book of life, sometimes as the Lamb's book of life (3:5; 13:8; 17:8; 20:12, 15; 21:27). Sometimes the Lamb is said to have been slain from the foundation of the world (13:8; cf. 17:8). At Revelation 19:11 the rider on the white horse is said to be faithful and true. Cf. also Gos.

Truth 21:23: He enrolled them in advance.

26:2-4:

It is a drawn sword, with two edges, cutting on either side.

Cf. Revelation 2:12; also 2:16; 19:15.

32:27-30:
... from the day from above, which has no night, and
from the light which does not sink because it is perfect.

This recalls, somewhat distantly, Revelation 22:5.

39:15-20:
But the one who exists exists also with his name, and
he knows himself [or; he is the only one who knows
it] And to give himself a name is (the prerogative of)
the Father. The Son is his name.

The Name is treated from 38:6 to 41:3. Cf. especially Revelation 19:12
(a name which no one knows but he himself).

42:18-22
... nor have they envy nor groaning nor death within
them, but they rest in him who is at rest.

This recalls Revelation 21:4; cf. 7:17; 20:14.
        It seems very probable that the author of the Gospel of Truth
had read Revelation and occasionally recalled its language. We eannot
say so much of any other Gnostic author though from time to time there
are hints of possible acquaintance.[21] It would be rash to claim too
much, but it is probably safe to say that Gnostic writers did not regard
Revelation as an anti-Gnostic work.[22] Their attitude to Apocalyptic as a
form of literature and theology is perhaps best indicated by the fact that
in the Nag Hammadi Library five works are described as apocalypses
(of Paul, first of James, second of James, of Adam, of Peter; possibly
we should add Zostrianos). The fact is important, though Yvonne Jans-
sens may exaggerate when she writes,[23] "What is very clear is that the
Gnostics had a fondness for the literary *genre* of Apocalyptic (at least a
fifth of the Nag Hammadi library is 'apocalypses'!), doubtless to aid
the presentation of their teaching. The form of these apocalypses is in
general, I think, near enough to Judaeo-Christian Apocalyptic. Yet
there is a difference in the secret which is often entrusted to the seer
and which cannot be revealed except to chosen Gnostics or fellow 'spiritual' persons."[24] This minimizes the difference between the Gnostic

and other apocalypses, which is considerable. It remains, however, true that the Gnostics did not avoid apocalyptic on principle; a corresponding truth is that the great anti-Gnostic writers, notably Irenaeus and Hippolytus, use Apocalyptic (quoting Revelation freely) not to rebut the arguments of the Gnostics but to describe the unpleasant destiny in store for them.[25]

A second approach to the question before us is by way of analogy. Revelation is a Christian work with deep roots in Judaism. Does non-Christian Judaism provide us with information about the relation between Apocalyptic and Gnosticism?

It need not be said that Apocalyptic, though taken up and to a great extent preserved in Christian circles, is a Jewish phenomenon, with origins in the Old Testament. It has too often been treated as a singular line of development unrelated to other movements in Judaism and calling for separate treatment. That this is an error was long ago decisively demonstrated by W.D. Davies in relation to rabbinic Judaism. In his still important article of over thirty years ago[25] Dr Davies made three points. (1) "In its piety and in its attitude to the Torah Apocalyptic was at one with Pharisaism" (op. cit., 22). (2) "There is a community of eschatological doctrine between the Pharisees and the Apocalyptists" (op. cit., 23). Dr Davies mentions Akiba's championing of the cause of Bar Kokba, and comments, "Nothing could more point to the reality of eschatological beliefs among the Rabbis and to the falsity of the customary distinction between fanatic Apocalypticism and sober orthodoxy" (ibidem). (3) "The view is to be suspected that Apocalyptic stands for a popular interest, while Pharisaism is 'scholastic.' By its very nature Apocalyptic is a gnosis meant for the initiated: it dealt with visions given to the elect: it had an esoteric character however much its ideas might be diffused by preachers like the 'ober gᵉlila'ah" (op. cit., 24).[27] It is no doubt true that in this passage Dr Davies is not using the word "gnosis" in the narrow sense, that is, with reference to what is commonly understood by the Gnostic movement; it remains significant, and may in fact lead beyond the point that Dr Davies himself was concerned to make. For the main content of Pharisaism, of academic Judaism, is not a private gnosis but a legal system practised in the courts and taught openly by public instruction. It presupposes the existence of an intellectual élite, but the only limitations imposed upon its dissemination were the inward limitations of mental capacity. Pharisaism, Rabbinism, did however have a mystical element, frowned upon,[28] but in fact contributing significantly to the development of Judaism. "Nun ist bekannt, dass die leitenden Kreise der alten Synagoge allezeit mit einem gewissen Argwohn über der Reinerhaltung des monotheistischen Gottesgedankens gewacht haben. Aber trotz aller Vorsicht drangen gnostische Irrlehren selbst in die Kreise der Schriftgelehrten ein."[29] For the connection between such speculations, mystical experiences, and apocalyptic, it is perhaps sufficient to quote the fundamental Mishnah text.[30]

> Chagigah 2:1:
> The forbidden degrees may not be expounded before
> three persons, nor the Story of Creation before two,
> nor [the chapter of] the Chariot before one alone, un-
> less he is a Sage that understands of his own knowl-
> edge. Whosoever gives his mind to four things it
> were better for him if he had not come into the
> world—what is above? what is beneath? what was
> beforetime? and what will be hereafter?

There is no space here for a full discussion of the matter, but there is
much to support the conclusion recently drawn by Dr Rowland: "While
fully accepting the problems presented by the rabbinic material and the
dangers of building too much on an insecure foundation, it seems to me
that there was probably an essential continuity between the religious
outlook of the apocalypticists and that of the earliest exponents of *mer-
kabah*-mysticism among the rabbis. Both seem to bear witness to the
possibility that the study of Scripture could, in certain instances, lead to
direct apprehension of the divine world" (op. cit., 444; see also 306-
348).

This conclusion, that in Judaism there is a kinship and propin-
quity between Apocalyptic and the sort of mystical speculation that is
one, and indeed a major, component among the phenomena of Gnosticism, will lead to one more observation.

This may begin from the fact that there is at least some contact
between Revelation and the chapter of the Chariot (Ezekiel 1; cf. also 8;
10) which rabbinic Judaism handled with such caution. The following
parallels, some clearer than others, are worth noting.

Revelation	Ezekiel
1:13	1:26
1:15	1:24
1:17	1:28
4:2	1:26
4:3	1:27f.
4:5	1:13
4:6	1:5, 18, 22; 10:12
4:7	1:10
4:8	1:18; 10:12
8:5	10:2

These parallels. though of varying weight, are sufficient to show that
the Chariot vision was familiar to John and that he wrote with it in
mind.[32] The Old Testament picture of the Garden of Eden is also used
to supply some of the imagery of Revelation.[32] These observations

could, of course, have no more than literary significance, but in the circumstances of the first century it is unlikely that the material had no deeper meaning. John stands within a tradition that combined mystical and apocalyptic-eschatological elements.

John's world-view, and not least his imaginative understanding of God, have not a little in common with developed Gnosticism. The universe is controlled by good and evil hierarchies of spiritual beings. There is indeed one God, of whom little can be said save that he is *ho ōn kai ho ēn kai ho erchomenos* (1:4)—an expression (intentionally) beyond both declining and construing. But this God shares his throne[33] with another, a slain lamb (5:6). In the vicinity of the throne are twenty-four elders, four living creatures, and seven spirits. Except that they are not provided with names they recall the aeons and emanations that stand between the ineffable Gnostic God and creation.[34] There are corresponding evil powers, which fortunately this paper need not attempt to sort out or arrange in order: the snake, the dragon, the devil, Satan, the beast, another beast, the great harlot, the false prophet, an assortment of demons.

Again, in both Gnosticism and Revelation salvation consists in the ultimate separation of two sets of beings. "If anyone was not found written in the book of life he was cast into the lake of fire" (20:15; cf. 21:8; 22:3-5, 14, 15). It is true that there is a marked difference here. The elect whose destiny is to be in the city of God are what they are, not because of an innate pneumatic purity, but because they have washed their robes and made them white in the blood of the Lamb (7:14). Even among them, however, there appears to be an élite group who manifest a radical opposition to the flesh in that they are celibates: the 144,000 who follow the Lamb wherever he goes and who alone can learn the new song which they sing before the throne (14:1-5). And it is of course true that Revelation is about the unveiling of secrets. I quoted above (p. 144) words of Dr Rowland's; they may be said to call for an addition in the light of Revelation 5:5. After the letters to the seven churches the main substance of Revelation is introduced by the visions of chapters 4 and 5. Chapter 4 opens with the vision of the throne of God. God himself does not appear, but the various beings mentioned above surround the throne, and from it proceed thunders and lightnings. The Living Creatures sing the Trisagion (4:8), and the Elders, Worthy art thou (4:11). Next is introduced the sealed book (5:1-4), which is either the book of the living (that is, the saved), or the book of human destiny, which will include the names of the saved; and it is only the slain Lamb, who occupies the throne of God (5:6), who is able to open the book. It is the opening of its seals (6:1, 3, 5, 7, 9, 12; 8:1, leading to the seven angels, and so on) that sets the story of salvation in motion. The *style* of Revelation is to say: When the Lamb opened the first seal, I saw... and I heard.... The *style* of Gnosis would be to quote the contents of chapter 1 of the book, but the underlying sense is the same. Sal-

vation consists in the fact that the Lion of the tribe of Judah, the Root
of David, has overcome so as to open the book and thus disclose its
contents.[35]

If any general conclusion is to be drawn from this paper, in
which it has been impossible to study the contents of Revelation as a
whole, it must be that the religious thought of the early Christian period
constitutes a very complicated story. The sharp lines that are often
drawn between law and mysticism, Hellenism and Judaism, Gnosticism
and Apocalyptic, may possess a measure of didactic convenience, but
they run the risk of fostering serious error. How did the mind of John
the Divine work? That he abhorred idolatry (which for him, though not
for Paul, was necessarily involved in eating *eidōlothuta*) and sexual and
other kinds of immorality is clear. But he could fall into a trance (1:10)
and see many visions, and he regarded his book as having infallible and
incontestable authority (22:6, 18, 19); it would not be wrong to say that
it contained the true gnosis. To know this secret revelation was the way
to blessedness (1:3; 22:7). Not that reading it would benefit any but the
elect; the time for conversion was past (22:11). He wrote Apocalyptic.[36] This meant however that there was revealed to him the truth about
God and human destiny which is now visible in the heavenly world and
is to become universally known, truth by which those who can receive
it live; and what is this but Gnosticism? Certainly there is a great difference in emphasis. Apocalyptic including the Johannine Apocalypse, is
interested in the mysterious unfolding of history, which it sets against a
clear time-scale. It builds upon the sacred books of the past, noting
which of their prophecies had already been fulfilled and which retained
predictive force. It is thus not a flight from history, as some have maintained[37] and as Gnosticism is: salvation happens for the people of God
in, though at the end of, history. To become Christian, Gnosticism has
to be historicized; this is not necessary for Apocalyptic since it already
has a necessary historical element. To become Christian, Apocalyptic
has to give a share in God's throne to the slain Lamb, concerning itself
with the middle of history as well as its end. This John has done;
whether he has worked out all the implications of this move, and
whether his myths need demythologizing, are further questions. Perhaps this was the point at which his colleague in the Johannine Circle
thought it necessary to write a gospel.

NOTES

1. *The Johannine Epistles*, MNTC, London 1946.
2. *Die drei Johannesbriefe*, KEK, Göttingen 1967.
3. See, among a number of works, O. Cullmann, *Der johanneische*

Kreis, Tübingen 1975; R. E. Brown, *The Community of the Beloved Disciple*, London 1979.

4. *Church and Gnosis*, Cambridge 1932.

5. *Gnosticism and Early Christianity*, New York 1959. Cf. O. Cullmann, *Le Problème littéraire et historique du roman pseudo-clémentin*, Paris 1930, 201: "L'apocalyptique peut être considérée comme un côté particulier du gnosticisme"; also G. Kretschmar, in *RGG*³ II, 1657.

6. Material in square brackets is given by Grant in footnotes.

7. *The Open Heaven*, London 1982.

8. A notable supporter of a very different view was A. Schlatter. See *Die Theologie des Neuen Testaments*, 2. Teil, Calw and Stuttgart 1910, especially 138-142 ("Der Johanneische Dualismus"), 142-3 ("Die Johanneische Metaphysik"), and, with special reference to Jezebel and the Nicolaitans, *The Church in the New Testament Period*, London 1955, 293-5. H. Conzelmann, *Grundriss der Theologie des Neuen Testaments*, Munich 1967, 347-8, sets Apocalyptic and Gnosis over against each other as respectively right-wing and left-wing ways of expressing "die Jenseitigkeit des Heils."

9. C. K. Barrett, *Essays on John*, London 1982, 128-130.

10. A. Hilgenfeld, *Die Ketzergeschichte des Urchristentums*, repr. Hildesheim 1963, 408-11, is still a valuable collection of material. See also 250-77, "Die ophitischen Häresien."

11. N. Brox, *VigChr* 19, 1965, 23-30 (especially 30) thinks it more than conjecture.

12. See the opposite view in W. Bousset, *Die Offenbarung Johannis*, KEK, Göttingen 1906, 237 - not "eine ausgebildete gnostische Schule."

13. Clearly set out by R. H. Charles, *The Revelation of St John*, ICC, Edinburgh 1920, I, 73f. See also H. Schlier, *Bathos*, ThWNT I, 515f.

14. So Jeremiah 3:24; 11:13; Hosea 9:10; and in compounds.

15. For example in the scheme of Justin the Gnostic, Hippolytus, *Refutatio* V, 26:4.

16. R. Seeberg, *Lehrbuch der Dogmengeschichte* I, Leipzig and Erlangen 1920, 282-4.

17. See Hilgenfeld (n. 10).

18. Bibliography in *RGG*³ IV, 1659.

19. I have adjusted the references to those in *The Nag Hammadi Library in English*, translated under the direction of J.M. Robinson, Leiden 1977, and have used that translation.

20. See however G. W. MacRae in *The Nag Hammadi Library*, 256.

21. E.g., Gos. Thom. 32:10; 42:8-12; 43:12-23; 44:34, 35.

22. There were those who believed that the Gnostic Cerinthus wrote Revelation; see Eusebius, *Hist. Eccl.* VII,25:2 (III,28:2 has been taken to mean that Gaius taught that Cerinthus wrote Revelation, but this does not seem to be the meaning of the text). According to Grant, Gnosticism (n. 5), 98, Cerinthian Gnosticism was based on "Christian apocalyptic, primarily the Apocalypse of John."

23. Iı (ed.) J. Lambrecht, *L'Apocalypse johannique et l'Apocalyptique dans le Nouveau Testament*, BEThL 53, Gembloux 1980, 75.

24. See Wilson (p. 135), 130-139; also Grant, quoted on 136, 137.

25. E.g. Irenaeus, *Haer.* II, 31:3.

26. ET 59, 1948, 233-7, repr. in W. D. Davies, *Christian Origins and Judaism*, London 1962, 19-30.

27. See also the article by T. W. Manson in *Aux Sources de la tradition chrétienne, Mélanges offerts à M. Maurice Goguel,* Neuchâtel and Paris 1950, 139-145.

28. See the well-known passage about the four who "entered into Paradise" (T. Chag. 2:3; b.Chag. 14b; j.Chag. 77b; conveniently given in synoptic form in Rowland, *Heaven,* 310-12).

29. Str.-B. II, 307.

30. On this passage, taken with Aboth 3:1, see W. D. Davies in *Christian History and Interpretation: Studies presented to John Knox,* Cambridge 1967, 150f.

31. See a much fuller discussion in I. Gruenwald, *Apocalyptic and Merkavah Mysticism, AGJU* 14, Leiden/Köln 1980, 62-9.

32. Revelation 2:7; 12:9, 17; 22:1, 2.

33. Whether any other being may be said to share the throne of God was precisely the disputed issue in mystical Judaism and the controversies it evoked.

34. Note however the use of Amen as a name at Revelation 3:14, and cf. Hippolytus, *Refutatio* V, 26:3.

35. On the Gnostic side, cf. Burkitt (as in n.4), 90: "The Gnostics were, in the last resort, Christians and had no 'explanation' for Jesus. He remained more real to them as a 'Saviour' than the fantastic demonic organization from which they understood that He was saving them."

36. I believe that there is a difference between Apocalyptic and Prophecy, and that John wrote Apocalyptic, but cannot go into the question here.

37. Rowland, *Heaven,* 445, is rightly cautious on this matter, but it is doubtful whether John the Divine and his associates had much opportunity to escape from reality.

10

PAUL: MISSIONARY AND THEOLOGIAN

The starting-point of this lecture is the statement that I once read, "Paul was not a theologian; he was a missionary"—a statement incorrect both in principle and in history. It is wrong in principle, because there is no Christian theology that is not, in the broadest sense, kerygmatic theology; and it is wrong as a matter of fact, because the historical Paul wrote as a theologian and worked as a missionary.

So much is, in my opinion, clear, and it is not necessary to provide detailed proof of my two counter-propositions. Long ago, while I was an undergraduate, I read an article by Karl Barth on "The Basic Forms of Theological Thought." These, Barth said, were three. The *first* was exposition. The theologian quarries in Scripture the raw material of theology; of course, the text requires exegesis, exposition. The *second* form was criticism; by this word Barth meant that the theologian, having discovered biblical truth, will set it alongside the thought and the ethical behavior, which naturally implies conscious or unconscious thought, of the society in which he lives. He uses it as the criterion by which he judges human systems of thought. The *third* basic form of theological thought, without which the process would remain incomplete, was proclamation. Different theologians at different times would emphasize different elements and use them in different proportions, but always all three, including proclamation, must be present. Barth was right; and it follows that the Christian theologian must be a missionary. Naturally this does not mean that he must be an outstanding preacher or a world-traveler, but his subject requires that he should make the content of his subject known. Conversely, the missionary must be a theologian; this means that he must understand as well as possible what he is talking about. If Christian theology has a missionary content, the message of the Christian missionary has a theological base. It is good news of God; and that is theology.

The historical question also may be answered briefly. It is not necessary to go into the historical problems that are raised by the Acts of the Apostles. The epistles contain sufficient evidence. When Paul does not describe himself as δοῦλος Χριστοῦ (Christ's slave) he calls himself ἀπόστολος (apostle). Everyone knows that this Greek word has a very scanty background in pre-Christian use. We can hardly think that Paul meant to say that he was a naval expedition and must allow him to define the word for himself. The Cynic-Stoic use of κατάσκο–πος, the spy, sent out to investigate and illuminate the human situation, is only of limited usefulness. The use in late Hebrew of *shaliaḥ* and its cognates is important (and Paul may himself contribute something to our understanding of rabbinic practice), but in the end it is Paul himself whom we must hear.

He defines himself as doing ambassadorial service, as though God himself were making the appeal through him: "We beseech you on behalf of Christ, Be reconciled to God" (2 Cor 5:20). He is not content simply to make a verbal appeal; he will do anything to win men for Christ. "Though I am free from all I made myself a slave to all that I might win the more...I have become all things to all men, so that somehow I might save some" (1 Cor 9:19-22). This meant preaching, not running an institution. "Christ did not send me to baptize but to preach the Gospel" (1 Cor 1:17). He was a pioneer missionary who avoided the easy well-trodden tracks, eager "to preach the Gospel where Christ's name was not yet known, that I might not build on another's ground" (Rom 15:20). He was a hardened traveler who covered long distances and endured great hardships. But he was more than this. What he was doing was itself a part of the Gospel that he preached. The Gospel, he said, is the power of God which saves all who believe; in it the righteousness of God is revealed—ἀποκαλύπτεται, present tense (Rom 1:16f.). When Paul preached the Gospel the saving righteousness of God was revealed, power leading to salvation was in operation. When Paul spoke, the word of Christ was heard (Rom 10:14).

It would not be difficult to add more, but from this last observation it is easy to take the next step. Was Paul also a theologian? It may be that the author whom I have quoted intended to say, "Paul was not a systematic theologian." This has often been said, and it is possible to make a case for it. Certainly it is true that Paul never (so far as we know) wrote a textbook of systematic theology, setting out in regular order the usual chapters: Revelation, God, Christ, the Spirit, the Trinity, Sin, Redemption, and so forth. But it is not necessary to write a textbook in order to be a systematic theologian. It is necessary to think systematically, and one must have the ability to recognize the important traditional themes and to perceive their relation to one another. One must be able so to work with the Christian tradition as to express Christian truth in the light of contemporary philosophical thinking.

If we have here a reasonable definition Paul will qualify not only as a theologian but also as a systematic theologian. One must of course remember that for him the "Christian tradition" was something different from what it has become for us who have centuries of Christian theology behind us. For Paul the tradition scarcely existed. He became a Christian only a very short time after the resurrection; before him there had been no one capable of handling the story of Jesus in a seriously theological way. Paul had indeed received the outlines of belief, that Christ died for our sins according to the Scriptures, that he was buried and raised on the third day according to the Scriptures, and that he appeared to a number of people whose names could be listed (1 Cor 15:3-5). The importance of this report is not to be undervalued, but it shows hardly any trace of further reflection. It is asserted that Christ died for our sins; but how could his death achieve anything for the sins of others? He died and was raised up according to the Scriptures. Which Scriptures? And what concept of the fulfillment of Scripture is presupposed? These are questions that arise immediately; but it was Paul who articulated them, and Paul who first gave some indication how and where answers might be sought. Not only as a missionary but also as a theologian Paul was a pioneer. Again, the religious and philosophical atmosphere that he breathed was different from ours, so that it is certain that he provides us with no systematic theology for our own time. Even an apostle cannot do that, for a systematic theology for our time must speak to today's intellectual environment. What the apostle will do for us is of course something more than that; he will provide us with the raw material out of which every later generation can construct a systematic theology for its own time. It is however possible to collect out of the Pauline letters material for the conventional theological themes.

For example, Paul wrote about God. That was not difficult, for at this point he had Judaism and the Old Testament behind him. He had however to modify the Jewish inheritance. God was the creator, and as any artist is known through his creative work, so also is God; at least there is a potential knowledge of God in the things that God has made (Rom 1.20), even if it remains potential because those who ought to accept it are unwilling to do so on the only terms on which it can be had: they are unwilling to glorify God and give thanks to him (Rom 1:21). Instead, they choose to pass by their creator and in his place to worship their fellow creatures. The result is the darkening of their morals and of their minds. Creation goes out of joint as Paul sees most clearly in the perversion of human sexuality, and thought, not only moral but metaphysical thinking, is corrupted (Rom1:19-25). Broadly speaking, this is Paul's exegesis of the Old Testament story of creation, but it is necessary only to compare it with the parallels in the Wisdom of Solomon to see how much more profound it is than anything that his predecessors or contemporaries achieved. Also Jewish is the belief that God is judge, and that as judge he is righteous and always acts in righteousness (Rom 2:5; 3:6). Here too one recalls Genesis: Shall not the judge of all the earth do right? (Gen18:25). Abraham had asked the rhetorical question; but Paul has a problem. God, as a good judge, will duly distinguish between the innocent and the guilty. What then if there are no innocent? Paul can quote the Old Testament to prove that "there is none righteous, no, not so much as one" (Ps 14:1; Rom 3:10). Paul the theologian has grasped the supreme moral problem about God, which is not, How can God be righteous and yet permit suffering? but, How can God be righteous and yet fail to inflict suffering upon the whole of universally guilty humanity? How can God at the same time be both just and justifier—when there are none to justify but the ungodly (Rom 3:25; 4:5)? Paul is aware of the question, and also has an answer, though that is not to be dealt with now. It is at least clear that God loves, as Luther rightly said, with a love that "non invenit sed creat suum diligibile." The act of love took place while we were still sinners (Rom 5:8; 8:38f.). The paradoxical question can be dealt with only by a paradoxical answer. From first to last, from foreknowledge to glory (Rom 8:29f.), God is the author of salvation.

The conviction that God loves those who have no claim upon his love rests upon the fact that Christ died for us. It is the love of God which is in Christ Jesus our Lord from which nothing can separate us (Rom 8:38f.). Paul therefore must also write about Christ. And here is perhaps the hardest question of all: How can the death of another person benefit the rest of us? Or (to ask a different though related question), What sort of person is he whose death can benefit the rest of mankind? After the crucifixion and resurrection the conviction arose that it had so happened, and that Jesus was that sort of person. In the earliest days that conviction sufficed; and there are some for whom it suffices still. But for one who had a searching and analytic mind, and therewith a theological responsibility for his fellow Christians, it would not suffice. Here we can with a great deal of probability observe Paul developing the tradition that he had received. If time permitted we could in paragraphs such as Phil 2:6-11; Rom 1:3f. trace how Paul edited Christological formulations. Here we can only note that the theologian who takes his calling with full seriousness has many problems. Paul never ran away from them.

Here we can consider only one more theme, that we may observe how Paul's mind works, and how his thought develops. What has Paul to say about the Law?

Paul was a Jew; he never ceased to be a Jew. He loved the Law, as Jews did and do. It was easy for Paul to say, The Law is good; it came from God, it is spiritual, it gives commands which are still to be obeyed, it carries within itself its own self-transcending summary in the commandment of love; easy for him to say this, and leave it there. Paul was also a Gentile missionary. He knew that Gentiles were acceptable to God as they were, without any legal observance, that the grace of God was free and undiscriminating. It was easy for him to say, If you get yourselves circumcised, Christ will be no good to you. I testify again to every man who is getting himself circumcised that he is under obligation to do the whole Law. You are finished with Christ, you who would be justified by Law; you have fallen out of grace (Gal 5:2-4);

easy for Paul to say this, and to leave it there. It is characteristic of Paul, the theologian, that he insists on both propositions and refuses to take either easy way out. The key to his understanding of the matter is to be found in Rom 7:7-25, which handles the outrageous but unavoidable question, Is the Law sin? Here Paul insists most strongly on the divine excellence of the Law, which is holy, righteous, and good. Here he says that in his experience the Law means that the good he wants to do, he does not do; the evil that he does not want to do, he does. And it is here that he states in the plainest terms the answer to the problem. The Law itself is good but an evil power has taken hold of it and twisted it out of its proper use and purpose so as to form a ἕτερος νόμος, a different law, a different kind of law, which makes war upon the good Law that my mind approves. It is not for us at present to trace in detail the way in which Paul works this out; it is enough that we should see with what seriousness Paul wrestles with his problem. We can see too, though again not in detail, how Paul's thought advances. In Galatians the Law appears as essentially an interlude, filling the space between Abraham and Christ. Now that Christ has come we no longer need the παιδάγωγος, the child-minding slave who gets the boy to school. In Romans Paul does not contradict this but says even more explicitly than in Galatians that the Law slipped into this interval in order that transgression might abound (Rom 5:20); here too however he has seen how the Gospel establishes the Law (Rom 3:31). God is not contradicting himself; a self-contradicting God would not be God, and the whole theological enterprise would be at an end. The Gospel establishes the Law not as the Judaizers understood it but as God himself understood it. For Paul can now see that the Law is to be understood ἐκ πίστεως, by faith (Rom 9:30-33). Understanding the law in this way we can see that it proclaims the righteousness of faith.

We may conclude then that Paul sets us a proper example by being both theologian and missionary. That presents no serious difficulty. More difficult is a second question: How were these two aspects of Paul's life related to and bound up with each other? For he was one man, and his whole life was determined by one conviction: "All I do, I do for the sake of the Gospel (διὰ τὸ εὐαγγέλιον,1 Cor 9:23). The Gospel was at the same time message and theology; a theological message and a kerygmatic theology. Fresh theological insights furthered the mission; the mission required constantly fresh theological work. A circular relationship; but in this case the circle has a beginning. We call it conversion.

Conversion: but is this the right word? Should we not rather say, Vocation? The arguments for vocation are well known and are not without weight. It never occurred to Paul that, as a Christian, he was worshipping a different God from the one he had served as a Jew. When he describes most clearly the beginning of his Christian life he does so in terms that recall prophetic vocations in the Old Testament: "God who separated me from my mother's womb and called me through his grace" (Gal 1:15). On the other hand, at the end of the same chapter he speaks of the most radical of conversions: "He who once persecuted us is now preaching the faith which formerly he ravaged" (1:23). This is not merely a new course of action; it originates in a changed belief. What had seemed so wrong that it was necessary to use all possible means to stamp it out now seemed so right that it must be not only held but propagated. The fact is that every true conversion, especially in the Christian sense, is at the same time a vocation. And for Paul the vocation was "that I should preach Christ among the Gentiles" (1.16).

In his conversion Paul was presented with two theological problems, both of which were relevant to his call. I call them "problems"; they were in fact growing-points from which his thought developed. The content of his conversion was the discovery that the crucified Jesus was now alive. He could only be alive because God had raised him from death, and that God had done this was proof that Jesus had been right; his opponents had been wrong. The first consequence of this was that Paul had to reconstruct the eschatological framework of his Jewish theology. The eschatology was now realized, though only partially. The world, human society, was still subject to sin, suffering, and death. What in these paradoxical circumstances did God expect his people, and especially those who accepted the Messiahship and Lordship of Jesus, to do? Let us for a moment leave that question and notice, secondly, that Jesus had been cast out and rejected by the Law, or at least by its authorized exponents. But he had been right and they had been wrong. Had the Law, not Jesus, led Israel astray? Were the Gentiles, who had no Torah, better off than the Jews? In these two questions there is a great deal of theological substance; here they call for only one observation. Both questions as I have stated them lead us back to the Gentile mission.

We are inclined to take this Gentile mission for granted. To us it seems to be beyond question, but at that time it was a matter of radical questioning. Jesus had left neither a church constitution nor a liturgy, neither a theological system nor a missionary program. All this had to be improvised. That there should be a Jewish mission was self-evident. Jesus was the Messiah of Israel, and the Messiah was a national figure. True, most Jews had rejected him, but they now had an opportunity to change their minds. "Now, brothers, I know that you did it out of ignorance, as did also your rulers. But God has fulfilled what he announced through the mouth of all his prophets, that the Christ should suffer. Repent therefore, and turn, that your sins may be blotted out" (Acts 3:17-19). But what of the Gentiles? Probably there were some who said: The End will come soon; then God will do what he will. We have no time to evangelize the Gentiles. It is certain that there were some who said: First we must win all the Jews; after that we will turn to the Gentiles. We can be certain of this, first because it is presupposed by Paul's counter-proposal (to which I shall come in a moment), and secondly because it is confirmed by the speech attributed to James in Acts 15.13-18. James quotes Amos 9:11f.: "Afterwards I will return, and I will build up again the tent of David that had fallen down, and I will build up again its ruins, and I will raise it up, in order that the rest of mankind may seek the Lord, even all the Gentiles upon whom my name has been named." The interpretation of these words is disputed, but the quotation was probably taken to mean that Israel must first be re-established in order that others might then be incorporated into God's plan. This makes the best sense of the Apostolic Council. We must (so runs the argument that leads to the Apostolic Decree) retain so much of Judaism that the Jews may be satisfied now, and not so much that the Gentiles will later be offended. The counter-proposal, the third way forward, is set out in Romans 9-11, especially in 11:31f. There is no way to the mercy of God but the way of unbelief and disobedience. The Gentiles were always unbelieving and disobedient; therefore they may enter immediately into the realm of free, gratuitous mercy. They have deserved nothing from God; his approach to them cannot be based on any merit of theirs and they cannot pretend that it is. This the Jews had to learn through hard experience, as Paul himself had done when he came to regard his credits as debits and his righteousness as dung (Phil 3:7f.). The Jews' rejection of the Gospel thus served a double purpose. Its immediate result was the Gentile mission; as the Jewish door closed the Gentile door opened. The more remote result was that it gave to the Jews the possibility of understanding the mercy of God and accepting salvation. So the conversion of the Gentiles would make possible the deliverance of Israel.

I have spoken of improvisation. Paul was the great, creative improviser, and as Gentile missionary he had a trump card up his sleeve. For him, Jesus was not only the Christ but the last Adam, not only a national but a universal figure. "Or is God the God of the Jews only? Is he not also the God of the Gentiles?" (Rom 3:29). Once more, theology and mission, though distinguishable, form an inseparable unity. It is interesting here to compare the Pauline epistles with Acts. When Paul writes, "The Jews first and also the Greeks" (e.g. Rom 1:16), what he has in mind is primarily a theological proposition. In Acts we have the equivalent of it in a practical missionary program: Try the Synagogue first, and when the Jews throw you out move on to a neighboring lecture-hall. Between Luke and Paul there is a difference, but no contradiction: Paul may well have worked in this eminently sensible way. But it is characteristic of Paul to state the matter theologically, and of Luke to like his theology in the form of stories. The result is the integration of theology and mission.

Theology and mission: but we must return to the words with

which we began, Theologian and missionary. That is, we must ask, How could Paul hold the two functions together in his one person? What was the relation between the two? The question is in the first instance a historical one. How did Paul conduct his missionary work? It was his aim to preach only where the name of Christ was not yet known (Rom 15:20). How was that to be done? How did Paul do it? We know all too little about this. In Galatians 4, for example, Paul gives a fascinating account of his first encounter with the Galatians and of his reception by them, but in this chapter we have not a word of what Paul said in his preaching. The epistles can indeed be described as written preaching, but they are not mission preaching. There are sermons in Acts, but they give us little help. The sermon in Acts 13 is a synagogue sermon, and assumes a good deal. In the opening words, "the God of this people Israel" (13:17), it presupposes that there is one true God, who is active in history and especially in the election of the people to be his servant. It presupposes τὰς φωνὰς τῶν προφητῶν, since the prophetic books are publicly read Sabbath by Sabbath (13:27). Perhaps one might hope for more from the Areopagus address in Acts 17, but this address presents us with historical and theological problems. I shall however return to it shortly.

What can we learn from the epistles? The passage usually cited in this connection is 1 Thess 1:9f. There is no need for him, Paul says, to give anyone an account of the Thessalonians and their conversion. Everyone already knows how they accepted the Gospel. Their response had been that for which Paul hoped. They had turned to God from idols, to serve the living and true God and to await his Son from heaven, whom he raised from the dead, Jesus, who delivers us from the coming wrath. That seems to confirm what we might a priori expect, that Paul would as a beginning press the Gentiles to abandon their idolatry and turn to the true God, whom he had known from childhood through the Old Testament. But with what sort of proof would he convince his hearers? In 1 Thessalonians he reports the end but not the means. In order to learn more we move to Athens and to the speech in Acts 17. If the speech is read quickly it seems that Paul uses the same proofs that were used by contemporary philosophers. They—some of them—believed in one spiritual universal God, who had created all mankind from one origin, was not confined to material temples, and had no need of material gifts from his worshipers. All this can be found in ancient thinkers, not least in the Epicureans and the Stoics, who are mentioned in the passage. Epicurus (as Lucretius tells us) had delivered men from religion. The gods were distant and much too concerned with the enjoyment of their existence to interfere with ours. The Stoics knew that life had a meaning, a λόγος, and that this λόγος was a sort of god, the reality that lay behind the ridiculous mythologies of the uneducated and credulous. Such a god was not to be found in wood and stone. So did Paul use a philosophical natural theology of this kind when he preached to the Gentiles? Did he follow the philosophers as far as he could, in order at the end to supplement nature by grace, referring to Jesus—though not indeed by name (17:31)?

The objection that is usually—and rightly—brought against this view is that Paul seems to have had no high opinion of natural theology (Rom 1:18-23). "They have changed the truth of God into a lie, and honored and served the creation instead of the Creator" (1:25). Creation could give them at most the conception of an invisible and powerful Other. To this supreme Other they have preferred visible things, so that the only god they had in fact derived from the world of nature was an opposite to the true God. Their natural religion was bringing down upon them not the divine favour but the divine wrath. This is hardly the sort of gambit with which Paul would begin a missionary speech. We observe a difficult historical question with regard to Acts 17 and a theological uncertainty with respect to 1 Thess 1:9f.

There are further observations to make. In 1 Cor 1:18 Paul describes the Christian message as the word of the Cross. For Paul, Christ is God's power and wisdom, but he knows that to the Greeks his Gospel is nonsense. That means that his mission preaching to Gentiles was not constructed so as to be pleasing to the philosophers. "The word of the Cross is foolishness to those who are lost…We preach Christ crucified, to Jews an offence and to Gentiles a nonsense" (1 Cor 1:18, 23). In the next chapter he repeats the same theme: "When I came to you I did not come proclaiming my testimony about God with pre-eminent eloquence or wisdom. For I resolved that in the midst of you I would know nothing but Jesus Christ, and him crucified" (2.1f.). We may here recall Gal 3:1, where we have what is missing in Galatians 4. We know very well how Paul preached in Galatia. Before the eyes of the Galatians he placarded Jesus Christ, the crucified. The difference between these passages and Acts 17 is clear. In the Areopagus speech we have nothing at all about the Cross. Only at the end is Christ mentioned. All men must now repent because God has set a day on which he will judge the world in righteousness by a man whom he has appointed for the purpose (17:30f.). This man must have died, for God has raised him from the dead, but the manner, even the fact, of his death is not mentioned. One wonders, Is the word *difference* strong enough? Should we not say, *contradiction?*

We may note first that though Acts 17:22-29 contains philosophical thought, and a quotation from a Greek poet, it contains also the thought and the words with which Isaiah and Jeremiah attack the idolatry of their contemporaries. For Isaiah also, God is the Lord, the Creator of the ends of the earth, who calls the stars by name. He is not to be confined within material, man-made houses. "Heaven is my throne and the earth is my footstool; what is the house that you would build for me…? these things my hand has made" (Isa 66:1f.). The practices of human religiosity are scorned by the prophet as they are by Epicurus. "He who slaughters an ox is like him who kills a man; he who sacrifices a lamb, like him who breaks a dog's neck; he who presents a cereal offering, like him who offers swine's blood; he who makes a memorial offering of frankincense, like him who blesses an idol" (Isa 66.3). This paragraph in Acts 17 contains the Old Testament proclamation of the one, true God. In other words (though they put the matter too neatly to be entirely true), we may say that what we read in Acts 17 is not natural but revealed theology. He who wrote Acts 17 learned his theology not from the Greeks but from the Bible. And the result is perhaps not totally irreconcilable with Romans 1. Since the Fall, the *theologia naturalis*, the theology that sinful man draws from nature, is a fallen theology, idolatry, a flight from the true God who seeks from men service and obedience. This is the prophetic message, and the message of Romans 1, where the essential point is that man has set in the place of the true God god-substitutes which can never truly be his Lord and serve only to corrupt his thinking and his moral behavior. The recognition of the Old Testament influence on Acts 17 throws a different light on the Areopagus speech, though it probably came not from Paul but from a non-Pauline branch of the Gentile mission.

A second observation comes from a return to 1 Thess 1:9f. The Thessalonians learned to await Jesus who rescues us (τὸν ῥυόμενον ἡμᾶς) from the coming wrath. So Jesus is a rescuer, a deliverer. How, we may ask, does he deliver us? This question is not answered in 1 Thess 1:10. We must seek an answer elsewhere. We may begin with a passage in the same letter. In 1 Thess 5:10 Paul writes of Jesus that he "died for us that, whether we wake or sleep, we may live with him." Many similar passages can be quoted from the other letters. For example, Jesus "gave himself up for our sins that he might deliver us out of this present evil age" Gal 1:4); the Son of God "loved me and gave himself up for me" (Gal 2:20); "Christ died for our sins", (1 Cor 15:3). These passages show that Christ had delivered the Thessalonians by dying for them; so we come back to the "word of the Cross," to the "nothing but Christ and him crucified" (1 Cor 1:18; 2:2). If Paul told the Thessalonians to await the coming of God's Son from heaven, he was a Coming One who would be recognized by the marks of his passion.

We may be able to take a step further. Paul proclaimed the Christ, the crucified Christ. A Greek would probably be able to work back from *Christ*, Χριστός , to the verb χρίειν, to anoint, but the word would have no clear content. Who is this person smeared with oil? Paul cannot have preached Jesus as the Christ, the Messiah, without giving his hearers some preparatory instruction in Judaism. Only those Gentiles who had already been in the habit of attending the synagogue would find such instruction unnecessary. Once more the Old Testament is involved in the preaching. This means that the preaching of Christ already contains a requirement to abandon idolatry and turn to the true

God. It was the Jewish God, the God of the Old Testament, who had a Messiah, and the concept of Messiahship was inseparable from a God conceived in a particular way: a God who was unique and almighty; a God who was actively at work in history, anything but an Epicurean remoteness, anything other than a Stoic immanence; a God who had strangely set his choice upon that strange people the Jews, so that their history became the special locus of his work and of his revelation; a God who to this special people had made special promises, promises which he would be certain to fulfill; a God who made correspondingly special claims upon those who were his. All this says a good deal about God before one begins to consider the particular person whom Christians recognize as Messiah.

One further observation: Paul preached the crucified Christ. Why crucified? Even if his hearers did not understand the meaning of Χριστός they knew very well the meaning of ἐσταυρωμένος. It meant that the person was either a slave who had made his master unusually angry, or a political or military rebel. If Paul was unwilling to accept any of these explanations he must provide another. Such an explanation would require an account, however short, of the life of Jesus. Kähler was correct in the view that the gospels grew backwards: first the passion narrative, then stories, controversies, teaching, to make sense of the final scene. We note here questions both historical and theological. Why did they kill him? That is a hard question for the historian. Why did God allow him to die? For the theologian this is an even harder question. It is however no more than a beginning, for the New Testament does not represent the death of Jesus as simply part of the tragic fate of human mortality. It is a hard enough question when we ask, Why do the innocent suffer? But this is not an event that God permitted; it was God himself who caused it. "God did not spare his own Son" (Rom 8:32). Isaac might come out of his ordeal whole, but not Jesus. If this tells us anything about God, does it tell us that he is a monster? Certainly not; but what then? It must say something about the complexity of the being of God—at least (since the Holy Spirit is not in question and we cannot speak of a trinity) about God's twofoldness, for if the Crucified is not somehow God, as his Father also is, then the Father is inflicting suffering on an inferior—and this is monstrous. One does not treat inferiors so.

I shall not make the universal negative assertion that Paul never argued in the manner of a hellenistic-Jewish philosopher. Idolatry and polytheism do expose themselves to philosophical objection, and Paul may have argued that popular religion was mere superstition and that men ought to live in accordance with the Mind, the Logos, of God. He could have done this without enrolling Lucretius and Posidonius among the prophets, for the real prophets had themselves said something of the sort. But it was not necessary for him to do this, for simply to tell the story of the Cross poses all the questions about God, and on this basis the preacher could detach his hearers from their old belief (or unbelief) and lead them in a new direction. The Cross questions all conventional philosophical arguments, including the traditional Christian arguments, for the existence of God. The philosophical problem of verification is a real one, and the Cross means that God refuses to verify himself, to come down from the Cross and so to prove his case. It contradicts the cosmological and the teleological proof, for there is no event so disorderly, none that runs more plainly contrary to the notion of purpose in the ordering of the universe. It is the contradiction of the moral argument too, for the moral argument asks, Who but God can have set within me the voice that cries, I ought? And the Cross means that when it comes to the push, the inward voice cries, I ought, but I won't. There is no God, no President of the Immortals, who can make me surrender the search for my own happiness, comfort, and security.

It is not easy to believe in God. That is why Christian thought about God does not begin with Plato and Aristotle, with the consideration of creation (cosmology) or the consideration of history (teleology), but with the preaching of the Cross. It is in the obedience of Jesus that God is known, in the suffering of Jesus that God is glorified. Every other god is an idol, such a god as the Thessalonians had now given up. The Thessalonians were right. We can never be content with a god who wound up this watch of a universe and left it to tick. We need a God who wrestles with rebellion and overcomes resistance with love, a God who speaks to us from outside ourselves, so remote that we can confuse him with the thunder, yet speaks in language that we can understand, because we see him in one who would rather be the friend of sinners and die than give them up and live.

It is not my intention (as it was not Paul's) to construct a Christian metaphysic, though I do observe that we have come to a point where a true metaphysic is possible, for here we are indeed μετὰ τὰ φυσικά, beyond our normal experience, not in a world of fantasy but in the world of unsearchable divine love. Exegetically (and that is my concern) we must recognize that 1 Thess 1:9f. on the one hand and 1 Cor 1:18; 2:2 do not contradict each other; historically (and that also is my concern) we must say that Paul may well have won the Thessalonians from their false gods by preaching Christ crucified.

In our attempt to understand Paul in his double role as at once theologian and missionary there is one further line of investigation that we may follow. In his book *Jesus and the Transformation of Judaism* [London, 1980] John Riches has admirably brought out the way that must be followed by one who wishes to communicate a genuinely new message. He must use language that is essentially familiar to his hearers. If he uses a totally new vocabulary no one will understand him. If however he uses the old words with their old meanings he will achieve nothing more than a mere rearrangement of ideas. He must use the old vocabulary but he must also give to the old words a new meaning—a meaning that is related to the old one, so that there may be a point of contact, but also different, so that the new message is communicated. This procedure Professor Riches has pointed out in the gospels; it may also be seen in Paul. I give two examples.

In 2 Cor 4:16 Paul writes, "Though our outward self is liable to corruption (διαφθείρεται) yet our inward self is renewed day by day." A non-Christian Corinthian would have taken this up immediately. "We have heard this from the philosophers and we know what they mean. They are contrasting the frail bodily shell, which will soon perish, with the immortal spirit that dwells within." That was a common place; it was certainly not what Paul meant, but what he meant was not totally different. Paul too knew the meaning of mortality. Earlier in this epistle he had written of an experience that could only be described as a sentence of death (1:9). The bodily shell was indeed wearing out, and within was something that did not share this corruptibility. It was however no immortal human spirit, longing to be delivered from its prison. "We who are in the tent, burdened as we are, groan, because we do not wish to strip, but rather to put on over our body the habitation that comes from heaven" (5:4). So far as there is in man something that may be called Spirit, it is the Spirit of God which God himself has given.

From this starting-point we could, if time allowed, study a complex group of words used by Paul: the inward and the outward self; the old and the new self; flesh and spirit; the mind, the members, the body. Such study is impossible here; I can only state its conclusion. The new Christian eschatology makes possible a new application of the old terminology, and we perceive an important theological operation that enabled Paul the missionary to speak to the Gentile world.

A second example. Occasionally Paul uses the language and the cosmology of astrology. Powers and authorities, height and depth (Rom 8:38f.) are at home in this field. Related to astrology is Gnosis, and Paul uses also the language and cosmology of Gnosis, but always with a characteristic difference. This too we cannot study seriously; it is possible only to say, in all brevity, that the criterion Paul uses in Christianizing Gnosis is twofold. His gnosis (or wisdom, σοφία) is the Cross, the foolishness of God, which is wiser than men. And, secondly, Paul recognizes that in this age our knowledge is partial, and that in the end what is partial will be done away. "Now I know in part; then I shall know, as now I am known" (1 Cor 13:12).

Gnostic cosmology and the heavenly powers remain, but they serve a new purpose. They make clear that the Gospel is not only the possibility of an inward renewal, an existential transformation of human nature, but the external cosmic event that makes this possibility possible. The language of subjective mythology is re-applied so that it expresses the objectivity of a sequence of historical events.

Here I must close and sum up what I have said about Paul as theologian and missionary. Paul is both: it is hardly possible to read a page of his letters without recognizing him in both roles. As missionary he had a message that was a theology, as theologian, a theology that demanded to be communicated. This inverse relation focuses upon the figure of the last Adam, the universal Man, who was the instrument by which God worked out his plan for his human creatures. He was doubly universal in that he represented the universality of God and generalized the particularity of man and so became the Man for all men, in the breadth of his compassion and in his power to unite within himself every member of the human race. His particularity was a special particularity, for he was the unique representative of the unique race, the Messiah of the Jews. But he was not only Χριστός, he was also κύριος, for God is not the God of the Jews only but of the Gentiles too (Rom 8.29). Christ vindicates the truth of God by confirming the promises made to Israel, but this he does in such a way that the Gentiles may glorify God for his mercy (Rom 15:8f.). It is because God is what he is that Paul has both a theology and a mission.

11

THE SIGNIFICANCE OF THE
ADAM-CHRIST TYPOLOGY FOR THE
RESURRECTION OF THE DEAD:
1 Cor 15:20-22, 45-49

The passages proposed for discussion in this session may be said to raise the following questions:

(1) What part do these passages play in the development of the argument in 1 Cor 15? They cannot be simply abstracted from the rest of the chapter, in which Paul develops (we may provisionally assume) a connected and coherent case against Corinthian Christians with whom he disagreed. We must therefore give careful attention to the links between our two passages and those which precede and follow them.

(2) Why are the two passages separate? That is, Why is Adam mentioned twice, at an interval of more than twenty verses, in which a variety of topics, ranging from the practice of baptism for the dead (v. 29) to the nature of the resurrection body (v. 34) are discussed? Again we may make a provisional assumption, that the second passage is not simply an afterthought. Unless Paul is absentmindedly repeating himself the Adam-Christ material must play two different roles in the total argument; its significance will not be exactly the same in verses 45-49 as in 20-22.

(3) How are the two passages related to other Pauline passages in which Adam is mentioned, or appears to be alluded to? The most important passage to consider is Rom 5:12-21; there are others, notably Rom 1:18-32; Phil 2:5-11; and quite a number more. For the most part we shall use other passages in the attempt to explain our own, but the reverse process may occasionally become possible.

(4) What may be inferred from these two passages concerning the meaning of 1 Cor 15 as a whole? If it is possible to establish Paul's meaning at these two points, especially since they are separate, we should learn something about the meaning of the entire chapter. What was it that Paul wished to communicate to the Corinthian church? Clearly we shall not be able to give a complete answer to this question

till the whole chapter has been reviewed, but we may be able to attempt a tentative suggestion.

(5) If we have any success in answering Question 4 we shall be able to go on to a further question. How far do our verses help us to understand the Corinthian error which Paul was rebutting? I need not say that this is a notoriously disputed question, but it may be possible to suggest an answer, or answers.

It goes without saying that, if they can be answered at all, these questions will be answered only on the basis of careful exegesis conducted against the background of the speculations about Adam entertained by Paul's contemporaries.

Exegesis will start with the question, What is the relation between vv. 20-22 and that which precedes? How does v. 20 grow out of the earlier part of the chapter?

Unlike 7:1; 8:1; 11:2; 12:1; 16:1, chapter 15 does not begin with the hint that Paul is answering a question directed to him by the Corinthians. The specific motivation of the chapter does not appear till v. 12, though it is carefully prepared for in vv. 1-11. These verses do not prove that a "resurrection" either has happened, or will happen. The logical content of the paragraph is that the theme of resurrection is a vital and indispensable part of the Christian εὐαγγέλιον or λόγος of salvation (15:1.2), and that by whomsoever the proclamation is made. It is widely held, and is very probably correct, that vv. 3, 4 contain a traditional, pre-pauline, statement of Christian belief, and it is centered on the proposition Χριστὸς ἀπέθανεν...καὶ...ἐγήγερται. That he was raised, is not proved, hardly could be proved, by the sequence of appearances (showing traces of Semitic idiom) that follows; this is intended rather to lead up to the conclusion of v. 11. Cephas, James, and Paul all appear in the list of witnesses to the resurrection. Paul was by no means unaware of the practical and doctrinal differences that existed between himself and his colleagues, but he can say, εἴτε οὖν ἐγὼ εἴτε ἐκεῖνοι, οὕτως κηρύσσομεν. Not only did all Christian preachers proclaim this event, it was accepted by the Corinthians: οὕτως ἐπιστεύσατε. The aorist tense does not mean (even when contrasted with the present κηρύσσομεν) that you believed it once but do so no longer; it refers to the time of conversion when the Corinthians gave to the evangelists the hearing of faith. If any doubt is expressed in this paragraph it lies in the εἰ κατέχετε and the εἰκῇ of v. 2.

It was necessary first of all to establish (in vv. 1-11) and to repeat (in v. 12a) that Christian preaching is focused upon the resurrection of Christ in order to prepare for the astonishing statement of v. 12b that there are Corinthians who are prepared to contradict their faith and deny their existence as Christians by affirming that ἀνάστασις νεκρῶν οὐκ ἔστιν. How Paul was informed of this assertion we do not know. We may guess at the household of Chloe (1:11), or at Stephanas, Fortunatus, and Achaicus (16:17). And we may guess that Paul had been misinformed, or that he had misunderstood what he had been told. He certainly manifests astonishment, and is quick to point out that for Christians the Corinthian position is untenable. If the denial of resurrection is made in general terms it will include denial of the resurrection of Christ: οὐδὲ Χριστὸς ἐγήγερται (v. 13); but this contradicts the κήρυγμα and the πίστις of v. 11, and these have been represented there as matter of universal Christian agreement. Contradict the preaching and you make the preachers false witnesses (v. 15). The next three verses retrace the same logical steps, more or less in reverse direction. Let us accept the Corinthian proposition, now expressed in different words: νεκροὶ οὐκ ἐγείρονται. The changed wording is worth noting because it suggests that for Paul there is little significant difference between ἀνάστασις (ἀνιστάναι) and ἐγείρεσθαι. If the general proposition is true, the particular instance will follow: οὐδὲ Χριστὸς ἐγήγερται(v. 16, as in v. 13). If this is true, it follows (not this time, as in v. 15, that the preachers are false witnesses, but) that the Christian proclamation of salvation breaks down and those who have believed this misleading tale are still in their sins (since the death for sin of v. 3 applies only because of the resurrection). Because they remained under the power of their sins those who have died as Christians (ἐν Χριστῷ, v.18) are dead and done with. The wages of sin is death (Rom 6: 23); they are still in their sins; they get what they deserve and accordingly perish.

Throughout vv. 12-19 the logical factor has been the negative condition, εἰ δὲ Χριστὸς οὐκ ἐγήγερται (vv. 14, 17; cf. v. 19 εἰ ἐν τῇ ζωῇ ταύτῃ...μόνον). This negative condition has not been fulfilled: Χριστὸς ἐγήγερται, as is affirmed by Christian preachers in general and the witnesses listed in vv. 5-8 in particular. This assertion however does not in itself prove that there will be a resurrection of others as well as Christ. It asserts its possibility but not its certainty, for it would be quite reasonable to maintain that Christ, who was the Son of God (e.g. Gal 4:4) and sinless (2 Cor 5:21) was raised from the dead, but that the rest of mankind, who were human and nothing more and among whom was not even one righteous man (Rom 3:10), were consigned to the fate of everlasting death which they undoubtedly deserved. It is clear what the next step in the argument must be. Paul must prove that the resurrection of the rest of mankind (or perhaps of believers, of those who are in Christ) is not only a possibility but a fact. It may be that the difficult verse 19 was intended to prepare for this step. Suppose it to be true that Christ was indeed raised from the dead, as the preaching affirms, so that our sins are dealt with (v. 3); but suppose also that physical death is the end of our existence. Then we should have hope in Christ in this life only; the Gospel would be blocked by death; death, the wages of sin, would still be meted out by God even

though sin had been disposed of. Christ would (if we may put it so)
have led us up the garden path only for us to discover that the path ended in a brick wall. Far better never to have set out.

But this is not so: νυνὶ δέ, one of Paul's most characteristic
expressions. Cf. Rom 3:21; 6:22; 7:6; 1 Cor 12:18; 13:13, all significant
points of comparison because they lead to profound statements of the
Gospel. It is at this point that we must examine the details of vv. 20-22.
Not that every detail will prove to be significant. Anarthrous
Χριστός for example, is very frequent in the first part of this chapter
(11 times in vv. 1-34; in this section Χριστός has the article three
times), and indeed elsewhere in Paul. It would be difficult to maintain
that Paul sees in Χριστός a specific reference to the office of Messiahship. The word refers simply to "the person whom we call Χριστός,"
though of course it could not have been so used by anyone who believed that Jesus of Nazareth was not the Messiah. This observation is
important; Χριστός did not in itself ascribe to Jesus a representative
character; some other term was necessary if this was to be done. I have
already observed that it is difficult to establish any marked difference
between ἀνιστάναι and ἐγείρεσθαι. It is however fair to say that the
passive sense of ἐγείρεσθαι is available for use if needed, and that this
is occasionally brought out explicitly by the use of the active ([ὁ Θεὸς]
ἤγειρεν τὸν Χριστόν, v. 15). The resurrection of Christ is unthinkable apart from the action of God. He rose (and remains alive—this is
perhaps intended by the perfect ἐγήγερται) ἐκ νεκρῶν. This preposi-
tional phrase points to the fact that the single person in question was selected *out of* the whole company of the dead as the one to be raised up;
this was not (except in the sense about to be described) the resurrection
of the dead, but a resurrection *from* the dead. "Die νεκροί sind die Ge-
samtheit der Toten...die Totenwelt" (Conzelmann, ad loc.).

The hint at a selection from among a considerable number is
taken up in the next word, ἀπαρχή. In the New Testament this is pre-
eminently a Pauline word (in addition to Pauline passages see only
James 1:18; Rev 14:4; also perhaps 2 Thess 2:13, if this is not Pauline,
and if the original reading is not ἀπ' ἀρχῆς). In the present chapter it is
taken up, with unchanged meaning, in v. 23. In 16:15 the household of
Stephanas is described as the firstfruits of Achaea; in Rom 16:5 Epae-
netus is the firstfruits (unless again we are to read ἀπ' ἀρχῆς) of Asia.
In each of these two cases "first convert(s)" is meant; the first (and, we
may add, representative) member(s) of a group. These passages give a
sufficient explanation of ἀπαρχή as it is used here. Christ was the first,
and so far remains the only one, to be raised from the dead. Compare
Col 1:18; Rev 1:5: he is πρωτότοκος ἐκ [τῶν] νεκρῶν. Conzelmann
is unwilling to go further than this; but Paul could use the word in other
senses (e.g., Rom 8:23, the firstfruits (consisting) of the Spirit; 11:16, if
the firstfruits is holy so also is the lump), and these show, as is in any

case sufficiently probable, that Paul was aware of the use of the word in the Old Testament, so that occurrences of *reshith, terumah,* may have influenced him. At Passover, the firstfruit sheaf was offered on the day after the Sabbath that followed the feast (Lev 23:10f., ...you shall bring the sheaf of the firstfruits [*reshith*]) of your harvest to the priest, and he shall wave the sheaf before the Lord; on the morrow after the Sabbath [*mimohºrath ha-shabbath*] the priest shall wave it). This was to Christians Easter Day. Earlier in the epistle (5:7) Paul had written of Christ as τὸ πάσχα ἡμῶν, and it may be that he saw some analogy between the risen Christ and the sheaf which represented the offering to God, and thereby the sanctification of the whole crop, of which it was part. Philo allegorizes the same passage, though of course in a different sense (*de Spec. Leg.* 2. 163, The reason for this is that the Jewish nation is to the whole inhabited world what the priest is to the State). There is some attractiveness in the suggestion that Paul had this passage in mind, but if he had he must have been following the Sadducean interpretation of Lev 23:11 (the Sadducees, not unnaturally, took *shabbath* to mean Sabbath) rather than that of the Pharisees (who took it to mean the festival day—so also Philo, *de Spec. Leg.* 2.162; Josephus, *Ant.* 2.250; and the LXX, τῇ ἐπαύριον τῆς πρώτης). This is unlikely; Conzelmann is probably right.

Up to this point in the chapter the dead have been, six times, (οἱ) νεκροί; here they are οἱ κεκοιμημένοι (cf.v. 18, οἱ κοιμηθέν‐τες). The same perfect participle is used at 1 Thess 4:13, the aorist at 1 Thess 4:14,15 (cf. 1 Cor 7:39; 11:30 for the finite verb). Paul uses ἀποθνῄσκειν much more frequently (40 times; twice in Colossians), and it can hardly be a matter of accident that he prefers to use the image of sleep in passages where he is specifically affirming that there will be an awakening from death comparable with the daily awakening from sleep. We may be confident that the word is so used here: the risen Christ is the first of those who will awake from the sleep of death. A causal connection between Christ as the firstfruits and those who will rise subsequently is strongly hinted at, but we cannot say that it is directly stated, still less that it is proved. The argument so far has started from the factual, or allegedly factual, statement that Christ has been raised from the dead. This proves that the general possibility of resurrection cannot be ruled out; no one can say, ἀνάστασις νεκρῶν οὐκ ἔστιν. It is next stated, but not proved, that the resurrection of Christ was not, or is not in the end to be, a single isolated event. This is put in two ways: (a) Christ was raised as an ἀπαρχή; therefore there will be others; (b) the dead are now to be described as οἱ κεκοιμημένοι; therefore they may be expected to wake up (cf. Mark 5:39,41: οὐκ ἀ‐πέθανεν ἀλλὰ καθεύδει...σοὶ λέγω, ἔγειρε).

Before we go on to ask whether Paul can offer any sort of proof of what he has asserted one further question about the use of κοιμᾶσθαι must be considered. Does it apply to the dead in general, or only to dead Christians? It will be noted that in all the other passages (referred to above) it is either explicit or implicit that κοιμᾶσθαι is used of those who have died in the Lord—that is, of Christians. At v. 18 also this is explicit, οἱ κοιμηθέντες ἐν Χριστῷ. It seems very probable that the same will apply to v. 20. The question whether Paul has in this chapter anything to say about a general resurrection, applying to all, believers and unbelievers, may perhaps arise at v. 24, τὸ τέ-λος. The question does not arise in our verses, and in the chapter as a whole is at most a side issue. The problem with which Paul is wrestling is how the resurrection of One can become a ground for believing in the resurrection of many. An important step is taken in the next two verses.

Interest in the theme of resurrection arises through the fact of death—an observation sufficiently obvious but of first rate importance. An explanation of the origin of death will help the argument forward. Man cannot escape his mortality; his life in this world, as the Old Testament eventually discovered, cannot give a satisfactory account of the justice of God or of the victory of the good.[1] What then is the origin of death? Paul as a student of the Old Testament knew the answer to this question. "Through one man sin entered the world, and through sin death" (Rom 5:12). The next words of this verse present difficult grammatical and exegetical problems into which, fortunately, there is no need here to go in detail. The first man sinned, and through his sin death entered the world; the man died. Paul was probably thinking of Gen 2:17, "In the day that thou eatest thereof thou shalt surely die", and of the fulfilment, after the disobedient eating of the forbidden fruit, of that warning: "Dust thou art, and to dust thou shalt return" (Gen 3:19). Other Jewish writers took up the theme. "You gave him your one commandment to obey; he disobeyed it, and thereupon you made him subject to death, him and his descendants" (2 Esdras 3:7). "Adam sinned and death was decreed against those who should be born" (2 Bar 23:4). "There is none of the earthborn who has not dealt wickedly, and among those that exist who has not sinned" (4 Ezra 8:35). Thus, *by man came death* (as the result of sin; cf. vv. 17, 56); death originating with one disobedient man spreads from that one to the many. We may now turn back to Rom 5:12. Death reached (διῆλθεν εἰς) all men; all men sinned. The two features of man's existence, death and sin, were both inseparable and universal, so that though any subsequent individual might rail against Adam as the cause of his mortality ("O thou Adam, what hast thou done? For though it was thou that sinned, the fall was not thine alone, but ours also who are thy descendants!" (4 Ezra 7:118) he could not deny that death was the just punishment of his misdeeds ("For how does it profit us that the eternal age is promised to us, whereas we have done the works that bring death?" (4 Ezra 7:119). Just punishment, and indeed punishment necessary and inevitable, for as Paul makes very clear (so that there is no need here to set out the evidence) sin has its roots in an alienation from God, which though it results in moral evil originates in a pre-moral rebellion of the creature against his Creator. In being alienated from God man is alienated from the only source of life and is therefore subject to death. This line of argument, however, naturally suggests, at least in theory, the possibility of a reverse process. Suppose there were a man who achieved, corresponding to Adam's act of transgression (παράπτωμα), an act of righteousness (δικαίωμα, Rom 5:18); who instead of disobedience (παρακοή) offered to God a perfect obedience (ὑπακοή, Rom 5:19); who instead of counting life lived on equal terms with God a prize at which he must at all costs snatch chose rather the form of a servant and became obedient even unto death; who in consequence, instead of being made subject to beings and forces over which he should have ruled, was exalted so as to become the universal κύριος (Phil 2:5-11): suppose there were such a man, might it not be that, as death passed from one man to mankind as a whole, so resurrection would pass from this new man to a new plurality? Of course, it is not to be suggested that Paul's mind moved in this direction; it moved in precisely the opposite direction, not by way of speculative theology to the fact—or hope, or dream—of a new man who should reverse the work of the old, but from the realized fact to the theological explanation of the fact. Paul, however, chooses, not unnaturally, to set out his thought in chronological form. Death was sent into the world by God, but he sent it on the occasion and as the result of a human act; it thus came into the world δι᾽ ἀνθρώπου. Resurrection would come into the world only as God's gift, but it was appropriate that it should come in the same way, δι᾽ ἀνθρώπου. We shall see in a moment that it was not only appropriate but necessary that resurrection should come in this way. Paul does not say, As by man came death, by man came also life; this would be an inadequate statement. The given condition being universal death, what is needed is not simply life but resurrection.[2] In any case, this is in line with the argument that has led up to this point. This has shown that the resurrection of Jesus—the historic fact from which the whole train of thought proceeds—has made it possible to conceive resurrection in general though it has not proved that resurrection in general will happen.

The most important point to observe in relation to v. 21, with its twofold invocation of an ἄνθρωπος, is the connection between sin and death, righteousness and life. Death arises not from some natural mortality, the fact that human organs will after a time wear out; it comes from sin. It is because man sinned that the whole race is subject to death. If the process is to be reversed it must be reversed as a whole, and sin must be replaced by righteousness. But if righteousness is to be more than an abstraction it must be expressed in the righteous act, the δικαίωμα, of a man; only a man can offer to God an obedience to neutralize the disobedience of the man Adam. Thus Paul's argument builds up. It would however be mistaken to make much of the causality inherent in the construction of the verse, ἐπειδή...καί. ³ The degree of causality implied is reduced by the absence of a verb in both halves of the sentence, and the main point is the parallelism brought out by the repetition of δι᾽ ἀνθρώπου, which expresses that which Adam and Christ have in common; however they may differ in other respects, both are men. It was (to use the word I have already employed) appropriate that what was done by one man should be undone by another. It is so much the less likely that Paul intends any great measure of causality in v. 21 in that when he moves on to v. 22 he changes the construction, which now becomes the simple comparison, ὥσπερ...οὕτως καί. Since the main point is a simple parallelism it is unlikely that speculations about a Primal Man, or a god Anthropos, play any significant part here. We shall have to give more attention to these possibilities when we come to the second passage, vv. 45-49. Paul's thought develops as the chapter proceeds; the second passage does not simply repeat the first. We shall have to ask what the differences are, and what is their cause.

In v. 22 the word ἄνθρωπος disappears and the two men are identified by name; that is, the new verse, in contrast with v. 21, emphasises the difference rather than the resemblance between them. The parallelism remains, but it is even more clearly an antithetical parallelism. The two are named as Adam and Christ. Christ, as counterpart to Adam, is clearly a name rather than a title or office. Each has the article, ἐν τῷ Ἀδάμ, ἐν τῷ Χριστῷ. I noted earlier that so far in this chapter Χριστός has usually appeared without an article; does the different usage here suggest that we have in vv. 21-22 a prepauline traditional formulation?

> Since by man came death,
> By man came also the resurrection of the dead.
> For as in Adam all die,
> Even so in Christ shall all be made alive.

There is as good a case for prepauline formulation here as in many other passages where this has been alleged, but I see in the verses nothing that is clearly unpauline, and a good deal that is definitely Pauline, not least the contrasting interpretation of the figures of Adam and Christ. The verses fit, as we have seen and shall continue to see, into the general line of the argument, and there seems to be little ground for thinking that Paul did not himself write them specifically for the purpose they fulfill here. If the style is exalted and poetical, the theme is a lofty one, and Paul was capable of writing impressively.

All die (ἀποθνήσκουσιν) corresponds to the reference to death in v. 21; *all shall be made alive* (ζωοποιηθήσονται) to the reference to the resurrection of the dead. ζωοποιεῖν is a Pauline word (Rom 4:17; 8:11; 1 Cor 15:36, 45; 2 Cor 3:6; Gal 3:21), but the use of it here, in the future tense, is important because, unlike the verbless clause in v. 21, it enables Paul to make clear that he is thinking of a future event. All die; that is a fact of present experience. All shall be made alive; this is an event that is yet to come. All die, because of sin, the negative relation of mankind with God that has obtained since the time of Adam; all shall be made alive, because this negative relation has now been changed into the positive relation of righteousness—men are δίκαιοι by justification.[4]

Two related questions call for consideration before we leave this paragraph. (1) In what sense does Paul use πάντες? It is undoubtedly true that in the present state of mankind all men die, as did even Jesus Christ himself. Does Paul similarly assert that every human being, after passing through death, will be made alive? If so, he is either including non-Christians in his statement, or implying that at some point in the future all will have become Christians. Or does he mean only that all those who are ἐν τῷ Χριστῷ, that is, all Christians, will be raised up and given life? This question is related to the second, so that it will be convenient to discuss them together.

(2) How does Paul use the preposition ἐν? Again, on the side of Adam the problem is not severe. The whole human race is mortal. Adam—*adam*—is man; he is sentenced to death, and man generically dies.[5] *In* Adam may mean no more than this; it could refer to the seminal identity of the whole human race, all of whom could be said to be, however distantly, in the man Adam who was the father of all, so that they shared the death sentence that was passed on him. Related to this is the notion of a transmissible corruption, passed on from one generation to another. Alternatively, ἐν might have an instrumental sense; in this case ἐν τῷ Ἀδάμ would differ little from δι' ἀνθρώπου. If, however, ἐν τῷ Ἀδάμ was a phrase modelled on the basis of the already existing ἐν (τῷ) Χριστῷ, it will involve more than the necessary hereditary relationship; an element of choice, of decision, will be included. Men have taken Adam's side, they have joined the revolt against God, and for that reason die. This is (very nearly if not quite) the meaning of Rom 5:12: εἰς πάντας ἀνθρώπους ὁ θάνατος διῆλθεν ἐφ' ᾧ πάντες ἥμαρτον. What then of ἐν τῷ Χριστῷ? A full examination of the New Testament use of the phrase is clearly impossible here, but it is a common formula (though more usually anarthrous) in Paul, and expresses comprehensively the relation between Christ and the believer. It is eschatological rather than mystical[6]—an observation that fits the present verse well. Those are *in Christ* who are so united with him by faith that they die with him (Rom 6:8; see also below), and thus embark on the eschatological process which leads through the messianic affliction into the age to come. The process is not complete; hence the future, ζωοποιηθήσονται.

Does the promise of life refer to the whole human race? The order of words suggests that it does. ἐν τῷ Χριστῷ stands first adverbially: in this way, by this means, in virtue of this relationship. The rest of the sentence follows: all shall be made alive. Is it conceivable that Paul, who elsewhere (e.g. 1 Cor 1:18) writes of those who are perishing, οἱ ἀπολλύμενοι, should mean this? It seems improbable. The alternative is that ἐν τῷ Χριστῷ, was, notwithstanding the order of words, intended to limit πάντες: not *all* absolutely, but all who are in Christ. It may be that Paul was led by the parallelism with ἐν τῷ ᾿Αδάμ to write ἐν τῷ Χριστῷ πάντες when what he meant was πάντες οἱ ἐν τῷ Χριστῷ. Paul does sometimes appear to misplace words.

Again we must pause to note the point that Paul has reached in his exposition, and consider where he will go next. (1) He has made the point that no one who accepts the resurrection of Christ can assert that ἀνάστασις νεκρῶν οὐκ ἔστιν, for with one resurrection he has allowed in principle the general possibility of resurrection. (2) He has claimed that Christ's resurrection was in fact the first stage in a wider event; he was raised as an ἀπαρχή. (3) He has shown that the negative parallelism between Adam and Christ (which rests ultimately upon his belief that Christ is God's justifying agent) suggests that like Adam Christ was a representative person, so that as Adam's transgression led to sin and death for all who were in him, so Christ's act of righteousness led to justification and life for all who are in him. It will follow that there is a possibility, and more than a possibility, that Christians will be raised up.

This position is exposed to the comment: True. There is a resurrection of Christians, and it has already happened. This could very nearly be inferred from Paul's own words in Rom 6. We have died to sin (6:2); we were baptized into Christ's death (6:3); we were buried with him through baptism into death (6:4); we have been planted with him in the likeness of his death (6:5); our old man has been crucified with him (6:6); we died with Christ (6:8). Balancing these statements about the Christian's death are others that refer to life. How shall we any longer live in sin? (6:2); as Christ was raised from the dead through the glory of the Father so we also should walk in newness of life (6:4); we shall be planted with him in the likeness of his resurrection (6:5); we believe that we shall also live with him (6:8). A moment's examination of the passages shows, however, that whereas death is repeatedly referred to in past tenses (ἀπεθάνομεν, and the like), resurrection is referred to in the future, or in the subjunctive mood (ὅπως περιπατήσωμεν, συζήσομεν). The difference can hardly be accidental.[7] Certainly Paul believed that Christians experienced a new life through and in Christ; if we bear about in our body the νέκρωσις of Jesus it is that his life also may be manifested in our body (2 Cor 4:10); but the care with which Paul expresses himself shows that resurrection proper belongs to the future. In Rom 6:11 the believer must *consider himself* to be dead to sin and alive to righteousness; literal death and resurrection belong to the future. This was a point that Paul had reason to emphasize in Corinth, where there evidently was a tendency to think that the whole of Christian salvation had already been experienced (1 Cor 4:8). Does this mean (as has often been thought) that the error behind 1 Cor 15 was that of Hymenaeus and Philetus (2 Tim 2:18), the belief that ἀ-νάστασιν ἤδη γεγονέναι?

In the circumstances that I have described this is a possibility that must be taken very seriously.[8] Yet it is not entirely satisfactory, since there is a difference between asserting that resurrection has already happened, so that no resurrection remains in the future, and asserting that there is no resurrection at all. It is true, and this strongly supports the suggestion that there were Corinthians who embraced an error that was an anticipation of that of Hymenaeus and Philetus, that Paul's next step is to look into the future. In Christ shall all be made alive (v. 22); true, but not all at once; each will be quickened in his own order. Christ himself comes first, as ἀπαρχή (the word is repeated in v. 23); then, ἔπειτα, those who belong to Christ, not immediately but at his (future) coming (v. 23).

It is true and important that Paul in this context affirms not only the fact but the futurity of resurrection—it will happen, that is, when any ordinary person would expect it to happen. It is possible that "There is no resurrection" is a loose way of saying, "There is no resurrection still to come"; even so, it would be interesting to know what those who held this view (and they were Christians—v. 12) made of death and of the question what happened next. We may recall Justin's reference (*Trypho* 80) to those false Christians who thought that the future would see the souls of Christians translated at death immediately to heaven, without resurrection; such a belief could well accompany the anticipated eschatology that the Corinthians appear to have maintained, but maintained without the use of the language of resurrection. They may have held that Christians do enter upon a new life now and at death do not perish, but that neither now nor in the future is there anything that can be called resurrection. This could issue in the proposition, There is no resurrection. It does however seem (from the rest of the chapter) that Paul understood the persons in question to maintain that death was the end; it is possible (and we shall return to this question) that he may not have fully understood what they meant, but it is on the whole safer to assume that any failure to understand what was going on in Corinth is to be found with us rather than with Paul.

To return briefly to the sequence of vv. 22, 23, and the following verses: there is no doubt that Paul is concerned to place the resurrection in the future; presumably he believed that it was important to emphasize this point. Death will be destroyed as the last enemy of all to succumb to the power of Christ (v. 26). We should note in passing the use of both Ps 110:1 and Ps 8:7. The two Psalms speak in very similar language of the subjection of enemies, or of all things, under the feet of one whom New Testament writers (not only Paul) take to be Christ. This means the association of Christ as heavenly Lord with the term Son of man, which will prove to be significant when we reach vv. 45-49. The main theme however of vv. 23-34 is that Christian life and Christian rites make no sense except in the context of a future guaranteed by God himself. Practical considerations are introduced to enforce the argument; but all this is to be considered in its own right on another occasion.

There is no point in being a Christian if the dead are not raised; but this does not stifle questionings, which at this point (unless, as is possible though not probable, we are to think of them as simply doubts arising in Paul's own mind) will probably have come from Greek philosophical, or gnostic, sources. If dead men are to be raised up (and ἀνιστάναι, ἀνάστασις, ἐγείρειν, can be understood in a very literal sense) what becomes of their bodies? ποίῳ σώματι ἔρχονται; Paul's answer lies in the observation that there are several different kinds of body made of different kinds of flesh, each appropriate for the purpose for which God has designed it—flesh of fish for swimming, flesh of birds for flying, and so forth. The distinction to be used here, however, is that between σῶμα ψυχικόν and σῶμα πνευματικόν, the former appropriate to the present life before death, the latter to the life that will be lived after the parousia (cf. v. 50).[9] The distinction is a very convenient way of dealing with the problem and gives a clear answer to the question, ποίῳ σώματι; namely, σώματι πνευματικῷ. But Paul's partner in discussion will naturally ask where the expression comes from, what it means, and how Paul knows that there is such a thing as a σῶμα πνευματικόν. It is here that the figure of Adam is re-introduced, on the basis of the statement in Gen 2:7: *way^ehi ha^2adam l^enephesh ḥayyah*, καὶ ἐγένετο ὁ ἄνθρωπος εἰς ψυχὴν ζῶσαν.

The statement that Adam became a living ψυχή immediately supplies a link with the word ψυχικόν. Paul adds to this quotation the adjective πρῶτος and the name Adam. In the LXX the Hebrew' *adam* is properly rendered ἄνθρωπος; Paul needs the name (which he has already used in v. 22) in order to prepare for what he is to say next. He also needs the adjective πρῶτος since here (differing in this respect from v. 22) he intends not to use Christ as the counterpart to Adam but to speak of a *last* Adam. Thus he writes, The first man Adam became a living soul.[10] This (emended) quotation has taken Paul part way towards the justification of his ψυχικόν – πνευματικόν contrast, but only part way. He now adds to his quotation the parallel clause, ὁ ἔσχατος Ἀδάμ [ἐγένετο] εἰς πνεῦμα ζωοποιοῦν.[11] What is Paul's authority for this parallel statement? Is there any sense in which it can be regarded as an inference from or exposition of the text? It seems more probable that Paul is bringing ideas to his text than that he is deriving them from it.[12] For him, always, Jesus is a given historical fact rather than an inference from Scripture, though he regularly, as here, describes the historical fact in language based upon the Old Testament and makes use of concepts derived from the Old Testament. It will be necessary shortly to say something about speculations of Paul's time relating to the creation narratives and Primal Man, but it is important not to underestimate the effect of a straightforward reading of Gen 1-3, in which all the basic terms appear and are plainly related to one another: not only man, sin, and death, but also *nephesh –ψυχή, ruah– πνεῦμα, nᵉshama—πνοή*. An acute mind reflecting on these data, and on the questions of continuity and discontinuity in human existence raised by a firm insistence on σῶμα as the vehicle of man's life, could move a very long way towards the content and formulation of v. 45 without any additional pressure from contemporary speculation.

Before we leave v. 45 another question must be asked. The second clause in the verse lacks a verb. It is natural, and certainly correct, to supply the verb contained in the first, ἐγένετο, and to read, The last Adam became a lifegiving Spirit. We may ask, When did the last Adam become a lifegiving Spirit? There is no doubt that Paul is referring to Christ; what point of time does he have in mind? There are three possibilities (excluding, what otherwise would be attractive, the possibility that Paul is thinking of the parousia; if he had been referring to the future he would have had to supply a verb): the origin of the pre-existent heavenly man; the incarnation; the resurrection. None can be ruled out as completely impossible, but the last is the most likely, since for Paul it is with the resurrection that the lifegiving work of Christ begins.

So then v. 45 can be satisfactorily explained on the basis of the Old Testament alone; this observation however cannot be so convincingly applied to v. 46. The two adjectives appear in the neuter gender, τὸ πνευματικόν, τὸ ψυχικόν; that is, they are not applied in direct relation to the masculine noun ἄνθρωπος, though this is the substantive of the preceding sentence and of the following one, and cannot be entirely out of mind. The neuter noun in the context is σῶμα, and what Paul says in v. 46 must apply to this. He is however stating a matter of general principle: the natural precedes the spiritual, and not vice versa. Paul makes the point so emphatically, stating it first negatively and then positively, that it seems certain that he must be deliberately correcting the opposite view: the spiritual precedes the natural. There are two main areas in which this position was taken.

Of these, the first is in regard to the creation of man, and since Paul has just quoted Gen 2:7 it seems probable that this will have played at least some part in his thought. It is well known that Philo distinguished between the two accounts of the creation of man in Gen 1 and 2; a full account of his exegesis is impossible here but some fundamental passages must be quoted. In *Leg. Alleg.* 1:31f. Philo interprets the two (P and JE) accounts in terms of a Platonic world-view. Commenting on Gen 2:7 he says: "There are two types of men; the one a heavenly man (οὐράνιος ἄνθρωπος cf. v. 48, ἐπουράνιος), the other an earthly (γήϊνος). The heavenly man, being made after the image (κατ᾽ εἰκόνα, Gen 1:27) of God is altogether without part or lot in corruptible (φθαρτῆς; cf. 1 Cor 15:42,50,52,53,54) and terrestrial substance; but the earthly one was compacted out of the matter scattered here and there, which Moses calls 'clay' (χοῦν; cf. 1 Cor 15:48,49, χοϊκός). For this reason he says that the heavenly man was not moulded, but was stamped with the image of God; while the earthly is a moulded work of the Artificer (τοῦ τεχνίτου), but not His offspring. We must account the man made out of the earth to be mind mingling with, but not yet blended with (εἰσκρινόμενον...οὔπω δ᾽εἰσκεκριμένον), body. But this earthlike mind is in reality also corruptible, were not God to breathe into it a power of real life; when He does so, it does not any more undergo moulding, but becomes a soul (ψυχήν), not an inefficient and imperfectly formed soul but one endowed with mind (νοεράν) and actually alive; for he says, 'man became a living soul'." The relation of this to the man of Gen 1:26 is made clear in De Opif. 69. "Right well does he say this, for nothing earth-born is more like God than man. Let no one represent the likeness (ἐμφέρειαν) as one to a bodily form; for neither is God in human form, nor is the human body Godlike. No, it is in respect of the Mind (νοῦν), the sovereign element of the soul, that the word 'image' is used; for after the pattern of a single Mind, even the Mind of the Universe as an archetype, the mind in each of those who successively came into being was moulded." Philo's thought here rests on a base of Platonism; and it must be acknowledged that the order of Gen 1; 2, with εἰκών in chapter 1 and χόος in chapter 2, suits his purpose well. We cannot say what account Paul, who evidently rejects the Platonizing interpretation of Philo, would have given of the two Genesis creation narratives and of their relation to each other. His use of the neuter adjectives, which we have already observed as meaning that he is not speaking simply of the two "men," recalls to some extent Philo's argument in De Opif. 25: "Now if the part [Philo is referring to man] is an image of an image, it is manifest that the whole is so too, and if the whole creation, this entire world perceived by our senses (ὁ σύμπας αἰσθητὸς οὑτοσὶ κόσμος) (seeing that it is greater than any human image) is a copy of the Divine image, it is manifest that the archetypal seal (ἡ ἀρχέτυπος σφραγίς) also, which we aver to be the world descried by the mind (νοητὸν...κόσμον), would be the very Word of God (ὁ θεοῦ λόγος)" Cf. 134.

To say that Paul was simply rejecting a Platonic world-view (and I recognize that I have myself come near to saying this in the past) would go too far, though there is no reason (even if he had not himself read Philo) why he should not have been aware of, and rejected, the sort of understanding of creation that we have considered. The matter may not, however, have been so simple. In the first place, Philo's interpretation of Gen 1; 2 was more complex, and betrays, as much of his philosophizing does, a strong moral interest. This is well brought out by B. A. Pearson,[13] who cites other passages where Philo uses Gen 2:7. Of these perhaps the most important is *Quod Det. Pot.* 80-85, where Philo deals with the apparently contradictory statements that the element of life is blood (e.g. Lev 17:11), and that it was πνεῦμα that made man a living soul (Gen 2:7). The conclusion is that ἕκαστον ἡμῶν κατὰ τὰς προσεχεῖς τομὰς ἀριθμῷ δύο εἶναι συμβέβηκε, ζῷόν τε καὶ ἄνθρωπον (82). Hence the moral conflict in man; hence also the mortal and immortal elements in man which recall, though they are by no means identical with, Paul's σῶμα ψυχικόν and σῶμα πνευματικόν.

The second area we must consider is expressed in the related claim that in v. 46 Paul is rejecting the gnostic "Behauptung, das Pneumatische sei älter als das Psychische," which W. Schmithals[14] describes as "prägnantester Ausdruck des gesamten gnostischen Selbstverständnisses." That which is spiritual comes first, is primary existence; this has come to be imprisoned in the material, ψυχικόν, body; the salvation for which man longs is the release of the primary element from the secondary. As Schmithals rightly adds (p. 137), "Die Vorordnung des Pneumatischen vor das Psychische bedeutet ja das Ende der Predigt von Busse und Gnade, während umgekehrt die Nachstellung des Pneumatischen von dem Wissen getragen ist, dass das im Geschenk des Pneuma mitgeteilte Leben die freie Gabe Gottes ist, der sich zu dem sündigen und verlorenen Fleisch hinabneigt".

There is much of value in these observations, but I do not think that we have yet reached the heart of Paul's thought. As the following verses, and the whole apocalyptic framework of chapter 15, show, Paul is concerned (as Schmithals in the last quotation clearly hints) with a mobile, not a static scene. For him no metaphysical world-view is so important as the fact that, when the fullness of the time came, God, in fulfilment of his Old Testament promises, sent forth his Son, who, after a life on earth, was crucified and rose from the dead; who is yet to come in glory, gathering about him the living and the raised up elect. Was he really dealing with the crude criticism of the notion of resurrection, that if all dead bodies stood up again in their earthly form the earth would be able neither to contain nor to sustain them? This question must be answered on the basis of vv. 35-44; there is no sign in our verses that Paul was concerned with this. He is developing a different point: the transformation that men will undergo at the resurrection corresponds not to a transformation that Christ may have undergone at his (of this, Paul says nothing), but to a transference from the family of Adam to the family of Christ.

The crucial question arises in v. 47. The first half of this verse takes up again the Genesis creation narrative, in which Paul does not distinguish between but assimilates the two sources (Gen 1; Gen 2): ὁ πρῶτος ἄνθρωπος ἐκ γῆς χοϊκός. This is still the first man, Adam, of v. 45, and it will follow that the second half of v. 47 maintains the parallelism and describes the ἔσχατος 'Αδάμ.[15] This time he is the δεύτερος ἄνθρωπος, and is said to be ἐξ οὐρανοῦ. It is to be understood that the man who comes from heaven is not only ἐπουράνιος (vv. 48, 49), but πνευματικός; otherwise the paragraph loses logical cohesion. But why does Paul move from the expected *spiritual* to *heavenly*? There seems to be nothing in Gen 1; 2 to suggest the change, and one has to look for some other influence that may have affected Paul's thought. Philo indeed, as we have seen, referred to an οὐράνιος ἄν– θρωπος; but Paul has deliberately and emphatically turned away from Philo's approach. Philo's heavenly man came first, in a Platonic sense; it is Paul's δεύτερος ἄνθρωπος who is ἐξ οὐρανοῦ and is in consequence described as ἐπουράνιος. Similar considerations rule out most kinds of Urmensch speculation, which in any case have little definiteness in them. No suggestion seems to me so probable as that behind Paul's second man, last Adam, there lies the eschatological man of Dan 7:13. To turn aside here into a full discussion of Daniel's vision, together with other references to it in the New Testament and contemporary literature, is impossible. The following relevant points may however be briefly made.

(*a*) Paul knew very well that *bar* ꜣ*enash* meant ἄνθρωπος, that one described as *kᵉbar*ꜣᵉ*nash* meant a human figure, distinguished by his humanness from the beasts of the preceding vision. He must also have been aware of the other significant references in Daniel to beings " having the appearance of a man" (8:15,16,17; 9:21; 10:5,11,16,18,19; 12:6, 7).

(*b*) The human figure is described as moving ᶜ*im* ᶜᵃ*naney* shᵉ-*mayya*, ἐπὶ τῶν νεφελῶν τοῦ οὐρανοῦ; that is, whether, he is thought of as *coming* or *going* he may reasonably be described as ἐπ–ουράνιος.

(*c*) The human figure is in some sense (and it is not necessary here to inquire in what sense) representative. When he receives a kingdom, the people of the saints of the Most High receive a kingdom (Dan 7:18, 27).

(*d*) His appearance belongs to the future, to the time of the end.

(*e*) There is some evidence, though not much, for the identification of the rabbinic ᵃ*naney* the Cloud man, with the Messiah.[16]

(f) Most important is the general rabbinic interpretation of Dan 7:13; for which see Casey, op.cit., 80-90. Casey is concerned to play down the messianic interpretation, but recognizes that "the corporate view is outnumbered by the messianic" (89). It is not necessary to suppose that there was a "Son of man concept" (92) in Judaism. Paul does not claim, or suggest, that he is drawing upon a recognized concept. Nothing in fact is necessary beyond the supposition that he had read Daniel; and of that there can be little doubt.

(g) The vindication of the people of God signalled by the man-like figure includes the resurrection of at least some of them. ὑψωθή-σεται πᾶς ὁ λαός...καὶ πολλοὶ τῶν καθευδόντων (cf. Paul's use of κοιμᾶσθαι at 1 Cor 15:21)...ἀναστήσονται.

(h) Dan 7:13 figured in the gospel tradition. This point must be made with caution, for we do not know, and cannot here investigate, at what stage Dan 7:13 entered the tradition. It would be wrong to assume that it was used by Jesus, though for my part I think it probably was. Again, one must be careful not to overestimate Paul's knowledge of the tradition.

(i) Casey dismisses the suggestion that 1 Cor 15:47 is to be linked with Dan 7:13 on grounds that are surely quite inadequate (151f.). He fails to explain the use of ἐξ οὐρανοῦ, ἐπουράνιος—indeed he makes no attempt to do so. Why, after vv. 45, 46, does Paul not continue to say πνευματικός?

(j) If Paul is using Dan 7 he has the strongest reason for rejecting Philo's order and his Platonism. The figure of Dan 7 is nothing if not eschatological. He belongs to the time when, after all the horrors that the four evil beasts have brought with them, God finally ends the struggle in favor of his saints.

By using Dan 7 Paul accomplished several things at the same time. He changed (and the polemic of v. 46 shows that he knew that he was making a change) the time-scheme and implied world-view of Gen 1-2 as understood by Philo in an apocalyptic sense; that is, he firmly fixed resurrection in the future. He established the way in which Jesus is to be thought of as the Man, and his position vis-à-vis Adam: his presence signalizes salvation, not in the gnostic manner but as deliverance from sin and death. He also found scriptural authority for the belief that Jesus like Adam was a representative person, for the Son of man in Dan 7 represents the people of the saints of the Most High. In fact Paul has in this passage adopted both interpretations of the human figure, the messianic and the corporate, for it is clear that the heavenly Man is Jesus Christ, and equally clear that as the ἐπουράνιος he is inseparable from the ἐπουράνιοι who bear the same image. This is important because it brings together the two elements that compose, in their relation with each other, the theme of this paper, in which we are inquiring into the relation between the Adam-Christ typology and the resurrection. There is an inherent eschatology embedded in the Adam myth, for this contains the promise that the woman's seed will finally overcome the serpent, through whose guile man was robbed of his innocence and his immortality. Adam considered on his own could lead only to a completely pessimistic view of history, and the only escape from such pessimism is in the hope of a second Adam.

V. 48 places with the χοϊκός, who must be Adam, the χοϊκοί, and with the ἐπουράνιος, who must be Christ, the ἐπουράνιοι. This verse does not itself make clear what is meant by the two plural adjectives; they could be understood in terms of a gnostic determinism, setting over against each other the ὑλικοί and the πνευματικοί: there are those who are destined to sin and die like Adam, and there those who are destined to be righteous and to live, like Christ. That this is not Paul's meaning does not become clear till we reach v. 49, where it appears that "we"—Paul and his correspondents, the Christians—belong to both groups. We bore, ἐφορέσαμεν, the image of the earthy man. The aorist can hardly mean that we bore this image only at a single point in time; it is perhaps best thought of as an inceptive aorist. When we came into the world we took up the image of the earthy man. The life that we entered upon was Adam's life, characterized by the same physical limitations, marked by sin, and bounded as a deserved conclusion by death. We still live this life, of which the constituents are flesh and blood, and whose destiny is φθορά (v.50). But we—the same we—shall bear (φορέσομεν, future, not the subjunctive φορέσωμεν) the image of the heavenly Man; that is, of Christ. We shall see that this new life is taken up in the next paragraph; for the present we must note the use of the word εἰκών, which Paul uses elsewhere at 2 Cor 4:4 (cf. Col 1:15). In a context which is based primarily on Gen 1-3, *image* must be at least in part related to the use of the word in Gen 1:27, but it is not identical with this, and probably owes something to the Wisdom concept which is certainly in mind in 2 Cor 4:4. See also Col 3:10 for the closest parallel: the new man is renewed in the image of him who created him.

When do *we* assume this new image? To what point does the future tense apply? The language of v. 49 is not sufficient in itself to enable us to answer this question, and we can do so only by looking ahead into the next paragraph. The key phrase is in v. 51, πάντες δὲ ἀλλαγησόμεθα. The force of this is independent of the argument of Jeremias,[17] that, in v. 50, σὰρξ καὶ αἷμα refers to living human beings, and φθορά to the dead, though this is probably correct. Those who, at the coming of the Son of man, are still living cannot hope, being what they are, to inherit the kingdom of God. Those who, when that time comes, are already in the corruption of death, cannot hope, being what they are, to inherit incorruption. What will happen to any individual we do not know. We know, by the apocalyptic mystery that Paul is disclosing (v. 51), that not all will sleep (cf. v. 20) in death; but all, if they are to participate in the future planned by God, will be transformed. The dead will be raised so as to be ἄφθαρτοι; and we (Paul assumes that he will be one of the survivors) shall be changed. This will be the moment of ultimate triumph, when we bear the image of the heavenly man but for the moment we must go no further. This material will be dealt with later in the week.

What then can we say about the chapter as a whole, viewed from the two Adam-Christ passages which are our special responsibility in this session? The main point is quite clear. The Corinthians cannot deny, unless they choose to deny the Christian faith altogether, that Christ rose from the dead. This is the testimony of a variety of witnesses who all claim that they have actually seen Jesus alive after his death and burial, and it has been from the beginning a fundamental feature of all Christian preaching; of Paul's preaching but equally of the preaching of those who in many respects were his opponents. It was this preaching that the Corinthians accepted when they became Christians. The testimony and the preaching do not prove (in the sense of strict historical proof) that Jesus is alive; still less can they prove that (as Paul says) God raised him from the dead; God's action is not susceptible of this kind of proof. But they do prove that anyone who claims to be a Christian accepts Christ's resurrection. Therefore no Christian can say, ἀνάστασις νεκρῶν οὐκ ἔστιν. To claim however that one person, Jesus of Nazareth, was raised from the dead says nothing about any other person, beyond affirming bare possibility. I have deliberately said here, Jesus of Nazareth. Paul however says regularly not Jesus but Christ; that is, though he is not (see above) thinking in purely Jewish Messianic terms, he is thinking of Jesus as the one appointed by God to the supreme work of restoring the human race to the position for which it was created. Paul characteristically uses such "office" terms as a context requires, and here he moves rapidly to parallelism with Adam, in the latter of the two passages speaking explicitly of Christ as the last Adam, the second man, the man from heaven, that is, the human figure of Dan 7. Here too, of course, we have assertion rather than proof. It would be possible to reply, No; the Christ is a unique, not a representative figure. We cannot infer from his resurrection the resurrection of others. Paul's exegetical answer to this objection is that the last Adam is prophetically depicted in Dan 7:13 and is there said to be a representative and inclusive figure connected with the resurrection at the end of time. At the end of time: so the general resurrection belongs to the future. Christ is the only one for whom it has already happened; for the rest of mankind it is still to come, and its unfolding is a mystery. Only at the last day when the trumpet sounds will the dead be raised incorruptible and the survivors changed.

There is a close relation between vv. 20-22 and vv. 45-49; it could not be otherwise, since each turns upon a parallelism between Christ and Adam. Each passage argues that Christ is a representative person, and that it is therefore possible to move from his resurrection, which is assumed as an event in the past by all Christian preaching and believing, to the future resurrection of at least all those who are in him. It must always be borne in mind that, in Paul's view, death entered the world through sin, and that it is through Christ's dying for our sins

(1 Cor 15:3) that the possibility of resurrection arises, and precisely so far as sin has been overcome. This conviction is common to the two passages, and unites them. Yet they stand apart from each other, and in different contexts. This gives an important clue to the much disputed Corinthian error. It seems that there was not one error but two. The first Paul states bluntly in v. 12.There are those who say, ἀνάστασις νεκρῶν οὐκ ἔστιν. I suspect that this assertion was made but loosely expressed, that those who made it did not mean to deny the resurrection of Christ (οὕτως ἐπιστεύσατε:15:11), but a subsequent resurrection of others. The second error asks, πῶς ἐγείρονται οἱ νεκροί; ποίῳ δὲ σώματι ἔρχονται; This has often been taken as a sceptical question, designed to disprove the notion of resurrection by a reductio ad absurdum. It may however have been a quite genuine inquiry, leading, in Corinth, to the conclusion, The dead indeed are raised, but they are raised ἐκτὸς τοῦ σώματος, or χωρὶς τοῦ σώματος (2 Cor 12:2, 3). In his discussion of this point Paul is led on, as we have seen, to touch on a variety of issues, but his central concern in vv. 45-49 is to prove the proposition stated in v. 44b: εἰ ἔστιν σῶμα ψυχικόν, ἔστιν καὶ σῶμα πνευματικόν. The proof is scriptural: οὕτως καὶ γέγραπται ; and it consists in the quotation of Gen 2:7, elaborated in targumic fashion and interpreted in the light of Dan 7:13. There is no kind of existence independent of σῶμα; the two primal men, the first Adam and the last, had each of them a σῶμα, but their bodies are distinguished as ψυχικόν and πνευματικόν. We all share the likeness of the earthy man; salvation, without which resurrection is unthinkable, with which resurrection is certain, means that we come to share also the image of the heavenly Man.

Recognition that there were in Corinth two errors regarding resurrection solves a number of problems in 1 Cor 15. It explains the lay-out of the chapter, with its two references to the Adam-Christ relationship and its two apocalypses. It explains the unexpected break between v. 34 and v. 35. It explains the fact that the practical moral consequences of Christian belief are drawn in the middle of the chapter, with only a distant echo at the end in v. 58. Above all it explains the difficulty that generations of expositors have found in defining the Corinthian error. Was it a total denial of future life? Was it a preference for immortality over resurrection? Did Paul fail to understand what his opponents were saying? How is the resurrection error to be integrated into the Corinthian theology as a whole? All these questions, which can only be seriously dealt with on the basis of a study of the whole chapter and not of eight verses only, may, I believe, be illuminated by this hypothesis.

NOTES

1. "There are two passages in the Old Testament [Isa 26:19; Dan 12:2] which certainly and indubitably refer to a resurrection of the dead, and in each case it is the demand for justice which is the deciding factor". N. H. Snaith, *S.J.T.* 17 (1964), 317; see the whole paper, "Justice and Immortality," 309-324.

2. Cf. Gal 3:21; the defect of the law was that it was unable ζωοποιῆσαι.

3. H. Conzelmann, *Der erste Brief an die Korinther*, KEK (Göttingen 1969), ad loc. Also U. Wilckens, *Weisheit und Torheit*, BhTh 26 (Tübingen 1959), 29.

4. Snaith, op. cit., 323f.

5. I do not think that Paul would have been greatly concerned about Enoch and Elijah as exceptions.

6. Cf. R. Bultmann, *Theologie des Neuen Testaments* (Tübingen 1980), 312.

7. It is worth noting that the difference has disappeared in Col 3:1 (συνηγέρθητε); cf. however Col 3:3,4 (ἡ ζωὴ ὑμῶν κέκρυπται ...φανερωθήσεσθε.

8. See my own *Commentary on 1 Corinthians.*

9. There is no indication what kind of life will be lived, in what kind of body, between death and the parousia; there may be some information on this question in 2 Cor 5, but that is not a matter to be discussed at present.

10. I use *soul* as a rendering for *nephesh*-ψυχή, without claiming that it is satisfactory; in particular it fails to supply an adjective corresponding to the Greek ψυχικός.

11. Editors and copyists seem, to have had some scruples about Paul's treatment of the Old Testament text; in the first clause B and others omit ἄνθρωπος, and in the second P46 and Irenaeus omit ᾿Αδάμ.

12. Cf. Targ. Onk, which runs,...he breathed into his nostrils the breath of life, and it became in man a speaking spirit (*mᵉmalᵉlaʾlᵉruaḥ bᵉ ʾadam wahᵃwath*). Ps. Jonathan develops the thought much further.

13. *The Pneumatikos-Psychikos Terminology*, SBLDS 12 (Missoula 1973), 19.

14. *Die Gnosis in Korinth*, FRLANT, N.F. 48 (Göttingen 1956), 136.

15. In v. 47b, as in v. 45, there is a good deal of textual varia-

tion. Many MSS, somewhat unnecessarily, introduce the word κύριος to make the identification with Christ explicit.

16. See M. Casey, *Son of Man: the interpretation and influence of Daniel 7* (London 1979), 82, 83, 166.

17. J. Jeremias, *N.T.S.* 2 (1955-6), 151f.

12

THE GENTILE MISSION AS AN ESCHATOLOGICAL PHENOMENON

That the Christian Mission is directed to the whole world is today a proposition taken for granted without argument. It was not always so, and the early Christian mission to Gentiles constitutes a problem in more senses than one. That it was a problem to the first-century church is attested by the clearest firsthand evidence. There were those who would prevent Paul from speaking to the Gentiles that they might be saved (1 Thess 2:16). These were Jews, apparently not Christians. But there were also Christians who would consent to the inclusion of Gentiles among the people of God only on terms that would have excluded many: they wished all converts to be circumcised (Gal 6:12). This leads to the somewhat less direct evidence of Acts, where the same demand is made: "Unless you are circumcised in accordance with the custom of Moses you cannot be saved...It is necessary to circumcise them [Gentile converts] and order them to keep the law of Moses" (Acts 15:1, 5). Already Peter's approach to Cornelius had attracted criticism (11:3), and it was only by a vision that he had himself been persuaded that God had no favorites and that he must call no one profane or unclean (10:28, 34). It was by no means clear to the earliest Christians (for we have no reason to question the sincerity of those who opposed the movement into the Gentile world) that Christian missionaries should be free to present the gospel to those who were Jews neither by birth nor by proselytization. Hence a second sense in which the Gentile mission constitutes a problem: it is a problem to the historian of Christian thought and action, who is bound to ask why so many of the first Christians adopted this limiting attitude; what arguments and what events convinced them, or a majority of them, to abandon it; and how, in this controversial situation, the mission proceeded.

Like many problems and controversies, this, though it evoked strong feeling and sharp dispute, proved in the end to be creative. It would suffice to refer to Paul, whose understanding of law, faith, and grace was sharpened by the debate in which he found himself involved; beyond Paul lies the unquestioned universal scope of Christian evangelism which ultimately emerged—threatened though it regrettably was in the later stages by the opposite danger of neglecting, despising, and even hating the Jews. The missionary problem moreover interacted with another of the major problems of the early years, that of eschatology. The reconstruction of the earliest Christian outlook upon the future affords plenty of room for controversy and debate (to which Dr. Beasley-Murray has made a distinguished contribution), but few are likely to disagree with the moderate proposition that in the first years of the church there were at least some, perhaps many, who believed that the time before the end was too short to admit any extension of the mission beyond the confines of Israel. Such an extension might or might not be desirable, permitted, or illicit; it was simply impossible. It was a natural inference that what God's plans did not permit he cannot have desired. How widespread this view was, and whether it went back to Jesus, are questions that will be briefly touched upon below; if it existed at all, that is sufficient to demonstrate the association that has been made between the problem of the Gentile mission and the problem of eschatology, and goes some way towards vindicating the description of the Gentile mission as an eschatological phenomenon.

What follows is anything but a full discussion of the question in what sense the Gentile mission may be spoken of as an eschatological phenomenon. Its main intention is to consider the bearing on the matter of some passages in Acts, but it is necessary first to glance briefly at the teaching of Jesus and Paul—briefly, because the essential points are not unfamiliar.

Jesus

Did Jesus himself carry out, plan, or desire a mission to the non-Jewish world? The correct answer to this question has, in my opinion, been given by Joachim Jeremias in *Jesus' Promise to the Nations*. The evidence contained in the Gospels appears to lead to a contradiction.

> We have found, on the one hand, that Jesus limited his activity to Israel, and imposed the same limitation upon his disciples. On the other hand, it has been established that Jesus expressly promised the Gentiles a share in the Kingdom of God, and even warned his Jewish hearers that their own place might be taken by the Gentiles.[1]

The contradiction is resolved by the recognition that "the gathering in of the Gentiles occurs in the hour of the final judgement."[2] Jesus believed that the Gentiles would be drawn (as the Old Testament had foretold[3]) at the end of time to the Mount of God. It was God's intention that they should eventually share his kingdom with the Jews, but this would not happen as the result of a mission conducted in the course of history. It would be in the strictest sense a matter of eschatology, not of "realized eschatology" but of that ultimate future which, however near, lies beyond the present span of time.

Jeremias recognizes that Mark and the other synoptic evangelists do contemplate a mission in historical terms; this was inevitable since they lived in the midst of the mission; but where they allow this to appear they are reinterpreting sayings of Jesus which may originally have borne a different meaning. The two most important passages are Mk 13:10 and 14:9. Each of these must be interpreted in terms of the angelic proclamation of good news described in Rev 14:6f., "where, in the hour of final fulfillment, an angelic voice proclaims 'the everlasting gospel of triumph.'"4 This belongs to the last day, when the Gentiles are included in God's people at God's own instance. This is Jesus' view, modified by the Gospel editor, who knew that a historical mission was in fact taking place. Whether Jeremias had rightly interpreted the Marcan passages is a fair question, and one that can be properly treated only in the context of a general discussion of the eschatology of Jesus and of the evangelists. Of the teaching of Jesus it would be hard to affirm anything with complete conviction beyond the fact that he believed that his ministry would culminate in an eschatological crisis of rejection by the people and vindication by God. The vindication was expressed in various ways which appear to be alternative images rather than sequential stages. The image of resurrection was used; the image of an appearance with the clouds of heaven was used also. The two never appear in the same prediction in such a way as to suggest that there would be an interval between them.

If it is indeed true that Jesus (whatever he may himself have thought inwardly) gave no explicit instruction about such an interval, two things, otherwise difficult to explain, become clear. In the first place, it is easy to see why there was much hesitation and not a little dispute about the inauguration of a mission to the Gentiles. If Jesus had in fact given orders that such a mission should take place in the interval between his resurrection and his return, his followers could hardly have disputed whether it was right to undertake it. If, on the other hand, resurrection happened and the expected parousia did not, the disciples must have asked themselves in some bewilderment what they were expected to do—wait another week or two in Jerusalem, doing nothing? They can hardly be blamed if they found a worldwide mission not immediately obvious. In the second place, the diversity of attempts to fill the gap is accounted for. There are passages, such as Mk 13:10 and 14:9, which speak fairly plainly of a mission to Gentiles, and Mk 7:19 claims that at least the laws regarding clean and unclean foods are abrogated. On the other hand, Mt 10:5, 6, 23 order missionaries to confine their work to Israel; they must not approach Gentiles. Matthew does not reproduce Mk 7:19, and Mt 5:17 requires the observance of even the least commandments. Matthew himself has reached a point at which variety can be accommodated. Along with the passages cited he gives (28:19) the commission to make disciples of πάντα τὰ ἔθνη ("all the nations") and appears to understand the restrictive commands as applying to the time of the ministry of Jesus, the universal commission to the post-resurrection interval.

The Gentile mission thus appears as a piece of "realized eschatology" belonging to the period between resurrection and parousia.

PAUL

Paul could describe himself as ἐθνῶν ἀπόστολος ("an apostle of the Gentiles," Rom 11:13), and it seems that he had to defend himself against the charge of neglecting his own people. His protestations in Rom 9:2f. and 10:1 are so strong that they are best understood as a reply to charges that had hurt his image. He was in truth willing to exchange Christ's blessing for his curse if that would benefit his fellow Jews. It was by agreement that he concentrated his mission on the Gentile world; at his meeting in Jerusalem with James, Cephas, and John, he and Barnabas had undertaken to "go to the Gentiles" leaving the Jewish mission field to the Jerusalem apostles (Gal 2:9). Exactly how this agreement was understood and how it was carried out cannot be discussed here; Paul certainly did not take it to mean that he might never offer the gospel to Jews or have Jews in his churches. He did, however, both practise and defend the mission to Gentiles, whom he received into the church without any demand that they should become Jews on the way.

Paul answered the charge that he was a renegade, neglecting his own people in the interests of others, not only with vehement assertion of his devotion to his kinsmen after the flesh but also by a reassessment of the eschatological situation. Those who took the line suggested by Mt 10:23 and applied it to the time after the resurrection must have argued, There is no time for a mission to the Gentiles. It will be hard enough to cover the cities of Israel before the coming of the Son of man; we must concentrate first on our fellow Jews. If God wishes to have some Gentiles among his chosen people he can bring them to Zion at the last day. They may well have continued, To go to the Gentiles at the same time as to the Jews will not only cost time and effort that we cannot afford; it will also make the conversion of Israel more difficult because Jews will not wish to be associated with Gentiles, probably of low ethical achievement and certainly unclean by the standards and requirements of the law. This argument Paul answered by a special divine "revelation," a μυστήριον (Rom 11:25). At least a partial failure of the mission to Israel is assumed; this is certainly in accordance with fact. It must already in the 50s have been clear that only a minority of Jews were accepting Jesus as Messiah. The answer to this was not to go on battering on a closed door but to turn, as Paul had done, to the Gentiles.

It was God's intention not to draw in the Gentiles as a sort of after-thought, with the intention of filling up the vacant places left by recalci-trant Jews, but to incorporate them first. First the πλήρωμα τῶν ἐθνῶν ("fullness of the Gentiles," 11:25), then Israel—πᾶς Ἰσραὴλ σωθήσεται ("all Israel will be saved," 11:26). The process is given a psychological explanation in 11:14: Paul will pursue his Gentile mis-sion with the utmost vigor: εἴ πως παραζηλώσω μου τὴν σάρκα καὶ σώσω τινὰς ἐξ αὐτῶν. To see Gentiles included and them-selves rejected will provoke the Jews to jealousy, and they will turn to claim their own. Later in the chapter Paul gives a theological explana-tion. This has two points. If God calls individuals (as he has certainly called Israel) he does not stop calling them even when he is rebuffed (11:28, 29). Israel is therefore not to be written off. But also: the only basis on which God deals with humanity is mercy. There is no person, Jew or Gentile, who can deserve salvation; as long as they suppose that they can deserve it they will not have it. Only out of a context of recog-nized unbelief and disobedience will people accept God's mercy. The Gentiles were, and knew that they were, already in this context. Hence the success of Paul's mission to them; they knew that they had no right-eousness of their own and were therefore prepared to accept the right-eousness offered them by the mercy of God in Christ. The Jews were seeking (according to Rom 10:3) to establish their own righteousness; only when their disobedience, proved by their rejection of the Messiah, was demonstrated would they recognize that they too had no hope ex-cept in the mercy of their own merciful God. Israel's salvation would come about only by the removal of sin (11:27, quoting Isa 59:21).

Paul's revelation[5] is put in an eschatological setting. Salvation is regularly for Paul a future event (cf. e.g., Rom 13:11). Here, howev-er, the future is represented as already invading the present. The Jews have *now* become disobedient and unbelieving (νῦν ἠπείθησαν), that they may *now* be dealt with in mercy (νῦν ἐλεηθῶσιν, 11:31). It is in the light of God's final action, not only of Paul's evangelistic mission, that πλήρωμα ("fullness") and πᾶς ("all") must be understood.

ACTS

Whether the "delay of the parousia" played a major part in the motivation of Acts is a disputed question which need not be considered here. What is clear beyond dispute is that had there been no interval be-tween resurrection and parousia there would have been no Christian history for Luke or anyone else to record. It is equally clear that the mission to the Gentiles was one of Luke's keenest interests. It forms the backbone of his book. If Philip's mission to the Samaritans and to an Ethiopian, the founding by Peter of an at least partly Gentile church in Caesarea, and the founding of a similar church in Antioch are removed from the first twelve chapters, little is left; and the rest of Acts (13-28) is an account of the work of the great Gentile missionary Paul, punctuated only by an account of the council, which both defended and regulated his work. Another observation regarding Acts is that though Luke has by no means abandoned futurist eschatology, he has it firmly under control so that it has no problems for him. In the opening chapter it is made clear that Jesus who ascends into heaven with a cloud will come in the same way (1:11); the story of the church and its mission will be terminated by the return of Christ. God knows when this will happen; he has established times and seasons by his own authority (1:7), and he has set a day when he will judge the world in righteousness (17:31). But no one else knows when the end will be. He leaves it to his Christians to get on with the job he has appointed for them; and this for Luke means the evangelization of both Jews and Gentiles, a process which is located within what remains of the present age. The sun has not yet been turned into darkness nor the moon into blood; the present is the time of vision and prophecy, in which everyone who invokes the Lord's name will be saved (Acts 2:17-21).

This was Luke's own view. The mission is not so much a matter of "realized eschatology" as of a substitute for an eschatology that has been deferred. But Luke, open to criticism though his historical work is, did not write the story of the church simply out of his own imagination but on the basis of traditions—some written, some oral, some trustworthy, others clearly fallible—helped out by his own reconstruction. It is for us to look among these traditions to detect, if we can, traces of earlier eschatological thought. They are not many; Luke absorbed and digested his material.

The interesting (and to me unexpected) result of this inquiry is that Luke shows here and there traces of the view that we have seen to be opposed to the conviction that Paul had reached by the time he wrote Romans 9-11. Acts confirms the view that there were those who held that the prime obligation of Christians before the End was to win the Jews.

We can lay little stress on the sequence Jerusalem, Judaea, Samaria, the end of the earth (1:8); this was probably Luke's own program for his work (cf. Lk 24:47) and in any case does little more than express an inevitable geographical expansion from the center.

The appointment of a twelfth witness in the place of Judas Iscariot has been well explained by K. H. Rengstorf.[6] The Twelve were to be the eschatological judges of Israel (Mt 19:28; Lk 22:30); the appointment of Matthias meant that notwithstanding the crucifixion the disciples were not abandoning their responsibility for and to Israel. The mission to the Jews must be reestablished before anything else was done, and it must be done in view of what was to happen at the παλιγ–γενεσία (the word is Matthew's but the sense of it is also in Luke 22).

The evidence of Acts 2 is difficult to handle and to harmonize. The list of names in 2:9-11 is so oddly assorted and arranged that one hesitates to draw the conclusion[7] that it represents the gathering of the Gentiles to Mount Zion, thus anticipating the End.[8] Did not Luke think that all concerned were Jews or proselytes? This seems to be the view expressed in the speech; note the reference to πᾶς οἶκος 'Ισραήλ in v. 36 ("all the house of Israel"). This in turn suggests that v. 39 means "to you Palestinian Jews and to your distant brethren in the Diaspora." It does, however seem probable that Luke wished to suggest by his list of names and the reference to οἱ εἰς μακράν ("those from afar") that gospel and church were from the beginning at least potentially universal.

It is only towards the close of the speech in ch. 3 that Peter begins to envisage the world outside Judaism and then in such a way as to suggest that the Gentiles take a second place. The word πρῶτον ("first," v. 26) is explicit, and it interprets the promise to Abraham quoted in v. 25: ἐν τῷ σπέρματι σου ἐνευλογηθήσονται πᾶσαι αἱ πατριαὶ τῆς γῆς. Instructed by Paul in Gal 3:16 we are accustomed to take the *seed of Abraham* as a reference to Christ, but in v. 25a *you*, the Jewish hearers of Peter's speech, have been described as οἱ υἱοὶ τῶν προφητῶν καὶ τῆς διαθήκης ἧς διέθετο ὁ θεὸς πρὸς τοὺς πατέρας ὑμῶν. They are the seed of Abraham; in them, once they have come to accept Jesus as the Messiah and to find in him the forgiveness of their sins, the Gentile families will be blessed. That is, the Gentiles will indeed be accepted, but in a second stage of the mission. For several reasons which are not to be discussed here it would be unwise to build a great deal on Acts 8:14 and 11:22, but if these verses are taken as they stand they indicate suspicion regarding any advance towards the Gentiles. The most interesting piece of evidence is the quotation from Amos 9:11f., attributed in Acts 15:16-18 to James. This has recently been discussed afresh by J. Dupont,[9] whose article contains a wealth of bibliographical references[10] which it is unnecessary to repeat here. He concludes,

> If it can be assumed that Luke has some consistency in his views, then when in Acts 15:16 he writes on the issue of the restoration of the tabernacle of David, presenting it as the point of departure for the offering of salvation to the Gentiles, one should not consider this simply (*simplement*) as a restoration of Israel that will be achieved in the Judaeo-Christian community. The "tabernacle" of David is none other than the "house" of David seen in the pathetic state in which it found itself at the time of the division of the monarchy. It must not be confused with the "house of Israel" (Acts 2:36; 7:42). This house of David was rebuilt and the throne of David reerected at the moment in which God raised Jesus to be seated at his right hand (2:34). From the perspective of Luke, the "uni-

versal" nature of Christian mission is rooted directly
in the mystery of Easter.[11]

With this proposition I should agree provided I were allowed
to lay great stress, greater stress, I suspect, than Père Dupont would
himself allow, on the word *simplement*. It is true that the very name David points in a messianic direction, and it is also true that Christian uni-
versalism is rooted in the "mystère de Pâques," though how far this entered into "l'optique de Luc" is another question. Père Dupont's view is
supported by his review of Jewish interpretation of Amos 9:11f.,[12] but
he does not, I think, allow sufficient weight to the context in which the
quotation appears, and, in particular, to the somewhat obscure argument conducted by James. This leads to a conclusion that James (no
doubt we should say, Luke) cannot have found easy to state. Acts
15:19, 20 could almost be paraphrased, I give my judgment that we
should not trouble (παρενοχλεῖν) Gentiles who are turning to God—at
least, that we should not trouble them too much. We will not ask them
to observe the whole law, but we will ask for certain limited observanc-
es. This is followed by the notoriously obscure v. 21, which gives a
ground (γάρ) for the "decree," but does not make clear whether it is defending it against the charge that it asks too much or the charge that it
asks too little. There are in fact two interests to be served, those of the
Jewish-Christian and those of the Gentile-Christian communities. With
this balance the quotation from Amos is well chosen to agree, and
though Père Dupont calls it a "curieuse considération" (31, n. 41), J.
Jervell's argument that as v. 17 has in mind the Gentile church so v. 16
will refer to the Jewish church is by no means without weight. His
point is given in the words, "Die Bekehrung der Heiden ist die
Erfüllung der Verheissungen an Israel . . . Dies stimmt mit dem
jüdischen Gedankengang überein, nachdem die Heiden in der Endzeit
sich dem wiederaufgerichteten Israel anschliessen werden."[13]

It would be natural to infer from this that Christians must take
as their priority the establishing of a renewed Jewish people, united in
the acceptance of the Messiah Jesus. Without this, to what could Gentile converts attach themselves? The practical consequence was that potential Jewish converts must not be frightened off by too strong a measure of Gentile freedom. This attitude and program correspond with
Paul's theological statement, "to the Jew first and also to the Greek,"[14]
but also with that whose existence was inferred from Paul's energetic
reply in Romans 9-11.[15]

Both attitudes, Paul's and the other, are intelligible, especially
if it is true that Jesus left his followers with no instructions about the
way they should conduct themselves in the interval between resurrection and parousia. That both existed helps to make intelligible the conflicts that lie under the surface of the narrative of Acts, and on the surface of the Pauline letters. Paul shows a greater readiness to respond to

the historical circumstances in which the eschatology of the Gospels and of the gospel is to be worked out, and a greater readiness to look to the future: it is neither circumcision nor uncircumcision that counts, but a new act of creation (Gal 6:15).

NOTES

1. J. Jeremias, *Jesus' Promise to the Nations*, (Philadelphia: Fortress, 1983), 55.
2. Ibid., 56.
3. Isa 2:2-4; Mic 4:1-3.
4. Jeremias, *Promise*, 22.
5. Cf. the use of μυστήριον in an apocalyptic setting in 1 Cor 15:51.
6. K. H. Rengstorf, "Die Zuwahl des Matthias," *Studia Theologica* 15 (1962): 35-67; idem, "The Election of Matthias," *Current Issues in New Testament Interpretation: Essays in Honor of Otto Piper*; ed. W. Klassen and G. F. Snyder (New York: Harper, 1962), 178-92, 293-96.
7. Notwithstanding H. J. Cadbury's view that Gentiles were intended.
8. See above, 186.
9. J. Dupont, " 'Je rabâtirai la cabane de David qui est tombée' Ac 15,16 = Am 9,11," in *Glaube und Eschatologie: Festschrift für W. G. Kümmel*, ed. E. Grässer and O. Merk (Tübingen: J. C. B. Mohr, 1985) 19-32 .
10. One could add now the commentary Ökemenischer Taschenbuch-Kommentar zum Neuen Testament, 5/1 and 5/2, 1981 and 1985, by A. Weiser; and a further article by J. Jervell, "Die Mitte der Schrift," *Die Mitte des Neuen Testaments: Festschrift für Eduard Schweizer*; ed. U. Luz and H. Weder (Göttingen: Vandenhoeck & Ruprecht, 1983) 79-96 published in English as "The Center of Scripture" in J. Jervell, *The Unknown Paul* (Minneapolis: Augsburg, 1984), 122-37, 179-83.
11. Dupont, "Je rebâtirai la cabane de David," 31f.
12. Dupont refers to Dan 11:14; CD 7:14-19; 4Q 174 1:10-13; b. Sanhedrin 96b.
13. J. Jervell, "Das gespaltene Israel und die Heidenvölker," *Studia Theologica* 19 (1965): 68-96; quotation from 80f. ET: "The conversion of the Gentiles is the fulfillment of the promises to Israel. . . . This corresponds with Jewish thinking, according to which in the endtime the Gentiles will be joined with reestablished Israel."
14. Rom 1:16; 2:9, 10. Can these have been a concession to opponents? Cf. also the allegory of the olive tree, Rom 11:17-24.
15. See above, 188f.

13

PAULINE CONTROVERSIES IN THE POST-PAULINE PERIOD*

The theme is one that could easily be allowed to develop into a history of the apostolic age. I hope to keep it within reasonable bounds by approaching it in the main from one angle only. Like most of the great figures of the past, Paul is known to us both as a historical and as a legendary figure, and it is my intention in this paper to consider in a small way not only how the real Paul and the legendary Paul illuminate each other, but also how, between them, they cast a measure of light upon an obscure period.

There is no safer historical proposition about Paul than that his career, and the letters through which his career is known to us, were deeply marked by controversy. He was the storm-center of his age, and even Acts, which notably dilutes the controversial element in his life, fails to remove it completely. He was a man born to trouble as the sparks fly upward, and inevitably generated controversy; at the same time, the controversies in which he was engaged helped to make him the man he was, and it was in debate that some of his most characteristic, and most important, doctrines were hammered out. It is for example doubtful whether we should have had in the form in which we know it his doctrine of justification by faith had it not been threatened before it was formulated by the judaizing movement. It is doubtful whether he would have thought through (though presumably he would have continued to practise) his own conception of apostleship if he had not been confronted by false apostles. It is doubtful whether his Christology would have developed as it did if he had not encountered gnostic and other attempts, mostly well-meaning but not for that reason adequate, to locate the figure of Jesus in history and the universe. He was the first and greatest but not the only Christian theologian to find that controversy made him creative. So much is fairly evident, and unlikely to be disputed.

---

* Presidential address read at the S.N.T.S. General Meeting at Southampton, August 1973.

With this observation the theologian might be content to stop, and proceed to deal with the doctrinal raw material which the controversies deposited in the epistles. He would, I think, be ill-advised, for in doing so he would lose not only the context that could make his theology intelligible but also a quantity of vital theological substance, for New Testament theology is not static but mobile, and is better seen as a moving picture than as a sequence of stills. The historian will be very unwilling to stop at this point, for once he has scented a controversy a historian will, if he can, follow it to the kill. Unfortunately, however, in the Pauline controversies it is not long before he encounters a check, and line after line peters out. Again and again we simply do not know how Paul's conflicts ended. We can hardly expect to know: the epistles cannot tell us how the conflicts ended for they are part of the controversy as Paul conducted it; Acts, which in general does not tell us that the battles began, can hardly inform us of their outcome.

Perhaps the most notable example of our ignorance is the dispute with Cephas at Antioch (Gal. 2: 11). What happened in the end? We may guess but we do not know. It is possible, though not altogether easy, to make out the ground and cause of the dispute, but once the theological issue has been brought to light Paul's interest in the event as such evaporates, and commentators are not even agreed where his words to Peter end and he resumes his discourse to his Galatian readers. The dispute begins with the message from James and Peter's success in bringing in on his side all his fellow-Jews, including even Barnabas. Did all the Gentile Christians side with Paul? Does his silence mean that they deserted him and accepted circumcision in order to remain in communion with the Jewish party? Did Paul retain the allegiance of the Gentiles and recapture the Jews? It would be helpful if we could be certain of the relative dates of Galatians and 1 Corinthians, where Cephas and Barnabas are referred to, though with no conspicuous warmth, as colleagues. But the date of Galatians is disputed. Tradition (questionable tradition, since Ignatius does not mention it) makes Peter bishop of Antioch before he was bishop of Rome; this might suggest that Paul was defeated. Antioch ceases to be the base of his mission, but this may mean no more than that it lay too far east, and would require too long lines of communication to serve as a center of supply for campaigns in Rome and Spain. Possibly the dispute was not ended, and Antioch not quiet, when Paul wrote Galatians, but we can hardly suppose that Peter was simply left to stand and wait for the resumption of Paul's dressing down.

This gap in our knowledge is only one of a sequence of gaps (a sequence so extensive that it reminds one of the definition of a net as a large number of holes fastened together with string). What was the outcome of Galatians itself? Did Paul win back the Galatians, who so grieved and baffled him (4:19)? We hear in Acts 18:23 that he passed through Galatian territory and Phrygia strengthening all the disciples;

otherwise only that Gaius of Derbe (20:4) accompanied him to Jerusalem; this may be significant (a) if you do not accept the Western variant Δουβέριος, and (b) if you think that Galatia includes Derbe. More important, but belonging probably to a later date, is the reference to Galatia in 1 Pet.1:1; it seems reasonable to conclude that Christianity of a more or less Pauline kind existed in Galatia at the time this epistle was written. But this observation tells us nothing about the course of events, or about the development of personal relations between Paul and the churches, and though 1 Peter is broadly Pauline in outlook its ascription to Paul's rival in Antioch, whether genuine or pseudonymous, can hardly be insignificant.

We are a little better informed about the outcome of Paul's conflicts in Corinth. Some indeed, taking the view that 2 Cor 10-13 is part of the " severe letter" and that it was written before the conciliatory parts of 2 Cor 1-9, would say that here we are actually informed by the epistles themselves and have on paper the record of Paul's reconciliation with his rebellious church: I am glad that I have every confidence in you (7:16). This conclusion must however be modified in two important respects. In the first place, it is far from certain that 2 Cor 10-13 is to be dated earlier than 1-9; and in the second, though Paul had trouble enough with the Christians of Corinth they were not the main object of his polemic. He was desperately anxious about them because they were being duped by servants of Satan disguised as apostles, but the false apostles themselves were the real enemy. It seems, not from 2 Corinthians but from the passing remark in Rom 15:26, that Achaea like Macedonia had made a contribution to the needs of the poor saints in Jerusalem, and thus that the Corinthians were sufficiently reconciled to Paul to trust him with their money, but it is by no means clear that the false apostles were penitent, or even that they had ceased their operations in Corinth.

The same passage in Romans that tells us that Achaea had contributed to the fund urges its readers to wrestle in prayer that the collection might prove acceptable in Jerusalem; the image (συναγωνί–σασθαι) is to some extent conventional, but it would be ridiculous if Paul knew that when he reached Jerusalem he was sure to be greeted by a polite Thank you. Achaea and Macedonia had contributed—he does not say that Galatia had; but the outcome remained quite uncertain.

It would be easy, if time permitted, to take up other controversial themes, such as the dissident groups in Corinth, the problem of the resurrection and, perhaps more significant, the conflict between the weak and the strong, of which there are traces in every Pauline mission-field. If any of these disputes was settled in Paul's lifetime we do not know on what terms. I shall however close this sketch with the observation that where Paul appears to take over Christological material, which he uses presumably because it was already familiar to his readers, and perhaps had been composed by some of them, he does so with alterations. The most familiar examples are Rom 1:3 f.; Phil 2:6-11; Col 1: 15-20. In all these passages it can be shown with considerable probability that Paul introduced comments of his own which, though verbally slight, had the effect of giving a radically new turn to the Christology he was using. In Rom 1 he brings the divine sonship of Christ into the pre-resurrection period; already as man Jesus was Son of God. In Phil 2 the deified Second Adam of the original becomes the heavenly being who, already of divine status, begins the story by coming down from heaven and becoming man, thereby exhibiting in the highest degree the humility and obedience which, as man, he continues to practise. In Col 1 Christ is not, or is not simply, the head of the cosmic σῶμα, an ontological mediator who bridges the gap between the invisible God and the material universe, but the Redeemer who reconciles the rebellious cosmos to God through the blood he shed on the cross, conveys to men the forgiveness of sins, and becomes the head of the church. So far, so good; but what was the reply? What did those who composed the original forms of these hymns make of Paul's additions and emendations? Did they accept them as improvements? Or did they use something like the tart (and not unjustified) words of John Wesley about those who treated his and his brother Charles's hymns in this way? "They are perfectly welcome [to reprint our hymns], provided they print them just as they are. But I desire they would not attempt to mend them—for they really are not able. None of them is able to mend either the sense or the verse."[1] Unfortunately, we have neither this nor any other kind of comment; we do not know what happened.

        If at this stage we may briefly sum up, there are two observations to make. One side of Paul's controversial activity is a frontier skirmishing with an inadequately Christianized gnosis. The clearest example of this is that which we have just considered. Behind Col 1:15-20 is an honest attempt at Christology: take the accepted framework of cosmic speculation and give to Christ the highest place within it. The trouble is that in Paul's view this place is neither high enough nor low enough. On the one hand it leaves Christ as no more than a sort of hybrid between God and men, and on the other it fails to bring him down to the historical depth of shedding blood in death. Corinthian gnosis did well enough when it emphasized that there was but one God, that idols therefore were nothing, and that food sacrificed to idols was nothing and might be freely eaten. But it needed sharp correction when it failed to observe that I ought to be more concerned about my brother's conscience than my freedom to compile my own shopping-list and menu, drew false analogies between freedom to eat and freedom to commit fornication, and applied its rationalist dialectic to the resurrection. Paul was a gnostic, but the sort of gnostic who exercised a very strict criticism on the various pieces of gnosis, speculative and moral, that he encountered and was invited to adopt.

        The counterpart of this sporadic encounter with gnosis was

something more like a pitched battle with the judaizing counter-mission that seems to have dogged Paul wherever he went, assuming different forms in different areas. In Galatia and Macedonia it demanded circumcision, apparently requiring that Gentile Christians become proselytes. In Corinth and the Lycus valley it entered into some kind of partnership with local religious life. Apostolic character was essential to it; hence Paul's most radical condemnation of its representatives as ψευδαπό–στολοι,[2] representatives of Satan, not (as they claimed) of Christ. Or did they make this claim? Certainly they understood apostleship in a different way from Paul and may have thought of themselves as servants of Christ but apostles of the Jerusalem church, charged by it to bring all the new communities which were growing up in the Empire into association with the mother church. We come back here to the confrontation between Paul and Peter. In this everything was at stake: the centrality and sufficiency of Jesus, a relation with God based on faith only, and an understanding of Christian life which, though focused most sharply in the figure of the apostle, meant for all a bearing about of the killing of Jesus, transformed by resurrection. The conflict was such that Paul was obliged to fight for his life, or rather for the life of his churches and of Christianity as he understood it. As we have seen, in Galatia at least we do not know the outcome of the struggle.[3]

Within a few years the situation was completely transformed. Paul, Peter, and James died as martyrs. The evidence is not as good as one could wish, but it is sufficient. For James we have the explicit accounts of Hegesippus and Josephus. These are not identical, but the only point of divergence to be noted here is the date of the event. According to Josephus (*Antiquities* xx. 200) this took place just before the accession of Albinus as procurator of Judaea (διὰ τὸ τεθνάναι μὲν φῆστον, Ἀλβῖνον δ᾽ ἔτι κατὰ τὴν ὁδὸν ὑπάρχειν), that is, in A.D. 62. According to Hegesippus (*apud* Eusebius, *Church History* II. xxiii.18), after James's death εὐθὺς Οὐεσπασιανὸς πολιορκεῖ αὐτούς. This is often taken to mean that Hegesippus put the event in A.D. 69, just before the siege of Jerusalem (though this was conducted not by Vespasian but by Titus), or in 66 or 67, just before Vespasian began military operations in Palestine. This however puts a heavy weight on εὐθύς, which Hegesippus may have used in the same loose way as Mark: "and the next thing, that is, the next significant thing, was that Vespasian besieged them." Eusebius's *Chronicle* and Jerome are in approximate agreement with Josephus, and A.D. 62 may be accepted with some confidence.

It is a surprising fact that there is no comparable early account of Peter's martyrdom. It seems very probable that Peter did reach Rome and die there as a martyr; the arguments of Lietzmann[4] have been supplemented but not disproved. The date of Peter's death is a good deal less well attested. W. M. Ramsay[5] may well be right in describing the statement that he perished in the Neronian persecution as not tradition but historical theory; his own view, that the martyrdom took place nearer A.D. 80, is also a theory, designed to reconcile the belief that 1 Peter cannot have been written in the sixties with the conviction that it must have been written by Peter. The Neronian date may be accepted, though not with complete conviction, as the more probable.

That Paul died after Peter is a belief that seems to rest on no better foundation than that Clement, in speaking of the deaths of the "good apostles" (1 Clem 5:3 ff.), mentions Peter first. This reason is hardly sufficient. Paul reached Jerusalem, bearing the collection for the poor, probably in A.D. 55; it was in the same year that Festus took office. How long Paul remained in Palestine is uncertain. His voyage to Rome started too late in the sailing season; it may have been as early as late summer 55, or perhaps a year later. According to Acts he would reach Rome in the early spring (28:11) of the next year—56 or 57. Then began the two-year period of house arrest (28:30), ending early in the year 58 or 59.[6] How did it end? According to old tradition—as old as the Pastorals—in release and further missionary activity; but perhaps in condemnation and execution. This is a difficult question, not to be resolved in a line or two of this paper. If it is argued that the tradition in 1 Clement of preaching in the far west refers to Spain and cannot have been altogether false because at the time Clement wrote some were still alive who knew what had happened thirty years earlier, this may be countered by the tradition of the Pastorals, which represents Paul as travelling back east and says nothing about a journey to the west. According to 1 Clement Paul perished διὰ φθόνον; this is compatible rather with action by Jews or Jewish Christians than with Nero's face-saving persecution. The familiar problem of the end of Acts could be solved if there was something discreditable in Paul's death (not necessarily to him). In 2 Cor 11:26 Paul refers to dangers he had experienced at the hands of false brothers; these occur as the climax of a list of physical perils—from Jewish and Roman beatings, from stoning, from shipwreck, from highwaymen. The false brothers were, or represented themselves as, Christians: they had already put Paul in danger of death. Did they join the Jews in accusing Paul (cf. Phil 1:15, διὰ φθόνον καὶ ἔριν)? Did James fail to offer the support he might have given? There is no hint in Acts 21-26 that he took much positive action on Paul's behalf. It would be wrong to build much on Clement's διὰ φθόνον, which is applied also to Peter, and may be a fiction based on Acts 3-5; 12;[7] it is however not unreasonable to think that Paul died as early as 58 or 59, and even if he was released after two years of confinement he may have died as early as James and some time before the Neronian persecution.

The important fact is that Paul, James and Peter were all within a short space removed from the scene.[8] It may well be true that the more extreme members of the trio, Paul and James, died first, leaving Peter in a dominating position. This could explain many things: the emergence, or re-emergence, of Peter as in fact the rock on which the church was to stand, and the characteristics of sub-apostolic Christianity, which was not judaizing, and yet did not adopt, probably no longer understood, the radicalism of Paul. We must add the fact that "before the war" (that is, not later than A.D. 66) the Christians in Jerusalem had left the city for Pella.[9] This must have robbed the counter-mission of its authority, for though it might be argued that all Christians should be in communion with Jerusalem, not only the scene of the Lord's death and resurrection and the seat of the first disciples but the ancient city of God's election to which the ancient promises were attached, no one could with any plausibility maintain that the Christians of, say, Philippi, Corinth, and Rome owed any special obligation to the Peraean city of Pella. Thus within a few years the whole situation was transformed; not only was it transformed, the means by which the old controversies could be understood were removed.[10] Suddenly a power-vacuum came into being, which was also, and this is more important, a theological vacuum. What happened? This is the question we should iike to answer, but there is no way of handling it by frontal approach. We must go round to the back door, and if this is to be done effectively we must be prepared to go a long way round.

More than 100 years after Paul's death we find a distinguished Christian writer still speaking of the apostle and his place in Christian theology in a somewhat defensive manner. Irenaeus is aware that the Pauline ark has to be brought back out of the land of the Philistines.

> It is necessary to subjoin. . . the doctrine oᶜ Paul. . ., to examine the opinion of this man, and expound the apostle, and to explain whatsoever [passages] have received other interpretation from the heretics, who have altogether misunderstood what Paul has spoken, and to point out the folly of their mad opinions; and to demonstrate from that same Paul, from whose [writings] they press questions upon us, that they are indeed utterers of falsehood, but that the apostle was a preacher of the truth, and that he taught all things agreeable to the preaching of the truth (*Adv. Haer.* IV. xli. 4).[11]

Irenaeus however marks the end of one stage, and the beginning of another. From the end of the second century Christian writers show no hesitation about the canonical status of the Pauline literature;[12] Paul, its author, was conclusively enrolled among the orthodox. The earlier defensiveness and hesitation had been due to the various pictures of Paul that circulated in the second century. We have it on the good authority of 2 Pet 3:16 that the heretics made use of the Pauline epistles, and this evidence is confirmed by such fragments of Marcion, Valentinus, and other heretics as we possess, and by the accounts of them given by orthodox writers such as Irenaeus.

It was thus that Paul came to be seen as the proto-gnostic, the enemy, the bogus apostle, the source of error and division. The clearest of the anti-Pauline legends appears in the caricature of Paul in the person of Simon Magus, which appears in the *Kerygmata Petrou*, as this document is reconstructed from the *Clementine Homilies and Recognitions*. It is impossible here to go into the complicated literary and historical problems involved; the existence of the picture is a sufficient witness to the mistrust of Paul, and to the complicated cross-currents, gnostic and anti-gnostic, Jewish and anti-Jewish, of the second century.[13]

This mistrust is reflected in the disuse of Paul by second-century figures nearer to the main stream of Christian thought: Hegesippus, Papias, and Justin.[14] Bauer[15] cites the quotation from Hegesippus in Eusebius, *Church History* iv. xxii. 2 f., in which Hegesippus describes the true faith which he found preached in every city as that which "is preached by the law and the prophets and the Lord." This, Bauer says, leaves no room for Paul as an authority. In the same context Eusebius records, in connection with Hegesippus's visit to Corinth, that he knew 1 Clement, but gives no indication that he used the Pauline letters to Corinth. Bauer refers also to a passage quoted by Photius,[16] in which Hegesippus disapproves of the words, "The good things prepared for the righteous neither eye saw nor ear heard, nor did they enter man's heart," setting over against them the Lord's saying, "Blessed are your eyes which see, and your ears which hear." Had Hegesippus then read 1 Corinthians (2: 9) and disapproved of it? The observation is weakened by the fact that after quoting the passage in question Paul goes on to say (1 Cor 2:10),ἡμῖν ἀπεκάλυψεν ὁ θεὸς διὰ τοῦ πνεύματος—in this respect at least Paul and Hegesippus are on the same side. But on the whole the conclusion stands: Hegesippus was a Jewish rather than a Pauline Christian, using (according to Eusebius) the "Syriac" Gospel according to the Hebrews and quoting it "in Hebrew," giving particulars about Jewish as well as Christian sects and parties, and information about the family of Jesus. Eusebius, however, would hardly have used Hegesippus as he does had he been a heretical Jewish Christian, and there is little or nothing to suggest that in his disuse of Paul he was reacting against Marcion. He could not have used 1 Clement and have radically disapproved of Paul, though he may have failed to understand him.

Bauer (op.cit. 217) notes that Eusebius quotes no information from Papias about Luke; he thinks, because this was Marcion's gospel. The extant fragments contain no reference to Paul, though Papias admired Revelation and (according to Eusebius) used 1 John and 1 Peter. This shows, says Bauer, that he confined himself to material of Palestinian origin (since he believed Mark to be dependent on Peter), and to documents of marked *Kirchlichkeit*—1 John because it was so strongly anti-gnostic, and 1 Peter because it emanated from Rome. Paul does not figure in Papias's list of apostolic and sub-apostolic authorities (Eusebius, *Church History III.* xxxix. 4). This is indeed a noteworthy silence,[17] but it is to some extent explained by Papias's aversion to books (Eusebius, *Church History* III. xxxix.4),[18] This implies however that even in the region of Ephesus oral tradition derived or purporting to be derived from Paul had already dried up.

An even more important figure is Justin, of whom Bauer (op.cit. 218) says, "Bei Paulus fehlt nicht nur der Name, sondern auch jedes Eingehen auf seine Briefe." He advances the strong arguments that when Justin claims that Christians are loyal subjects who pay their taxes (1 *Apology* 17) he makes no reference to Rom 13:1-7; when he discusses the conversion of the Gentiles and the rejection of the Jews (1 *Apology* 49) he does not use Rom 9 ff.; in his tract on the resurrection he makes no use of 1 Cor 15.[19] Justin was a responsible and learned Christian who lived in Rome; why does he make no reference to Paul? E. F. Osborn[20] finds more allusions, but even so they amount to little, especially in view of the fact (which Dr Osborn brings out) that there is often common Old Testament material that may account for the resemblances between Paul and Justin. Dr Osborn offers three explanations of Justin's disuse of Paul (and of other parts of the New Testament): "Justin's understanding of prophecy, his position as an apologist and the classical convention of indirect citation" (op.cit. 138). These explanations are not without weight, but it must remain probable that they were strongly reinforced by a measure of mistrust; Paul was the heretics' apostle, and it was wise to be cautious in using him.[21]

With the negative results achieved for Hegesippus, Papias, and Justin, Bauer does his best to accommodate the evidence to be found in Ignatius and Polycarp—not, I think, successfully. They show knowledge, he thinks, only of 1 Corinthians, "des am lehrhaften Gehalt so armen I. Korintherbriefes" (op. cit. 222). This judgment certainly undervalues the doctrinal content of 1 Corinthians, and probably undervalues also the number of Pauline allusions to be found in Ignatius and Polycarp. This is not the place to collect such allusions in detail; but Ignatius's reference to Paul "who in every epistle makes mention of you in the Lord" (*Eph* 12:2), though it need not refer to a ten-letter collection must refer to more than one letter, and it is hard not to see an allusion to the Pastorals (1 Tim 6:10, 7) in Polycarp 4:1 (cf. 9:2; 12:3). This is of vital importance, for it means that we must reject Bauer's conclusion, "dass die Pastoralbriefe in der Zeit, als sich Marcion über den Umfang der Paulusüberlieferung Klarheit verschaffte, noch nicht vorhanden gewesen sind" (op. cit. 225). Paul was used and approved before the disparaging legend became current.

This is borne out by the fact that, notwithstanding the evidence from Hegesippus, Papias, and Justin, the second century, as 2 Pet 3:16 shows, never rejected Paul altogether. For this, Wagenmann[22] gives three reasons. (1) The Corpus Paulinum already existed and was known and read in all the churches; it was now too late to excommunicate Paul, however desirable this may have appeared to some.[23] (2) From the letters it was known that Paul had been the universal missionary, responsible for establishing churches in the greater part of Christendom. It was impossible therefore to cast doubt on his doctrine and apostleship without casting doubt on one's own authenticity as church and Christian. (3) He was already too widely used for doctrinal purposes— not indeed that the post-apostolic authors really understood him, but all drew texts from his epistles (as the heretics did) to support their own doctrinal positions. These points call for some modification; Paul was not as widely read and used in the second century as Wagenmann suggests. It might be better to be content to say that the "good" Pauline legend was in existence at least as early as the bad, and did not altogether cease to be operative, and that in influential and important quarters. Within at most a decade or so of Justin's work in Rome, perhaps earlier, there were there τρόπαια of the two great apostles,[24] and hesitant as Justin may have been in his theological writing there is no mistaking the direction of popular piety, or the weight of ecclesiastical authority behind it. That Marcion contributed much to the formation and definition of the Pauline corpus is almost certainly true; but he did not initiate the collection, and if on the one hand he furthered the legend of the gnostic Paul, on the other his contribution to the Pauline canon helped to destroy it. He was in fact operating at a relatively advanced stage in the development of the legend, which in its positive form was already full-blown in Acts and the Pastorals before the time of Polycarp. Indeed, since neither Ignatius nor Polycarp substantially adds to it we may conclude that it was virtually complete by the end of the first century.

It was—and this should be said at the outset—a legend that was by no means entirely legendary. Acts in particular contains a quantity of material of real historical value. This is not unusual: for example, the historical Tiberius, though not quite the monster of Tacitus's legendary, or tendentious, description, was nevertheless not one of the most desirable acquaintances. It is not so much large-scale falsification as subtle variation that we must observe. The main sources are Ephesians, Acts, the Pastorals, and 1 Clement; we shall not expect them all to present the same variations on the one historical theme.[25]

Ephesians is probably the oldest of the Pauline pseudepigrapha; it is precisely because the picture of Paul that it implies is so like that of the other letters, that is, is so like the historical Paul, that it continues to be possible to make a strong, though not to my mind a convincing, case for its authenticity.[26] The personal note about Tychicus (6:21 f., lifted bodily from Col 4:7 f.) presents Paul as the busy missionary and pastor that he was, circulating among the churches, caring for those he has left behind as well as that in which he is now working, surrounded by assistants who carry news from one part of the field to another and represent the apostle in his absence. This vignette is consistent with the designation of Paul as apostle, which also is simply borrowed from the genuine letters. In particular, Paul is the apostle of the Gentiles, ὑπὲρ ὑμῶν τῶν ἐθνῶν (3:1); there is nothing strange in this, and it could be said to go no further than Gal 2: 9. In practise, however, in the other epistles, and by no means least in Galatians, Paul appears as the apostle of particular Gentiles, whereas in Ephesians the stress is on Gentiles as a body. As the apostle of the Gentile body Paul is the great architect of the unity of the church, for Ephesians looks back upon the gathering together in one of Jewish and Gentile Christians, all of whom are now reconciled to God in one body and have access to him in one Spirit (2:16,18). There are other more subtle distinctions, but this achieved unity of Jews and Gentiles is perhaps the most striking feature of the Ephesian legend. In the latest epistles we have Paul was still engaged in a life-and-death struggle with judaizing envoys; in Ephesians the counter-mission has come to an end. It is recognized that Jews and Gentiles are different, and that to unite them is a signal achievement, but there is little or no hint of the internal Christian quarrel that grieved Paul himself.

No one can turn from the epistles to Acts without noting the relative absence of controversy in the account of Paul's life. He is occasionally in trouble with Roman authorities, often attacked by Jews, but the only controversy he encounters within the church is disposed of quickly and successfully in Acts 15. Serious trouble is thrown into the future in the farewell speech of ch. 20; after Paul's departure grievous wolves will harry the flock. Paul is the universal missionary, who carries the Gospel throughout the world. He is not however represented as an apostle—14:4, 14 may be variously explained, and on the whole accentuate the failure of the book as a whole to apply the word ἀπόστο-λος to Paul. This unique feature of Acts (for no one else denies him the title who refers to him at length) is probably due to the fact that Luke had committed himself to a numerical identification of the twelve disciples of Jesus with the apostles; it certainly was not intended as disparagement. Paul is the outstanding bearer of the word of God; because he is the bearer of the triumphant and invincible word his own career partakes of these characteristics. Judaizers cannot pervert the Gospel; Jews cannot kill or even halt the preacher. Luke is in a difficulty here, for he knows, and knows that his readers know, that Paul died as a martyr, and he knows also that it will add to the effectiveness of his adulatory picture if he can introduce the shadows of martyrdom as they fall, not too darkly, across his hero's path, and can also indicate that Paul was aware of what was to happen. This in fact is what he does; and we may probably see here the reason why Acts stops where it does. An account of the martyrdom itself, especially if at the time Paul was deserted by his friends and the victim of some kind of treachery,[27] would not enhance the record of Paul's devotion and might detract from the sense of confidence, victory, and unity that permeates the book.

The Pastorals, in which Paul is not merely an apostle but the apostle *par excellence*, provide an important filling out of the picture in Acts (just as from another point of view Acts is a necessary completion of the Pastorals, in that it provides models for the minister who in the Pastorals is taught that it is his duty to preach). Acts avoids the controversial element in Paul's career; the Pastorals represent him as engaged in constant and violent controversy, and thus identify the grievous wolves of Acts 20:29. Paul also makes provision for the continuation of the controversy after his death, and for the teaching of the sound faith: he lays this charge upon Timothy and Titus, and they in turn must hand it on to others. Judaism, legalism, mythology, and gnosis are lumped together in a way that suggests rather that the author was concerned to omit no heresy he had heard of than that he wished, or was able, to analyze, sub-divide, and classify. Error was a mark of the last days, in which it was, or might have been, expected that men would no longer tolerate sound doctrine but turn aside after their own lusts. It is thus an eschatological phenomenon, but it is countered not by arguments based on the imminence of the end but by insistence on the form of sound words, the faithful sayings, the guarding of the deposit of faith, and its transmission to the next generation. Above all, perhaps, in the Pastorals Paul is represented as the martyr. His death, of course, cannot be described in documents purporting to have been written by his hand, but 2 Tim 4 brings Paul as close to death as possible: nothing more remains but the crown of righteousness which the Lord will give him.

The martyr theme reappears in 1 Clement, where the author is able to write freely as one who looks back on the event. Peter and Paul are named together, but it is not implied that they suffered at the same time. They are the good apostles; they suffered on account of jealousy and envy (the evils that were disturbing the Corinthian church); they were the greatest and most righteous pillars—a term rather surprisingly applied to Paul in view of Gal 2: 9, but evidently it had now lost the special sense it had had two generations earlier. Paul in particular is the great sufferer for the faith, traveler, and preacher to the Gentiles (for this is probably implied when Clement says (5:7) that he taught ὅλον τὸν κόσμον). The apostles, Paul presumably among them, foreseeing trouble to come, made provision for the continuance of the preaching ministry. In addition, Paul is appealed to as a letter-writer; the Corinthians can still learn from the letter he left.

It seems clear, and it is confirmed a few years later by Ignatius, that at the end of the century, or very soon afterwards, the church had already developed a hagiographical portrait of Paul. I have pointed out above that it was by no means a wholly fictitious picture. Inevitably the later account looked back to Paul and saw him as a martyr. He could hardly see himself in this way, though his longing to be conformed to the death of Christ could, in the circumstances, hardly lead to any other end. Acts and the Pastorals represent two different ways of relating Paul to current, end-of-the-century error. Acts takes the line that in Paul's time all was well; he foresaw error, but his own time was free from it; those therefore who lived when heresy had come into being had to look back to and imitate the good old days when, under Paul's guidance, the church was pure. The Pastorals handle the same situation by bringing Paul within it and allowing him to speak to the new circumstances in which heresy was rife. Clement tells the dissident Corinthians to read 1 Corinthians.

It is the controversial element in the legendary picture of Paul that we have to consider here, just as it was the controversial element in the historical picture that we considered at an earlier point. It is perhaps in this area that the difference between the two is greatest. The battle between Paul and the false apostles has disappeared. Jewish Christians and Gentile Christians are welded together in one body. There is a relic of the old controversy in the opposition to Jews which appears in the deuteropauline literature, but this is a different matter. It is not simply that Acts (in the "Apostolic Decree") and the Pastorals (especially in 1 Tim 1:7-11) represent Paul as taking up an attitude to the law different from that which we read in the genuine letters; there is a general impression of unreality in the references to Jews: either the author of the Pastorals has simply invented the material because he knows that the historical Paul was in some sense anti-Jewish and confuses Jews with judaizing Christians, or he is writing about a new Judaism, a gnosticizing Judaism. There may be truth in both possibilities.

The vehement struggle is now between Paul and gnostics. These are probably the grievous wolves of Acts 20:29; in the Pastorals they have come out into the open and are the true enemies of the deposit of truth. The hymn of the descending, conquering, and ascending Christ (1 Tim 3:16) bears witness to an earlier stage, when gnostic elements could be absorbed (cf. Phil 2:6-11); the epistle itself maintains a different attitude. The generous though not unguarded concessions to the proto-gnosticism of the strong which appear in Romans and 1 Corinthians have now given place to misgiving and defensiveness.

These changes are readily explained as what might have been expected after the deaths of Paul, James, and Peter. It is impossible that Ephesians should have been written at a time when the Jerusalem church was still sponsoring an anti-Pauline mission, but when not only James but his church also ceased to exist it was possible for the integration which Luke ascribed to the Apostolic Council to come into being, and to do so on the lines described in Acts 15. Along with the rapprochement between Jewish Christians and Gentile Christians there went an alienation between Jews—Jewish Jews—and Christians of all sorts, Jewish and Gentile, for the flight to Pella emphasized the fact that not even Jewish Christians would take any part in the Jewish war

against the Romans. This was a defection that Jews found hard to understand and forgive; Luke antedates it by bringing out the resistance of
Jews to the Gospel in the period dealt with in Acts. Jewish Christians
are ceasing to be a problem for the main body of the church. Not so
gnosticism. This was the great formative period of gnosticism, when
the incorporation of Jewish and Christian elements into speculative systems that had originated further east and had already made some contact with Hellenism was supplying backbone and giving firm shape to
what had previously been nebulous and variable. There was some
ground for greater Christian caution than Paul had shown, though the
transformation of his freedom is a clear mark both of the changing environment and also of the lower potential of his successors—especially
of the latter, for the next great Christian theologian, the Fourth Evangelist, was able to resume the old freedom.

The positive Pauline legend was already well developed with
Ephesians, Acts, the Pastorals and 1 Clement.[28] There were complicated developments in the second century, at some of which I have hinted,
and this age witnessed developed tension between the historical Paul of
the letters, the gnosticized Paul, and the anti-gnostic Paul—a tension in
which popular piety as well as theology played its part; but these were
developments, and fresh interrelations, of components that were already present at an earlier date and are to be found in the New Testament itself. This is perhaps the most important example of the general
truth that "the New Testament must be appraised as controversy before
it can be used as history."[29] The historical study of the last 100 years
has not shown that the conflicts, tensions, and resolutions described by
F. C. Baur are imaginary; it has shown that they belong to earlier dates
than those to which Baur assigned them.[30] A similar observation could
be made with regard to Walter Bauer's work on orthodoxy and heresy,
and in particular to his distinction between Paul and the *Pauluswort*:
"Erst als Bestandteil einer in der Kirche anerkannten Hl. Schrift wird
sich, nicht die Persönlichkeit des Heidenapostels und seine Verkündigung, sondern das Paulus*wort*, da wo man es zur Ausbildung und
Sicherung der Kirchenlehre brauchen kann, einigermassen in Geltung
setzen" (op. cit. 230). Bauer himself makes this statement with reference to a period later than that with which he is expressly dealing; *mutatis mutandis* it could be applied to an earlier period, at least if by the
"Pauluswort" we may understand something like what I have called the
Pauline legend. The historical development was rapid and compressed,
and the period between A.D. 60 and 100 a very complicated one.

We have already seen that the legendary Paul could not have
come into being except on the basis of the historical. It also serves to
bring out features of the historical Paul that might otherwise have been
lost. It may for example over-emphasize Paul's work as organizer and
administrator; yet the historical Paul did organize and administer, even
though his letters often give the impression of a disorganized and even

chaotic church life. But most important is the combined light the two pictures throw on the difficult period in which the clear relation between theology and history which is manifest in the story of Jesus and of Paul, and again with John, is obscured. We know little enough of either the theology or the history of this period, and the writers who follow seem to have lost the clue to Paul's controversial theology. New controversies, which retained some of the old terminology, were described, but the old judaizing controversy with the new eschatological and gnostic controversies of the end of the century produced in combination an amalgam lacking in realism and creativity, and Christian theology does not thrive on shadow-boxing. This observation will lead to a brief consideration of our last theme. Our New Testament canonizes both the historical and the legendary Paul; what bearing has this fact on our understanding of the canon? That the legend no longer represents Paul as fighting against a judaizing agency that had ceased to exist can hardly be brought as an accusation against those who wrote rather to edify than to supply historical information. Indeed, the fiction evolved out of the fact under historical pressures that must have affected Paul himself if he had survived to witness the deaths of James and Peter, and the collapse from its center of the organized judaizing opposition. This is not to say that Paul would in any circumstances have adopted the safe and moralizing churchmanship of the Pastorals, but that this could never have existed without Paul, and was a natural evolution from him.

More: the fictitious Paul is in a different sense "safe," that is, harmless to the true being of Scripture and the church, because it has carried with it into the canon the genuine historical Paul. It is not for nothing that in the opening words of *Adversus Haereses* Irenaeus alludes to Luke and quotes the Pastorals:

> Inasmuch as certain men have set the truth aside, and bring in lying words and vain genealogies, which, as the apostle says, "minister questions rather than godly edifying which is in faith," and by means of their craftily-constructed plausibilities draw away the minds of the inexperienced and take them captive, I have felt constrained, my dear friend, to compose the following treatise in order to expose and counteract their machinations.

The establishing of the Pauline canon towards the close of the second century means in effect that the church corrected the Marcionite perversion of the historical Paul by adding to it the legendary Paul of the Pastorals and Acts, seeing, or perhaps instinctively feeling without understanding, that, as Dr Käsemann[31] has said, "Das Evangelium bleibt nicht länger es selbst, wenn es allein auf dem Plan steht." This was not merely a correction but a rescue, for apart from the legend Marcion and the gnostics might well have destroyed the historical Paul.

Put in this way, it may seem that the legendary Paul is the price we have to pay for the historical; but this would be an inadequate and misleading judgment. The legendary figure contains too many historical elements to be dismissed in this way, and in the post-Marcionite period was a step back in the direction of the historical, which it carried with it into the canon, so that the legendary stands always under the correction of the historical Paul. The process however is one that operates in both directions, and both figures exercise a critical and questioning function for the reader. Moreover, their contiguity in the canon saves us from the ill effects of canonmaking, well described by L. E. Keck[32] and summed up by him in a quotation from Harnack: "Canonising works like whitewash; it hides the original colours and obliterates all the contours."[33] Canon is not a set of eternal propositions; one way of describing it would be a way of perpetuating the fundamental controversies, and thus the essential mobility, of the Gospel, and of demonstrating its powers of renewal even in the hands of the epigoni.

NOTES

1. Preface to the 1779 "Collection of Hymns for the Use of the People called Methodists."
2. See "ΨΕΥΔΑΠΟΣΤΟΛΟΙ (2 Cor. 11:13)," in *Mélanges Bibliques en hommage au R.P. Béda Rigaux* (1970), 377-96.
3. This view seems to me much more probable than that which sees all Paul's opponents as gnostics.
4. *Petrus und Paulus in Rom* (1915).
5. W. M. Ramsay, *The Church in the Roman Empire before A.D. 170* (10th edition, no date); cf. 282 f.: "While the tradition that St. Peter perished in Rome is strong and early, the tradition about the date of his death is not so clear."
6. S. Dockx, *Nov. T.* XIII, 304, gives the two years as A.D. 56-8.
7. Morton Smith, *N. T. S.* VII, 86 ff. But had Clement read Acts?
8. There is much of importance in S. G. F. Brandon's discussion of this situation in *The Fall of Jerusalem and the Christian Church* (1951); but that from A.D. 55 Paul was out of contact with his churches, and discredited in their eyes, is contradicted by Philippians and Colossians, if these were written from Rome. Brandon is surprisingly conservative in his use of Acts 21.
9. Eusebius, *Church History* III. v. 3. J. Munck (*N. T. S.* vi, 103 f.) thinks the story a fiction—the city could not be destroyed while any of the righteous remained within it; Brandon (op. cit. 177 f.) that the flight was not to Pella but to Alexandria. The latter view does not affect my argument; the former does not adequately account for the origin of the tradition.
10. Munck (op. cit. 114 f.) rightly points out that later Jewish Christianity was not a lineal descendant of the Jewish Christianity that Paul encountered.

11. Translation by A. Roberts and W. H. Rambaut, in the Ante-Nicene Christian Library. Cf. the Muratorian Canon, lines 63-8.
12. Except, of course, Hebrews.
13. On this important subject, which can only be touched on here, see G. Strecker's translation of the text in E. Hennecke and W. Schneemelcher, *Neutestamentliche Apokryphen* II (1964), 76 ff., and his introduction, op. cit. 63-9; the same author's *Das Judenchristentum in den Pseudoklementinen* (1958) L. Goppelt, *Christentum und Judentum im ersten und zweiten Jahrhundert* (1954), 171-6; H.J. Schoeps *Theologie und Geschichte des Judenchristentums* (1949); *Aus frühchristlicher Zeit* (1950); *Urgemeinde, Judenchristentum, Gnosis* (1956); O. Cullmann, *Le Problème littéraire et historique du Roman Pseudo-Clémentin* (1930).
14. See W. Bauer, *Rechtgläubigkeit und Ketzerei im ältesten Christentum* (1934), 215-30.
15. Op. cit. 199. For the texts of Hegesippus see M. J. Routh, *Reliquiae Sacrae* I (1846), 205-19.
16. For details see Routh, op. cit. 219. A quotation taken by Photius (in the ninth century) from Stephen Gobarus (in the sixth century) is hardly the highest authority for the views of Hegesippus (in the second century).
17. It is scarcely mitigated by Routh's conjectural attribution (op. cit. 10 f.) to Papias of the passage which is ascribed by Irenaeus (*Adv. Haer.*, V. xxxvi. I f.) to οἱ πρεσβύτεροι and contains a quotation from I Cor 15:25-8.
18. One must also bear in mind that, at least according to Eusebius (*Church History* III. xxxix 13), Papias was σφόδρα σμικρὸς τὸν νοῦν.
19. But is there not in *De Resurrectione* 10 an allusion to I Cor. 15: 53?
20. *Justin Martyr* (Beiträge zur historischen Theologie, 47; 1973), 135 f.
21. J. Knox, *Marcion and the New Testament* (1942), passim, but especially 115 f., supports Bauer in his view not only of Justin but of the general suspicion of Paul in the second century.
22. J. Wagenmann, *Die Stellung des Apostels Paulus neben den Zwölf in den ersten zwei Jahrhunderten* (Beihefte zur Z.N.W. 3; 1926), 154f.
23. The Clementines attack Paul under cover of Simon Magus.
24. See the words of Gaius quoted in Eusebius, *Church History* II. xxv. 6f., and, for the date, among other publications, J. Toynbee and J. W. Perkins, *The Shrine of St. Peter and the Vatican Excavations* (1956), 128f., 154f.
25. See R. M. Grant, *Gnosticism and Early Christianity* (1959), 160f.
26. It is reasonable to think of a Pauline school, such as E. Lohse posits for Colossians (*N. T. S.* xv, 211-20, and the same author's commentary, 1968).
27. See above, 200. An alternative possibility is that Paul's imprisonment ended with the failure of his accusers to appear and his departure through the back door of the gaol—an anticlimax that would have spoilt Luke's book in a different way.
28. A full discussion would seek traces of it elsewhere, e.g. in the gospels.
29. E. L. Allen, in *N. T. S.* I, 143.
30. See *Durham University Journal* lxiv (new series xxxiii), 198-203.
31. E. Käsemann (ed.) *Das Neue Testament als Kanon* (1970), 408. Cf. 407: " . . . dass es geschichtlich Jahwe nur im Streit mit Baal, Jakob nur in

Bindung und Auseinandersetzung gegenüber Esau gibt, Christ und Antichrist stets gleichzeitig auf dem Plane sind, deshalb auch Glaube und Aberglaube, Kirche und Gegenkirche zwar unterschieden, aber nicht irdisch sauber getrennt werden können. Man verkennt den Kanon, wenn man sich einbildet, in ihm sei dieser Streit nicht im Gange, deshalb ihm gegenüber die Prüfung der Geister nicht notwendig."

32. *Nov. T.* vii, 224.
33. A. von Harnack, *The Origin of the New Testament* (1925), 141.

14

JESUS AND THE WORD

It may not be known to all the readers of this book, published in Germany, and written for the most part in German, that *Jesus and the Word* is the title of the English translation of Bultmann's *Jesus*. The original was published in Germany in 1926 (2nd edition, 1929). The translation, made by two American ladies, L. P. Smith and E. Huntress,[1] was published in England by Ivor Nicholson & Watson in 1935. It seems to have made hardly any impression on the English public. It is true that I acquired a copy very soon after I began the study of theology in 1936, but in the short time available to me since I undertook this essay[2] I have been unable to find a review in any of the well known British theological periodicals.[3] It is good to know that it was reissued in 1980 by T. & T. Clark, of Edinburgh. In their Preface (v) the translators explain that both they and the publishers felt "that the present title, *Jesus and the Word*, would in this country [America] convey a more definite idea of the content and viewpoint of the book than the original title *Jesus*." They add, "This change was made with the approval of the author." Unfortunately they do not explain what they understand by "the Word"; does it mean the message, teaching, proclamation, of Jesus himself? or the preached word of the Christian church, which, after Easter, proclaimed a Word, a Gospel, of which Jesus was the theme? Perhaps it was intended to cover both,[4] and to suggest the question how each is related to the other, and to Jesus, and to New Testament theology. The question is one that Bultmann has raised in an unescapable and provocative way, and it is this question, and Bultmann's answer to it, that I hope, not indeed to do justice to but to comment on, in this short paper. What is the relation between the word of Jesus and the word about Jesus?

It is probably true that no single sentence of Bultmann's has attracted more attention, and, at least in England, more disagreement, than the opening words of his *New Testament Theology*[5]: "Die Verkündigung Jesu gehört zu den Voraussetzungen der Theologie des NT und ist nicht ein Teil dieser selbst" (1). The sentence is, of course, logically impeccable if it is true (as Bultmann goes on to say) that New Testament theology consists in reflection on faith in Jesus crucified and risen, and if it is further true that this faith arose first in the primitive church, since Jesus himself did not speak of his death and resurrection. With this proposition in the Theology there is often, and rightly, put one from Bultmann's book on primitive Christianity in its historical setting.[6] "The proclamation of Jesus must be considered within the framework of Judaism. Jesus was not a "Christian," but a Jew, and his preaching is couched in the thought forms and imagery of Judaism."[7] It follows that Jesus, if he may be thought of as a theologian at all, is not a Christian but a Jewish theologian.

This view is both a product of that critical study of the gospels of which Bultmann was so notable an exponent, and a way of dealing with the problems that arise from that study. It is not *Formgeschichte*, understood in a narrow sense, alone, but a general consideration of the preliterary tradition that underlies the gospels, that leads to the conclusion that such genuine tradition about Jesus of Nazareth as may once have existed has been permeated at every, or nearly every, point by the theological ideas of the primitive church.[8] This means that any reconstruction of the life, characteristics, and teaching of Jesus must be fraught with uncertainty, and can never be more than tentative. There is indeed a fair measure of probability[9] about some features of the life and teaching of Jesus, perhaps a greater measure than Bultmann himself was prepared to allow; but once it is conceded that a dogmatic, kerygmatic, interest existed in primitive Christianity (and it is impossible to deny this) it is unnecessary to go on to show that no corresponding historical interest existed too. If there was no historical interest, historical reminiscence must always have been dominated by dogmatic concerns; if there was a historical interest, and a genuine desire to keep alive the story of Jesus of Nazareth, there will have been constant interplay between this and the theological interest, and the resultant gospel material will show the effect of pressure from each side. It is failure to recognize the pervasive theological element in the tradition that leads many ancient historians, as well as conservative New Testament scholars, to chide Bultmann, and those who practise the same methods, for undue scepticism. The fact remains that attempts to build Christian theology upon the ipsissima vox of Jesus must always be open to critical argument and debate,[10] and pose problems ιor which there is no ready solution—except one. This is to recognize that what we *know* about the historical Jesus is that he was a Jew, who shared the beliefs about God which he and his fellow Jews inherited from the Old Testament through the channels of post-biblical Judaism. This Jewish theology formed indeed a most significant presupposition for Christian theology, which could not have existed without it. But Christian theology, as witnessed for example by Paul, was a word of the cross. It was "Christ Jesus that died, yea rather, that was raised from the dead" who stood at its heart. According to John, he, and he alone, was the way to the Father; and these were themes that Bultmann could not find in any teaching that he

could plausibly attribute to Jesus—the Jew. The position, even when
thus sketched with great brevity, shows something of the logical consis-
tency that Bultmann himself gave it. All we can really *know* about Jesus is *that* he existed; we cannot with the same confidence know the
what and the *how* of his earthly life because in these the tradition
showed no interest, or at least no single-minded interest, uncorrupted
by theological elements. This the student of the New Testament must in
his capacity as historian recognize. But in his other capacity as theologian he may be content, for it is precisely this *that*, and no more, that
the New Testament theologians need. Paul ignores the life of Jesus
completely;[11] John tells a story determined by sovereign theological
freedom. *That* Jesus existed, *that* he was believed in and proclaimed as
the exalted Lord, constitutes God's claim for man's decision to live in
faith and obedience, and thereby to discover his own authentic existence.

In Great Britain most of Bultmann's contemporaries reacted
strongly against this position, on grounds both historical and theological. The latter we need not consider except insofar as they arose out of
the former. A bitterly ironical attack was made by T. W. Manson in a
Commemoration Address at Westminster College, Cambridge.[12] I cannot avoid the impression that it betrays a refusal to take seriously the
believing environment in which the gospels arose and the tradition on
which they were based was handed down. "I venture to think that this
kind of thing has gone on too long. It may be granted that the stories in
the Gospels have forms. It may also be granted that the early Church
found the stories useful for all kinds of purposes. It may even be granted that the Church *might* have invented them. But it is a long way from
what the Church might have done to what the Church in fact did; and
there is a good deal to be said for abandoning the study of the branch of
fiction known as Überlieferungsgeschichte in favour of an unbiased examination of the evidence supplied by the Gospels" (8). The theme of
the present paper is dismissed as follows: "I may remark in passing that
the disseminated incredulity of Bultmann's *Geschichte der synoptischen Tradition* has its nemesis thirty years later in his *Theologie des
Neuen Testament* [sic!], in which a perfunctory thirty pages or so is devoted to the theology of Jesus himself, while a hundred or more are occupied with an imaginary account of the theology of the anonymous
and otherwise unknown 'Hellenistic Communities' " (6 f.). This sar-
casm is so unlike Manson's kindly nature that it bears eloquent testimony to the violent antipathy that Bultmann aroused in him. It is sad that
he and his contemporary C. H. Dodd were so antipathetic to their great
German colleague.[13] There seems to me to be no future in this kind of
reaction. There may be a great deal of future in arguing with Bultmann
about *Überlieferungsgeschichte*; he may have been mistaken in many
of his judgments; but there is no question that a process of
Überlieferung underlies the gospels, or that one influence (along with

others, some perhaps reflecting serious historical interest) upon the traditionary process was theological.

The reaction to Bultmann that I have described was not the only one. What has been called the New Quest of the Historical Jesus arose among New Testament scholars who were critics as radical as Bultmann himself, the most notable of them in fact his own pupils. It is with this reaction that Bultmann was concerned in a paper given to the Heidelberg Academy, "Das Verhältnis der urchristlichen Christusbotschaft zum historischen Jesus."[14] A detailed discussion of this paper would be rewarding, but would also exceed the limits of this essay and throw it out of balance. I must indicate briefly what Bultmann says, and confine myself to a few comments. Bultmann begins with the observation that the motivation of the new quest reverses that of the old. Formerly the desire was to free the picture of the historical Jesus from the dogmatic material that had been painted over it; now men are concerned to bring out the unity of the historical Jesus and the Christ of the kerygma. This involves two questions: (1) the question of historical continuity—no great problem here since the continuity is satisfied by the *that* of the historical Jesus; and (2) the question of substantial relationship. This is a more difficult question, and it has been attacked on two lines. "(1) Indem gezeigt wird, dass das Kerygma nicht nur das Dass, sondern auch das Was und Wie des historischen Jesus voraussetzt und zu seinem Verständnis wie zu seiner Glaubwürdigkeit bedarf; (2) indem gezeigt wird, dass in Jesu Wirken in Tat und Wort das Kerygma schon in nuce enthalten ist" (*Verhältnis*, 10). The first line of argument attempts to show, "dass das Personbild des historischen Jesus und seines Wirkens implizit im Kerygma enthalten ist" (ibidem). But this is just what historical criticism that takes seriously the influence of theology and faith upon the tradition cannot show. We cannot, for example, know how Jesus understood his death because critical study shows that all the predictions of the passion are *vaticinia ex eventu* (*Verhältnis*, 12). Will the second line of argument then succeed in showing that "Jesu Verkündigung bereits 'kerygmatischen' Charakter hat" (*Verhältnis*, 15)? It is at this point that Bultmann considers the work of some of his most notable successors in the world of New Testament theology— G. Bornkamm, H. Braun, H. Conzelmann, G. Ebeling, E. Fuchs, E. Käsemann, and J. M. Robinson—and here also that it would be desirable to go into detail in a way forbidden by time and space. Of course, Jesus' proclamation is "kerygmatic"; the question is how his kerygma is related to the "Christus-Kerygma" of the church (ibidem). The latter is Christological; was his? That he understood himself as an eschatological phenomenon perhaps implies a Christology; but the authority of the historical Jesus is not the same as the authority claimed by the church's kerygma for the exalted Christ. A more significant step is taken when the history is given an interpretation, "die auf der geschichtlichen d. h. existentiellen Begegnung mit der Geschichte beruht"

(*Verhältnis*, 18).

Fuchs (as summarized by Bultmann) begins hopefully with the claim that the continuity between Jesus and the kerygma is to be found in the paradoxical truth, "dass ein Mensch in demselben Gott, den er sonst flieht oder fliehen müsste, eine Zuflucht gefunden hat, die er jetzt liebt" (quoted in *Verhältnis*, 18), but in turning and appealing to the faith of Jesus he falls off into historical-psychological interpretation. Ebeling goes a similar way when he finds a continuity in the fact that Jesus as the "Zeuge des Glaubens" becomes the "Grund des Glaubens" (*Verhältnis*, 20).

Bornkamm and Käsemann both seek the understanding of existence that is contained in the words of Jesus, but neither gets beyond a description of Jesus as a historical phenomenon. Braun carries through the intention of finding an existential interpretation and contact more logically. We must look, he says, not for continuity but for a constant element (*Konstanz*); and he finds in all forms of the kerygma (that of Jesus, that of the *Urgemeinde*, that of the hellenistic communities) "das Selbstverständnis des Menschen vor Gott" (*Verhältnis*, 21). This is determined by the words of Jesus. "Diese lehren die paradoxe Einheit der radikalisierten Tora und der radikalen Gnade, der verschärften Forderung und der schrankenlosen Annahme des Menschen als Sünder, die 'Kontrapunktik' der Offenheit für den Nächsten und der totalen Angewiesenheit des Menschen auf Gott...Die Konstante ist das Selbstverständnis des Glaubenden; die Christologie ist das Variable" (*Verhältnis*, 21 f.). Somewhat similarly Robinson reaches the conclusion that the identity between the work of Jesus and the kerygma consists in the fact that "Jesu Wirken in Wort und Tat den Menschen in gleicher Weise vor die Entscheidung stellt wie das Christus-Kerygma" (*Verhältnis*, 22).

It might seem that a solution of the problem had now been reached, but a further question presents itself. How is it that the person who proclaimed (der Verkündiger) becomes the person who is proclaimed (der Verkündigte)? More sharply, "Hat dann das Christuskerygma nicht seinen Sinn verloren, ist es dann nicht überflüssig geworden?" (*Verhältnis*, 24).[15] The answer to the question lies in the claim that in the kerygma Christ himself is present, which means that the church has put itself in the place of the historical Jesus, and represents him. "Dann gibt es keinen Glauben an Christus, der nicht zugleich Glaube an die Kirche als Trägerin des Kerygmas wäre, d. h. in der dogmatischen Terminologie: an den Heiligen Geist" (*Verhältnis*, 26). It is therefore correct to draw the conclusion that Jesus has risen in the kerygma, provided that this is correctly understood. "Er setzt voraus, dass das Kerygma selbst eschatologisches Geschehen ist; und er besagt, dass Jesus im Kerygma wirklich gegenwärtig ist, dass es *sein* Wort ist, das den Hörer im Kerygma trifft" (*Verhältnis*, 27).

This Heidelberg Academy paper may be said to mark the end

of the road that begins with "Die Geschichte der synoptischen Tradition" and on which "Jesus and the Word" was a notable milestone. It seems to me that it nearly but not quite justifies the sentence that I have quoted from the first page of Bultmann's *Theologie des Neuen Testaments*. The following points are perhaps worth making in a critical survey of this part of Bultmann's "Werk und Wirkung."

(1) It is clear that Bultmann is not able to maintain his own intention to confine himself to the *that*, and exclude the *what* and the *how*, of the life and work of Jesus. It would be impossible even to discuss the question (for example) whether Braun's existential interpretation of the words of Jesus does or does not form a constant in relation to the content of the kerygma, if it were impossible to determine with sufficient confidence what words Jesus actually spoke. This is a more significant observation than the one that is commonly made, namely, that even "Die Geschichte der synoptischen Tradition" leaves a residuum of sayings that Bultmann ascribes to Jesus, and that these are used in the exposition contained in "Jesus and the Word." As a historical critic Bultmann was well aware that a historical tradition was open to investigation and that its contents could be graded into various degrees of historical probability. Provided the historian expresses himself with the appropriate measure of tentativeness, accounts of the teaching of figures such as Socrates and Pythagoras, Jeremiah and Jesus, can be given. But for agreement between one and another of them, *that* will not suffice. *What* was Jesus? Perhaps not the Messiah; perhaps not (in a special sense) the Son of God; perhaps not the son of man; but to think of him as, for example, a witness, even to think of him as a Jew, is to import some measure of content into the *that* of his historical being, especially if we are to think of him as a Jew who both sharpened the demand of the law and at the same time set beside it the sovereign grace of God. Bultmann invokes Paul as a proof that *that* suffices for the theological kerygma, and he is at least partly right when he says that for Paul the cross is a *Heilsereignis* and that obedience and selflessness (Phil 2:6-9; Rom 15:3; 2 Cor 8:9) are "das Verhalten des Praëxistenten, nicht des historischen Jesus" (*Verhältnis*, 9). Yet the crucifixion as *Heilsereignis* took place sub Pontio Pilato and implies a pre-history. The crucifixion of the two malefactors was not a *Heilsereignis*, and if that of Jesus was this must have been because the life that preceded this death was of a certain character.

This reference to the death of Jesus may suggest an appropriate example of a further line of thought which cannot be worked out in detail but should at least be alluded to in this context. It is proper to take into account the influence of the post-resurrection faith upon the tradition of the life of Jesus, but it is proper also to ask what this faith had to work on and in particular why the figure of Jesus of Nazareth was selected as its focus. It does not quite suffice to say, because it was he who was believed to have risen from the dead, for if the appearances

were hallucinations and the stories of the empty tomb legends we still
have to ask why they were attached to him; if they were not, the historical Jesus must have been a very extraordinary person indeed. The effect
of the post-resurrection faith will sometimes at least have been develop-
mental rather than creative. For example: I have elsewhere[16] argued
that though Mark 10:45 presents a theologically developed statement
about the purpose of the death of Jesus, reminiscent of other more explicitly theological passages in the New Testament (1 Cor 15:3; 2 Cor
5:15; Gal 1:4; 2:20; Eph 5:25; 1 Tim 2:6; Tit 2:14) it is probable that
there lies behind it a saying of Jesus in which he expressed his devotion
to the outcasts of his people, the *am ha'ares*. The original saying may
well have borne a theological implication; in the process of the tradition
the theology became explicit. Bultmann (*Verhältnis*, 12, n.20) quotes
Conzelmann's argument that the genuineness of the passion predictions
cannot be defended on the grounds that Jesus must have foreseen a
coming catastrophe[17]: "Denn diese Worte sprechen nicht eine scharf-
sichtige Analyse der Lage aus, sondern eine göttliche Notwendigkeit
des Leidens." This observation is undoubtedly correct. There is however no logical basis for the continuation: "D. h. sie enthalten bereits die
Deutung der Passion von Ostern her." Jesus would not have had to be
particularly scharfsichtig to see that trouble was brewing. In itself this
does not mean that he would ascribe the coming trouble to the absolute
authority of the divine will, but it does mean that unless he could so ascribe it he must have withdrawn from his ministry, recognizing that his
proclamation of the kingdom of God had been a mistake.

(2) It is not simply that Paul and John were theologians whereas Jesus was not. Jesus certainly did not have a technical training in theology, but lack of theological training does not prevent him from being
a theologian, if a theologian is one who interprets existence—his own,
his neighbours', the world's—in terms of God.[18] That Jesus did this,
and in this sense was a theologian, will appear below; it is in any case
allowed if he is described (as in "Jesus and the Word") as a Jewish theologian. The difference was rather one of historical perspective. It can
be seen in the *that* of Jesus' historical work, but it is hard to illustrate it
without drawing to some extent on *what*. The safest course will be to
use the one narrative that Paul recounts from the life of Jesus, the Last
Supper. He relates this narrative to the communal meal that his converts in Corinth (and no doubt elsewhere) were in the habit of eating,
and places the Christian meal within a specific interval of time. "As often as you eat this loaf and drink the cup you proclaim the Lord's death
[which therefore serves as a terminus a quo for the Christian custom]
until he come [so that his coming provides a corresponding terminus ad
quem]" (1 Cor 11:26). In the same context he defines the original meal
as being held before this terminus a quo: the Lord Jesus took loaf and
cup, and spoke words over them, in the night in which he was betrayed
(or handed over to death, 11:23-25). This was a tradition Paul claims to

have received from the Lord himself (11:23). This claim of his does not guarantee the historical accuracy of what he reports, but it does mean that the story was being told very soon indeed after the resurrection. In the original meal, whatever may have happened, it was impossible to proclaim the Lord's death, for it had not happened; or, if it was proclaimed, it was proclaimed in a different way, not as something to which men looked back but as something to which Jesus himself looked forward. Probably no piece of tradition was so frequently repeated; none was so exposed to modification. But the change of perspective itself was independent of such modification,[19] and the change of perspective is more significant than verbal variation.[20] There is no need to attempt the historical problem of defining what Jesus looked forward to; for Paul, part but not the whole of what was originally to be looked forward to had now happened (the Lord's death but not the Lord's coming). He was a "Denker der postmessianischen Situation."[21] It is this change of perspective, of balance, that creates the essential continuity and discontinuity between the teaching of Jesus and the post-resurrection proclamation of the church,[22] and it affects the whole of the tradition. The preaching of Jesus, including his radicalized Jewish theology, becomes New Testament theology when it is seen from this new angle, in this new light.

(3) I have indicated elsewhere[23] the development from Bultmann through Conzelmann to Käsemann in the interpretation of Johannine theology, and argued that, though it is impossible to miss his concentration on the figure of Jesus and his acceptance of him as Lord and God (John 20:28), John's ultimate concern is with the unseen eternal God, whom Jesus has expressed in the form of a story (ἐξηγήσατο John 1:18). Jesus is the sent Son of the sending Father, the revelation of the revealing God, the obedient servant of the One who commands. With his ἐγώ εἰμι he proclaims not that he himself is the God of the Old Testament but that he who has seen him has thereby seen the Father. That there is *Christ*ology in the Johannine literature is beyond question, but it, and especially the gospel, reaches its fulfillment in *the*ology. Much the same can be said of Paul. Christ is indeed wisdom, righteousness, sanctification, and redemption, but these things he is as God's gift (1 Cor 1:30).

It is in the same sense that Jesus himself is a theologian; the evidence for this is fully given in "Jesus and the Word" and need not be repeated here. Bultmann will of course reply that the teaching about God that is ascribed to Jesus is essentially Jewish teaching, sharpened and carried to its logical conclusion. In this however he hardly does justice to himself. There is a particularly significant passage in *"Verhältnis"* (8f.): "Nun wird aber—besonders nachdrücklich von Käsemann — bestritten, dass man Jesus dem Judentum zurechnen darf, da er doch die Grenzen der jüdischen Religion entscheidend durchbrochen habe. Dazu ist zu sagen, dass er nur als Jude das Judentum radikal überwinden

konnte. Es scheint mir dann ein Wortstreit zu sein, ob man ihn als Ju-
den bezeichnet oder nicht; jedenfalls kann man ihn nicht einen Christen
nennen. Als historische Gestalt steht er innerhalb des Judentums; und
wenn er innerhalb des Judentums eine einzigartige Gestalt ist als dessen
Überwinder, so ist doch nicht nur seine Sprache und Begrifflichkeit die
jüdische, sondern sowohl seine eschatologische Verkündigung wie
seine ethische Predigt sind in der Sache auf die jüdische Eschatologie
und Gesetzlichkeit bezogen, nehmen deren Problematik auf und sind
ohne sie gar nicht denkbar."[24] For Jesus God remains the transcendent,
distant God of Judaism, but he is also the coming God, and therefore always near. Where Jesus is, God is not far away. To say this is not to affirm that Jesus held "correct" Chalcedonian views about himself. There
is no reason for supposing that he did, and there are many reasons for
believing that he did not. My point is the much simpler one, that whereas a common, or similar, existential approach to man and his situation
in this world goes some way towards establishing a continuity between
Jesus and the Christian theologians Paul and John, a more important
constant factor is the understanding of God which proves to be common to Jesus on the one hand, Paul and John on the other.[25] Moreover,
the change of perspective, mentioned above, is sufficient to account for
the change from Proclaimer to Proclaimed. In the earlier stage Jesus
proclaimed what the God he believed in, the God of Judaism and the
Old Testament as he understood them, would do for his people. This
was the eschatological element in his proclamation. As soon as men believed that Jesus had been raised from the dead, and understood the crucifixion in the light of that belief, they were bound to believe that Jesus
himself was the one in whom God would fulfill his eschatological purpose—had already fulfilled part of it, and would in due course fulfill
the rest.

No one, I suppose, is likely to contribute to this book unless he
wishes his contribution to be understood as an acknowledgement of a
very great debt. At the same time, no one who has learned from Bultmann (even though mainly through his books, and with a minimum of
personal contact) can think his debt discharged by dutifully repeating
the master's words, or providing new words to express his thoughts.
The first duty of a student of the New Testament, along with learning
all that he can, is to think for himself and to question all the arguments
and conclusions laid before him—including the arguments and conclusions of Rudolf Bultmann. He made unescapable the question that lies
at the heart of any understanding of primitive Christianity—the question how the transition from Jesus to the church was made. No progress
will be made in reference to this question if his statement of it is ignored, or if we seek to find ways of avoiding or circumventing it. The
new generation will thank him best by taking him seriously and arguing
with him with as close an approximation to his learning and clarity of
thought as they can achieve.

NOTES

1. I should be glad to know more about these ladies, who, recognizing that Bultmann's book was "stimulating and thought-provoking" (v), seem to have been more percipient than many of their contemporaries. Dr Smith was born in 1887, wrote a small work on *The Messianic Ideal of Isaiah,* and contributed to a translation of Calvin's commentaries. Dr Huntress was born in 1907, and translated F. A. Stepun's *The Russian Soul and Revolution.* Their Preface is written from Wellesley, Massachusetts.

2. It is a matter of great regret to me that limited time and other commitments have made it impossible for me to contribute to this volume such an essay as I should wish to write. The brevity and slightness of my contribution in no way represent my indebtedness to Rudolf Bultmann and my profound respect for him as scholar and as man.

3. In a "Survey of Theological Literature" in the *HibJ* 33 (1934/35) 618f., James Moffatt wrote: "Bultmann's *Jesus and the Word* (Nicholson & Smith [sic!], 6s.), now translated, will enable English readers to appreciate the stimulating radicalism of his position and at the same time his Barthian affinities."

4. Like εὐαγγέλιον in Mark 1.1? See M. E. Glasswell in E. A. Livingstone (ed.), *Studia Biblica* 1978, JSNT, Supplement Series, 2 (1980) 115-127, especially 118.

5. *Theologie des Neuen Testaments,* Tübingen [8]1980.

6. *Primitive Christianity in its Contemporary Setting,* London 1956.

7. 71 f. For the continuation of his quotation see n. 24.

8. I need not point out that behind *Jesus and the Word* lies Bultmann's *Die Geschichte der synoptischen Tradition* (FRLANT, NF 12), Göttingen (1921) [9]1979.

9. It is interesting to note that the translators of *Jesus and the Word* wrote in their Preface (viii f.), "Professor Bultmann uses 'know' and 'certain' in almost an absolute sense; consequently he is forced to use 'probably' where most of us say 'certainly', and 'possibly' stands often for 'probably'."

10. I take the phrase *ipsissima vox,* of course, from J. Jeremias, consistent opponent of Bultmann, and, like him, a scholar for whom it is impossible not to feel the highest possible respect. It must however be pointed out that as soon as one begins, for example, to consider the changes to which the parables have been subjected in the course of transmission, or to discuss which *Abendmahlsworte* are the oldest, and in which form, one opens the door to argument and debate, and thereby to uncertainty. Even the greatest experts in Aramaic and Rabbinics will on occasion disagree with one another on such matters.

11. The narrative of the Last Supper (1 Cor 11:23-25) has pastoral rather than historical motivation. See however below, 219f.

12. In *Studies in the Gospels and Epistles,* Manchester 1962, 3-12. Manson is another scholar for whose erudition and insight I have very high respect, and I should perhaps apologize for taking as example this wittily mordant but occasional piece. But it is eminently quotable, and I do not think Manson would disown it. Much of the same material appears in his contribution (Present-day research in the life of Jesus) to W. D. Davies and D. Daube (eds.), *The Background of the New Testament and its Eschatology, in honour of C. H. Dodd,* Cambridge 1956, 211-221.

13. "Where scholars like Dodd, Taylor, and Manson have done so much to enhance our understanding of the New Testament, it is perhaps improper . . . to carp at what they have not done. Yet one feels that they have not always faced as openly as they might the constraints and challenges presented to the historical and critical standpoint by the Continental theologians' critique of historicism. Native British reaction against the 'extremism' in Continental theology, of the swing away from the 'Jesus of history' movement has not infrequently meant a premature dismissal of the issues raised by the other side" (H. Anderson, *Jesus and Christian Origins*, Oxford 1964, 94). In *The Interpretation of the Fourth Gospel*, Cambridge 1953, 121, C. H. Dodd observes that Bultmann's *Commentary on John* as a whole reached him only after his own book was complete. He told me that, having read it, he found himself unable to make any use of it. In *Historical Tradition in the Fourth Gospel*, Cambridge 1963, Dodd refers to Bultmann nine times (seven times to the *Commentary on John*) but nowhere attempts to deal seriously with his historical judgment of the gospel.

14. SHAW. PH Jg. 1960, 3. Abh., Heidelberg 1960 (³1962), now in: *Exegetica*, 445-469.

15. Cf. the quotation from R. H. Fuller on the same page: "The effort to demonstrate the continuity between Jesus and the Kerygma may so blur the difference between them, that in effect it will make the Kerygma unnecessary."

16. *New Testament Essays*, London 1972, 20-26.

17. So e.g. C. H. Dodd, *The Parables of the Kingdom*, London 1935, 57: "It needed, not supernatural prescience, but the ordinary insight of an intelligent person, to see whither things were tending, at least during the later stages of the ministry."

18. Bultmann, *Jesus and the Word*, 190, cf. 176, says that for Jesus faith is not part of a world-view; this may mean that Jesus was not a philosopher, but it cannot mean that he was not a theologian. In fact, though Bultmann develops his account of Jesus' teaching in terms that owe much to existentialist thought, the account that he gives is theological rather than philosophical, and thus supports the view that I have taken on 220f.

19. Cf. the rabbinic distinction between the "Passover of Egypt" and the "Passover of the generations that followed after"(*Pes.* 9. 5).

20. The addition of "given for you," and the like.

21. H. J. Schoeps, *Paulus*, Tübingen 1959, 95.

22. This is not to deny that many other distorting and originating factors were at work. None however is so fundamental as this, and this is not so much distorting as creative at once of continuity and discontinuity.

23. C, K. Barrett, *The Gospel according to St John*, London ²1978, 97; also "Christocentric or theocentric?", in J. Coppens (ed.), *La Notion biblique de Dieu*, Gembloux and Leuven 1976, 361-363.

24. It is at this point that I may continue the quotation begun in n. 7: "It [the proclamation of Jesus] is in fact a tremendous protest against contemporary Jewish legalism."

25. Substantial traces of it are to be found in the Old Testament also; the new element is the notion of fulfillment.

15

SCHOOL, CONVENTICLE, AND CHURCH
IN THE NEW TESTAMENT

School is a word with a long history, a history that has in it a curious twist. This is well known, and there is no need to recall it with more than the greatest brevity. Liddell and Scott list twenty Greek words beginning with the root syllable σχολ—. With few exceptions their primary meaning is related to leisure; there is even σχολεῖον, which when it does not mean *school* appears to refer to the place of unending leisure where there will never be anything to do—one's grave. σχολάζειν means *to have nothing to do*. This is neatly illustrated by Aristotle's ἀσχολούμεθα ἵνα σχολάζωμεν[1] from which it is but a short step to the same author's σχολάζειν καλῶς[2] and to the more developed ἄνδρες ἀκριβῶς φιλοσοφίᾳ σχολάζοντες[3]. *Having leisure* comes to be having leisure for a worthwhile pursuit.[4] Similarly σχολή, originally *leisure, rest, ease*, moves on to mean that on which one's leisure is employed, and eventually not only, or often, to a *school* (as a place where one studies, which is σχολεῖον) but to a group of disciples who learn a way of life from a common master. The word group is seldom used in the LXX, but the pattern of meaning is substantially the same as that which is found elsewhere in Greek. At Exod 5:8, 17; Prov 28:19 it[6] means laziness, idleness: at Gen 33:14 it denotes a *leisurely pace*. A better sense appears at Ps 45(46):11, where it is used of those who wait upon God[7] and at Sir 38:24 the wisdom of the scribe depends upon his having *leisure* (σχολή), which evidently he will not spend in idleness. Latin borrowed the word and used it plentifully, taking it up at the end of its development. There is no verb corresponding to σχολάζειν, but *schola* means (according to Lewis and Short) *leisure given to learning, a learned conversation or debate, a disputation, lecture, dissertation*; thence a place where such learned events take place; also *the disciples or followers of a teacher, a school, sect*.

The verbal stem continues in respectable and mainly academic use in English.[8] It suffices to quote the relevant part of the definition in the *Shorter Oxford English Dictionary*[9]: "The body of persons that are or have been taught by a particular master (in philosophy, science, art, etc.); hence, a body or succession of persons who are disciples of the same master, or who are united by a general similarity of principles or methods." The existence of a *school* (in this sense) without a master is well illustrated in a recent account of the so-called Religionsgeschicht-liche Schule.[10] *Conventicle* has no such interesting ancient history. The word is evidently Latin.[11] *Convenio* means *to come together; conventus* is a *coming together,* a *meeting* or *assembly,* and is used in a variety of senses. *Conventiculum* is a diminutive, but does not seem to be used pejoratively; *conventiunculla* is a further diminutive. It is in English[12] that development takes place, for there *conventicle* carries nearly always a disparaging tone, which reflects, in English history, the Conventicle Act of 1664, which forbade any religious meeting of more than four persons if not held in accordance with and under the authority of the Church of England. Thus a *conventicle* becomes "A meeting (*esp.* a religious meeting), of a private, clandestine, or illegal kind, as of Non-conformists or Dissenters in England, or of Covenanters in Scotland during the reigns of Charles II and James II...*contempt(uously)* A 'hole-and-corner' meeting...a place of meeting...*esp.* a nonconformist or dissenting meetinghouse. (Now *rhet(orical)* or *contempt(uous)*)."[13]

Both school and conventicle have been used in recent accounts of the history of early Christianity. For example, as long ago as 1954 K. Stendahl published *The School of St. Matthew,*[14] which was based upon a study of the Old Testament quotations in Matthew. It was one of the earliest New Testament studies to make serious comparative use of the Qumran pesher on Habakkuk. Our attention at present must however be focused on the chapter headed "The Gospel of Matthew as a handbook issued by a school" (20-29). Stendahl begins by questioning the adequacy of liturgy and the catechumenate as descriptions of the setting in which the gospel took its ordered form. Von Dobschütz and Bultmann had already described the book as a "manual of discipline" before the discovery of the now familiar Qumran Manual of Discipline.[15] There are similarities in form and compass between the two documents. Another manual has been longer known—the Didache. Stendahl takes up Bacon's fivefold division of Matthew, in which teaching on five themes—Ethics (5-7), Apostleship, Mission, and Martyrdom (10:5-42), the Kingdom of God (13:1-52), Church discipline (17:24-18:35), Eschatology (and Farewell Address) (24:1-25:46)—is combined with appropriate narrative. In 1QS there are "counterparts to the first, third and fourth points in Matthew's five-fold pattern, and in the Didache to the first, fourth and fifth. Some of the rules concerning itinerant teachers in Didache have affinity to the second discourse of Matthew" (27). This basic observation, together with a number of detailed considerations, led Stendahl to the conclusion that, in comparison with liturgy and pre-baptismal catechesis, "the school may be invoked as a more natural *Sitz im Leben.* The systematizing work, the adaptation towards casuistry instead of broad statements of principles, the reflection on the position of church leaders and their duties, and many other similar features, all point to a milieu of study and instruction" (29). Hence the school of St Matthew, in whose activities the interpretation of the Old Testament played a prominent part.

A little before the publication of Stendahl's book E. Käsemann was giving his inaugural lecture at Göttingen (30 June 1951).[16] This, "Ketzer und Zeuge," examined the background out of which the Johannine literature, and especially the Johannine epistles, arose. Briefly, Käsemann's conclusion was that the writer was an enthusiast (185) and the community in which he worked was an *ecclesiola in ecclesia.* "Immerhin würde eine Untersuchung der eigenartigen Terminologie unserer Briefe, die bereits von Harnack 'höchst konstant geistlich' genannt wurde, vielleicht doch darauf hindeuten, dass man sich in diesem Stande einzurichten beginnt und die Briefe insofern auch mit einem gewissen sachlichen Recht als die ersten Zeugnisse christlicher Konventikelbildung angesprochen werden dürfen" (179). The same observation about the Johannine community is made by Käsemann in *Jesu letzter Wille nach Johannes17*[17]: "Die Gemeinde, die sich lebendig vom Geist regiert weiss, kann Apostolat, Amt und Organisation in den Schatten treten lassen, sich selber in der Weise eines Konventikels verstehen, der durch seine einzelnen Glieder konstituiert wird und sich als den Kreis der Freunde und Brüder bezeichnet" (72f.). This account of the environment in which the Johannine literature originated is taken up in a qualified way by for example O. Cullmann[18] and R. E. Brown.[19] Of these (and many other names could be added) the latter is particularly careful to explain the sense in which he thinks that the word *sect* (he does not say *conventicle*) may be applied to the Johannine community, and both deny any radical separation between it and the main body of Christians.

With these observations may be set the much older recognition of a body of Deutero-Pauline literature. There are few students of the New Testament who would not recognize some or all of the following, which all bear Paul's name, as not having been written by the apostle himself: Ephesians, Colossians, 2 Thessalonians, 1 and 2 Timothy, Titus. With these we may put Acts, with its account of Paul's life and work. A body of pseudepigraphical literature is not the same thing as a school, but we may reasonably infer a number (and from that it is not a long step to a group) of Christian leaders who all looked to Paul as the outstanding Christian authority, regarded him as a model to be imitated, and wrote in a manner which they hoped would have had his approval. The list could be extended to the non-pseudepigraphical works 1 Clement and the Epistles of Ignatius.

It will be seen that the widely held views that have now been sketched are all based almost entirely on what may be called internal evidence. We read Matthew and infer a school-like process. We read, for example, Ephesians and note its ascription to Paul but infer from its contents that he did not write it. We come nearer to straight-forward historical evidence with the Johannine conventicle, for the letters themselves bear direct witness to the existence of two groups that excommunicated each other.[20] Even here however there is little direct evidence for the make-up and structure of the various social groups that undoubtedly existed in the early years of the Christian movement—as such groups have continued to exist ever since. The fact is that the early Christian writers were not sociologists and took little thought for the sociologists of the twentieth century. In this they shared the interest (or lack of interest) of most of their non-Christian contemporaries.[21] This is not to say that the inferences are false. They are in a sense so obvious and necessary that they can hardly fail to be broadly true. Something of the kind was observed long ago by E. Troeltsch.[22] "The Gospel of Jesus was a free personal piety...Only when faith in Jesus, the Risen and Exalted Lord, became the central point of worship in a new religious community did the necessity for organization arise. From the very beginning there appeared the three main types of the sociological development of Christian thought: the Church, the sect, and mysticism. The Church is an institution which has been endowed with grace and salvation as the result of the work of Redemption...The sect is a voluntary society, composed of strict and definite Christian believers bound to each other by the fact that all have experienced 'the new birth.' These 'believers' live apart from the world, are limited to small groups, emphasize the law instead of grace, and in varying degrees within their own circle set up the Christian order, based on love...Mysticism means that the world of ideas which had hardened into formal worship and doctrine is transformed into a purely personal and inward experience; this leads to the formation of groups on a purely personal basis, with no permanent form, which also tend to weaken the significance of forms of worship, doctrine, and the historical element."

This passage has today a somewhat dated appearance and needs correction here and there. For our present purpose it needs the addition of school; but it is a percipient statement, and in the body of his huge book Troeltsch is able to show the interplay of the various types of Christian association and the variety in detail that they exhibit. It illustrates a variety that is bound to interest both the student of the New Testament and those who are concerned with the modern ecclesiastical and ecumenical scene.[23] *Church* (especially if we begin with an only half-examined definition of the word in terms of a national, or supranational, body) and *sect* though distinguishable are nevertheless related terms, but mysticism is a psychological rather than a sociological term, and does not really fit with the other two. No more is it a theological term, and the New Testament is much more concerned with the theological meaning of the words it uses and the organizations it describes than with their structure; this is true even when (as in the Pastorals) some attention is given to structural details.[24] It was inevitable, or nearly so, that Christian development should in its earliest years manifest some of the characteristics of *school* and of *conventicle*, or *sect*, if only because there was in the environment of the first Christians abundant precedent for both, and that both in Palestine, where the new movement began, and in the wider Hellenistic world, into which it speedily moved. It will suffice to point out, first, that (apart from the Temple hierarchy) the leading figures in Judaism were *hᵃkamim*, who in their wisdom taught and applied traditional truth[25] and were surrounded by *talmidim*, who were still learning it. This is precisely the picture of a *school*. Secondly, and closely related both in language and in fact, there are the groups made up of *hᵃberim*. *ḥaber* was "a scholar's title, less than *ḥakkim*[26] or *zaken*,"[27] but denoted also a "member of a religious or charitable association, esp(ecially) a member of the order for the observance of levitical laws in daily intercourse" (422). The second meaning, with the corresponding community word *hᵃburah*, points directly to *conventicle*. *hᵃburoth* were precisely groups of the pious, which existed in order to foster the practice of piety. No love was lost between them and the ʿam haʾareṣ, who surrounded them. Behind both the *talmidim* and the *hᵃberim* was Torah, which required study and required also obedience. Divergent interpretations of Torah led to differences between the groups; thus Josephus is able to speak of various Jewish αἱρέσεις.[28] The Greek word calls to mind the fact that the Greek world also had schools and sects. Philosophers taught, and since they did not all teach the same thing sects, αἱρέσεις, came into being. Pseudo-Diogenes writing to Hipparchia congratulates her on the fact that, though a woman, she longed for philosophy (φιλοσοφίας ὠρέχθης) and became one of "our party," or school (τῆς ἡμετέρας αἱρέσεως ἐγενήθης).[29] Josephus[30] compares the Pharisees with the Stoic school. Religions, especially when they turned upon the celebration of a mystery, tended inevitably to become inward-looking, self-contained groups—conventicles, to whom all the rest of the world were outsiders. "The [Mithraic] order was divided into a multitude of little circles, strongly knit together and practising the same rites in the same sanctuaries. The size of the temples in which they worshipped is proof that the number of members was always very limited. . .it is impossible that these societies should have counted more than one hundred members."[31]

There is thus an inherent probability that the early history of Christianity would manifest social formations recognizable as schools and conventicles, and there is a measure of confirmation of this in the fact that the gospels present a clear picture of Jesus as a teacher, addressed in conventional terms as Rabbi (e.g. Mark 9:5) and surrounded by a group of μαθηταί, who were divided into an outer, ill-defined company, and an inner group selected out of the outer (Mark 3.13f.), very conscious of itself and of its distinction from those who did not very conscious of itself and of its distinction from those who did not belong to it (Mark 4:11). These synoptic passages ostensibly describe circumstances belonging to the ministry of Jesus; the extent to which this is correct is a disputed question that cannot be discussed here. That they correspond more or less closely to circumstances after the crucifixion and resurrection is highly probable and hardly open to dispute. This however remains an inference, and we still lack concrete evidence for Christian schools and conventicles. It is natural to seek such evidence in the only early Christian history that we possess; and the greater part of this essay will be devoted to an examination of Acts. Even here the evidence is not considerable, and has to be searched for; this suggests either that our a priori considerations have been misleading or more probably that Luke was concerned to minimize rather than to emphasize this aspect of the story.

I shall look for evidence along two lines: first by examining relevant parts of Luke's vocabulary, and secondly by considering relevant features of his narrative.

Luke in Acts provides us with the fundamental features of a school. The word σχολή itself occurs (19.9) but its only significance is that it shows Luke's awareness of schools as an institution in the world in which Paul and his colleagues did their work. His interest in the passage in question is to show Paul's movement from the Jewish world of the synagogue into the non-Jewish world of secular institutions. When the synagogue was closed to him he found another place in which to continue his teaching. The σχολή was a convenient place for assembling a class for instruction. More important are the words that describe or imply the process of teaching. There were teachers (διδάσκαλοι, 13:1 only; the word was probably little used in Luke's own church); the action of teaching is much more frequently mentioned (διδάσκειν: 4:2, 18; 5:21, 25, 28, 42; 11:26; 15:1, 35; 18:11, 25; 20:20; 21:21, 28; 28:31). It appears that the word is sometimes used almost indistinguishably from κηρύσσειν and refers to the public, evangelistic, proclamation of the Gospel; thus at 4:2 it is used along with the proclamation of the resurrection; at 15:35 it is parallel to εὐαγγελιζόμενοι. Elsewhere it seems to mean (as one would expect) such instruction as would naturally take place in a school, that is, in a Christian company that is being taken further in the understanding and application of Christian truth; so for example at 15:1 and 21:21—it is interesting to note that in the former passage the persons concerned are teaching what Luke certainly believed to be false and that in the latter Paul is accused of teaching what (according to Luke) he did not teach. Other related words occur. Paul in particular is said to argue (διαλέγεσθαι[32]) and in parallel with this (at 17:3) to open (the Scriptures? διανοίγειν). He discusses matters with the Hellenists (9:29).

The other side of teaching is learning, and this is represented by the word μαθητής (6:1, 2, 7; 9:1, 10, 19, 25, 26 (bis), 38; 11:26, 29;

13:52; 14:20, 22, 28; 15:10; 16:1; 18:23, 27; 19:1, 9, 30; 20:1, 30; 21:4, 16 (bis); cf. the feminine form μαθήτρια, 9:36, and the verb μαθητεύειν, 14:21). The verbal count is complicated by the fact that the word was established by its use in the gospels as meaning simply *Christian* and the consequent fact that to become a μαθητής sometimes means not *to learn* in the ordinary sense of the term, but *to accept the Gospel, to become a believer* (e.g. 6:7; 9:1). In some places however the μαθηταί appear to be under instruction; so for example 14:22; 18:23, where Paul strengthens (ἐπιστηρίζειν, στηρίζειν) (the souls of) the disciples, presumably by further instruction and exhortation. 9:25 is particularly interesting. The reading is in doubt, but there is a strong case for οἱ μαθηταὶ αὐτοῦ (P⁷⁴ ℵ A B C 81* *pc* vgˢᵗ), *his* (that is, Paul's) *disciples*. This would imply disciples who owed a special loyalty to Paul; not merely Christian disciples but Paulinists, men who accepted the Gospel as understood and taught by Paul: the seed of a Pauline school. It would however be mistaken to build much on this unique passage. The reading may be due to "scribal inadvertence"[33]; if it is original, in view of the otherwise uniform use of μαθηταί in Acts to mean *disciples of Jesus,* that is, Christians, it probably means "Paul's converts," men whom he had won not for himself but for Christ.

        That which was taught and learned could be described as a ὁδός (9:2; 19:9, 23; 22:4; 24:14, 22; cf. 2:28; 13:10; 16:17; 18:25, 26), though the use of this word is by no means uniform. It seems in general to refer to a way of life, which could be taught and accepted, but it is also used (22:4) for those who practised the Christian way that they had learned. The Greek word does not exactly translate but certainly recalls the Rabbinic *hᵃlakah,* which in general and in particular examples was taught and handed on from teacher to pupil in a scholastic process, and it has a fairly precise equivalent in the use of *derek* in some of the Qumran writings.[34]

        In their work the teachers were joined by prophets (11:27; 13:1; 15:32; 21:10; cf. 19:6; 21:9) and apostles (1:2, 26; *et passim*, but not after 16:4); it is not possible (or here necessary) to distinguish between the functions of the various offices.[35] The whole operation in which they were engaged can be described as a διακονία τοῦ λόγου.[36] This is probably best understood as the work of preaching, but it has been given an interpretation that brings it close to the work of rabbinic schools. According to B. Gerhardsson[37] "there is no doubt that their work on the logos is to a large extent a matter of 'doctrinal discussion,' based on the reading of a text of Scripture and perhaps the reciting of the tradition of Christ as well, or on concrete problems which have been posed and discussed during the process of 'taking stock' of that which is given in the Scriptures and the tradition of Christ, and that which was 'revealed' in the as yet unfinished miraculous course of salvation." He thinks the Council of Acts 15 to be an example of such a session. It is unfortunate for this view that Luke does not describe the Council as a διακονία τοῦ λόγου. Gerhardsson's view is not convincing; it must however be noted because if it can be accepted it gives the clearest example of a school-like process; if it cannot, it tells us something about Luke—he had little interest in representing the scholastic aspect of Christianity.

The result of the teaching of the Way is the production of a αἵρεσις. The word is used six times in Acts, three times with reference to Judaism. Thus 5:17 refers to the local (ἡ οὖσα) αἵρεσις of the Sadducees; 15:5 to the party of the Pharisees; at 26:5 Paul refers to Pharisaism as τὴν ἀκριβεστάτην αἵρεσιν of Judaism. 24:14 quotes an identification of the (Christian) way with a αἵρεσις: κατὰ τὴν ὁδὸν ἥν λέγουσιν αἵρεσιν: at 24:5 the Jewish accusation associates Paul with the αἵρεσις of the Nazarenes; at 28:22 the Roman Jews claim to know nothing about Christianity except that it is a universally disliked αἵρεσις. It is clear from these passages that Luke is familiar with the application[38] of αἵρεσις to such Jewish groups as Pharisees and Sadducees, and that he does not himself choose to apply it to Christianity, though he knows that others did so.

The word αἵρεσις provides a convenient link to the theme of *conventicle*, as also does ὁδός when considered in the light of the *derek* chosen[39] by the men of Qumran. Shared belief is one of the factors that can lead to the formation of a small group of like-minded thinkers, or believers, who by their shared convictions separate themselves from the world around them.[40] When the same group of people are looked at, however, in this light not only do new aspects of their common life appear, a new vocabulary sheds a different light on both the leadership and the membership of the group. Teachers, prophets, and apostles wear a somewhat different aspect, and other words, notably ἐπίσκοποι (20:28), πρεσβύτεροι (11:30; 14:23; 15:2, 4, 6, 22, 23; 16:4; 20:17; 21:18), ἡγούμενοι (15:22), appear. Presbyters in particular have a supervising and administrative rather than a teaching position. ὑπηρέτης[41] may mean not, as is sometimes suggested, one who taught the tradition about Jesus, but one who acted as general assistant to his missionary leaders. The apostles themselves have each an *allotment* (κλῆρος, 1:17) of duty and responsibility.

The words by which the members themselves are described are even more significant. They are brothers (ἀδελφοί: 1:15, 16; 6:3; 9:17, 30; 10:23; 11:1, 12, 29; 14:2; 15:1, 3,7, 13, 22, 23, 32, 33, 36, 40; 16:2, 40; 17:6, 10, 14; 18:18, 27 (si vera lectio); 21:7, 17, 20; 22:13; 28:14, 15),[42] they are *beloved* (ἀγαπητοί:15:25), and *saints* (ἅγιοι: 9:13, 32, 41). The very frequent use of ἀδελφός is particularly striking and characteristic of the small, closely-knit, group that comes to think of itself as a spiritual family. The bonds that unite them to one another serve at the same time to separate them from surrounding society. They have been baptized,[43] they come before long to bear a special and distinctive name (Χριστιανός: 11:26), they (or at least some of their leaders) are what they are and do what they do as the result of God's special choice (ἐκλέγεσθαι: 1:2, 24; 15:7; ἐκλογή: 9:15). 5:13, the more important because it is probably an editorial note by Luke himself, is very striking. The clearly defined and separate group of Christians was magnified by the people (ἐμεγάλυμεν αὐτοὺς ὁ λαός), but no one dared join (κολλᾶσθαι) them. The sentence is oddly worded[44] but Luke's meaning is clear enough; it was no light step to cross the frontier and join the Christians, however warmly one might admire them.

It was characteristic of the Christians according to Acts that they sought one another's company. One of Luke's most characteristic words is ὁμοθυμαδόν (1:14; 2:46; 4:24; 5:12; 15:25) and it is rightly pointed out[45] that the word has more than its customary meaning of unity of mind; for Luke it means physically together. Corresponding to this is Luke's use of διακονία (the διακονία τοῦ λόγου was accompanied by a material, eleemosynary διακονία: 6:1; see also 11:29; 12:25) and of κοινωνία (2:42, interpreted by 2:44; 4:32—the Christians held all things κοινά). They engaged not only in common prayer (προσευχή: 1:14; 2:42; 6:4; 12:5; προσεύχεσθαι: 6:6; 8:15; 12:12; 13:3; 14:23; 16:25; 20:36; 21:5) but also in common meals (breaking of bread: 2:42, 46; 20:7, 11; 27:35; τροφή: 2:46; 27:36).

This survey of Lucan vocabulary has inevitably touched upon much of the narrative material that calls for notice. One negative point may be made at the outset. From time to time in the course of his book Luke has occasion to refer back to the story of the historical Jesus, which he had told in his earlier volume. It is striking that he does not often refer to Jesus' work as a teacher. It is true that he does so in the summary at 1:1, where he speaks of all that Jesus began ποιεῖν τε καὶ διδάσκειν, but at 1:21 he does not say what Jesus did as he went in and out among us. In the Pentecost sermon Peter speaks only of Jesus' miracles; the same is true of Peter's sermon in Caesarea (10:36-38, with obscure references to "preaching peace" and to John the Baptist). At 13:23-25, 33 Paul seems to be on the verge of telling his hearers something more than that Jesus existed but scarcely does so. Beyond this we are told frequently that Jesus was killed, subsequently raised by God from death, and exalted to heaven; the only piece of teaching ascribed to him is the agraphon of 20:35. It cannot be said that Luke in Acts describes or thinks of Jesus as the teaching head of a school. There are however διδάσκαλοι, and the verb διδάσκειν is common; see above (230). Little is given to suggest the content of the teaching so far as this went beyond the evangelistic proclamation of Jesus as Lord and Savior. Whether or not the meeting of Acts 15 is rightly described as διακονία τοῦ λόγου (see above, 231f.) it does describe an occasion when a proposition regarding Christian behavior (15:1, 5) is dis-

cussed in terms of the Old Testament and the experience of Christians
(but not—*pace* Gerhardsson—in terms of the tradition of the teaching
of Jesus) and a conclusion reached. This picture bears some relation to
the activity of a school but in substance it comes nearer to the discipline
of a conventicle or sect which prescribes the conditions under which
converts may join it and the rules they must thereafter observe.

It is in fact characteristic of a sect or conventicle[46] that it is
particularly conscious of the boundary between itself and the surrounding world; and the Christians in Acts frequently betray an interest of
this kind. We have already noticed the use of κολλᾶσθαι in Acts
5:13; this verse portrays very clearly the self-awareness of a community of marked men who stand out among their contemporaries, are respected, perhaps a little disliked, and left to themselves, because it is
only the exceptional person who can pluck up the courage to join them.
This is the essence of a conventicle. The conventicle is conscious of its
numbers; and twice in the early chapters (2:41; 4:4) Acts mentions the
numbers of converts won by the apostolic preachers; later there are other less precise references to growth (e.g. 6:7). Frequently, though not
invariably, conversion and entry into the Christian conventicle are
marked by baptism.[47] Paul's speech to the Ephesian elders in 20:18-35
reveals the concern of a pastor for his flock and lays upon the elders the
charge that they should tend God's flock; nothing is said about searching for the lost sheep.[48]

The summaries that Luke interposes from point to point in his
narrative are of special importance because they are probably Luke's
own composition and reveal his own picture of the church of the first
generation. Its members are united by the practices of piety and of charity. Teaching and learning are part of their life (2:42)—as ever, school
and conventicle are closely related. They pray together as well as in the
Temple (2:42; 4:24-30), and religion and practical concern are united in
the common shared meal (2:42, 46; 20:7-12; 27:33-6). At 2:42 this is
mentioned along with κοινωνία—*fellowship*, but it is unlikely that
Luke would use the word without recalling its connection with the adjective κοινός and his statement that the first Christians had all things
κοινά (2:44-46; 4:32-35). This shared life is characteristic of the small,
enclosed group; not perhaps entirely uncharacteristic is the occasional
breakdown of this sharing in difficult circumstances. This occurs in
Acts 6:1, a verse full of difficulties, but one that bears witness to Hebrew and Hellenist groups,[49] led (we may perhaps infer) respectively
by the Twelve and the Seven. The originally single cell develops internal stresses and splits into two.

At this point we may review the evidence that we have considered and try to see it as Luke wishes us to see it, in the light of the
whole story that he has to tell. His intention in 6.1-7 is not to describe
two Christian factions but to show that any tendency to fissiparousness
that early Christians may have shown was immediately overcome by

the apostles who acted in harmony with the mass (πλῆθος, 6:2, 5) of the people, and moreover, after this prompt action, led not to the dissolution but to the further great expansion of the number of believers: many even of the priests accepted the faith (6:7). It is possible to dig out of Acts, as we have done, evidences of the school and the conventicle as forms of early Christianity, but these are not terms that Luke likes to use. As we have seen, the word σχολή is used (19:9), but only of a building. We may think of a Pauline or Johannine school but Luke does not. The word αἵρεσις is also used, but (as we have seen) at 5:17; 15:5; 26:5 of Jewish parties; of Christians only at 24:5,14; 28:22, and always in such a way as to show a measure of dissatisfaction "a promoter of the sect of the Nazarenes" (said by Tertullus); "the Way, which *they* call a sect," "concerning this sect, we know that everywhere it is spoken against." Luke's own word for the local Christian community is ἐκκλησία; and *local community*, as has often been observed, is what he does mean by this word.[50] There is one passage (20:28) where Luke appears to mean something more like the *una sancta catholica et apostolica ecclesia*, but this is a concept that he arrives at[51] by a summation of the various local ἐκκλησίαι. A pointer to this is to be found in 9:31,[52] where Luke speaks of an ἐκκλησία (singular) in Judaea, Galilee, and Samaria. He has not told us of the institution of a church in Galilee, but he has told us of one in Jerusalem (5:11; 8:1, 3), and implied the existence of one in Judaea (1:8; 8:1) and of one in Samaria (8:12, 13, 17). These taken together are the ἐκκλησία of 9.31. That of 20:28 covers of course a much wider area. It is not surprising that Luke, whatever, and however remote, his relation with Paul may have been, should have chosen in this respect to use Paul's church vocabulary, describing Christians collectively as ἐκκλησία and individually as ἅγιοι. These two words, and ἀδελφός also, had for him the specific advantage of pointing to the ancient people of God (as at 7:38) and to what he and his readers could recognize as the organized people of a city (as at 19:39). They were words that had a potentiality for emphasizing the unity of the totality of Christians, even though this totality might be thought of as no more than a summation of local ἐκκλησίαι, of local groups of ἅγιοι, of local families of ἀδελφοί. Luke did not see the existence of an ἐκκλησία in Jerusalem, another in Antioch, and others in various cities of the Hellenistic world, as a threat to the unity of the one ἐκκλησία; a school of James, a conventicle of Peter, might have constituted such a threat. This is not a matter of conjecture or hypothesis. There is good reason to consider Acts[53] as a monument of the Christian consensus that arose in the second half of the first century at the close of a period in which the church had been racked by those disputes between contending factions which can be traced with some clarity in the Pauline epistles. It was—subconsciously perhaps—part of Luke's intention to minimize the role of school and conventicle in the period of which he treats, as he undoubtedly fails to depict in all their gravity the conflicts between, for example, the Pauline and Judaizing groups.

It is true that these fierce undercurrents can here and there be traced beneath the smooth surface of Luke's writing. There were those who said, "Unless you are circumcised in accordance with Mosaic custom you cannot be saved" (15:1). Paul did perhaps have to be informed (21:25) of the existence of a decree he had had no hand in formulating, and received a less than cordial welcome from James and his party (21:20-24). In the same way, as we have seen, it is possible to discern in Acts traces of the school and of the conventicle, and in fact only hints at the significance—at the existence—of the *una sancta*. This is by no means to be regretted. The supersession of other terms by ἐκκλησία-*church* should not be allowed to obscure the fact that *school* and *conventicle* express and preserve elements of Christian existence that the Christian community can abandon only with serious loss.

In itself, *school* gives an inadequate account of the household of faith. Christianity is not simply a lesson to be learned or a tradition to be transmitted. Yet the Gospel is the word of God, a theology, and though there is a sense in which it can be apprehended by the simplest and least intelligent person it contains depths that the profoundest mind cannot fathom and it calls for constant re-application to a constantly changing society in ways that require a great deal of thought. It is easy to speak (Acts 28:31) of teaching the things concerning the Lord Jesus Christ; it takes a good deal of instruction and study to begin to understand what these things mean. Since the theological basis of Christianity is so rich it is unlikely that everyone will understand it in precisely the same terms; this may (though it need not) lead to contradiction and consequent separation of school from school. A school of nominalists and a school of realists (let us say) cannot both be right; but a Johannine school and a Pauline school may. Schools, as phenomena of intellectual history, always tend with time to lose momentum and edge. This appears in the New Testament. The Deutero-Pauline writers, great as their admiration for their head and great as our debt to them may be, do not show the intellectual and spiritual power of Paul himself: the Pastorals do not stand on the same level as Romans. The Johannine epistles do not show the flexibility and strength of the Fourth Gospel,[54] and indeed seem to peter out in the use of orthodox slogans accompanied by a measure of backbiting. But the Deutero-Pauline and Johannine schools, if they achieved no other purpose (and in fact they achieved a great deal) at least preserved for our benefit the work of their founders. From the beginning the *school* has played an important part in the understanding, transmission, and extension of the Christian faith, and this appears already in the New Testament.

It is not necessary (though it may perhaps be helpful) to stand in the line of those who suffered through the Conventicle Act of 1664 to recognize that the characteristics of the *conventicle* are characteristic of the New Testament church and must in consequence be characteristic of any valid manifestation of Christian community. It is quite clear in the New Testament that there is a difference between the Christian brotherhood of disciples and the world. "If you were of the world, the world would love what belonged to it; but because you are not of the world, but I chose you out of the world, because of this the world hates you" (John 15:19). "I pray not for the world, but for those whom thou gavest me" (John 17:9). Paul's terminology is different but he expresses the same thought, and as John sees love as the mark of discipleship so Paul recognizes that to join the Christian fellowship involves moral transformation. "Or do you not know that unrighteous men shall not inherit the kingdom of God? Do not be misled. Fornicators, idolaters, adulterers, catamites, sodomites, thieves, rapacious men, drunkards, abusive men, and robbers—none of these shall inherit the kingdom of God. And that is what you were, some of you; but you were washed, you were sanctified, you were justified, in the name of the Lord Jesus Christ and in the Spirit of our God" (1 Cor 6:9-11). To become a Christian means crossing a frontier, to belong to those who are saved and not to those who perish (1 Cor 1:18; 2 Cor 2:15). This transference sometimes is, sometimes is not, associated with baptism; always it is a conscious and deliberate choice. In the choice the initiating, activating force is the mercy of God (Rom. 9:16) and the work of the Holy Spirit (1 Cor 2:4), but these are expressed in the abandonment of idolatry (whatever form that may take) and the determination of life by the Lord Jesus (1 Thess 1:9,10). The danger of the local conventicle is that it tends to become inward-looking, to turn ethical principles into rigid rules, and to become narrow in its apprehension of truth. It is the whole church, the *una sancta,* that is one great conventicle, and its seat is Mount Sion, the heavenly Jerusalem (Heb 12:22, 23). Perhaps this is what Luke means when he uses the same word for the local and for the universal church.

NOTES

1. *Ethica Nicomachea* 1177ᵇ 5.
2. *Politica* 1337ᵇ 31.
3. Lucian, *Macrobii* 4.
4. Which to a Greek could not be commerce or industry; politics or agriculture perhaps.
5. See however Acts 19:9, σχολή.
6. The words used are σχολάζειν, σχολαστής, σχολή.
7. Hebrew *harpu.*
8. And, I believe, in most modern languages: Schule, école, scuola, school.

9. Oxford 1964, 1805.
10. "Von der Bildung einer Schule im konventionellen Sinn mit einer ausgemachten Führungspersönlichkeit und einer Schülergefolgschaft kann trotz des Namens 'Religionsgeschichtliche Schule' in diesem Fall nicht gesprochen werden." G. Lüdemann and M. Schröder, *Die Religionsgeschichtliche Schule in Göttingen*, Göttingen 1987, 7.
11. The few Greek words based on σύναγειν provide no true parallel.
12. Italian *conventicola* seems to have a similar sense.
13. *Shorter Oxford English Dictionary*, 386.
14. Acta Seminarii Neotestamentici Upsaliensis XX; Uppsala, Lund, and Copenhagen, 1954.
15. DSD, now denoted by lQS. Stendahl refers to E. Von Dobschütz, "Matthäus als Rabbi und Katechet," *ZNW* 27 (1928), 338-348 and to R. Bultmann, *Die Geschichte der synoptischen Tradition*, Göttingen 1931, 382f., where the word *Gemeindekatechismus* is used.
16. See *Exegetische Versuche und Besinnungen* 1, Göttingen 1960, 168-187.
17. Tübingen 1971 (third edition).
18. "Mit E. Käsemann mag man von einer 'ecclesiola in ecclesia' sprechen." *Der johanneische Kreis*, Tübingen 1975, 15.
19. *The Community of the Beloved Disciple*, London 1979, especially 13-24.
20. See 2 John 10, 11; 3. John 9, 10. On these small epistles see J. M. Lieu, *The Second and Third Epistles of John*, Edinburgh 1986.
21. I have drawn attention to this in J. Becker (Ed.), *Die Anfänge des Christentums*, Stuttgart 1987, 255-8.
22. *The Social Teaching of the Christian Churches* (tr. O. Wyon), London 1931, II 993.
23. And of course those who, like Eduard Lohse, are deeply concerned and active in both.
24. C. K. Barrett, *The Pastoral Epistles* (The New Clarendon Bible), Oxford 1963, 29, 30, and elsewhere.
25. *sopherim* was used for earlier generations of teachers; see E. Schürer, *The History of the Jewish People in the Age of Jesus Christ*, Rev. by G. Vermes, F. Millar, and M. Black, Vol. ii, Edinburgh 1979, 325.
26. Aramaic; Hebrew *hakam*.
27. M. Jastrow, *A Dictionary of the Targumin*, etc., New York, Berlin, London, 1926, 421.
28. E.g. *Vita* 10. On party differences see *Mélanges Béda Rigaux*, Gembloux 1970, 391-5.
29. A. J. Malherbe, *The Cynic Epistles*, SBL Sources for Biblical Study 12, Missoula 1977, 94.3.
30. *Vita* 12.
31. F. Cumont, *The Mysteries of Mithra* (ET, T. J. McCormack), London 1956, 170. On 171 Cumont speaks of "the interior life of the Mithraic conventicles". Cf. A. D. Nock, *Early Gentile Christianity and its Hellenistic Background*. New York, Evanston, and London, 1964, 13: In the Hellenistic age "we become aware of interesting esoteric rites carried on by small private societies. The cult society as a corporation is an old institution in Greece: now it becomes important as affording suitable soil for the growth of religious ideas."

32. When the word is used at 17:17 it is probably intended to recall the figure of Socrates.

33. B. M. Metzger, *A Textual Commentary on the Greek New Testament*, United Bible Societies 1971, 366; αὐτοῦ was mistakenly written instead of αὐτόν.

34. E.g. 1QS 9:17, 18; 10:21; CD 1:13; 2:6. At Qumran "the way" was understood as strict observance of the Mosaic law; not so even the most conservative Jewish Christian groups, but the two have in common the notion of the exact performance of what is believed to be the revealed will of God.

35. Note also the use of ὑπηρέτης at 13:5; cf. 26:16.

36. 6:4. λόγος, alone or with a genitive θεοῦ or κυρίου), is frequently used for the Christian message as proclaimed by apostles (e.g. 4:4) and others.

37. *Memory and Manuscript*, Acta Seminarii Neotestamentici Upsaliensis 22, Uppsala, Lund, Copenhagen, 1961, 245.

38. Noted above (note 28) in Josephus.

39. Note the use of *baḥar* at 1QS 9:17.

40. Chrysippus, *S.V.F.* 2:37:8: εἰ δὲ αἵρεσίς ἐστι πρόσκλισις δογμάτων ἥ, ὥς τινες, πρόσκλισις δόγμασι πολλοῖς...

41. See note 35.

42. 1.14 refers to members of the earthly family of Jesus.

43. References to baptism are by no means uniform in Acts; for example, no baptisms are recorded in the missionary travels of chs. 13 and 14, though churches are founded and supplied with presbyters. It cannot be assumed on the basis of Acts that all converts were baptized.

44. "Der scheinbare Widerspruch zwischen 13 und 14 ist eine blosse Ungeschicklichkeit des Erzählers"—H. Conzelmann, *Die Apostelgeschichte*, HNT 7, Tübingen 1963, 41.

45. As long ago as by E. Hatch, *Essays in Biblical Greek*, Oxford 1889, 63f.

46. Witness Troeltsch's definition, above, 228.

47. See above, note 43.

48. Note however the use of ἐκκλησία in 20:28, on which see below, 235.

49. For the meaning of ʿΕλληνιστής see my essay in *Context: Essays in Honour of P. Borgen*, ed. by P. W. Bockman and R. E. Kristiansen, Trondheim 1987, 19-33.

50. The New English Bible translates ἐκκλησία as *congregation* except at 20:28 and where it refers to the Christians of Jerusalem.

51. As perhaps did Paul, who by ἐκκλησία usually means a local church, but is able to sum all local churches in the plural ἐκκλησίαι (e.g. Rom 16:16), but also (probably Gal 1:13 and other persecution passages) in the singular ἐκκλησία.

52. If the singular is read, with P⁷⁴ ℵ A B C (Ψ) 81 323 453 945 1175 1739 *pc* vg (syᴾ) co Dionysius and against (E Ψ) η it syʰ boᵐˢˢ.

53. See the essay referred to in note 49.

54. C. K. Barrett, *Essays on John*, London 1982, 127-130.

16

WHAT IS NEW TESTAMENT THEOLOGY? SOME REFLECTIONS

Few who remember Cambridge theology between the wars are likely to question the outstanding significance of Sir Edwyn Hoskyns's lectures on the Theology and Ethics of the New Testament. "It is no dishonour to the Divinity Professors to record how men, and women, came to Cambridge for the sake of Hoskyns."[1] Hoskyns died, still a young man, in 1937; I had the good fortune to hear him lecture in his last year, 1936-1937, and then, and later, to be supervised by his pupil, Noel Davey, perhaps a more profound though less extrovert theologian than Hoskyns himself. I can bear witness to the truth of a further remark contained in Charles Smyth's *Memoir*, which I have already quoted. "You may generally recognise a pupil of Hoskyns by the fact that, when he says 'theology,' what he means is 'New Testament theology' " (xx). I need not say that this does not mean that either Hoskyns, or his pupils, were unaware of the existence, and the significance, of other subdivisions of the total theological undertaking: Systematic Theology, Philosophical Theology, Moral Theology, and the like. The translator of Karl Barth, even though it was the *Commentary on Romans* that was translated, and at a time when the *Kirchliche Dogmatik* had scarcely begun to appear,[2] is hardly likely to have continued in ignorance of the discipline of Dogmatics, even if he had known little about it to begin with. The fact is rather that in Hoskyns's hands New Testament theology was so fascinating, absorbing, exciting, that most of us, though from time to time we had to turn our attention to other fields, knew that the New Testament was the one area in which we had to work. After 42 years the fascination and the excitement remain.

"When he says 'theology,' what he means is 'New Testament theology'." But what does he mean when he says "New Testament theology"? I do not recall that Hoskyns ever told us.[3] Perhaps it was enough that wherever you opened the New Testament, whether at the Synoptic Gospels, or Paul, or 2 Peter, you found that it was talking theology; but that will scarcely suffice for a definition of a fundamental department of theological study. It is a curious fact, indicative, it may be, of national characteristics, that English-speaking, and especially

English, theologians, though they have not been unmindful of the theology of the New Testament, have produced very few "New Testament Theologies."[4] I must myself confess that though I have for many years lectured on the theology of the New Testament it is only recently, and in part under the stimulus of younger scholars, such as, notably, Robert Morgan,[5] not to mention friends and colleagues in other countries,[6] that I have come to ask myself what New Testament theology is. Hence this paper, which is no more than a groping towards an answer to the question that it poses.

New Testament theology as a separate discipline is a relatively new department of theological study. Through most of Christian history theologians have taken it for granted that theology that was not biblical could not be Christian; at the same time they have recognized that the task of theology was not completed by the repetition, or even the rearrangement, of the words of Scripture. Athanasius, for example, in defending the use of such unscriptural terms as ἐκ τῆς οὐσίας and ὁ– μοούσιος, declared that it was the business of the bishops in council to "collect the sense of the Scriptures,"[7] and collecting evidently included repacking the material in new bags bearing new labels. The substance of the scriptural message had to be collected from the various places in which it was expressed and re-expressed in a new terminology suitable to the controversies and to the philosophical habits of speech and mind of the age. But this did not mean that theology was divided into two distinct operations, biblical theology and dogmatic theology. It is arguable that in the Middle Ages there was a tendency for the biblical element in Christian thought to diminish and for the non-biblical philosophical element to increase, for the dogmatic tail to wag the biblical dog. It would be wrong, indeed ludicrous, to claim that theologians such as Anselm and Thomas abandoned the final authority of Scripture,[8] but it is certainly true that the Reformation rested upon a reassertion of this authority and a critical application of it: if current ecclesiastical practices and current ecclesiastical thought were not consistent with Scripture, so much the worse for them; they must be abandoned or amended. *Sola Scriptura*, as a critical principle, was not new; at least, *Scriptura* was not new. But it was enforced with a new rigor, and discovered to be creative as well as critical. This however did not establish Biblical Theology as an autonomous branch of theological study. It was reasserted that all theology must be fundamentally biblical, and the effect of this was rather to suppress than to encourage a special activity of biblical theology.[9]

It is not to the period of the Reformation but rather to that of the Enlightenment[10] that we must look for the origins of "New Testament theology." There were several reasons for the development of biblical theology at this time. One was discontent with the limitations imposed by dogmatic orthodoxy. This had now been developing among Protestants as well as Catholics for many years, and scepticism and pietism joined forces in the desire for something simpler and less hidebound. The best way of blowing away the cobwebs of the ages was simply to go back through the centuries to the origins of Christian dogma, thus cutting off masses of what seemed to be unnecessary, and clogging, accretions. It is not accidental that the study of biblical theology, and the use of that term, go back to about the same period as the origins of what we call the quest of the historical Jesus.[11] "Back to Jesus" was in fact the "back to the theology of the Bible" movement in its most radical form. Those who wished to be free from the fetters of current dogmatics, and those who sought a warmer and more intimate faith in communion with the Lord, might combine in the study of the apostles and their witness to Jesus. All this, of course, grossly simplifies a complex picture; at the moment I am drawing attention to a negative motive in the movement towards a New Testament theology, distinct from what theology had become.

There was a positive side too. *Dogmengeschichte* as a discipline, a historical discipline, arose at the time of the Enlightenment. "Die Dogmengeschichte ist ein Kind der deutschen Aufklärungszeit."[12] The context of this pronouncement goes on to mention, among others, Lessing (1729-1781) and Semler (1725-1791), who were notable figures in the early Quest and in the development of New Testament theology.[13] The development of *Dogmengeschichte* was part of a general development of historical awareness which contributed to the view that there might be a theology of the Bible with a historical distinctiveness as well as a special authority. It is at least approximately true that at about the same time, or a little later, scholars became aware of "the theology of" other periods too. Migne published the great *Patrologiae*,[14] recognizing the patristic period as an isolable entity in a far fuller way than the more dogmatic, less historical, classical Anglican appeal to the authority of the great councils of the undivided church. G. J. Planck began in 1781 to publish what was (as far as I know) the first history of Protestant Theology; Dorner's better known history followed in the next century.[15] My point is a simple one: a clearer, sharper, more critical awareness of history was among the factors that led to the recognition that the New Testament marked off a period of history which might be expected to have a theology of its own and to be worth investigating for that reason.[16]

Negative and positive motives for the study of New Testament theology thus combined with each other, as, well as with the polemical motive of proving that one brand of dogmatics was correct over against all the rest. It is not my intention to take the history of New Testament theology further[17] but, on this basis, to resume the inquiry into what New Testament theology is. In this sketch of origins at least three possibilities have presented themselves. (1) New Testament theology is the foundation of dogmatics, the basis of Systematic Theology, still requiring to be rethought and reformulated in the light of the philosophical fashions of the day but providing, as it were, the basic material which the systematic theologian will recycle. (2) It is a way of escape from dogma, an escape into an ampler, freer air. (3) It is a totally independent historical discipline.[18] I see no reason why any one of these propositions should be taken to represent the whole truth to the exclusion of the other two.

It is of primary importance that New Testament theology should retain full independence as a critical historical process. Hoskyns, as I have said, did not define New Testament theology; but in *The Riddle*[19] Noel Davey, after quoting the second article of the Nicene Creed, wrote,

> When the Catholic Christian kneels at the words *incarnatus est* or at the words *and was incarnate*, he marks with proper solemnity his recognition that the Christian Religion has its origin neither in general religious experience, nor in some peculiar esoteric mysticism, nor in a dogma, and he declares his faith to rest upon a particular event in history. Nor is the Catholic Christian peculiar in this concentration of faith. This is Christian Orthodoxy, both Catholic and Protestant. In consequence, the Christian Religion is not merely open to historical investigation, but demands it, and its piety depends upon it. Inadequate or false reconstruction of the history of Jesus of Nazareth cuts at the heart of Christianity. The critical and historical study of the New Testament is therefore the prime activity of the Church. (10)

This passage does not mention New Testament theology, but it does provide a pointer to the sort of thing that New Testament theology may turn out to be; and it is clear that it is rooted in critical historical study of the New Testament. In fact, this passage makes the same claim that Wrede makes, though with a quite different application. Wrede was one of the earliest and most radical members of the *religionsgeschichtliche Schule;* Hoskyns and Davey rejected "religion" and "religious experience" as the basis and content of Christianity (notwithstanding the repeated use in the passage quoted above of the term "the Christian Religion"). Further, the core of the New Testament is not a religious experience but a historical event; but this event is such that the critical study of it generates theology. The historian begins by asserting the crown rights of his own subject: history is and must be independent, and the historian serves but one mistress. Yet precisely in practising his own trade as a historian he finds that he becomes, whether he will or no, a theologian. Thus Wrede himself, as a historian, discovered that his sources (the gospels) were theologically rather than historically motivated; and this is not the end of the story.[20] If the record of what religious men do in the interests of their religion is *Reli-*

gionsgeschichte, then the New Testament historian must practise *Religionsgeschichte*, but his proper subject, pursued with all the integrity and rigor proper to historical investigation, turns out to be not *Religionsgeschichte* but theology.

New Testament theology is thus generated internally; I mean, within the general field of New Testament studies, as a kind of by-product, and (unless we are to withdraw to the mere collection of *dicta probantia*) it cannot be divorced from the literary criticism by which the books of the New Testament are analyzed and the historical criticism by which the events of the New Testament period are assessed in regard to their historical probability and arranged in plausible sequence and relation to one another. Yet, notwithstanding its origins, it turns out to belong within the operation of the Faculty of Divinity, and it is proper to consider its relation with other aspects of theological study. Whether it is best regarded as the foundation of dogmatics or as an escape from dogmatics[21] is a question that may be deferred until we have turned over the facts and examined them further.

Let us begin by allowing that both New Testament theology and Systematic Theology exist. How may they be compared with each other? The former may be characterized by the word process, the latter by the word result. I do not mean by this that the work of Systematic Theology is ever finished; by definition it never is. Each generation, each distinct intellectual climate, calls for its own Systematics, precisely because Systematics involves the relation between unchanging truth and varying philosophical modes. We await the next 13 volume set of *Kirchliche Dogmatik*. Yet Systematics means the production of a system, and this is a result, an end-product, and if it is not relatively final—final, that is, in relation to the environment for which it was designed—it has simply failed to achieve that which it was designed to accomplish. A truly satisfactory Systematics would be the system of Christian truth appropriate to today's date. Over against this, New Testament theology is a matter of process.[22] May we then think of it as the process that leads to the systematic result? There is some value in this suggestion, but in truth New Testament theology is both less and more, and cannot simply be dropped in some middle point between the text of the New Testament and modern reconstruction of the New Testament message. There is a famous passage in which K. Barth contrasts the great commentators on Romans in the early years of the twentieth century with Calvin.[23]

> For example, place the work of Julicher side by side with that of Calvin: how energetically Calvin, having first established what stands in the text, sets himself to re-think the whole material and to wrestle with it, till the walls which separate the sixteenth century from the first become transparent! Paul speaks, and the man of the sixteenth century hears.

Here is one contrast: Jülicher and his company (we will not stop to ask if Barth is entirely fair to them, or whether the walls that separate the first century from the twentieth are not very much thicker than those that separate it from the sixteenth) are content to take up the language of the New Testament and adduce parallels to it from Greek philosophy, Hellenistic Judaism, and the Rabbis (how fortunate we are to have the rich fields of Qumran and Nag Hammadi to draw on too!), and suppose that they have thereby done their duty to the text, whereas Calvin inquires what the text has to say to him in his own age. There is another contrast: that between Calvin and the man who is not content until he hears the text speaking the language of his own time—Luther, for example, who is not happy till he hears the text pronouncing judgment on the Papacy and the Scholastics,—and, it may be, Barth himself (here and there in *Romans*) till he can hear Paul speaking in terms of Kierkegaardian existentialism. Where does authentic New Testament theology, not badly represented, perhaps, by Calvin, though I think the work has to be done rather differently today, stand?

Part of the answer to this question is negative. It is the business of New Testament theology to check the systematic theologian when his enthusiasm runs away with him. Consider a very familiar New Testament term, kingdom of God. It is well known that this has been subjected to classical misinterpretations; for example, "the corporate human God-consciousness which is the existence of God in human nature and which comes into being as a result of Christ's God-consciousness."[24] When we read this we know that it is time to call up all the information acquired by the first-year student of theology—'*adonai malak; malkutha dash*e*maya*; and so on—to demonstrate that though Schleiermacher may be saying something true and important he is not saying anything that Jesus could conceivably have communicated to his fellow Jews in first-century Palestine. For him and for them the kingdom belonged to the realm of eschatology. But what does that mean? There are two questions, or groups of questions, here. The first group asks what were the eschatological beliefs of Jesus' audience, and how Jesus appropriated, negated, or modified them so as to create a new eschatological world view. The second group of questions inquires what, if anything, this eschatological world view can mean to a new generation that has abandoned the presuppositions of eschatology in that it no longer finds it possible to contemplate or assign any meaning to a "last day" whether near or distant. It may seem that the wheel has come full circle from Schleiermacher when Perrin writes at the end of a later book,[25] "Kingdom of God is a symbol evoking a myth; the hermeneutical possibilities vary enormously according to the viability of the myth and the functional possibilities of the symbol." Schleiermacher and Perrin are not saying the same thing, but each has abandoned biblical language (except for the actual symbol, kingdom of God, which is being defined) in favor of terminology appropriate to his own time.

The practitioner of biblical theology can hardly allow himself so free a hand. Yet the quotation from Perrin may serve the useful purpose of pointing us on from the negative to the positive function of biblical theology. Perrin's recognition of a variety of hermeneutical possibilities lying beyond his own work indicates the kind of service New Testament theology may perform. There is an analogy to the point I have in mind in what Albert Schweitzer said about Paul. Paul, according to Schweitzer,[26] did not hellenize Christianity, but did express it in a form in which it could be hellenized—brought, that is, into direct relation with, and set out in terms of, the philosophies and culture patterns of the hellenistic world into which it had been introduced. Whether Schweitzer was right or wrong about Paul does not concern us; we may however claim that it is not the business of the New Testament theologian as such to deal directly with the thought forms of his own time, but that it is his business to liberate the contents of the New Testament from their original setting that they may be made intelligible and thus applied in a new one—or rather in an indefinite number of new ones. How, it may be asked, is this liberation to be achieved? An answer to this question must wait till a later point in the discussion.

I have used the word "process" to describe New Testament theology, and outlined one sense in which the word may be understood. A second observation, which may take the argument further, is that the New Testament itself is a process; that is, it describes a historical process. It begins with the story of Jesus, running back to and indeed before his birth and continuing up to his death. It proceeds with the resurrection and the story of the early church, reaching in explicit narrative as far as about A.D. 60, and, by implication, to the end of the century. This is not a long stretch of time compared with what might be involved in, say, "The Theology of the Middle Ages," but it is the classical and formative period; it would perhaps not at this stage be right to say, the authoritative period.[27] I shall consider two aspects of it. The first is the great watershed which, on the Christian view, divides all history in two: the death and resurrection of Jesus. In the New Testament this separates the story of the life and teaching of Jesus of Nazareth from the history of the primitive church—separates, but also unites them. The second aspect of the period that will be considered is the story of the church itself.

The first of these points may be introduced by quoting two well known propositions; they are often used, but are too important to be neglected. There is Loisy's dictum: "Jesus foretold the kingdom, and it was the Church that came."[28] Before the epigram is dismissed the critic should take the simple step of consulting the concordance under the words βασιλεία, so common in the Synoptic Gospels and relatively rare elsewhere, and ἐκκλησία, hardly occurring in the gospels and frequent in the rest of the New Testament. Moreover, though the synoptic teaching on the kingdom is more complex than Loisy appears to allow, it does include a vivid urgent eschatological element—there are some of those who stand here who shall not taste death till they see the kingdom of God come in power (Mark 9:1)—which suggests an outlook that was already becoming an embarrassment in the first century and has in the twentieth, after 1900 years of Christian history, become frankly impossible. Is there a historical continuity between Jesus and the church? The second proposition is Bultmann's: "Die Verkündigung Jesu gehört zu den Voraussetzungen der Theologie des Neuen Testaments und ist nicht ein Teil dieser selbst."[29] This leads us to put our question in a different way: Is there a theological continuity between Jesus and the church? Examination of these questions may in the end contribute to an answer to the wider question, What is New Testament theology?

In a short paper the material available at this point must be handled selectively. We shall take the fact that, in the gospels, the ministry of Jesus ends with the account of a supper that he took with his disciples shortly before his arrest.[30] From one point of view this was a failure. To eat with someone, especially to be united with him by blood, was to pledge an absolute loyalty. This the disciples recognized. "If I should have to die with you, I will not deny you," said Peter; and so said they all (Mark 14:31). Correspondingly, the horror of the betrayal was that it was "one of you," εἷς ἐξ ὑμῶν, who shall betray me, "he who is eating with me," ὁ ἐσθίων μετ᾽ ἐμοῦ (Mark 14:18). But they did break their commitment, betray, deny, and desert him, and Jesus died, not in the company of his friends but alone. This of course is not the end of the gospel story, and before long the meals were resumed; the followers of Jesus continued to hold their supper party, and it was a κυριακὸν δεῖπνον because the κύριος was there; and Paul taught them at their supper to recall what the Lord had done in the night in which he was betrayed (1 Cor 11: 23). Yet it was not the Last Supper they observed. That was rightly defined as the last, the end-point of a series, and though a new series related with the former might begin, the last was the last. It is akin to the mishnaic distinction between the "Passover of Egypt," which could never happen again, and the "Passover of the generations that followed after" (*Pesahim* 9:5). The continuing supper provided a connection with the past, but the connection was neither simple identity nor bare recollection. The same words might be spoken, the same actions performed, but they were spoken and performed in a new context, in a different eschatological setting, between the resurrection of Jesus as the firstfruits of those who slept, and his coming.

It would be possible, and perhaps profitable, to follow this observation in an exposition either of the Last Supper itself or of eucharistic theology. This however is not the present task. I wish rather to draw out the analogy between the act of eating and drinking, transposed into a new period in the eschatological process, and the tradition of the words and deeds of Jesus, used, as it was after the resurrection, for theological rather than purely historical purposes. The event that revolutionized the supper by putting it into a new setting necessarily affected the teaching of Jesus too, which could no more be repeated identically than the supper. Even when the words were most accurately remembered they took on a new meaning.

The resurrection proved to the disciples in a way they could not doubt that Jesus had been right in the great issues—such as kingdom of God and Torah—of his ministry, and immediately they began to find new ways of expressing the fact that he had been right. These found their way progressively into the tradition. They began to label him with dignified titles—χριστός, κύριος, υἱὸς τοῦ θεοῦ—and to work out in theological terms the effect and significance of his death. They did not discard the historical tradition, but they could see that merely to repeat it would not make the point that had to be made. What had been reticent and allusive had to become explicit and challenging. It was necessary now to preach "Jesus *and* the resurrection,"[31] though this had not been prepared for and was certainly not a ready-made form of the Gospel. The propositional form of the preaching, like the structural form of the church, was not laid down in advance, and both had to be improvised in a new period of history whose very existence had not been foreseen; for this reason much in both was bound to be provisional. There is another pointer here to the nature of New Testament theology, at once permanently authoritative and transitional.

It is true that the gospels themselves are preaching. Units of tradition were used for this purpose, but it may well be that on this point Bultmann (who thought that the material was used for a variety of catechetical purposes) was more nearly right than Dibelius (who thought it was used in mission preaching).[32] If preaching, as we encounter it in Acts and Paul, means preaching Jesus and the resurrection, then the gospels are preaching if they are read as wholes, up to and including their last chapters; the individual pericope is complete only when put by the preacher in the new post-resurrection context. In the gospels themselves we see signs of this process; it constitutes the principal difference between the Synoptics and John. Perhaps we may conclude that the Synoptic Gospels (not quite the same thing as "Die Verkündigung Jesu," though related to it) are New Testament theology when we take them in their entirety; that the teaching of Jesus is New Testament theology when it is transposed out of its pre-crucifixion setting and placed where it can be seen in the light of the resurrection. For this reason we may be glad of all the modifications—even if they amount to historical falsifications—that entered the tradition in the course of its transmission.

There is a further inference of great importance. What we see in the process I have just described, whereby units of tradition were given a new form and context which made them usable as preaching material, is New Testament theology, beginning within the New Testament itself—very notably in the relation between John and the Synoptic Gospels[33]—and from this we may infer what the task of New Testament theology is. Its function is to relate all parts of the New Testament to its (the New Testament's) centre, and to interpret them in the light of that centre. What is the centre of the New Testament? That is a question that each New Testament theologian must in the end answer for himself, and until there is an agreed answer New Testament theologies will differ not only in detail but in fundamental conception. Our own generation has seen two outstanding opinions. For Bultmann the centre was justification by faith; this led him to interpret the New Testament as an anthropology, with existentialism as his hermeneutical principle. More recent theologians[34] have focused on Jesus, and New Testament theology becomes essentially a Christology. In fact, the two centres, justification by faith (*sola fide*), and Jesus crucified and risen (*solus Christus*), are if not identical at least so closely related as to be indivisible. This was already seen by Luther,[35] and (to pursue the geometrical image) an ellipse based on these two points as foci will turn out to be not very different from a circle. But the image matters little; what is important is the establishing of the principle on which New Testament theology works.

We have now considered, and drawn certain conclusions from, one aspect of that historical process which the New Testament describes. We must now turn to the second, the story of the post-resurrection church. I propose to mention two related senses in which this story bears upon New Testament theology. In the first place, the history itself is the record not of peaceful development but of strife and controversy; in the second place, and arising out of the controversy, the books that make up the New Testament bear traces of disagreement, or at least of diversity, to such an extent that we are bound to ask whether "the theology of the New Testament" is a proper expression; should we not rather speak of "the theologies of the New Testament"?

I may at this point recall a remark that I made earlier. I said that when applied to the New Testament critical and historical study itself becomes a theological operation. It might seem enough to say that the New Testament is such a thoroughly theological work that any method of study is bound to unearth theology in it; but there is more than this. It is critical historical investigation that brings to light the controversies that underlie the New Testament, and critical literary investigation that lays bare the various literary units and groups that constitute the New Testament. Thus these processes bring to light both the intensity and conviction, and the variety, that are characteristic of New Testament thought.

At present, however, I am concerned not with these characteristics but with the bare facts, and of these the first is that the New Testament is a record of strife and controversy. This is familiar to all students of the New Testament, though I suspect that they do not always recognize the violence of the strife and the heat of the controversy—the fact, for example, that Paul alleges that the majority of Christian preachers are untrustworthy cheats (2 Cor 2:17; cf. 4:2), and that the false brothers (who must at least have claimed to be Christians) appear to have threatened his life (2 Cor 11:24-26).[36] No wonder; they were in truth servants of Satan (2 Cor 11:15). Paul's apostleship was disputed (1 Cor 9:2; 15:8f.); but he could stand up for himself, and when envoys from James turned Peter from the straight path he did not hesitate to resist him (Gal 2:11). So much by way of illustration; a serious New Testament history would have to be both fuller and more cautious. It must not be assumed that Paul's opponents in Galatia, Corinth, and Jerusalem were the same; we must distinguish between Pillars, such as James and Cephas, and false apostles. What is important is that it was out of this clash of opinion and personality that Paul's theology grew. It has been said that we should not heed Galatians as a source for Paul's view of the law; it springs out of a controversy and therefore expresses a biased, one-sided opinion. I cannot accept so low a view of Paul's intelligence and integrity—or, as it seems to me, so low a view of Scripture. The opposite is the truth. Paul said what he had to say, neither more nor less. He may say it more violently in Galatians than in Romans, but what he says he means, and the effect of controversy is to sharpen the edge of his argument. We may be grateful to the false brothers for the statement of the doctrine of justification that they elicited, to those in Corinth who challenged Paul's apostleship for the exposition they provoked of what it means to be an apostle, to those in Colossae who did not "hold fast the Head" and thereby made Paul work out afresh a Christology in which Christ is head of both universe and church.

It is not simply that controversy sharpens men's wits, though this is true, and doubtless Paul's mind acquired a keener edge as he debated with Judaizers, Gnostics, and others. Controversy develops a special kind of theology, a critical theology which is seen already in the New Testament and especially in Paul and John. It is a function of theology to submit systems of thought, including well-meant systems of religious thought, to critical examination, to probe and to inquire; to say on occasion a sharp No. Truth is best defined over against error; creeds may need the sting of anathemas in their tail. This observation is needed as a supplement to W. Bauer's study of orthodoxy and heresy in the early church.[37] If it is true that Paul conducted no heresy hunts it is equally true—and this is the point of the preceding paragraph—that he was constantly at work establishing truth over against what he took to be error. This is not the same thing as drawing a straight line and excommunicating all who stand on the wrong side of it; that is a static, Maginot-line kind of warfare, whereas Paul's battles, and those of the New Testament in general, are full of movement, with a good deal of overlapping and interlocking of opposed forces.

It is the critical historical study of the New Testament that brings this critical theology to light as the creative thought of the New Testament period; an uncritical, unhistorical reading will miss it. It is of vital importance to the New Testament theologian that he should pursue this historical study and by entering into the history of the New Testament grasp the genesis of its theology. Yet, when all is done, we are not contemporaries of the apostles; we do not stand in Jerusalem or on Mars'Hill and join in the debates there. Our contact with these debates is literary, and we must therefore turn to the second aspect of the post-resurrection history. The New Testament consists of a considerable number of books which are, to say the least, not identical in their approach to and expression of theological truth. We have a variety of sources, and it is this variety that makes critical thought possible for us, whether in the realm of history or of theology.

The shortest way of illustrating this will be to consider Luke-Acts. For its first readers this was probably all the New Testament they had. Mark had been absorbed into the longer gospel, and could therefore be discarded; the author of Acts shows no knowledge of Paul's letters, and it would be surprising if his readers were aware of them. At this point critical thought is not impossible, but it is both difficult and limited. If Acts, for example, is read on its own it is possible to ask such outworn questions as How did Christianity reach Damascus? and such not uninteresting historico-theological questions as whether Peter's vision (10:9-16) originally had to do with clean and unclean animals or with clean and unclean men, and whether the decree of 15:29 deals with the challenge of 15:1,5 or with some other matter; but it is only when the Pauline epistles are brought into the discussion that questions about the opposition in Galatia and in Corinth, and the issues of the law, and of natural theology and heathen worship, become vivid and significant. It is by the comparison of document with document that we engage in the work of critical history and of critical theology too. Not that the comparison of one New Testament document with another opens the way to the kind of dispute Paul had with his enemies; the New Testament writers are on the same side, even though, like the armies in *King John*, in attacking the same city from opposite points they sometimes succeed in shooting at each other. The point is that critical, question-asking history provides an approach to the more difficult concept of critical, question-asking theology; and not only so, in New Testament study the two are inseparable. They belong together and can only be forced apart by violence.

The immediate practical consequence of this is to be found in the lay-out of a book on New Testament theology. This must in some way express the variety of New Testament thought. There is, of course, no single "right" way of setting out the sections and chapters of a book, but broadly speaking one may say that Bultmann's method, in which the proclamation of Jesus, the kerygma of the primitive church, the kerygma of the Hellenistic church, the theology of Paul, the theology of John, and the development towards the ancient church, are successively studied, is correct, and that of Alan Richardson's *Introduction to the Theology of the New Testament* (London, 1958), which results in a topically arranged book resembling a systematic theology, is wrong.

More important is the fact that we here return (*see* 250) to the principle by which each theological statement is related to the "centre"; this now appears however in a fuller and more complex form. There the centre was defined in doctrinal terms; it may now be sought (though probably not found) in personal, or rather literary terms. Is the centre of New Testament theology to be found in Paul? or in John? or should we simply say, corresponding to the *Solus Christus*, in Jesus? Clearly the word "centre" will not do. Paul must be related to Jesus, and to John; John must be related to the synoptic tradition, and to Paul; Hebrews must be related to John and to Paul; and so on. This is not only an essential process in a critical theology; it provides a vital clue to that liberation of New Testament theology desiderated above (247). The New Testament theologian traces the development of Christian thought from its origins—or presuppositions—in the ministry of Jesus through a variety of religious and intellectual contexts. This should enable him to distinguish between the essential and the peripheral, the constant and the variable; more than this, he should learn a great deal about proper and improper kinds of variation and adaptation. There is sufficient variety in the New Testament for general principles both positive and negative[39] to be established. For example, the New Testament gives us clear enough hints about the extent to which the mythical element in it may be demythologized, and the handling of the synoptic tradition in John[40] provides a pointer to the way in which primitive eschatology has to be modified as time runs out. In yet another sense, New Testament theology is a matter of process. It does not simply reproduce the content of the New Testament; it does not simply differentiate between the various theologies in the New Testament, or attempt a neat harmony of them; it describes and analyzes the process by which one theology, or mode of theology, is transposed into another, and thus on the one hand liberates the essential theological content of the New Testament from the various settings in which it was formulated, and on the other hand indicates to the systematic theologian the methods by which and the limits within which he may set to work to reformulate Christian truth in the current idiom—reminding him, however, at the same time, that however successful he may be he is not adding to the canon.

It is time to draw these reflections, which are no more than a preliminary attempt to answer the question at the head of this paper, to a close. I do this under three heads.

First, it may be asked what authority a New Testament theology thus conceived may have. It has been described in terms of a critical process, involving historical reconstruction with all its manifold uncertainties. If conflict and variety play an essential part in it, can it be in any sense authoritative? We may begin (but it is only a beginning) by returning to the Enlightenment and to Pietism. There is a sense in which Biblical Theology has always meant a release from authority, a sense in which it has always signified a turning to the immediate and personal in religion. It would be a mistake to regard either of these motivations as simply misleading. Indeed, they suggest the first point—a negative one, it is true, yet important—that is to be made here. The authority of New Testament theology means deliverance from various false authorities to which from time to time Christian life has been subjected. This could be illustrated not only from the period of the Reformation, but also, as I have said, from that of Enlightenment and Pietism. More important than these illustrations, and indeed the most fundamental observation of all, is that the New Testament itself reveals precisely this kind of deliverance. The gospels record a conflict between two kinds of authority, the authority of law as administered by Jewish institutions and the liberating authority of Jesus. It is essentially the same conflict, though transposed to different circumstances, that flares up in the story of Paul. The false brothers, to whom not even for a moment would he yield, crept in "to spy out our liberty which we have in Christ, in order that they might enslave us" (Gal. 2.4); at the same time, Paul does not stand for anarchy—he has authority, but it is authority "for building you up and not for throwing you down" (2 Cor 10:8; 13:10). Whatever is to be said about the authority of a theology based on the New Testament, it is not the kind of authority that lies in the rigid constitution of an ecclesiastical body which men question at their peril. Equally it is not the authority of a worked out and carefully formulated set of dogmatic propositions, which those who do not accept must be expelled from the community. This kind of authority makes itself felt on the margin of the New Testament (2, 3 John), but it is not to be found at the centre, where Paul, contending to the last ditch for the purity of the Gospel, asks only if a man loves the Lord (1 Cor 16:22), and proposes only the corresponding formula, κύριος Ἰησοῦς (1 Cor 12:3).

Two points may be added to this note on the authority of New Testament theology.

(a) "There is a riddle in the New Testament. And it is a riddle neither of literary criticism, nor of date and authorship, nor of the historicity of this or that episode. The riddle is a theological riddle, which is insoluble apart from the solution of a historical problem. What was the relation between Jesus of Nazareth and the Primitive Christian Church? That is the riddle."[41] Since the theological riddle is bound up with the historical problem the answer can be found only in New Testament theology. There are no independent historical traditions about Jesus of Nazareth that are of any value; the witness of the New Testament church enshrined in the New Testament books is decisive and authoritative. This does not in itself mean that the New Testament witness is right; we may reject it as mistaken. It does not mean that it is unitary; as we have seen, the New Testament is marked by variety. It does not mean that it is self-evident; we have to search for it with all the tools of the trade. It does not mean that, when we find it, we shall find it expressed in terminology that pleases us; the whole task of reformulation remains. It means simply that if we do not like the account, given by the New Testament and brought out in New Testament theology, of the relation between the New Testament church and Jesus, we must lump it; there is nowhere else to go. This is the sort of authority New Testament theology has.

(b) The authority of the New Testament (and thus of New Testament theology so far as it is genuine) is creative. I have already quoted Paul's "authority for building you up, not for throwing you down." The same man wrote to the same church, "You are the seal of my apostleship in the Lord" (1 Cor 9:2). Their very existence was a visible token of his apostleship, of his authority (though in the context he might well have disclaimed the word) as an apostle. Authority within the New Testament does not consist in occupying a position of dignity but in accomplishing a task. The authority of the New Testament does not consist in a doctrine of inspiration but in its apostolic effectiveness. The authority of New Testament theology within the whole theological operation does not consist in having the last word, but in having the first, creative word.

So Professor X's "Theology of the New Testament" has no authority save that which is conferred on it by its faithfulness to its subject-matter and theme; but New Testament theology—as a process, an unachieved process—has a paradoxical authority of its own. The second and third concluding points may now be set out in little space. The second follows from what I have just written, and I need do no more than recall the argument (247) that it is the task of New Testament theology to set the theological content of the New Testament free so that it can be re-expressed in the language of any age and place. It is often supposed that the contribution of New Testament scholars to Christian preaching consists in turning the Greek of their text into plain, easy English (or whatever it may be). The truth is the reverse of this. The New Testament scholar must put the New Testament into English as difficult, as full of problems and offence, as the original Greek; the smoother, the easier, the more inoffensive his rendering the greater his failure. Releasing the New Testament for assimilation in the modern world does not mean presenting something that the modern world will be glad to hear, and New Testament theology means making available the full content of New Testament thought and conviction in all its offensiveness.

It follows, and this is the third concluding point, that New Testament theology must be a free and independent operation (see 244). It

does not set out to please either the church or the world; it will often offend both. This is essentially a theological observation, but its effect is
to make New Testament theology academically respectable, and to do
so more effectively than Wrede's arguments, which stood on a different
foundation. Any trimming of the sails to prevailing winds would be
treachery both to scholarship and to the subject-matter of the discipline
itself. There are no limits to the questions that may be asked, or to the
sources to which the questions may be directed. Provided that the principle of judgment "by the centre" (250, 253) is maintained there is no
reason why there should be any trouble over the precise limits of the
canon; it will soon enough appear that Ignatius is further from the centre than John.[42] It does however follow from this that New Testament
theology is indeed theology, and not *Religionsgeschichte*; and the theology turns out to be one that expresses its integrity in a firm criticism of
religion—as Hoskyns never tired of saying. But this is only part of the
fact that New Testament Theology is always critical theology.

NOTES

1. Charles Smyth, in *Cambridge Sermons*, by Edwyn Clement Hoskyns (London, 1938), xix.
2. Hoskyns's translation of Barth's *Commentary on Romans* was published in 1933 (Oxford); the first volume of *Christliche Dogmatik* appeared in
1928, revised as *Kirchliche Dogmatik* in 1932.
3. This will to some extent be remedied when (it is hoped in the summer of 1980 [published 1981]) S.P.C.K. publish *Crucifixion—Resurrection: A
Study of the Essential Pattern of New Testament Theology and Ethics*, begun by
Hoskyns, continued by Davey, and edited by G. S. Wakefield.
4. O. Merk, in *Biblische Theologie des Neuen Testaments in ihrer An-
fangszeit* (Marburg, 1972), a book to which I am much indebted, in sketching
"Probleme neutestamentlicher Theologie seit F. C. Baur" devotes 5 out of 34
pages to "die Entwicklung im angelsächsischen Sprachbereich." The proportion
is both correct and misleading. See my review in *Journal of Theological Studies* 28 (1977), 245-7.
5. Robert Morgan, *The Nature of New Testament Theology* (Studies
in Biblical Theology, Second Series, 25; London, 1973). This book contains a
long and very valuable essay by Morgan, together with translations of W.
Wrede's *Über Aufgabe und Methode der sogenannten neutestamentlichen Theologie* (1897) and A. Schlatter's "Die Theologie des Neuen Testaments und die
Dogmatik" (1909).
6. Of whom, let it here be gratefully said, by no means the least or
least valued is Markus Barth. I wish I had known him at the time when I was
hearing Hoskyns in Cambridge and he was reading theology in Bern and Basel.
7. συναγαγεῖν ἐκ τῶν γραφῶν τὴν διάνοιαν (*de Decretis Nice-
nis* 20), said with special reference to the hypocrisy of their adversaries (Ari-
ans).
8. For example, Anselm, *Cur Deus Homo* I 18 (388A): Certus enim
sum, si quid dico quod sacrae Scripturae absque dubio contradicat, quia falsum

est; nec illud tenere volo si cognovero; Thomas, *Summa Theologica*, Qn 1, Art.
1,2: Necessarium fuit homini ad salutem, quod ei nota fierent quaedam per re-
velationem divinam, quae rationem humanam excedunt;—see the whole context.
   9. Collections of *dicta probantia* (see, e.g., Merk, op. cit. 15f., and
elsewhere) can hardly be called theologies.
   10. See Merk, op. cit. 21-8.
   11. A. Schweitzer, *The Quest of the Historical Jesus* (E. T., London,
1910, 1936). Schweitzer begins his account with Reimarus (1694-1768).
   12. F. Loofs, *Leitfaden zum Studium der Dogmengeschichte,* 5th edition edited by K. Aland, 1. Teil (Halle-Saale, 1951), 1.
   13. It was G. E. Lessing who published the "Wolfenbüttel Fragments" (of Reimarus's work) in 1778. J. S. Semler replied to this in 1779.
   14. The Latin series began in 1844; the Greek concluded in 1866.
   15. I. A. Dorner, *A History of Protestant Theology* (Edinburgh,
1871), a translation of *Geschichte der protestantischen Theologie* (Munich,
1864).
   16. It is no coincidence that F. C. Baur, whose critical sense of history was unsurpassed, contributed both to *Dogmengeschichte* in general and to
New Testament theology as well. The first edition of his *Lehrbuch der christlichen Dogmengeschichte* appeared in 1847. *Vorlesungen über die christliche
Dogmengeschichte* was published posthumously (1865-7), and so was *Vorlesungen über neutestamentliche Theologie* (1864).
   17. See, in addition to Merk, op. cit., the Epilegomena in R. Bultmann, *Theologie des Neuen Testaments*[7] (Tübingen, 1977), 585-99; N. A. Dahl,
in *Theologische Rundschau* 22 (1954), 21-49; G. Bornkamm, in *Theologische
Rundschau* 29 (1963), 33-141; G. E. Ladd, *A Theology of the New Testament*
(Guildford and London, 1975), 13-33.
   18. This is the view of Wrede; see the book by Morgan (note 5). So
for example: "How the systematic theologian gets on with its results and deals
with them—that is his own affair. Like every other real science, New Testament theology has its goal simply in itself, and is totally indifferent to all dogma and systematic theology" (69).
   19. E. Hoskyns and N. Davey, *The Riddle of the New Testament*
(London, 1931).
   20. See *Expository Times* 87 (1975-6), 8f.
   21. See (1) and (2) on 243f.; also 253-255.
   22. It is, I trust, unnecessary to point out that I am not talking about
"process theology."
   23. K. Barth, *The Epistle to the Romans* (E. T. by E. C. Hoskyns, Oxford, 1933), 7.
   24. Not Schleiermacher himself, but Norman Perrin summarizing
Schleiermacher in *The Kingdom of God in the Teaching of Jesus* (London,
1963), 14.
   25. *Jesus and the Language of the Kingdom* (Philadelphia, 1976),
203.
   26. *The Mysticism of Paul the Apostle* (E. T., London, 1931), especially 334: "Paul did not Hellenize Christianity; but he prepared the way for its
Hellenization."
   27. On the question of authority see below, 253-255.
   28. A. Loisy, *The Gospel and the Church* (E. T., London, 1903),

166.

29. Bultmann, op. cit., 1.

30. In what follows I shall draw upon what I have written in *Jesus and the Gospel Tradition* (London, 1967), 50f.

31. The words are precisely those of Acts 17:18, but significantly enough the same sense, in similar wording, is found at Rom. 10:9.

32. R. Bultmann, *Die Geschichte der synoptischen Tradition²* (Göttingen, 1931), 64: "Apologetik und Polemik wie Gemeindebildung und Disziplin sind ebenso in Rechnung zu setzen und daneben schriftgelehrte Arbeit." M. Dibelius, *From Tradition to Gospel* (E. T., London, 1934), 13: "Missionary purpose was the cause and preaching was the means of spreading abroad that which the disciples of Jesus possessed as recollections." Bultmann does not exclude preaching as part of the setting in life of the gospel material. On the difference see especially P. Vielhauer, *Geschichte der urchristlichen Literatur* (Berlin, 1975), 285-9.

33. This point is not dependent on the view (which I hold; see *The Gospel according to St John²* [London, 1978], 42-6; *Expository Times* 85 [1973-4], 228-33) that John probably knew Mark.

34. See my "Christocentric or Theocentric? Observations on the Theological Method of the Fourth Gospel," in *La Notion biblique de Dieu*, edited by J. Coppens (Bibliotheca Ephemeridum Theologicarum Lovaniensium XLI; Gembloux, 1976), especially 361-3. I go on in this paper to show that for John Christology is not the last word; the gospel is in the strictest sense theological.

35. See for example the 1522 Preface in which, though he praises the Epistle of James, he sets side by side the two complaints that it ascribes righteousness to works, and makes no mention of the suffering, resurrection, and Spirit of Christ.

36. See my *Second Epistle to the Corinthians* (London, 1973), 299f.

37. W. Bauer, *Rechtgläubigkeit und Ketzerei im ältesten Christentum* (Tübingen, 1934; second edition, 1964; E. T., Philadelphia, 1971).

38. James (see note 35) is not really an exception, though there may well be misunderstanding of Paul on the part of the writer, or of other persons known to him.

39. Again (see notes 35, 38), James comes to mind; see also E. Käsemann's discussion of 2 Peter (in *Exegetische Versuche und Besinnungen* I [Göttingen, 1960], 135-57).

40. See note 33; I am not assuming a literary connection, though such a connection may well exist.

41. *The Riddle of the New Testament* (note 19, above), 14.

42. This is not intended as a complete answer to the problem of the canon, only as a claim that in practice no harm but good results if we look at all the literary products of the apostolic and sub-apostolic ages.

17

THE CENTER OF THE NEW TESTAMENT
AND THE CANON

It is understandable and proper that a Festschrift for Eduard Schweizer should be published under the title *Die Mitte des Neuen Testaments*. In innumerable publications, and in many lectures and discussions, even when he has begun from a point on the periphery of the New Testament, he has led his readers or hearers to what they could recognize (even if they could not define) as the heart of the matter. And he has insisted that behind the variety of the New Testament there lies a creative core which gives life and meaning to the whole. I am glad therefore to take up the suggested topic for his sake as well as because it enables me to pursue a rather belated attempt to clarify the meaning, scope, purpose, and structure of that which we call "New Testament Theology"[1]—a subject on which I have been lecturing for many years. The New Testament is a book conditioned by the linguistic, social, and religious environment within which it arose, or better: the various environments in which the several parts of it arose, for variety is not a superficial but an integral characteristic of it. It is impossible to understand it without an awareness of this variety (so that the New Testament theologian must practise literary criticism) and impossible to grasp its essential message without knowledge of the languages, and of the social and religious history involved (so that the New Testament theologian must be a linguist and a historian). Yet the work of the New Testament theologian is not exhausted in literary, linguistic, and historical processes, fundamental and indispensable as these are. It is not within the province of New Testament theology as such (though some New Testament theologians, not least Eduard Schweizer, have done it very ably) to rephrase, to reconceptualize, the Christian Gospel in the thought forms appropriate to today: this is the work of systematic theology and apologetics. It is, however, the task of New Testament theology so to delineate the relation of any part of the New Testament message to its original environment as to make it detachable from that background and thus available for restatement in terms of a new environment; not perhaps actually to universalize it but to make it potentially universal in intelligibility and application. The core of this operation is to be found (so I argued in the earlier paper to which I have referred) in the relating of each unit of the New Testament to the centre of the New Testament. "What we see in the process that I have just described, whereby units of tradition [in the gospels] were given a new form and context which made them usable as preaching material, is New Testament theology, beginning within the New Testament itself. . . and from this we may infer what the task of New Testament theology is. Its function is to relate all parts of the New Testament to its (the New Testament's) center, and to interpret them in the light of that centre" (*NTTh*, 10f.).

But what is the center of the New Testament? I was not able in the paper I have referred to to pursue this question at length. I mentioned (250) the familiar phrases *sola fide* and *solus Christus*, and went on to show (253) that the answer was likely to turn out to be more complicated. Later, arguing that the process I had described gave to New Testament theology the academic independence and integrity that Wrede[2] had demanded (but sought in a different way), I wrote: "There are no limits to the questions that may be asked, or to the sources to which the questions may be directed. Provided that the principle of judgement 'by the centre'. . . is maintained there is no reason why there should be any trouble over the precise limits of the canon; it will soon enough appear that Ignatius is further from the centre than John" (*NTTh*, 256). I was prudent enough to add a footnote (42): "This is not intended as a complete answer to the problem of the canon, only as a claim that *in practice* no harm but good results if we look at all the literary products of the apostolic and sub-apostolic ages." There is however a problem of the canon, and though "judgement by the center" may provide a practical means of handling the problem it also accentuates and sharpens it.[3] If it is laid down that the twenty seven books constitute a canon, that is, a measuring-rod, a means of testing theological propositions, a *norma normans* that determines Christian truth, this definition will apply and apply equally to all the twenty seven books; if at the outset all are to be normative it cannot be said that some are more normative than others. A book is normative, in which case it is canon; or it is not, in which case it is not canon. It may be said, in the now famous sentence, "All animals are equal, but some are more equal than others"; but it can hardly be said, with reference to a measuring-rod, that all inches are equal, but some inches are more equal than others. This does not have even the intelligibility of an epigram. If we speak of the "centre of the New Testament" we intend to refer to some part or aspect of it which expresses the content of the whole with special clarity, force, or precision. We cannot, if we have regard to the meaning of the adjective, mean that it is "more canonical" than other parts, since there cannot be degrees of canonicity; we must mean that it is canonical in a sense or senses in which other parts are not. [4] The logical conclusion is put in the form of rhetorical questions at the close of Dr. Käsemann's essay on 2 Peter.[5] "Was ist es um eine Eschatologie, die

wie diejenige unseres Briefes nur noch die Hoffnung auf den siegrei-
chen Einmarsch der Gläubigen in das ewige Reich und die Vernichtung
der Gottlosen kennt?. . .Was ist es um eine Kirche, welche sich der Ketzer so erwehrt, dass sie selber zwischen Geist und Buchstaben nicht
mehr unterscheidet, das Evangelium mit ihrer Tradition und tatsächlich
mit einer religiösen Weltanschauung identifiziert, die Schriftauslegung
durch Lehrgesetz reguliert und aus dem Glauben das Jasagen zur ortho-
doxen Dogmatik macht?" (*EVB* I, 157). Käsemann of course sees how
this is connected with the question of the canon. "Was ist es um den
Kanon, in welchem der 2 Petr als klarstes Zeugnis des Frühkatholizismus Platz hat?" (ibidem). It is not at present my intention to attempt
to answer these rhetorical questions, but simply to note the process by
which they are reached. Käsemann's paper is for the most part a
straightforward exposition of the substance of 2 Peter itself, but it is
clear that at the vital points he is making a comparison, especially between "then" and "now". "Als vorhandener Besitz der Gemeinde ist Offenbarung *jetzt* die 'christliche Religion', wie Pistis den Christenstand
bezeichnete" (*EVB* I, 140; my italics). "Der Begriff des Apostels hat
sich also *gewandelt*: Der Bote des Evangeliums ist zum Garanten der
Tradition, der Zeuge der Auferstehung zum Zeugen der historia sacra,
der Träger eschatologischen Gotteshandelns zum Fundament der Heil-
sanstalt, der Angefochtene zum Bringer der securitas *geworden*"(*EVB*
I, 141; my italics). This structural change "bestimmt nicht weniger die
Lehre von der Kirche, die aus der creatura verbi zur Hüterin der vor-
handenen Wahrheit *wird*, vom Geist, der in der Lehrtradition aufgeht
und darum dem Buchstaben *nicht mehr* kritisch entgegensteht, vom
Glauben, der zur Entscheidung für die Integrität der Überlieferung
wird, und vom Worte Gottes, das nach *urchristlicher* Anschauung doch
nie abgeschlossen vorliegt, sondern je und je . . . sich neu offenbart, ubi
et quando visum est deo" (*EVB* I, 142; my italics).

It would be instructive, especially because it would make the
observations still clearer, to carry out a similar process with regard to 1
Peter, also in all probability a pseudonymous work.[6] The apostle Peter
is indeed represented as a witness of the sufferings of Christ (5:1), but
when he describes them (2:22-4) he makes no claim to be writing of
what he has seen (contrast 2 Peter 1:16-18), and is content to address
the elders as a fellow elder.[7] He writes as one who is living in the last
days; see not only the explicit statement of 4:7 but also 4:17 and 5:8—
the present persecution is to be thought of as the beginning of God's final judgement (he begins with his own household) and as the final rag-
ing of the devil before his overthrow. Regeneration is not effected by
baptism but by the preached word of the Gospel;[8] baptism is rather a
prayer to God for a good conscience (3:21), and this (though the wording is different and perhaps less unambiguous) is not widely different
from the Pauline doctrine of justification. As an epistle of suffering and
hope it could almost be regarded as a sermon based on Rom 8:18. In-

struction in Christian living, though cast in part in the form of household rules (2:13-3:9), is based on the belief that men are now living in the last days. Other elements enter into it: an apologetic element (2:12) and an evangelistic (3:1), but they supplement rather than qualify the fundamental principle.

It will be clear, even from this summary account, that 2 Peter and 1 Peter have both been compared with the theology of the Pauline epistles; it is by this standard that the "formerly", the "now", the "has become", have been defined. And it is almost certainly true that the chronological sequence is Paul—1 Peter—2 Peter. The comparison however would stand even if the chronology were different. This may be brought out by instituting a further set of comparisons.[9] 2 and 3 John depict one of the most striking situations in the New Testament—two groups of Christians in a state of mutual excommunication. In 3 John the prime actor is Diotrephes. Whether or not he should be described as a bishop[10] is not important. He does not receive "us" (3 John 9)—the Elder who writes the epistle. This means that he does not accept the Elder's version of Christian doctrine, spreads evil tales about him, and provides no facilities for members of the Elder's congregation who have, it seems, been travelling as missionaries. But the Elder behaves in the same way towards those of whom he disapproves. Many deceivers have gone out "into the world" (2 John 7); they too are probably missionaries. But their doctrine, the message they preach, is wrong (2 John 7, 9); they must not be received into the house, and must not even be given a courteous conventional greeting (2 John 10). It is not altogether clear what was the issue between the two groups. Almost certainly it was in part personal; so far as it was doctrinal it seems to have turned on a docetic view of Christ (2 John 7). The point is an important one; the New Testament as a whole is confident of the real humanity of Christ, but it does not elsewhere commend this kind of exclusiveness. The first epistle does not go so far. It knows that there are those who "have gone out from us" (2:19), thereby proving that they never "belonged to us" (2:19); these people speak "of the world" and world "listens to them" (4:5); that is, they too were, or at least regarded themselves as, missionaries, enlightened missionaries who were able to use the language of the world in order to commend the Gospel. They never belonged to us, says the author of 1 John; it may be that they said the same of him, but the conflict does not appear to have reached the pitch we see in the two shorter letters, though there is a tendency for the disagreements to crystallize in slogans (e.g.1 John 4,2.15) which were doubtless bandied about, and there are limits beyond which orthodox Christians ought not to pray for the lapsed (5:16.17). The Fourth Gospel is different. Although it is one of the most highly charged theological works in the New Testament it is not orthodoxy that it requires of its readers. "If anyone loves me, he will keep my word, and my Father will love him, and we will come to him and make our dwelling with him" (John 14:23; cf. 1 Cor 16:22 for the negative side of the same criterion). Discipleship is manifested not in exclusiveness but in love: "This is how all men will know that you are my disciples, if you have love among yourselves" (13:35).[11] One wonders if either the Elder or Diotrephes qualified. The gospel is moreover notoriously two-sided in its teaching: Hellenistic and Jewish, docetic and anti-docetic, predestinarian and universalist.[12] It would be rash in this case to speak of chronological development: the chronological order of John; 1;2;3 John is not easy to determine (though this sequence is in fact quite probable). But whatever the chronology may be, if the Fourth Gospel is reckoned to stand near the centre of the New Testament, 2 and 3 John are not far from the circumference.

We thus return to the question of the centre of the New Testament, and with it to the notion of a canon within the canon. It is evidently impossible in what must be a brief paper to deal with this topic in the way in which it is treated in the volume edited by Dr. Käsemann.[13] It will, however, be necessary to review some of the possibilities that have been suggested.

It is natural to begin with the proposition that the center of the New Testament is Jesus, and there is indeed a sense in which this is undoubtedly true. It is essentially Luther's criterion of canonicity, the significance of which is well brought out by G. Gloege.[14] "Ist Christus 'Herr und König der gesamten Schrift', so bedeutet das *positiv*: Luther übernimmt den Kanon der Kirche...nicht aus Gründen der Pietät, sondern von seinem Christusverständnis her...Das christozentrische Kriterium bedeutet *kritisch*: als Herr der Schrift ist Christus nicht nur Grund, sondern auch Grenze ihrer Autorität: Kanon im Kanon." To this theological principle we shall return;[15] but it is not without problems, easy to state but not easy to deal with. The record of the life and teaching of Jesus occupies half of the New Testament, and the other books refer to him frequently—most of them very frequently. But simply to say this will not satisfy anyone who has a historical as well as a theological conscience. Do we know what Jesus taught? If the word *know* is stressed and given the strictest possible interpretation the answer must be in the negative. Every student of the New Testament can construct a body of teaching, larger or smaller, which he believes can be ascribed with very great probability to Jesus. But probability is not certainty, and everyone knows that the tradition of Jesus' words passed through an uncharted period of about forty years before the earliest of our gospels was written. How much of the earliest tradition was lost, how much was distorted, how much was added to it from extraneous sources of various kinds, we may guess, and guess with some confidence, but we cannot know. So much for what he said; what he did (since he wrote no autobiography) is necessarily the witness of others, not necessarily false, but open at every point to the influence of interest and special pleading. Moreover, what he did would hardly stand as "center" unless it were interpreted and its significance drawn out, and this interpretation is almost certainly the work of others, not of Jesus himself; at least, to distinguish between interpretation that goes back to him and interpretation that is the product of subsequent theological reflection is a problem of notorious difficulty.

A second possibility (clearly, as we have seen, adopted by Käsemann in his discussion of 2 Peter) is to take Paul, the first great theological interpreter of Jesus, as the centre of the New Testament. There is much to be said for this choice. Even those who agree with him least cannot fail to recognize the theological energy with which Paul wrestles with the situation created by the emergence of Jesus within Judaism; to remove his letters, especially the four *Hauptbriefe,* from the New Testament would leave it emasculated, and the existence of a body of Deutero-Pauline literature shows that many in the subapostolic age looked back to him as the apostle and teacher *par excellence,* shows also that they were prepared to have their work judged in terms of his, and indeed invited such comparison. Simply however to take Paul as the normative centre of the New Testament is open to objection. It would ignore the fact that Paul, on his own showing, was a controversial figure. There were those who preached a different Gospel (Gal 1:6; 2 Cor 11:4); and the very fact that Paul expresses himself in this way shows that his adversaries were, at least in their own estimation, Christians, who doubtless believed that their Gospel was the true one and that Paul's was the different Gospel which was to be anathematized as no Gospel at all. The problem however does not lie with those whom Paul describes as false brothers, false apostles, ministers of Satan. If the New Testament is to be taken as in any sense an authoritative work such men cannot be regarded as candidates for the position of center or norm. The problem arises rather in the grey area between these false apostles and Paul. The false apostles seem to have been in some way related to the original group of Jerusalem apostles[16] with whom Paul (according to his own account in Gal. 2) reached a measure of agreement. The agreement was substantial but incomplete. It was not such as to prevent a break between Paul and Peter at Antioch (Gal 2:11) or to inhibit the heavy irony with which Paul speaks of those who thought of themselves as "pillars" (Gal. 2:9) and could be called the "superapostles" (2 Cor 11:5; 12:11). Paul maintained his equality with them; he did his best to preserve unity between his Gentile churches and Jerusalem; he did not question that they were servants of Christ; he and they preached the same Gospel of the crucified and risen Jesus. But it cannot be held that he and they developed this shared message in the same theological directions. In fact, if Paul is selected as the centre of the New Testament we are probably choosing a minority element. Up to the time of his own death and the deaths of Peter and James he and his followers may well have been outnumbered by Jewish Christians who understood the Gospel in a somewhat different way; whether in the next generation anyone fully understood him and perpetuated his work on precisely his lines is doubtful: the authors of Ephesians, Acts, the Pastorals, Clement of Rome, and Ignatius, for all their admiration of him, did not.

Paul then, though an outstanding figure, cannot be taken as the normative centre without raising problems, especially with regard to Jewish Christianity. Should we do better with John?[17] Again we have a theologian of outstanding power. He stands at the close[18] of the development of the theology in the New Testament, and if there are difficulties in using as norm the beginning of a process there is not a little to be said for using its termination. There is however more to be said against this course. The beginning of the Christian process—Jesus—is of such unique importance that John's remoteness from it is bound to give rise to serious doubt. It is not merely a matter of the lapse of time. Estimates of the historical value of the Fourth Gospel, and of the historical intentions of its author, have varied and do vary a good deal, but it is not open to dispute that its account of Jesus, when looked at in comparison with that of the Synoptic Gospels and from a historical point of view, raises considerable difficulty. It is also a syncretistic work. Again, opinions differ, and it would be impossible, even if it were relevant, here to list them all, but most would agree that the Gospel is the fruit of contact between the original Christian message and the environment in which, in the last quarter of the first century, or later, the message was proclaimed. The Fourth Gospel may serve[19] as a centre and norm within the Johannine literature, but objections could be brought against a wider use.

What has just been said might suggest the use of a number of sub-centres to serve as norms over limited areas, Mark, say, for the Synoptic Gospels, Paul (in the Great Letters) for the Deutero-Pauline material (including perhaps Hebrews), the Fourth Gospel for the Johannine literature. This might be better than nothing, but it would hardly be complete without a further stage in which the sub-norms were compared with one another.[20] For the present we may ask if a Jesus-Paul-John axis might serve as a centre of comparison, combining the virtues and avoiding the defects of the suggestions I have already made. It is to be feared not only that all the defects would reappear, reinforcing one another—the uncertainty of our information about Jesus, the one-sidedness of Paul, the eccentricity of John—but that we should find ourselves with a centre that occupied more than half the circle.[21] Suppose, then, we were to take our Jesus-Paul-John axis to mean the agreement of Jesus, Paul, and John, the theological material that is common to them all. The suggestion may seem attractive, but we should encounter further difficulties. Do these authorities agree? Two or three generations ago a widespread opinion was that they had little in common. Wrede, for example, held that Paul virtually contradicted Jesus at all essential points.[22] Many would give a different answer today,[23] and the demonstration of a common platform shared by Jesus, Paul, and John

may seem a possible undertaking, perhaps in the form of "Paul the interpreter of Jesus, John the interpreter of Paul", the whole forming an
axis running through the New Testament as a book and as a period in
history. This however is an over-simplification if it fails to recognize a
direct relation of some kind (not necessarily an independent line of tradition) between Jesus and John. Nevertheless it remains true that the
agreement of these *Hauptzeugen*[24] forms as attractive a possibility as
we have yet found. Unfortunately it also raises new problems. To speak
of picking out the agreements between Jesus, Paul, and John implies
that there are also disagreements, or at least differences, between them;
and what sort of position are we in if, by definition, our chief authorities prove to be in disagreement? Even to recognize that such disagreements do, or may, exist means that we are setting each of our authorities against each of the others as a standard: Jesus is judged by Paul,
Paul by John, and so on. This in turn leads to a further problem.

The critical process would have to be taken down into a Jesus-
Paul-John axis; in the same way it would have to be taken into each
unit or group of units taken to be authoritative. If, for example, Paul
and John are found to be in disagreement it follows that either at least
part of Paul is in error, or at least part of John is in error, or at least
parts of both Paul and John are in error; or, if we choose not to say "are
in error", we mean that they are not in harmony with what we have selected as our standard, our "center". This is a conclusion that may give
us trouble with our definition of what we mean by a "center", but it is a
conclusion that we should not hesitate to draw; indeed it is a conclusion
that is necessarily required by the process on which we have embarked.
Once it is agreed that theological criticism may be applied to the contents of Scripture it is impossible to be content with the comparison of
one book with another; the critical process must be applied within the
several books. This has been well brought out by Dr. Kümmel himself:[25] "Ja, es findet sich bei Vertretern des zentralen Kerygmas dur-
chaus auch 'apokryphes' Einzelgut, und es finden sich dort sachliche
Widersprüche gegen das ursprüngliche Christuszeugnis. Die eigentliche
Grenze des Kanons läuft also durch den Kanon mitten hindurch, und
nur wo dieser Sachverhalt wirklich erkannt und anerkannt wird, kann
die Berufung katholischer oder sektiererischer Lehren auf bestimmte
*Einzel*stellen des Kanons mit wirklich begründeten Argumenten abge-
wehrt werden. Diese 'innere Grenze' des Kanons kann nur durch
ständig neue Besinnung auf die zentrale Christusverkundigung *und*
durch Prüfung des gesamten neutestamentlichen und ausserkanonis-
chen fruhkirchlichen Schrifttums an dieser zentralen Verkündigung erkannt und gesichert werden."

This is well observed, but it is not certain either that
Kümmel's examples are satisfactory or that he has carried his argument
to its logical conclusion. Two of his illustrations require him to contrast
works by different authors: he turns from Acts 17:28f, which appears to

teach that man is naturally related to God, to the denial of any such relation in the rest of the New Testament; and claims that "die Vorstellung von der *Nachweisbarkeit* der Auferstehung Christi durch die Tatsache des Essens des Auferstandenen mit den Jüngern (Luke 24,36 ff) und durch die Wirklichkeit des leeren Grabes (Matt 27,62 ff; 28,11 ff) widerspricht der ursprünglichen Verkündigung, die nur eine *Bezeugung* der Auferstehung Christi kennt" (op. cit., 96, n.94). These observations do indeed raise the question of the canon in general terms but not the question I have in mind here (unless it is held that Acts 17:28 f. is an exact report of words uttered by Paul; but I do not think Kümmel would maintain this). He has one other example, which is more effective, for he contrasts 1 Cor 11:2 ff with Gal 3:28; here we have one author, but must ask whether the two passages really contradict each other. It can be reasonably maintained that 1 Cor 11 describes the position of woman in creation, Gal 3 the new position she receives through the Gospel; it is *in Christ* that there is neither male nor female.

For Paul a better example might be found in his account (based on traditional material) of the resurrection appearances (1 Cor 15:5-8), when this is set in the context of his general understanding of faith. If [26] Paul supposed that simple historical observation could demonstrate the truth of the resurrection he was making of faith something other than the divine gift of which he writes elsewhere. It is not, however, clear that this was his intention. He adds to the traditional list the appearance to himself and thus is provided with an argument that Christian preaching always and everywhere included the proclamation of the resurrection. Nevertheless, it can be plausibly maintained that in this passage he expressed himself with some obscurity and in a way likely to lead to misunderstanding. This conclusion is reached by means of that internal criticism of which I am speaking here, and is the kind of semicontradiction that is most likely to appear within the work of a reasonably careful writer who may at times allow his concentration to flag. Another example is perhaps to be found in Paul's treatment of the Jews. In the early 1 Thessalonians it appears to be Paul's view that God's wrath has finally fallen upon them (2:16). Does he not himself criticize this belief in the more mature discussion of Rom 11?

The Fourth Gospel is full of dialectical distinctions and opposites[27] and I have shown elsewhere that it is unwise to ascribe certain passages, which may superficially appear to contradict others, to an ecclesiastical redactor.[28] The two possibilities, of simple excision of difficult passages by the processes of literary criticism, and the transcending of apparent differences by theological interpretation, can be made to go a long way toward mitigating the force of internal criticism in John, and of course in the New Testament as a whole. The question, however, is bound to arise whether the theological harmonization that is able to produce a measure of unity is justified. Thus in regard to the signs it seems that John's main view is that a faith based upon signs, upon observable historical phenomena, is, though real and better than nothing, an inferior kind of faith (4:48; 14:11; 20:29), yet the first (2:11) and the last (20:30f) references to signs take a different line: by a sign Jesus manifested his glory and his disciples believed; the signs in the gospel are recorded there that the reader may believe.

It is particularly easy to rid the teaching of Jesus of these inner inconsistencies that form the basis of internal theological criticism; it is easy to put them down to divergent elements and strains in the tradition. It might in fact be wise to speak not of the teaching of Jesus himself but of the tradition of his words. We are then free to raise the question of his attitude (as the tradition presents this) to the law and to its Jewish expositors. Within for example the Matthean tradition he affirms the eternal validity of the law and the low standing of those who do not keep and teach it (5:18 f); but the same chapter not only expands the law (e.g. with regard to murder, 5:21 f) but also contradicts the *lex talionis* (5:38 f). The scribes and Pharisees are said to sit in Moses' seat, so that their teaching must be observed (23:2 f); yet not only are they described as hypocrites, their teaching is contradicted (23:16-22).

Enough has been said to show that the processes of critical theology apply not only to the comparison of book with book but also to the examination of individual books. This may seem to amount to the accusation that the New Testament authors were incapable of maintaining a consistent line of argument. This would be too harsh a judgement, for several reasons. In the first place, it must be remembered that these authors belong to a very early stage in the development of doctrine. Confronted in the ministry, crucifixion, and resurrection of Jesus with astounding and unheard-of facts and assertions, they were for the first time attempting to strike out coordinations and interpretations; it is not surprising that they should make various attempts to set out the meaning of their faith or that these attempts should sometimes be inconsistent with each other. Moreover, none of them was a wholly independent theologian. Each of them was to some extent, and some of them were to a very great extent, dependent upon traditional material that had been handed down to them by others. The traditions were often diverse. It is possible to study the redactional activity by which the several authors sought to accommodate the various lines of tradition to one another and to their own theological viewpoints, but the process was seldom if ever complete. This was inevitable at a time that was not only formative but one in which clear-cut lines separating orthodoxy from heresy and not yet been drawn. In addition, most of the New Testament writers were by no means accomplished literary workmen. We may be glad that they were not, and that they have left us in their work clear traces of the crosscurrents of theological thought that disturbed the surface, and the depths, of first-century Christianity. We must, however, use with caution such terms as "das ursprüngliche Christuszeugnis" and "die zentrale Verkündigung." This is an observation to which it will be necessary to return.

Before we leave this point it will be well to observe that the application of theological criticism to the books of the New Testament does not always work in one direction. It may suggest from time to time that Homer—the gospel tradition, Paul, John—nods; but it may also show that some books often regarded as peripheral are nearer to the center than some suppose. In *NTK* H. Küng and H. Braun, approaching the matter from different angles, find Catholicism in the New Testament, and notably in Acts and the Pastorals. "Das Katholische (im Verständnis des Amtes, der apostolischen Sukzession, der Ordination, der Lehre usw.) findet sich bereits im Neuen Testament."[29] "Die drei bisher besprochenen Kreise[30] haben gezeigt: der fromme Anspruch erhebt wieder sein Haupt, die Naherwartung wird in die Prolongierung der Eschatologie aufgelöst, die Kirche versteht sich am Ende des ersten Jahrhunderts institutionell. All diese Linien schiessen zusammen in einem Statischwerden von Glaubensinhalt und Lehre: die 'gesunde Lehre' der Pastoralbriefe, die 'vorhandene Wahrheit' (2 Petr 1,12) und der 'einmal überlieferte Glaube' (Judas 3) bestimmen das Bild der fruhkatholischen Schriften des Neuen Testaments."[31] Both writers have in mind and refer to the essay by Dr.Käsemann, "Begründet der neutestamentliche Kanon die Einheit der Kirche?"[32] Küng complains that Käsemann, and Protestants in general, establish their view of the church by making a selection from the New Testament; if they would accept the whole (as the canon they profess to accept obliges them to do) they would be bound to accept a catholic view of the church.[33] Braun, writing under the title "Hebt die heutige neutestamentlich-exegetische Forschung den Kanon auf?" reaches the conclusion: "Die Exegese, die auf die Botschaft merkt, paralysiert die Schlacken im Kanon und macht die Begrenzung des Kanons, was das einzelne anlangt, fraglich. Sie sagt also nicht Ja zum Kanon als ganzen, nicht Ja, weil es der Kanon ist. Sie nimmt ihn kritisch, aber unter Verwendung *jenes* Sachkriteriums, das dem Neuen Testament selber entstammt. Und darum hängt sie am Kanon, was seine Mitte, was das neutestamentliche Grundphänomen betrifft. Sie hat dies ja nur *im* Kanon, später doch schon gar nicht; wenn auch im Kanon nicht rein und nicht unvermischt. So paradox es klingt: sie respektiert den Kanon dann am gründlichsten, am sachgemäßBesten, wenn sie an ihm als Kanon, als einer formalen Grösse, als einer genau abgegrenzten Grösse nur relativ interessiert ist; wenn sie vielmehr ihre Leidenschaft völlig auf die Mitte richtet, von der die Hauptteile des Kanons regiert werden, auf jene Schriften, bei deren Abfassung an Kanonisierung noch kein Gedanke war."[34] There is much in each of these conclusions of great importance, and I have cited them here partly in order that they may be kept in mind throughout the rest of our discussion. My main object at present, however, is to point out[35] that there is in the Pastorals and in Acts a great deal less of Frühkatholizismus than is often supposed. There is Frühkatholizismus

in the New Testament; its "unacceptable face"[36] appears in 2 and 3
John (see above). It is always, however, first century (or early second-
century) Frühkatholizismus, and is a token of the fact that the church,
the bearer of the Gospel, settled down, as it had to do, to life in this
world, and in doing so recognized that institutions, however dangerous,
were nevertheless essential; and the books in question reveal the tension that must exist between the people of God, who are constituted by
the Gospel and by definition have in this world no continuing city, and
the framework of their continuing life in this world.

So far we have spoken of the "centre of the New Testament"
in literary terms; and have not been successful in finding a way of defining it. It is also possible to think of it doctrinally, and one thinks immediately of the familiar phrases *sola fide* and *solus Christus*. Here two
questions arise. First, what is the origin of these phrases? It is clear that
solus Christus, though not identical with the proposition that the figure,
or the teaching, of Jesus, or the traditions about Jesus, should be regarded as the centre of the New Testament, is very closely related to it and
could hardly be thought of independently of it—unless *Christus* were to
be understood in the gnostic manner as a heavenly emanation. In the
context in which *solus Christus* is used *Christus* is the *Christus* of the
New Testament as a whole, the heavenly being who was incarnate in
the man Jesus. The *solus Christus* thus focuses upon the man in whom
the Son of God is known and upon the action of the God-man in re-
deeming mankind. This does in fact take more seriously than a literary
selection of material can do the centrality of Jesus in the New Testament. It means, however, that for practical purposes the phrase is of little use as a measure of authority and canonicity, for, with scarcely an
exception, all the documents of the New Testament affirm this centrality. It may be argued (and this would be a significant observation) that
some of them, even when they give an apparently central place to Jesus
Christ, derogate from this centrality in practice by assigning too much
importance to other considerations, such as ecclesiastical institutions.
Such an imbalance would, for example, operate against any claim that
might be made for the canonicity of the epistles of Ignatius. Thus *solus
Christus*, though closely related to the gospels, is in fact derived from
the New Testament as a whole.

Sola fide, on the other hand, is unquestionably based on Paul,
and preeminently on Romans and Galatians; it thus corresponds very
closely to the literary selection of the Pauline *Hauptbriefe* as the centre
of the New Testament. Its use therefore turns, in the first place, on the
question whether it is a valid summary of the essential content of these
epistles, and, in the second place, on all those questions that were raised
above concerning the eligibility of Paul himself as a centre. The latter
questions need not be discussed again; the former may be answered in
the affirmative, especially if we understand *sola fide* as an abbreviation
of the fuller formula, *justificatio impiorum, sola gratia, sola fide. Sola*

fide can in fact be regarded (and in this way it expands far beyond its narrowly Pauline verbal limits) as a variant form of *solus Christus,* since it means that "none but Jesus can do helpless sinners good", and that to him must be given all the glory and praise. The connection between the two is brought out in Luther's well-known criticism of James. "... achte ich sie für keines Apostels Schrift, und ist das meine Ursache: Aufs erste, dass sie stracks wider S. Paulum und alle andre Schrift den Werken die Gerechtigkeit giebt ... Aufs andere, dass sie will Christenleute lehren, und gedenkt nicht einmal in solch langer Lehre des Leidens, der Auferstehung, des Geistes Christi."[37] It is in this context that Luther develops explicitly not the *sola fide* but the *solus Christus* test. "Was Christum nicht lehret, das ist noch nicht apostolisch, wenn's gleich S.Petrus oder S.Paulus lehrete. Wiederum, was Christum prediget, das wäre apostolisch, wenn's gleich Judas, Hannas, Pilatus und Herodes thäte" (Kleinert, 173). To claim (if James does in fact do this) that man's relation with God can be put right by his obedience to the law is implicitly to deny the all-sufficiency of Christ and James becomes an epistle of straw *gegen sie*—in comparison, that is, not only with Paul, who formulates the *sola fide,* but with John, 1 John, and 1 Peter, "the books that show you Christ."[38]

This comparison may introduce the second question regarding the *sola fide* and *solus Christus*: for what purpose are they used? They have been introduced here as an alternative form of the "canon within the canon", and that they can be used in this way is shown very clearly by Luther's characteristically vigorous definition of the apostolic and the non-apostolic (terms which for him subsume a good deal more than literary authorship).Yet it is an interesting fact that, although he set them in a group by themselves, he continued to print Hebrews, James, Jude, and Revelation in his New Testament, and wrote of James: "Darum kann ich ihn nicht unter die rechten Hauptbücher setzen. Will aber damit niemand wehren, dass er ihn setze und erhebe, wie es ihn gelüstet; denn viel gute Sprüche sonst darinnen sind".[39] That is, Luther did not use these formulas as an instrument for determining, or abridging, the canon;[40] they function rather as a hermeneutical principle, or guideline, for the interpretation of Scripture. It is Christ (and, with him, the message of justification by faith) that Scripture proclaims, Christ who is the authority within Scripture who lends authority to Scripture. Hence Luther can write: "Wenn die Gegner die Schrift treiben gegen Christus, so treiben wir Christus gegen die Schrift".[41] This characteristically exaggerated remark liberates Luther from all literalistic biblicism; but that is another matter, with which we are not at present concerned. Nor is it possible here to pursue the question how Luther used and interpreted the Scriptures. There is some substance in the criticism that his *sola Scriptura* must be supplemented by *tota Scriptura*.[42] It would, however, be a damaging criticism only if Luther had excluded passages of Scripture which did not use the Pauline language of justification by faith, and this, as we have seen, he did not do. *Sola fide* gave him access to Scripture, a position form which he could approach it and understand it; and since it denotes the approach of God to sinful man— that is, to man as he is—on the basis of nothing but his own gracious will, it was a well chosen position.

Sola fide and *solus Christus*, then, are not reductions of the whole Bible, aimed at accommodating Scripture either to a party line (whether Catholic or Protestant) or to the requirements of those who do not mean to take their religion to excess. They are not to be equated with "das ursprungliche Christuszeugnis" or "die zentrale Verkündigung", though they may turn out to be not very different from them. This observation will lead us at length to draw our discussion to a close and to ask in specific terms what we are seeking—not least, what we are seeking in a canon. For myself, I am still seeking to understand the meaning of "New Testament theology", and to find the best way of dealing with the subject. This undertaking must include an attempt to describe the various currents of theological thought in the New Testament period, and if this is to be done all the available sources must be used;[43] in the end the reader will have to decide for himself, as in any case he must do unless he is prepared to wear ecclesiastical blinkers, whether he prefers Paul or Clement, John or Ignatius. *Sola fide* and *solus Christus* do have an exclusive force, though this is not their only or perhaps their most important effect, and from the point of view of biblical theology and biblical preaching the penumbra of the canon need cause no great anxiety. In the penumbra of a total eclipse we do not suppose that we see the sun's full face.

For biblical theology is not dogmatic theology, though (as we have noted in regard to a number of pairs which it has been necessary to distinguish) they are intimately related to each other; and it is in relation to dogmatic theology that canon has traditionally acquired its special significance. Which scriptures may be used as foundation on which to establish dogma? Which may not? It is canonical scripture only that has binding force upon the dogmatic theologian. After listing the thirty nine books of the Hebrew canon of the Old Testament the sixth of the Church of England's Articles of Religion, referring to the so-called apocryphal books, says: "The other Books (as Hierome saith) the Church doth read for example of life and instruction of manners; but yet doth it not apply them to establish any doctrine" Conversely, canonical texts are used to establish doctrine, and the dogmatician requires a canon defined as precisely as possible and is likely to be impatient with a hazy canon within a canon which each man defines for himself. Dr. Braun's question (see above, 269), "Hebt die heutige neutestamentlich-exegetische Forschung den Kanon auf?", is one that is not easily disposed of. Christianity would be incomprehensible without its sacred Scripture; the canonical books retain their place; but it may be that some, even many, theologians have mistaken their significance, and that the dogmaticians have taken over what was not originally theirs. Is there any part of the New Testament that advertises itself as dogmatics, or even as the substructure of a dogmatics yet to be constructed? Braun's reference (above, 269) to "jene Schriften, bei deren Abfassung an Kanonisierung noch kein Gedanke war," will be recalled. It would probably be true to say of the same writings that their authors had no intention of writing dogmatic theology or even of laying down a series of propositions out of which dogmatic theology might develop. The writings that do adopt a more dogmatic style, notably 2 Peter, are those whose canonicity is called in question on other grounds.

Most of the New Testament books have the form of preaching rather than of dogmatics; though it is right to add to this not only that preaching, thus understood, contains a considerable number of sub-forms (there is a good deal of difference between Mark and Romans) but also that all preaching necessarily contains a dogmatic element. W. Bauer's picture of an early Christianity that did not distinguish, or at least did not distinguish as we do, between *Ketzerei* and *Recht-gläubigkeit*[44] requires one qualification. Paul, who was tolerant of variant dogmatic opinions, was emphatic in his denunciation of false preaching. "If we or an angel from heaven should preach to you a Gospel different from that which we preached to you, let him be anathema" (Gal 1:8; cf. 1:9; 2 Cor 11:4). It is with pure preaching rather than with a sound dogmatic system that he is concerned. Of course it is true that a false dogmatic system will produce preaching that is not faithful to the Gospel; but the system is a means, not an end. And a canon that is the authority for preaching is not quite the same thing as a canon that is intended to be the authority for dogma.

Die Mitte des Neuen Testaments: it may be that we have been looking for the wrong thing, or perhaps picturing it in the wrong way. The phrase is apt to suggest a series of concentric circles: James and 2 Peter, perhaps, at the outer edge, Romans and the Fourth Gospel very near to the common centre. Perhaps we should think rather of a spiral, where every point is on a curving line that winds inward towards the origin. At every point the direction of motion is tangential, but in such a way that the motion ends at the centre; that is, our preaching today, if it lies on the curve, however far continued, is directly linked with the point from which the Gospel emanates. *Praedicatio verbi divini est verbum divinum.* The image of the spiral (which doubtless like all images runs the risk of obscuring what it is intended to clarify) will call to mind the history of the canon itself. This is not the place to go into details, which are, of course, familiar to all. At the end of the first century the gospel tradition and certain epistles (Romans, 1 Corinthians, and Hebrews at least) are known and used. Early in the second century we begin to find traces of Matthew, and of other epistles; before long of John too. By the end of the second century, if we may take the Muratorianum as a sample list of this period, the only absentees are 1 and 2 Peter, possibly one epistle of John, James, and Hebrews. This recalls Eusebius's enumeration of *antilegomena*: James, Jude, 2 Peter, 2 and 3 John.[45] If we trace our way back through the history of the canon we find that we are moving along a spiral which takes us back through works of institutional ecclesiasticism (2 and 3 John), of intolerant dogmatism (2 Peter and perhaps Jude), and of moralism into the realm of Gospel preaching. This movement reflects a development from a preaching to a dogmatic canon.

Something like this has been said by Strathmann.[46] "Das Verhältnis der christlichen Gemeinde zum Neuen Testament (und seiner Vorstufe im Alten Testament) ist nicht dem Verhältnis des Staats zu seinem Grundgesetz oder einer Körperschaft zu ihrer Satzung vergleichbar. Es ist ein lebendig-religiöses Verhältnis. Es kann deshalb nicht historisch-dogmatisch, sondern nur geschichtlich-religiös, nämlich aus der tatsächlichen Lebensbeziehung der Kirche und ihrer Glieder zum Neuen Testament begründet werden." The negative part of this statement seems to me to be precisely correct; it is not however clear exactly what Strathmann means by *geschichtlich-religiös* and *Lebensbeziehung*. He goes on to repeat his negative definition and adds a reference to "Zeugnisse der kirchengründenden Predigt" (M.Kähler), with the note that "Das Zentrum dieser Zeugnisse bildet die Gestalt Christi—und sonst nichts,—deren erlösende, lebensspendende Macht die Zeugen als erlebte Wirklichkeit bekunden" (*NTK*, 60). The weakness of this definition is its subjective character, which is only partially mitigated by Strathmann's reference to the historical traditions about Jesus. To some extent this is no doubt inevitable. It may, however, be better to express the matter by saying that though the church is constantly engaged in conversation with itself—within the several confessions and between the several confessions, within any given period and between the various periods—when it turns to Scripture it finds itself engaged in conversation with the Lord and his apostles. It is not dogmatic orthodoxy that either he or they demand; they point to him and he points to himself (*ego eimi*), and seek the obedience of faith. *Solus Christus; sola fide*.

NOTES

1. See "What is New Testament Theology? Some Reflections", in *Intergerini Parietis Septum* (Eph. 2,14), Essays presented to Markus Barth, ed. D. Y. Hadidian (Pittsburgh 1981) 1-22; reprinted in *Horizons in Biblical Theology* 3, 1981, 1-22. I shall refer to this essay as NT Th .
2. W. Wrede translated in R. Morgan, *The Nature of NT Theology* (London 1973) 69, 116. On the question of the canon in general, and especially on the "canon within the canon" which is not far re-

moved from the "centre of the NT", the collection of essays, *Das NT als Kanon*, edited with a critical analysis and summing up by E. Käsemann (Göttingen 1970) is invaluable. In this paper I shall be able to refer to it only occasionally, but if the paper were to grow into a monograph it would be necessary to enter into serious conversation with each contributor. I refer to this book as *NTK*.

4. For Luther's list of secondary NT books see below, 271.

5. In *Exegetische Versuche und Besinnungen* (to be cited as EVB), I, (Göttingen 1960), 135-157.

6. It would make no essential difference if 1 Peter were written by Peter towards the end of his life.

7. It may be that here the word πρεσβύτερος is not used technically but means simply "older man".

8. The usual view seems to me to be plainly contradicted by 1,23-5.

9. I have gone into rather more detail in this matter in my *Essays on John* (London 1982), 126-130.

10. See Käsemann, EVB 1, 186; much earlier, B. H. Streeter, *The Primitive Church* (London 1929), 85.

11. If, as some think, the Evangelist reduced Christian love to a narrow, sectarian relation, existing only within the Christian brotherhood, the difference between gospel and epistles is not so great.

12. See *Essays on John*, 128-130.

13. See note 3.

14. *NTK*, 29.

15. See 270f.

16. See my *2 Corinthians* (London 1973), 28-32.

17. The Evangelist; on the epistles and their author see above.

18. Not in a strictly chronological sense; at least 2 Peter and Jude are later .

19. See above, 262f.

20. See *NTTh*, 14.

21. Synoptic Gospels + John + Romans + 1 & 2 Corinthians + Galatians =414 out of 680 pages in Nestle[26]; if we reduce the Synoptic Gospels to Mark the total is 224.

22. See W.Wrede, *Paulus* (Tübingen 1907), 90-97.

23. For example, on justification by faith, see J. Jeremias, *The Central Message of the New Testament* (London,1965), 70, and E. Käsemann, EVB II (Göttingen 1964), 102 f; for the connection with John, see Th. Preiss, *Life in Christ* (London 1954), 9- 31.

24. I borrow the term from the title of the book by W. G. Kümmel, *Die Theologie des NTs nach seinen Hauptzeugen, NTD* Erg. 3 (Göttingen, 1969). The mere existence of this book, by so distinguished an author, is itself significant; but see especially the Schluss, which bears the heading, *Jesus-Paulus-Johannes; Die Mitte des Neuen Testaments.*

25. *NTK*, 95 f.
26. See R. Bultmann, *Theologie des NTs*[3] (Tübingen 1980), 295; 305; also my *1 Corinthians* (London 1968), 341.
27. See note 12.
28. See my *Commentary on St John*[2] (London 1978), 283f., and references given there.
29. H. Küng, *NTK*, 196.
30. These are Gesetz; Eschatologie; Kirche und Amt.
31. H.Braun, *NTK*, 22f.
32. In *NTK*, 124-133.
33. See note 42.
34. H. Braun in *NTK*, 231f.
35. It is impossible here to give details; see however my essays in the Festschrifts for N. A. Dahl and E.Dinkler. I hope to go into the matter fully in a commentary on Acts.
36. The phrase, used in a different connection, goes back to Mr Edward Heath.
37. In the Septembertestament. I use the modernized version of P . Kleinert (Berlin 1883), 172.
38. In the Septembertestament; Kleinert, 173.
40. Note the use K. Barth makes of this in *Church Dogmatics* 1.2 (Edinburgh 1956), 599-601.
41. Weimar Edition (39tl) 47; quoted by Gloege, NTK, 29.
42. For the fundamental criticism see Concilium Tridentinum, Sessio IV(8 April 1546); Denzinger[21-3], 279-81. See G. Ebeling, *Luther* (London 1972), 112.
43. As, from the literary point of view, in P. Vielhauer's excellent *Geschichte der urchristlichen Literatur* (Berlin 1975).
44. In his well known book, first published in 1934.
45. The position of Revelation, either a *homologoumenon* or a *nothos*, is a well known *crux*.
46. In *NTK*, 59.